6/15/60

DATE DUE

Student Personnel Work
as Deeper Teaching

Student Personnel Work
as Deeper Teaching

EDITED BY ESTHER LLOYD-JONES, Ph.D.

PROFESSOR OF EDUCATION
TEACHERS COLLEGE, COLUMBIA UNIVERSITY

AND MARGARET RUTH SMITH, Ph.D.

ASSISTANT PROFESSOR AND DIVISIONAL ANALYST
WAYNE UNIVERSITY

HARPER & BROTHERS
Publishers . New York

Library of Congress catalog card number: 53-11851

"Perhaps the greatest single shortcoming of our school system is its tendency to concern itself almost exclusively with the dissemination of information. School should be the most important influence outside of the home for the molding of whole persons. Yet individual purpose, character, and values, the bases of which are laid in the home, are often inadequately developed by institutions which could, by precept and *deeper teaching*, assume a major share in supporting them most successfully."

REPORT OF THE TRUSTEES OF THE FORD FOUNDATION
September 27, 1950

v

Contributors

LUCILE ALLEN, Ed.D.
Dean, Pennsylvania College for Women, Pittsburgh, Pennsylvania

FRANK BALDWIN, M.A.
Dean of Men, Cornell University, Ithaca, New York

MARK BARLOW, Jr., M.A.
Assistant to Dean of Men, Cornell University, Ithaca, New York

JOHN L. BERGSTRESSER, Ph.D.
Dean of Students, San Francisco State College, San Francisco, California

DOROTHY V. N. BROOKS, Ed.D.
Dean of Women, Cornell University, Ithaca, New York

PAUL G. BULGER, Ed.D.
Associate Professor of Education and Assistant Provost, Teachers College, Columbia University, New York, New York

MARION J. CROSBY, Ph.D.
Director, Placement Bureau, Graduate Division, Hunter College, New York, New York

DANIEL J. GRIER, Ed.D.
Assistant to the Dean of Men, Purdue University, Lafayette, Indiana

ROBERT J. HAVIGHURST, Ph.D.
Committee on Human Development, University of Chicago, Chicago, Illinois

ANNA L. ROSE HAWKES, Ph.D.
Dean of Students, Mills College, Oakland, California

WILLIAM L. HUGHES, Ph.D.
Director, Department of Health and Physical Education, Temple University, Philadelphia, Pennsylvania

NORMAN KIELL, Ed.D.
Counselor to Students, Department of Personnel Services, Brooklyn College, Brooklyn, New York

MARY F. LANGMUIR, Ph.D.
Chairman, Department of Child Study, Vassar College, Poughkeepsie, New York

ESTHER LLOYD-JONES, Ph.D.
Professor of Education, Teachers College, Columbia University, New York

GEORGE E. McCABE, Ed.D.
Assistant Professor of Psychology and Education, San Francisco State College, San Francisco, California

ELIZABETH McHOSE, Ed.D.
Associate Professor of Health

and Physical Education, Temple University, Philadelphia, Pennsylvania

CHARLES EUGENE MORRIS, Ed.D.
Assistant Professor of Guidance, Springfield College, Springfield, Massachusetts

MARY I. OMER, M.A.
Research Associate in Residence Counseling, Stephens College, Columbia, Missouri

RAYMOND A. PATOUILLET, Ed.D.
Assistant Professor of Education, Teachers College, Columbia University, New York, New York

ISABELLE J. PEARD, Ph.D.
Director of Student Deans, Cornell University, Ithaca, New York

EUGENE L. SHEPARD, Ph.D.
Dean of Student Personnel, Stephens College, Columbia, Missouri

THOMAS B. SHREWSBURY, Ed.D.
Assistant Dean of Students, School of Business and Civic Administration, City College of New York, New York, New York

MARGARET RUTH SMITH, Ph.D.
Assistant Professor and Divisional Analyst, Wayne University, Detroit, Michigan

RUTH STRANG, Ph.D.
Professor of Education, Teachers College, Columbia University, New York, New York

ORDWAY TEAD, LL.D.
Editor, Social and Economic Books, Harper and Brothers, New York, New York

DOROTHY E. WELLS, Ed.D.
Assistant Dean of Students, San Francisco State College, San Francisco, California

Contents

Preface

In recent writings Arnold J. Toynbee, the great British historian, has stated that three hundred years from now historians will assess the twentieth century's values not so much in terms of the discovery of the atom, the development of air travel, or even in terms of the horrifying crimes that have been committed during this century against human ideals. He says this century will stand out preeminently as having been the first age since the dawn of civilization, some 5000 or 6000 years ago, in which people dared to think it practicable to make the benefits of civilization available for the whole human race.

Toynbee's "benefits of civilization" are predominantly in terms of material welfare. But even as we are inspired with Toynbee's description of this great achievement, we recognize that even greater is another ideal which is pushing education beyond any goal hitherto envisioned. This ideal is the development of each person in all ways to his fullest possible extent. To appreciate how revolutionary an ideal this is, one need only travel in foreign countries and talk with educators from outside of the United States. If the ideal of material welfare for all is a great idea, this is an even greater one. This is the idea, fundamentally, that has provided the personnel movement in American education with its great lifting power. It is this idea that explains the great potential contribution that personnel work can make to education.

The time was gone, the editors of this book believed, when any one or two authors could produce an adequate treatment of personnel work. The cooperative efforts of many carefully selected persons were needed. It was the hope that these chapters would not be mere compilations, no matter how competently done, of what has already been said by others. Other books in the personnel field provide this kind of resource. Furthermore, they expressly wished to avoid describing how to do in more effective ways the little things that personnel workers are commonly expected to do.

Anyone trying to clear away accustomed ways of thinking and doing is apt to have a rough time. Moreover, the end product will probably not be as clearly understood as are efforts in a more familiar pattern. The many distinguished people who contributed chapters to this book were painstaking and persistent in their attempts to get beneath the surface of the more conventional interpretations of personnel work. They brought to their writing fine qualifications for cooperating in this undertaking and for writing the particular chapter that each has produced. They have contributed much fresh thinking, and the editors think that each chapter makes a significant contribution to what seems to be a remarkably unified volume. The editors admire the quality of thinking that these collaborators have shown and are grateful to them for it.

Those who have generously read and criticized the manuscript have pointed out some weaknesses. One reader said his institution painfully redrew organization charts a few years ago, developed budget plans to implement the charts, sold trustees on the changes, hired and fired people, promoted and demoted, realigned office space, and generally tore the college apart to put into operation a new plan they had thought was "best practice." Now how could he possibly upset all of this and move toward the ideas here presented, even though he saw values in so doing. He found here, he says, no suggestions to help him.

A number of people who report that they work in situations that violate many principles of fine human relations say the book suggests idealistic practice but doesn't give enough help on what they can do to improve their situations.

The editors discovered that more than another chapter would have been needed to describe adequately how group procedures, skillfully designed and executed for the educational ends described in this book, could be developed in a personnel program. They are of the opinion, however, that it will be possible to discuss group procedures more authoritatively and more helpfully after more situations have experimented with them more thoroughly.

The full development of human resources—the fullest development of each person—is the great idea that stirs American education. Human relations—man's relationship to man—constitutes the central problem of our time. Education is the primary instrument for progressively improving the quality of human relations. Personnel work, if it stays close to its purposes, has an opportunity to make significant contributions to education as it moves forward along new frontiers.

ESTHER LLOYD-JONES
MARGARET RUTH SMITH

Student Personnel Work as Deeper Teaching

1. Changing Concepts of Student Personnel Work

ESTHER LLOYD-JONES

WHEN one examines all that has thus far been written about student personnel work, he cannot but conclude that it is considered by most to be essentially a collection of specialized services for students. He will find many descriptions of each of the numerous services. He will read much of how important it is that these services be well fitted together. He will find much discussion of who is to coordinate these services. He will learn that in the past thirty years student personnel work has been the fastest growing development within the broad context of education. He will easily recognize that some feel this is a great achievement, in and of itself an index of progress; that others view this growth differently, as an excrescence, a development that calls for careful study and critical evaluation. He will, however, find only a few discussions of how the theories, insights, emphases, and skills that personnel workers have compounded from many fields (the social sciences, medicine, and religion, among others) can be made to contribute more directly to educational objectives.

It is to this problem—how personnel work can contribute more directly to the broad objectives which education holds for each individual—that this book addresses itself.

Present Concepts, "Genealogically" Viewed

Student personnel work, as represented in most books on the subject, started in Boston about 1908 with Frank Parsons and the vocational guidance movement. It continued on in greater force as psychological testing developed rapidly after 1910. World War I, with its use of psychological tests for classification and assignment of men, led on, after 1918, to the work of Taylor, Scott, Bingham,

Paterson, and others who thought that man could and should be scientifically managed for greater industrial efficiency and individual productivity.

Vocational guidance, stimulated by the overwhelming economic complexity of our country and supported by the amazing growth of psychological testing, gripped the imagination and faith of so many to such a degree and for so long that there were some thoughtful leaders who feared that guidance—or personnel work—(we shall use the two terms interchangeably) would fail to bring to education the full contribution that might be possible or needed.*

Alongside the vocational guidance movement, however, sparked by the dynamic book, *A Mind That Found Itself*, written by Clifford Beers in 1909, the mental hygiene movement was gathering power. This might be thought of as another great tributary to the student personnel movement, flowing along almost parallel to vocational guidance and psychological testing until the 1930's.

Progressive education and child development, working in close conjunction in the 1920's and 1930's, borrowed heavily from the ideas developing in the field of mental hygiene, with a good deal of

---

* This danger was accentuated by certain developments on a national level, a threat that has been felt more directly by elementary and secondary schools than it has by colleges and universities. In 1938, a ruling of the Commission of Education permitted the Vocational Education Branch of the United States Office of Education to use federal funds for occupational information and guidance. Accordingly an officer in charge of Occupational Information and Guidance was appointed to the Vocational Education Branch of the United States Office of Education, and federal funds were allocated for programs of occupational information and guidance to the vocational education divisions of the states and, further, to local systems. These funds were to be used explicitly to serve the purposes of occupational information and vocational guidance. Through the active interest and cooperation of the American Vocational Education Association and the National Vocational Guidance Association, the Congress of the United States permitted the use of a portion of federal funds provided by the George-Barden Law (1946) to be spent for vocational guidance and counseling activities. Recently much of this federal program has been discontinued, and, as yet, no broader provision—and as a matter of fact, no provision at all—has been made for a program of guidance as part of the work of the United States Office of Education. The effect of all of this vocational guidance emphasis, however, on the concepts and programs of guidance is not to be underestimated. It has served through the appointment of State Supervisors of Guidance and Occupational Information in forty-two states to link guidance with occupations. Furthermore, through the certification requirements for secondary school guidance workers that these supervisors have sometimes dictated, and through vocation-education-linked limitations of the use of funds for "guidance," concepts of guidance have been molded and restricted in a very definite way.

reliance on tests and measurements and only a minor concern for vocational guidance as such.

The 1930's saw another component of guidance mushroom in this country. Psychoanalysts, fleeing from Europe before the Hitler tide associated themselves with mental hygiene organizations and leadership groups in progressive education and child development. It is interesting to trace the stream of psychoanalysis in this country through its orthodox Freudian phase and on into adaptations by Rank, Horney, Plant, Taft, Rogers, Sullivan, May, and others. The result in what we are identifying as the guidance or student personnel movement was a strong emphasis—almost an obsession during the 1940's— on individual counseling. Guidance during this time, for many, was almost completely identified with counseling, and vast floods of literature resulted that dwelt on the mysteries and untold possibilities in an infinite variety of counseling approaches. Counseling has been so revered and so completely identified with guidance in the thinking of many that titles of guidance workers on the high school level almost everywhere changed over during the 1940's from "dean" to "counselor." Only feebly, as yet, are suggestions heard that perhaps the title of "counselor" and the function of counseling too narrowly connote the contributions a general guidance worker should make to education.

Student personnel work drew heavily on psychology throughout the decades described above. In the 1940's, however, reports of research and experimentation in the area of group interaction attracted more and more attention, and student personnel workers, probably first on the college level and then on the level of secondary education, began to recognize that the social sciences might have much to contribute to the broadening objectives of their field. This appears to many to be the next big tributary which will flow into the guidance movement to modify its concepts and contribute to its power.

Even now the person who starts out with an interest in vocational guidance, with testing as a means to more effective results, seems soon to realize that the success of the person whom he counsels vocationally will also depend importantly upon his emotional adjustment and his mental hygiene. This leads the vocational counselor to an interest in a broader kind of counseling, which professes to deal with such matters. But then comes the realization that emotional and social development are made up of feelings about self and about others and of knowledge and skills that have been learned through many years of interacting with others in what might be thought of as a curriculum of social experience. Thus the personnel worker, even though he may begin with a concern for helping persons with their vocational planning and preparation, and with their work placement and advancement, comes eventually to an appreciation of the necessity for breadth in his personnel work if his professional objectives are to be achieved.

Emphasis on Specialization

It is not always possible, however, for one who has gained this realization to do more than practice in one small area of the field. Organizationally, one of the results of this step-by-step development of the student personnel field has been the development of many specializations and specialists. There are specialists in vocational guidance; there are specialists in testing; there are specialists in educational guidance; there are specialists in counseling, per se, who sit in counseling bureaus and do nothing but counsel—sometimes about only one or two kinds of problems, sometimes with little regard for the kind of problem the student presents—feeling that the important thing is that the counselor strengthen the student to solve his own problems. There are specialists in housing, in the selection and admission of students, in student activities, in fraternity and sorority problems, in remedial reading, in social activities, etc.

Yet all of this proliferation into specialties has not been due solely to the way in which the field of student personnel work has developed. Much of it has been due to the fact that about half of all the students in higher education in this country have chosen to flock to only about 160 of our some 1800 colleges and universities. These some 160 institutions represent such huge units that one natural consequence has been the breaking up of duties of staff into finer and finer functions, just as has been done in giant industries. Each person's duties have been carefully delineated by some administratively superior person who writes job descriptions and administers worker relationships. The prestige and glorification that Americans tend to assign to the very fact of "bigness," furthermore, has meant that the other some 1600 smaller colleges and universities that could perhaps have met their needs in a better manner, have tended to fall in line with the big university pattern, feeling that this must be right and best because of the importance of the institutions by which this pattern has been adopted.

Common Beliefs

Always, however, in spite of different emphases, various degrees of expertness, different approaches, and even limited views of the total field, those who profess themselves as student personnel workers have seemed able to agree on certain common beliefs:

1. A belief in the worth of the individual; that human values are of the greatest importance; that the common good can be promoted best by helping each individual to develop to the utmost in accordance with his abilities. There is growing agreement that the mores, the way in which groups subtly and unconsciously assign roles to persons, and the social expectancies to which individuals respond are powerfully controlling in stimulating or inhibiting an individual in the development of his abilities.

2. The belief in the equal dignity of thinking and feeling and working; that these aspects are inseparable. Personnel work is interested in the whole person and not merely in his mind or his economic productivity or some other one of his aspects.

3. The belief that the world has a place for everybody: a place in the social world, a place in the civic world, a place in family life, and a place in the vocational world; that it is education's task to offer youth not only an invitation but also positive stimulation carefully adapted to his needs to help him to grow to full stature in all of these roles. A stimulating and rich environment provides for the exploration of resources (relationships: who and what he is); and for the accomplishment of developmental tasks appropriate for his age level which will carry the young person into effective adult life, and on further into a rich later life.

4. The belief that what an individual gathers from his experiences continues on in time; it is not what is imposed, but what is absorbed that persists. Personnel workers see the person—at whatever age—not as a single moment independent of the past and the future, but as a transition point in a stream of experience that goes back to infancy and will continue on into the future; they believe that each person can move progressively from dependence toward independence, from interest to responsibility, from casual concern to good work habits, from superficial to logical associations, from egocentric to social behavior.

Threats to Principle

With these beliefs or principles so widely professed, it is interesting to note the contradictions to them that have sprung up in practice. Take, for instance, the important points proclaimed vigorously in every book on student personnel work: that personnel work is interested in the *whole* person, not only his mind or his economic productivity, and that personnel work contributes to the personalization of education. The very specialization, however, to which personnel work itself has fallen victim, as described above, has threatened to nullify these basic claims of personnel work. On the one hand, we talk piously of the whole student, and on the other we proceed, because of the way our professional expertness has developed, because of the size of the units within which we work, and because of the organizational forms personnel work has taken, to divide the student up amongst the experts, thus contributing directly to the depersonalization of personnel work and education.

Education—including both the curriculum and student personnel work—is not the only field in which specialization threatens important values. Much has been written in the field of medicine about extremes to which specialization has gone; about the way in which the patient has been sectioned up into small areas of anatomy, as well as into brief time spans so that few persons any longer have a medical doctor who can follow them through from birth to death.

Most recently, action taken by the Football Rules Committee of the National Collegiate Athletic Association has revealed the extent to which athletics also had fallen victim to specialization. Daley in discussing the scuttling of the two-platoon system in football, analyzes the situation thus:

There was a coach for the offensive ends, the defensive ends and every which phase of the sport until there was almost a special coach to teach the fellow who held the ball for field goal attempts only when there was a crosswind blowing from a southeasterly direction.

These specialists not only rolled up costs but played before a slowly shrinking group of spectators. Individual personality was stamped from the game in favor of mob scenes of faceless robots. Even the coaches couldn't keep track of what went on because there were many instances of ten-man or twelve-man teams taking the field. What chance did the spectator have? He never knew who was playing and after a while he didn't even care. He just stayed away.

The coach ceased to be a coach. He was just a coordinator of assistants. Now he'll have to go back to work and teach blocking to tacklers and tackling to blockers. He'll have to produce genuine football players, whole football players. . . .

The smartest move the Football Rules Committee yet has made is legislating out of existence the controversial two-platoon system.[1]

Another consequence of specialization is the wholesale and uncritical way in which student personnel work has now come to be thought of as a collection of services to students. Every book and article about personnel work that has been analyzed has implicit in it the idea that this is exactly what student personnel work is: a collection of expert services which every self-respecting educational institution should offer to its students. On the face of it, this sounds entirely moral and quite innocuous when viewed this way. A natural conclusion is that these services need to be coordinated. This has sounded sensible and quite acceptable to most people. Other consequences then follow in terms of organizational patterns, budget problems, relations with curriculum, human relations, the accentuation of a dualistic philosophy of education, etc.—which now require careful analysis in terms of their educational implications.

When the idea of special services was adopted the belief was strong, of course, that this was the best way of making functional in education the great ideas that were central to personnel work. The time has come to examine critically whether specialization, the multiplication of special services to students, high expertness, coordination, preoccupation with administrative efficiency—all predominant characteristics of the kinds of personnel programs that have been advocated for the last fifteen or twenty years—are really essential to accomplish the high aims which personnel workers hold. It is possible that they may be means and methods, possessing an inner consistency among themselves, but which actually constitute undesirable obstructions to the fulfillment of the educational objectives of personnel work.

At this point it might be well to admit that one of the first books to describe and analyze student personnel work predominantly in terms of services was the Lloyd-Jones and Smith book of 1938, A Student Personnel Program for Higher Education. It was reassuring recently to come across the following words written by a man far surpassing the present writers in his wisdom:

[1] Arthur Daley: "Sports of the Times." The New York Times, January 16, 1953.

I am not myself in any degree ashamed of having changed my opinions. What physicist who was already active in 1900 would dream of boasting that his opinions had not changed during the last half century? . . . The kind of philosophy that I value and have endeavored to pursue is scientific in the sense that there is definite knowledge to be obtained and that new discoveries can make the admission of former error inevitable to any candid mind. For what I have said, whether early or late, I do not claim the kind of truth which theologians claim for their creeds. I claim only, at best, that the opinion expressed was a sensible one to hold at the time when it was expressed. I should be much surprised if subsequent research did not show that it needed to be modified. I hope, therefore, that whoever uses this dictionary will not suppose the remarks which it quotes to be intended as pontifical pronouncements, but only as the best I could do at the time toward the promotion of clear and accurate thinking.[2]

Perhaps the main reason programs of student personnel work have developed as they have is because of the concepts of personnel work that have "just growed" throughout the last half century. One is reminded of the way an idea that is in the mind of a pediatrician gets into the stomach of a baby. A pediatrician decides how often a baby he is supervising should be fed. Within two or three days the pediatrician's idea is operating in the stomach of the baby so that it begins its contractions, and the baby wants to eat at the intervals that the pediatrician has thought he should eat—every three hours, every four hours, even only three times a day. If we were able to set aside the near-sighted view as traced in the first part of this chapter and could gain a longer perspective on education, its goals, its methods, its strengths and weaknesses, we might be able to see personnel work in an entirely new light, unblinded by the forms and organizational problems that now seem to loom so large that we forget the fundamental principles and purposes which should be our main concern. It would be well if we could catch a fresh view of how personnel work might more surely contribute to education the important values it seeks to serve. Perhaps this new idea would get into the way we carry out personnel work.

Educational Philosophies and Personnel Work

Education in this country has represented a back-and-forth struggle, compromise, and regrouping of the ideas exemplified in French, German, and English education, with additional fresh emphases and

[2] Bertrand Russell: *Bertrand Russell's Dictionary of Mind, Matter, and Morals.* New York, Philosophical Library, Inc., 1952, Preface.

new ideas that are indigenous to American education itself. Beliefs in rationalism, pure intellect, secularism, absolutism, educational authoritarianism, impersonality, idealism, educational *laissez faire*, naturalism, instrumentalism, pragmatism, experimentalism, relativism, reconstructionism, and the religious and personal can be discovered in varying amounts and combinations at various times in every educational institution.

Taylor has categorized the philosophical principles that underlie programs of education into three general divisions, with which most educational philosophers would agree, in general, although some would break them down into more than three. Taylor calls his three divisions the rationalist, the neo-humanist, and the instrumentalist. He points out that

No philosophical concept or philosophy of education ever appears in actual existence as a pure form, and no matter how an educator tries, he cannot build an educational institution upon conceptions which then reproduce themselves in reality. Any idea for education . . . becomes so modified in practice by the character of the individuals who make up the institution that it would be fairer to say that what we have is a set of leading ideas which are then recreated in various forms by those who teach and those who learn.[3]

It is fruitful, however, to an understanding of what may be the deeper significance of personnel work to take a look at these main philosophies of education.*

Rationalism and Personnel Work

The rationalist holds that the sole aim of education is to cultivate man's reason. In spite of the high sounding pretensions of personnel workers, if they work in a situation largely rationalistic in nature, and especially if they themselves have not critically explored the educational outcomes of the various philosophies of education, they will probably find themselves consigned to certain roles that support the rationalistic character of the educational program and also provide a narrow and inadequate scope for their efforts as personnel workers who are interested in "the whole man." They will find themselves using tests to sift out only those with the highest amount of academic

[3] Harold Taylor: "The Philosophical Foundations of General Education" *General Education*, Fifty-first Yearbook. 1952, Part I, pp. 22-3.
* For a further discussion, see the paper by Esther Lloyd-Jones: "Personnel Work and General Education," *General Education*, National Society for the Study of Education, Fifty-first Yearbook, 1952, Part I, pp. 214-229.

intelligence. They may very possibly practice public relations and recruitment skills to attract more applicants from which the intellectual cream may be skimmed off thicker. It would almost be fair to say that the whole effort required of these personnel workers is to attract, select, and deliver to the classroom students whom the professors will find stimulating to teach; and, furthermore, to deliver the student to the classroom in the best condition to learn. This might imply that personnel workers would have to do something about seeing that the students were housed and fed, that they did not misbehave, thus disturbing the academic tranquility of the classrooms, and that they received remedial help if they were not in good shape to profit from the professor's efforts on their behalf.

Neo-Humanism and Personnel Work

There are many educators, however—possibly the majority at the present time—who cannot accept the rationalistic as an adequate philosophy of education. They cannot overlook the fact that the young person who comes to them has a body that may be energetic and full of life, or feeble and even sick. They recognize the strong influence that motivation has on their students' learning, and that motivation is inseparably tied up with the student's emotional life. They recognize that each student has many needs as a person that may seem quite unrelated to the subject matter which he studies in classes. As kindly and humanitarian people, or even in their own self-interest because they enjoy having students who are free to learn well, many teachers want not only to teach the student but also to have him taken care of in ways to which they feel they cannot contribute. These educators, having themselves grown up in a rationalistic setting (especially during their years of graduate study) usually feel strongly that their responsibility is to teach subject matter to students. They support the idea, however, that the school or college should provide for these other aspects of their students' lives. They readily have bought the idea that personnel people have been selling them for the last twenty-five or thirty years that personnel workers are needed, and in substantial numbers, to take care of the many needs students have about which they, as specialists in subject matter, can be expected to know little. Furthermore, as products themselves of specialist education[4] they accept uncritically the specialist system that has developed within the field of personnel work.

[4] Howard Mumford Jones: *Education and World Tragedy*. Cambridge, Massachusetts, Harvard University Press, 1946.

The neo-humanists are essentially dualistic in their philosophy: they recognize both mind and body, reason and emotion, thought and action. They also tend to think in terms of classroom and extra-class activity, curriculum and student personnel work, teaching by faculty on the one hand and counseling by student personnel workers on the other.

This is the philosophy that prevails most widely in education at the present time. It provides a situation that has given personnel work a wide open field. The rapid growth and proliferation of personnel services, as already mentioned, is a phenomenon in education that has come about so suddenly that only now are we getting around to looking at the situation critically from a standpoint of its fundamental meaning for education.

One of the outstanding characteristics of the neo-humanist is his reliance on the fitting together externally of pieces and parts to bring about the desired result of inner unity and harmony. In the curriculum he depends upon the careful selection of pieces or areas of subject matter and their arrangement into some kind of pattern that shows logical relationships. For the education of the whole man he relies, as already described, upon supplementing the curriculum and classroom by the efforts of personnel workers in their various specialized activities to take care of all that for which the curriculum and teaching staff do not provide. And the personnel worker who holds a neo-humanistic philosophy believes that students' needs can be met by analyzing each special need, supplying a specialist to meet that need, and then relating these specialists in some kind of firm pattern of relationship that appears administratively logical. The assumption seems to be that if the connections and relationships exist externally between and among the pieces and parts, these can then be transferred inward by the student to reinforce the unity and harmony of his experiences and contribute to his growth.

Some consequences of the neo-humanistic philosophy in education are to draw attention away from the actual process of student growth and learning while directing professional interest toward the rearrangement of subject matter, reading materials, greater specialization, and the organizational relationship of personnel specialists to each other.

Instrumentalism and Personnel Work

The instrumentalist philosophy of education puts its chief emphasis on the uses of knowledge and experience. The ultimate value upon which it rests is the quality of experience within the individual. Taylor quotes the *Report of the President's Commission on Higher Education*, which he says gives us one of the most recent expositions of the ideas upon which the instrumentalist philosophy rests:

The first goal in education for democracy is the full, rounded, and continuing development of the person. The discovery, training, and utilization of individual talents is of fundamental importance in a free society. To liberate and perfect the intrinsic powers of every citizen is the central purpose of democracy, and its furtherance of individual self-realization is its greatest glory.

To quote further directly from Taylor:

. . . If this is the goal for democracy and for education, it is to be served by an education which rests on a philosophy of individualism, not individualism as a doctrine of enlightened self-interest, but individualism as the full development of the individual in the development of his society. In order to fulfill himself in the context of this moral philosophy, the individual must give part of himself to the others with whom he lives and works.[5]

The instrumentalist philosophy, much more than that of rationalism or neo-humanism, seems to represent the principles in which student personnel workers have protested they believe. To compare the writings of the instrumentalists with the four principles outlined on page 5 is to find almost complete agreement.

Personnel Work and Deeper Teaching

But how is education to gain from student personnel work the full values that it offers? Must student personnel work continue in education as a collection of special services designed ostensibly to correct the mistakes of educators or, at best, to do what the rest of education cannot do in a system that is frankly dualistic? Is there some better way to conceive of student personnel work—perhaps of education itself—that will eventuate in greater growth and development of each student for life in a society that he will by his living improve?

This book attempts to set forth the view that student personnel workers should not so much be expert technicians as they should be educators in a somewhat unconventional and new sense. Student personnel workers have many opportunities through their work to

[5] Harold Taylor: *Op. cit.*, pp. 42-3.

contribute to the development of students, to help them learn many lessons and skills of vital importance for their fulfillment as whole persons within a democratic society. Perhaps their most important opportunities are more indirect than direct and exist in their collaborative work with faculty members toward these ends.

The book shows clearly that teachers of subject matter have magnificent opportunities to contribute to this kind of deeper learning by their students. As they strive to know their students as individuals, to help them find significant experiences inside and outside of the classroom, in reading books, in relationships with their peers, in conversations with their teachers, in service to the community, teachers are clearly seen to be the pivotal persons around whom more effective programs for deeper learnings must be developed.

Emphases coming from many other sources besides personnel work are reshaping curricula and influencing teachers to see education as the all-round development of their students. These other emphases are similar to those that have been stressed by personnel workers. The United States Office of Education has for some years been discussing objectives of Life Adjustment Education, which are also similar to those of education as set forth by the President's Commission on Higher Education. These objectives are generally described as: (1) the development of saleable skills, work experience, etc.; (2) good mental and physical health, physical fitness; (3) citizenship; (4) family living; (5) the purchase and intelligent use of goods; (6) the understanding of science; (7) esthetic appreciation; (8) leisure time (socially useful activity); (9) respect for other persons, to live and work cooperatively with others; and (10) to think rationally, to listen, think, communicate. General education, which has been gaining many adherents, states its objectives in a similar way.

In the next nineteen chapters there is much that has to do with most of these objectives. There is also a chapter on developing spiritual insights. How to build spiritual capital, stated in one way or another, is a concern of most personnel workers, and also, in fact, of most educators. Each of these nineteen chapters has been written by one or more thoughtful persons who have attempted to show how various facets of what is usually considered by personnel workers to be a part of personnel work and which could almost certainly be concerns of all educators, may contribute effectively to the breadth and depth of education.

The final chapter in the book sets forth suggestions for ways and means whereby we might attempt to modify the dualistic, specialist system that is now advocated in most books about personnel work to one that will be productive of surer outcomes in terms of the educational growth of students. It is hoped, however, that not only personnel workers themselves but also other educators will find a challenge in these discussions to the end that they and personnel workers and administrators and students will all together improve the educational experiences in which our society as a whole has so great a stake.

BIBLIOGRAPHY

American Council on Education: *The Student Personnel Point of View,* 8, No. 13, Series 6. Washington, D. C., American Council on Education, September, 1949.

Brouwer, Paul J.: *Student Personnel Services in General Education.* Washington, D. C., American Council on Education, 1949.

Cantor, Nathaniel: *Dynamics of Learning.* Buffalo, New York, Foster and Stewart Publishing Corp., 1946.

Lloyd-Jones, Esther: "Social Competence and College Students." Washington, D. C., American Council on Education Studies, Series VI, Vol. IV, No. 3, September, 1940.

Lloyd-Jones, Esther: "Personnel Work and General Education." Chicago, National Society for the Study of Education, Fifty-first Yearbook: *General Education,* Part I, P. 214, 1952.

Lloyd-Jones, Esther, and Smith, M. R.: *A Student Personnel Program for Higher Education.* New York, McGraw-Hill Book Company, Inc., 1938.

Roethlisberger, F. J., and Dickson, W. J.: *Management and The Worker.* Cambridge, Mass., Harvard University Press, 1943.

Taylor, Harold: "The Philosophical Foundations of General Education." Chicago, National Society for the Study of Education, Fifty-first Yearbook: *General Education,* Part I, p. 20, 1952.

Williamson, E. G. (ed.): *Trends in Student Personnel Work.* Minneapolis, University of Minnesota Press, 1949.

Wrenn, C. Gilbert: *Student Personnel Work in College.* New York, Ronald Press, 1951.

2. Who Should Go Where to College?

ROBERT J. HAVIGHURST

SINCE World War II it has become evident that the proportion of boys and girls going to college is and will probably remain substantially greater than it was before the war. The trend of increase which went on all through the twenties and thirties has been resumed, and the end is not in sight. How many young people will eventually go to college? What kind of persons will they be, in terms of intelligence, sex, and socio-economic status? What kinds of colleges will the new college students choose? These are the questions discussed in this chapter, with their implications for personnel work.

There are three major alternative answers to the question, "How many young people will eventually go to college?"

1. *Half of the population for two years; one third for four years.* This is the most expansive proposal yet made by a responsible and substantial group of people. The President's Advisory Commission on Higher Education in 1947 urged that a national policy be adopted which would bring all boys and girls of average intelligence or higher into college for two years, and would keep a third of the total age group in college throughout a four-year course.

2. *Those who want to go to college, and are in the upper half of the population in intellectual ability.* This answer takes account of the fact that many able boys and girls do not wish to go to college. (About four out of ten in the top ten per cent of ability do not have a strong desire to go to college; and motivation for college attendance becomes lower as we go down the intelligence scale.)* This would bring about 30 per cent of the age-group to college, and would keep about 15 per cent there for four years.

---

* For justification of these and other estimates in this chapter, see the writer's Appendix to the book, *Who Should Go to College in America?*, by Byron Hollingshead.

3. *Those in the upper quarter of intellectual ability who possess a strong and clear motivation for college education.* Again, taking account of the facts of motivation for college-going, this would bring at the most 15 per cent of the age group into college and would graduate about 12 per cent. These numbers are close to the present situation in terms of numbers but not in terms of selectivity for intellectual talent. With the aid of the GI Bill, about 20 per cent of young people entered a post-high school institution, but they ranged over the upper half of the age group in terms of intellectual ability.

During the next decade, barring war or other catastrophe, we probably shall see a situation moving toward Answer 2, assuming that substantial scholarship assistance is available to poor but able young people. As we move in this direction, there will be a number of developments of interest in the area of personnel work. Some of these are:

a. *A considerable influx of boys and girls from working-class homes into the colleges.* Any substantial increase in college attendance must come from the homes of people in clerical and manual work, as is shown in Table 1. In this Table, it will be seen that in 1940 the young people entering college were predominantly from middle-class families. Children in the upper middle and upper socio-economic groups generally went to college unless they went to an upper-class finishing school or unless they were simply too dull to have a chance of succeeding in college. Only a minority of children from families in the lower white-collar occupations went to college, however, and they were mainly bright, ambitious youngsters. From working-class homes only about one in twenty children started college, and this group constituted a small minority of the total college population.

The two estimates in Table I are based on the proposals already outlined for increasing the proportion of youth going to college. The conservative estimate would draw heavily from the abler third or quarter of the lower middle and working groups. It would bring about 28 per cent of this age group into college, which is not much of an extension of the present trend, in which about 20 per cent of this age group enter some sort of post-high school institution of learning. Furthermore, if things should proceed according to this conservative estimate, a drastic change in the composition of the student population will take place. Instead of being dominated by boys and girls of upper middle and lower middle-class economic status, the

TABLE 1. COLLEGE ATTENDANCE OF THE VARIOUS SOCIO-ECONOMIC GROUPS

Socio-economic group	Percentage of total age group	1940		Possible future situations			
		Percentage of group going to college	Percentage of total age group in college	Conservative Estimate		Liberal Estimate	
				Percentage going to college	Percentage of total group in college	Percentage going to college	Percentage of total group in college
Upper and upper middle	8	80	6.4	80	6.4	80	6.4
Lower middle	32	20	6.4	30	9.6	50	16.0
Working class	60	5	3.0	20	12.0	40	24.0
Totals			15.8		28.0		46.4

average student body will be dominated numerically by boys and girls from working-class families.

To say the least, this will present a challenge to the college agencies which adapt the college to the student and the student to the college. For the working-class home typically provides a different culture from that of the upper middle-class home, and provides their children with different expectations in life, different values, different manners and mores.

Should the liberal estimate come closer to the reality, the shift in socio-economic complexion of the student body would be even more complete, with as few as one in six or seven students coming from upper middle-class homes. The liberal estimate, however, is hardly a possibility for the near future, although certain colleges in big cities even now approximate this socio-economic distribution.

The present reality is not far from the conservative estimate since in many colleges today the students of working-class and lower middle-class origin outnumber those of upper middle-class origin, to whom the colleges originally were adapted.

The situation is a very good one for the purpose of keeping democratic fluidity in the social structure. It is evidence that we are in the process of realizing the democratic ideal of equality of opportunity. It is a situation for which some colleges are not well prepared, however, nor of which they are aware.

The reason some colleges are not well prepared for such a situation is that the American college has been founded on the tacit assumption that its students will have middle-class values, habits, and vocational expectations. The typical college boy, based on these assumptions, will be like John Chesney.

John is the son of a lawyer who has always expected John to go to college and to prepare for a business or professional career. John has been taught that he has a long period of preparation for adult life ahead of him. He expects to be fairly well established in his vocation before he gets married, perhaps at the age of 25 or 30. He has learned to give up immediate pleasures for the sake of greater gains to him in the future. He can work all summer and save his money for college. He can say no to a group of fellows who want him to go to the movies when he has a hard lesson to prepare for the next day. John has grown up in a home where books and magazines were much in evidence, and he has learned to expect good results from reading. He has learned the table manners, the language manners, and the sexual attitudes of his family.

Although a variant to John Chesney, the college is also accustomed to a boy like Walter Olson, whose father works in the office of the public service company as a clerk. Walter's father and mother graduated from high school, and they have raised their three children to be studious, church-going young people with a serious outlook toward life. Walter is the brightest of the three and the whole family will sacrifice to help him get through college, while the other two children will go to work as soon as they finish high school. Walter has a great respect for books, although he must use the public library for his reading material, since the home does not afford him either a wide selection of books or an example of wide reading in the person of one or both parents.

The Olson family expect Walter to become a doctor, or a teacher, or an engineer, to make a good living for himself, and to bring credit to the family. They expect him to remain a loyal church member.

Walter will not join a fraternity where he could live with boys like John Chesney. He would feel somewhat uncomfortable if he had to take a girl to a dinner party with these boys. He would not feel sure that he had the right clothes, or that his conversation would fit in the fraternity pattern, or that he used the correct utensils for eating in the correct way.

Walter's studious work habits will get him ahead in college. He will enjoy church activities. His taste in amusements will be simple. Once out of college and in his first job, he may find himself up against competition in his profession that will puzzle him. Although his professional knowledge will be adequate for success, he and his wife may feel that they are under some social handicaps in meeting and getting along with the people who can further Walter's career. They will study this problem as seriously as they have studied other problems, and either they will learn how to move in the new social circles into which they are introduced, or they will admit it is not worth while, and will be content with family friends in their old church, and with a limited vocational success.

Newer and less familiar on the college scene is Tony Panetsky. A football star in high school, with above average intelligence and a pleasing personality, Tony went on a scholarship to the State University. The only one of eight children in the Panetsky family to enter college, Tony cannot quite explain to his steel-worker father what college is. Yet, one thing the elder Panetsky and Tony agree on is that Tony is going to get an easier job than his father, a steadier job, and he will be some kind of boss. Tony thinks he may coach athletics for a while, and then go into some kind of business.

Tony is still unconscious of many of the differences between himself and the boys in his classes. He does not know that he has an accent that people notice, and that his choice of sweaters and socks and sport shirts is somewhat different from that of the fellows who are "big men on the campus." He tries to be like them, and succeeds in the more obvious ways but misses the subtle points. He does not grasp some of the discussions of literature and the drama in his sophomore English class, but he gets enough out of his textbooks and the required reading from the reserve shelf in the library to get fairly good grades. If Tony was not having such a good time with the girls and his athletics it would be hard for him to stay in school and graduate, because his studies mean little to him, and he could make good money by playing professional football.

Taking the differences among these boys in family background and in motivation for education, and adding these differences to those between other boys and girls also in college, it is easy to see that college life is complex and is not growing any simpler.

b. *A substantially expanded program of scholarship grants, with appropriate means of selecting students and steering them to appropriate colleges.* If as many as 20 per cent of the age group enter college, a great many of them must have scholarship aid. Whether this aid comes from private or from governmental sources, there will be a problem of awarding scholarships fairly, and of helping each boy and girl to find the colleges best for them. These matters will generally be referred to personnel workers.

If scholarships should continue to be paid primarily to veterans of the armed services there would, of course, be no problem of selecting boys and girls to whom the awards would be made. Any long-term, peacetime scholarship program, however, will have to be based on methods of selection which are fair to girls as well as boys, and to young people of all races, nationalities, and socio-economic backgrounds. Scholarship examinations of the scholastic aptitude or intelligence test type might at first sight seem to promise the most fairness in a system of awards. It seems clear, however, that such tests are systematically biased in favor of middle-class youth, since the vocabulary and problems in these tests are more familiar to this socio-economic group than to any other. On the other hand, interviews with candidates and recommendations by their teachers and other adults who know them would almost surely tend to favor youth with middle-class attitudes and habits. Thus the problem is a complex one and deserves attention from people in the personnel field. It should get increased attention if a large-scale scholarship program is developed in this country.

c. *Efforts at motivating the many able high school students who do not now want to go to college.* Studies of the reasons why boys and girls of superior intelligence drop out of school or stop their education with high school graduation show that about twice as many stop because of lack of desire to go to college as compared with the number who would like to go but cannot afford it. Table 2 reports

TABLE 2. REASONS OF SUPERIOR AND HIGH AVERAGE STUDENTS FOR NOT GOING TO COLLEGE

	Superior IQ (115+)	High average IQ (101–114)
Percentage of total youth now entering post-high school institutions	7	8
Percentage who would continue education if scholarship aid was available	4	4
Percentage who lack sufficient motivation for further education	7	20
Percentage of total age group in this intelligence range	18	32

results from a series of studies of the reasons superior youth do not go to college. The studies were made in a number of states by several different methods, and they indicate clearly that a scholarship program alone, without attempts at improving the motivation for college-going, would not be effective in bringing many more of the able boys and girls into college.

The motivational reasons for not going to college may be summarized as follows: practically all of the superior youth who do not continue their education beyond high school are children of people who have had less than a high school education. These families participate in a culture which has little personal contact with higher education. They value a job and an earning career highly for their young people. They are not accustomed to postponing the earning of money in favor of a long and costly period of vocational preparation. They favor early marriage, especially for their daughters. ("It gets them over a fool's hill early.") While these people have come to look favorably on high school graduation for their children, they do not regard college as really within the reach of their aspirations or their financial means. The majority of children growing up in these families will have little desire for higher education. Only a minority of the children of these families will have sufficient motivation to make the sacrifices necessary to get to college.

Any program aimed to increase the motivation for education of boys and girls from working-class and lower middle-class homes obviously will involve high school teachers and guidance counselors. Fortunately there is an increasing number of such programs in operation, successful and stimulating.

d. *Motivation and guidance of boys and girls after they reach college, to help them adjust their aspirations to college standards.* Even after youth reach college, many of them fail to understand what college life requires in the way of systematic work and study habits, and what it affords in terms of vocational and intellectual goals. Many of them have drifted with the tide into college, and will drift out again unless they fit their aims and goals to what the college requires and what it has to offer—and unless the college fits itself to them. This discrepancy between personal aspirations and college standards will appear more frequently as more working-class youth enter college. It can also take the form of a lack of social skills and leisure-time interests that are in keeping with the cultural aims of the college.

e. *The question of marriage while still in college will arise with increased urgency—especially for college girls.* With the lowering of the age of marriage that has been such a striking phenomenon recently in America, half of American girls are now married by the time they are 20. And these are not the more stupid half, by any means. Consequently, any substantial increase in college attendance by girls will present more and more insistently the following questions:

1. What shall we advise when freshman or sophomore girls come to ask our advice about getting married immediately?
2. How shall we deal with the social activities, the dating and parties, in a student body where a good proportion of the couples are married, while others in the same social groups are just beginning to learn the arts of courtship?
3. What kind of housing provisions should the college make for young married students?

What Colleges for What Students?

Does the personnel worker commence his work with the student after the student has made his decision to enter X College? Or is there a prior question for personnel workers—namely, to what kind of college should the student go?

The prior question is a proper one for the personnel worker to raise, even though he may not do much about this question if he deals with students only after they have made their choice of a college. The question of what kind of college for this or that kind of student will arise more insistently as college enrollments expand to include more young people from lower-status homes and with a wider range of vocational interests. It may become an important function of the admissions staff to guide boys and girls into the right kind of college for them, and to help them transfer to other colleges if they make bad first choices.

Two principles might be stated as guides in answering the question, "What colleges for what students?"

1. The student should go to a college which helps him to develop and mature intellectually. If the college standards are so low that a particular student is not stimulated to grow intellectually, he should not go there; yet, the same college might be a good place for a slower student who would be stimulated by this college and might be overwhelmed and discouraged by the intellectual pace set in a college with higher academic standards.

2. The student should go to a college which helps him to develop and mature personally and socially. This means that the student should find friendship and social acceptance from at least a small group of his fellows. He should find spiritul stimulation (through religious or ethical or artistic influences in some combination) that makes him a wiser and better person.

This second principle is important in its own right and in its relation to the first. If we say that the college is primarily a place for intellectual development and maturing, we do so with the knowledge that the intellect does not develop soundly except as it does so in harmony with personal and social development. Therefore a reasonable degree of happiness in his social life is a desirable and necessary goal for the student who wants to develop and mature intellectually. The personnel officer ought in some cases to help a student get out of a college in which he is leading an unhappy social life, even though he appears to be making satisfactory academic progress. Personnel workers should be as concerned with helping a student make a happier social adjustment in college as they would be with helping him make satisfactory academic progress.

Another aspect of the second principle is that the student may need help from the college in achieving individual social mobility. As more and more children from working-class families enter college, more and more will the college be a place where young men and women are learning middle-class social skills and responsibilities as well as middle-class vocational skills.

These principles can be applied on the basis of study of the individual student, his abilities, his goals, and his past experience. For admission to college the admission officers need information which tells them whether the applicant can probably achieve the level of academic excellence expected by the particular college, and they also need information which tells them whether the applicant has the life goals which are honored in the college, whether he is reasonably well geared to the kind of social life lived by the students in this particular college, or whether he has the personal flexibility to enable him to adjust to such a social life.

There are possibilities in this connection in the use of inventories of interests, health, life goals, and in the deeper and more sophisticated use of the usual application and personal history forms. The personal history blank is now being used in some business corporations to aid in selecting employees for job assignments and promotions. The blank in this case is analyzed by a psychologist who has learned what characteristics of response to the personal history questions signify success or failure in one or another kind of business activity. The same procedure probably could be used to predict whether a college applicant is likely to succeed in one or another kind of college.

One type of analysis could be made on the basis of the "mobility-orientation" of the student. Carson McGuire has pointed out that the boy or girl who goes to college is probably in one of the following categories:

1. *The high status static.* This is a person of upper or upper middle socio-economic level who has the typical educational attitudes of his social group. Though not upward mobile, he will go on to college because that is normal for his group.

2. *The climber.* This is a lower middle or a working-class youth who has a solid and realistic ambition to "get ahead" in life. This person has friends among boys and girls of higher social status, spends

time in their homes, and absorbs their educational attitudes. He has a good mind, a strong personality, understands that self-control and hard work will be required of him, and is prepared internally to make the sacrifices necessary for the achievement of higher education and consequently of social mobility.

3. *The strainer.* This is a lower middle or a working-class youth whose goals in life are mixed, and whose own personality is vacillating. He wants to "make good," yet is not sure within himself what this means. He makes friends with boys and girls higher on the social ladder but is never sure that he desires their way of life. In the end it is something external to him, such as a GI Bill of Rights, that decides whether he shall go on with his education.

To the counselor these three mobility orientations have implications for college selection. The *high status static* is a good risk in any college. But the *climber* can be ruined by the wrong college. He needs a college which will help him to develop socially, and reward him with honors and encouragement and scholarship aid, if necessary, for his good mind and his good work habits. He cannot profit fully from a college in which social lines are drawn tightly to exclude from college social life those who do not have the "right" background. The *strainer* is a poor risk in any college, and a sure failure in the college with rigid and high academic standards combined with a laissez-faire guidance policy which allows the student to sink or swim, depending on his own power.

TABLE 3. FAMILY SOCIO-ECONOMIC STATUS OF STUDENTS IN VARIOUS TYPES OF UNIVERSITIES (PERCENTAGE DISTRIBUTIONS)

Family Status	Cosmopolitan Univ.	Ivy College	Opportunity College	Warnell
Upper and upper middle	25	75	5	40
Lower middle	50	20	40	50
Working class	25	5	55	10

Some Typical Colleges

In order to see more clearly how the nature of the college is related to the chances of success and failure of the various kinds of students, let us look at three typical colleges.

COSMOPOLITAN UNIVERSITY. This university is either a midwestern or western state university or a large municipal university. It charges little or no tuition. It maintains high academic standards by flunking out a large proportion of the freshman class every year, although it has a liberal admissions policy. In socio-economic status its students, as shown in Table 3, range over almost the whole social spectrum, with the campus life dominated by upper middle and a few lower middle-class students. A large and growing group of boys and girls from working-class families is contributing to the rather inarticulate mass of youngsters who follow the patterns set by campus leaders.

Intellectual growth is mainly the result of the working of a curriculum which is broad and diverse and taught by competent scholars. Although many of the elementary courses are large and run by an impersonal staff of one or two professors and a corps of assistants, the more advanced courses are small enough to permit a good deal of personal contact between teacher and student.

Informal intellectual and esthetic stimulation is there for those who seek it, in the form of occasional off-campus lectures, departmental clubs, student union programs, and church foundation classes and discussion groups.

This type of institution is especially good for the *climber*, the person who knows what he wants and will keep looking until he finds it. The middle-class static does reasonably well here, but the strainer is likely to have difficulty. Uncertain about his own goals, inadequately equipped with work habits and attitudes that will carry him through academic difficulties, he is likely to get lost in the impersonal bigness of Cosmopolitan University.

The social life of this campus is diverse. There are conventional fraternities and sororities which draw upper middle-class youth and a few mobile ones from lower middle and working-class homes. There are the newer fraternities and clubs, designed expressly for groups of certain races or religions. The church foundations provide social centers for youth of all statuses who do not care for the beer-drinking and petting of the more sophisticated social organizations. The student union offers organized activities and informal recreation for boys and girls of all degrees of social affiliation and sophistication.

When this university is located in a large city, there are large numbers of commuters whose college life is limited to the day-time hours, and also many students who are supporting themselves completely with jobs that limit their participation in campus life to class attendance only.

The personnel worker in Cosmopolitan University is likely to discover many boys and girls whose goals are diffuse or whose own drive and sense of direction are inadequate to enable them to make headway toward their goals. They need counseling, individually and in groups. Some of them probably should be assisted to transfer to a smaller and more personalized college, such as Opportunity College or Warnell, where they may profit from the greater amount of supervision that the individual student may get in those colleges.

Also in Cosmopolitan University the personnel worker may find it necessary to help students find their way into the social groups that will be most advantageous to them. This applies especially to the shy ones, and those whose own social backgrounds have given them little experience with club and party life.

OPPORTUNITY COLLEGE. This college appears in several versions, always characterized by low costs, easy admission standards, and a predominance of students from working-class families. It may be a city junior college, with all its students commuters. It may be a state teachers college with most of its students living in dormitories. Or it may be a small "self-help" college, with a number of cooperative work enterprises in which students earn their board and lodging.

This college draws the poor but ambitious youngster, usually of high average but not superior academic ability. The sons and daughters of salespeople, office clerks, railway brakemen, construction workers, factory workers, and tenant farmers predominate. Their vocational goals are often vague, characterized by the notion that education will help them to something better, but without a realistic or intimate knowledge of what it means to become a lawyer, or an engineer, or a teacher—the kind of knowledge that comes from seeing such people in one's own home and knowing them as relatives or neighbors.

This college has a high drop-out rate, due to transfer of students to other colleges, to lack of finances, to poor learning ability, and to lack of clarity of educational purpose.

The social life of this college is not highly developed, and consists either of faculty-organized or supervised parties and dances, or of rather crude copies of the clubs and proms at the neighboring state university. The campus leaders among the students tend to be ambitious and energetic working-class and lower middle-class youth whose enthusiasm is not matched by their *savoir-faire*.

To a considerable extent, Opportunity College is a collection of students who want to go somewhere but are not sure just where this is, and who lack guides among themselves. The small group of upper middle-class students are likely to be atypical of that group and not adequate examples or guides.

Consequently the personnel worker in this college must be a guide or must discover and develop guides in the faculty and student body. There is need for more benevolent paternalism in this kind of college than in others.

Opportunity College is primarily a place for youth who desire social mobility. This they hope to attain by learning material skills and by learning the middle-class social skills. The college is better equipped to help them with vocational skills than with social skills, as a rule.

The personnel worker in Opportunity College will find that his work with groups will be aimed primarily at the social development of youth through social activities which prepare them for association in middle-class service clubs, civic associations, and professional and business organizations, as well as the informal middle-class clique activities of dining together, card playing, play-reading, and dancing.

At the same time his work with individuals will consist largely of counseling about the problems of the boy or girl who is feeling his way uncertainly toward a vocational position that he cannot envisage clearly. Typical topics will be vocational choice, choice of subjects in college, organization of study hours, adjusting the demands of part-time employment to a study schedule, shifting to Cosmopolitan University for the last two years of college work.

IVY COLLEGE. This is the generic name of the high status college with an old tradition, selective in its admissions policy, likely to be a college for men or for women only, but occasionally coeducational. Ivy College extends from the top of the liberal arts hierarchy down to the midwestern church-related college with a waiting list and a fine record of sending students on to graduate work.

This is the only type of college in America that has a literal majority of students from upper and upper middle-class families. Added to these are a minority of ambitious, hard-working boys and girls from lower middle-class families and a scattering of working-class youth with similar motivations. Social life centers around exclusive clubs and fraternities, and informal dormitory activities. The social interests of the students are likely to be organized on a family or summer home basis that makes the college relatively unimportant, especially for association with the opposite sex.

For the minority of upward mobile youth in Ivy College there are tremendous learning opportunities, both intellectual and social. The intellectual opportunities are open to all, through a stimulating campus life and through personal relationships with competent and personally attractive scholars. The social opportunities favor upward mobile youth with unusually attractive social talents, or with special artistic or athletic abilities. Some of the highly intelligent but less scintillating students fail to find their way into the social life of the campus.

One question with which personnel workers and admissions officers are concerned is whether Ivy College should deliberately seek a greater degree of heterogeneity, whether through scholarships the proportion of lower middle and working-class youth should be increased. One consequence of such a development probably would be to reduce still further the participation of upper status youth in campus social life, although the desire is to preserve social heterogeneity, with the personnel staff working deliberately to encourage campus-wide social participation.

In any event, it seems that the personnel worker in Ivy College will find his easiest and most rewarding activities in his work with upward mobile boys and girls. Some personnel workers, of course, will find themselves challenged by the situation and find ingenious new ways of deepening the learnings with the result that far more of their students will gain from college life.

WARNELL COLLEGE. There are several hundred Warnells, most of them church-related now or in the past. They tend to be found in the cities of ten to a hundred thousand, where they are regarded as the chief cultural asset of the community. They are, now as in the past, essentially middle-class institutions, as much lower middle as upper middle. By location and by tradition they tend to remain culturally homogeneous. They may be largely Methodist, or Presbyterian, or Baptist, or Lutheran, or Catholic. There are some Negro Warnells in the South, but few Negro students in the northern Warnells. Jewish students are absent, or present only in a small minority.

Warnell has her eye fixed on Ivy College, but a number of Warnells have moved into the Opportunity College category in the past generation.

Warnell is a much more comfortable place than Ivy College for boys and girls of lower middle and working-class status. It is the easiest kind of place for them to learn upper middle-class ways. They can make their way into fraternities and clubs easily, but they can also be comfortable if they stay out and belong to eating clubs, church groups, and local fraternities.

The student deans at Warnell are likely to find that mediocrity, intellectual and social, is the principal danger to worry about. Mediocrity tends to produce few personal problems, and consequently the counselor seems not to be needed so much. His role may have to be that of a gadfly stinging the abler students and faculty to greater and more critical intellectual activity, and to more creative social activity.

At the same time personnel work at Warnell will have a considerable responsibility for helping the "strainers" as distinct from the "climbers" to organize their lives and to set their goals on what the college can give them. Group guidance for freshmen and sophomores who are not achieving up to expectation should work well at Warnell.

The collegiate admissions officer or the personnel staff dealing with admissions will do well to look at their institutions in terms of their type of college, the distribution of their student body according to classes and types, and the consequences in terms both of group dynamics and individual growth that result from these factors. Such an analysis should help personnel workers become more realistic, discerning, and intelligent in their work. Intelligent appraisals of the needs of students and the needs of colleges based on the background here presented should bring greater benefits to students, to colleges, and to society than is possible when admissions hinge on scholastic aptitude alone. Society is fluid and changing; colleges and universities can become more so, to their benefit and to that of the communities which they serve. Rigid patterns often need to be broken, yet the wise admissions officer will not attempt to break them and leave them there. He will discuss with the faculty and with the student body issues that need consideration in relation to a more democratic philosophy of who should go to college. He will interpret the students he admits to the personnel staff and faculty. He will interpret the college to the students. In these ways he will be contributing in a vital way to deeper teaching and learning in his college.

BIBLIOGRAPHY

SOCIAL STRUCTURE AND EDUCATION

"Amherst College; Problems in American Civilization." *Education for Democracy*—The Debate Over the Report of the President's Commission on Higher Education. Boston, D. C. Heath, 1952.

Davis, Allison: *Social Class Influences Upon Learning.* Cambridge, Mass., Harvard University Press, 1948.

Hollingshead, A. B.: *Elmtown's Youth.* New York, Wiley, 1949.

The President's Advisory Commission on Higher Education: *Higher Education for American Democracy.* New York, Harper & Brothers, 1948.

Warner, W. L., Havighurst, Robert J., and Loeb, Martin B.: *Who Shall Be Educated?* New York, Harper & Brothers, 1944.

Warner, W. L., and Lunt, Paul S.: *The Social Life of a Modern Community.* New Haven, Yale University Press, 1941.

WHO GOES TO COLLEGE AND WHY

American Council on Education: *On Getting Into College: A Study of Discrimination in College Admissions.* Washington, American Council on Education, 1949.

Barber, Leroy E.: "Why some able high school graduates do not go to college," *School Review* 49:93-96, Feb., 1950.

Burack, Marvin: *Relation of the Social Status of Students to Their Retention and Progress at the Junior College Level.* Chicago, University of Chicago Library, 1951, unpublished Ph.D. dissertation.

Goetsch, Helen B.: *Parental Income and College Opportunity.* Teachers College, Columbia University, Contributions to Education, 1940.

Havighurst, Robert J.: "Social implications of the Report of the President's Commission on Higher Education," *School and Society* 67:257-261, 1948.

Hollingshead, Byron S.: *Who Should Go to College in America?* New York, Columbia University Press, 1952.

McGuire, Carson: *Adolescent Society and Social Mobility.* Chicago, University of Chicago Library, 1949, unpublished Ph.D. dissertation.

Mook, John: *Social Class and Social Mobility in a Midwestern College.* Chicago, University of Chicago Library, 1949, unpublished Ph.D. dissertation.

Mulligan, Raymond A.: "Socio-economic background and college enrollment," *American Sociol. Review* 16:188-196, 1951.

Phearman, Leo T.: "Comparisons of high school graduates who go to college with those who do not," *J. Ed. Psych.* 40:405-14, Nov., 1949.

Reeves, Floyd: "Barriers to higher education," *Phi Delta Kappan* 31:214-24, Jan., 1950.

Roper, Elmo: *Factors Affecting the Admission of High School Seniors to College.* Washington, American Council on Education, 1950.

3. Continuity in the Educational Process

RAYMOND A. PATOUILLET

ARTICULATION between high school and college is a problem in continuity. It involves making school and college part of an ongoing continuous educational experience. In order to be continuous, however, a process must have consistency of purpose. Schools and colleges rarely have common purposes, however, and that is the core of the problem of articulation.

Articulation and a Philosophy of Education

A philosophy of education determines purposes and procedures. This concept is well developed in a chapter by Taylor[1] and has already been discussed in Chapter 1 of this book. However, there are certain implications of philosophy for the articulation process which deserve mention. Instrumentalism, for example, is more generally accepted as a philosophy of education at the public secondary level than in private secondary schools and colleges. In the latter, rationalism and neo-humanism, as described by Taylor, are the guiding philosophies. This difference in philosophical orientation constitutes the basic difficulty in the articulation process.

The question may now be raised, "Which philosophy tends to provide the setting in which articulation has the maximum opportunity for realization?"

The rationalists can argue that since education should be everywhere the same, the problem of articulation does not really exist. The purpose of education is to train the intellect and the only articulation necessary is to agree upon some order and sequence of

[1] Harold Taylor: "The Philosophical Foundations of General Education," pp. 20-45.

selected subject matter and admit to college the intellectual élite who can involve themselves with profit in the abstractions of the "great books." Assuming, however, that such a restrictive concept of education is tenable, the fact remains that a student brings more to college than his intellect. He comes as a whole person with all kinds of psychophysical needs. If these are disregarded, the problem of articulation must necessarily assume serious proportions as a student tries to adjust to college life.

The dualism of the neo-humanist is clearly evident in the following quotation from a committee report by members of the faculties of three preparatory schools and three colleges working on the problem of articulation:

Finally, we are modern enough to be concerned with the intimate connection of *the mind and the emotions.* This report concerns primarily the mind. It assumes that what goes on in the classroom is the center of the educational process, although we are aware that often it is not; and it treats purely curricular problems with the seriousness which they deserve. But we know that a student's mind does not develop in isolation from his physical, social, and emotional development.[2]

While recognizing a connection between "the mind and the emotions," this report frankly states its primary concern with the mind. The same problem in articulation persists here as it does with the philosophy of rationalism. Continuity is impossible to achieve where only part of the personality, i.e., the mind, is selected to participate in a continuous educational experience. In this connection it is interesting to point out that it is partly because studies in articulation have for the most part been restricted to subject matter articulation that the problem of articulation continues to exist.

A philosophy is needed which holds that education is concerned with the whole person. It is the whole person who is making the transition from school to college. Such a philosophy enjoins colleges to look upon articulation as an area worthy of serious study in non-subject matter as well as subject matter areas. Instrumentalism provides a framework within which such study is not only possible but mandatory.

[2] *General Education in School and College.* A committee report by members of the faculties of Andover, Exeter, Lawrenceville, Harvard, Princeton, and Yale, p. 10.

A Brief History of Articulation

As has been noted briefly elsewhere in this chapter, articulation has up to now concerned itself primarily with subject matter. This emphasis is clearly evident as one studies the historical development of articulation in this country.

COLONIAL AMERICA

In colonial times the function of the Latin grammar schools was to prepare young men for college. The curriculum in the colleges was narrowly conceived and students followed a common course of study. Subject matter articulation was a relatively easy task.

THE ACADEMY

A demand for a more practical type of education developed midway through the eighteenth century, with Benjamin Franklin its most eloquent supporter. This movement led to the establishment of the academy. Most academies presented both the more traditional Latin curriculum and the new, more practical English curriculum. This broadened approach to secondary education helped the colleges broaden their own requirements and curriculum articulation was never to become the simple process it once had been. Every student could no longer take all the content offered by the schools and colleges.

PUBLIC EDUCATION

With the rise of the public high school and state universities after 1825 the problem of articulation entered into its third phase. Academies began to assume more and more the function of college preparatory institutions while the public high schools, although dominated by college requirements, helped meet the need for a terminal type of education. "State Universities, in ideal established for the people, in practice continued to cater to a small group who could afford the luxury of a higher classical education."[3]

With the increasing variety of secondary school offerings, curriculum articulation was becoming a more and more difficult task.

ACCREDITATION

When the University of Michigan around 1870 evolved a plan of accreditation with the high schools of the state, articulation moved

[3] R. Freeman Butts and Lawrence Cremin: A History of Education in American Culture, p. 356.

into a fourth phase. According to this plan the holder of a diploma from an accredited high school could attend the state university without further examination.[4]

Six regional associations of colleges and secondary schools have been established since the original Michigan agreement. The purpose of these associations is to promote the welfare of the colleges and secondary schools through better articulation. Although the associations have come to devote considerable study to non-subject matter areas, these areas are not yet part of the articulation process in the sense that the curriculum is.

STANDARDIZATION

Toward the end of the last century school-college relations were probably at their worst and articulation entered its fifth phase. Colleges could not agree among themselves on general entrance requirements and the secondary schools reacted against what they felt to be domination by the colleges. It had become difficult, for example, for a school to prepare its students for more than one college.

This state of affairs led to the formation by the National Education Association of the Committee of Ten in 1892. The report of this committee stressed the fact that the high school was not and should not be a college preparatory institution but at the same time proposed certain subjects for those students who were planning to go on to college.

In 1899 the Committee on College Entrance Requirements made a report which tended to standardize high school curricula and increase the emphasis on college preparation. The work of this committee led directly to the formation of the College Entrance Examination Board.

LIBERALIZATION

The underlying philosophy behind the approaches to the problem of articulation discussed in the preceding paragraphs seems to be that college should be an educational experience limited to the more intellectually capable in certain academic subjects. There were those, on the other hand, who believed that the purpose of all education is to educate for effective citizenship in a democracy. This more liberal view found expression after the turn of the century and articulation entered a sixth phase with the junior college movement and the

[4] Burke A. Hinsdale: *History of the University of Michigan*, p. 60.

publication in 1918 of the *Cardinal Principles of Secondary Education*.

The junior college movement gained strength because it met the need for more functional education which the state universities as well as the private colleges were not providing. California has taken the lead in this movement to the extent that today more than half of our junior colleges are in that state and are operating, in most instances, as part of their respective public school systems.

The *Cardinal Principles* formed one of several reports of the Commission on the Reorganization of Secondary Education which in turn evolved from the work of a Committee on the Articulation of High Schools and Colleges. This report stressed the belief that the purpose of education is to meet the needs of a democracy. Indirectly, then, it is a sort of declaration of independence on the part of high schools.

Although the high schools first revolted against college domination around 1890, and issued their declaration of independence in 1918 in the form of the *Cardinal Principles*, it was not until 1942 that a bold and practical step was taken. The *Cardinal Principles*, by stressing the needs of democracy, implied that any curriculum that meets the needs of students, is well planned, and of high quality is acceptable college preparation. The famous *Eight-Year Study* is a practical implementation of this concept and two of its basic conclusions are quoted below:

First, the assumption that preparation for the liberal arts college depends upon the study of certain prescribed subjects in the secondary school is no longer tenable.[5]

The second major implication of the results of the Eight-Year Study is that secondary schools can be trusted with a greater measure of freedom than college requirements now permit.[6]

The *Eight-Year Study* showed that the students from the experimental schools did better scholastically than students from other secondary schools, and in general were able to meet their problems of adjustment with greater resourcefulness. The problem of articulation was most easily met by those students whose interests and needs had furnished the bases for their high school curriculum.

In 1947, Michigan, once again exhibiting leadership in the field, evolved a program of articulation which seems extremely promising. Parts of the program are reproduced here:

[5] Wilford M. Aiken: *The Story of the Eight-Year Study*, p. 118.
[6] *Ibid.*, p. 124.

The college agrees to disregard the pattern of subjects pursued in considering for admission the graduates of selected accredited high schools, provided they are recommended by the school from among the more able students in the graduating class. This agreement does not imply that students must be admitted to certain college courses or curricula for which they cannot give evidence of adequate preparation.

. . . .

High Schools which seek to be governed by this Agreement shall assume responsibility for and shall furnish evidence that they are initiating and continuing such procedures as the following:

a. A program involving the building of an adequate personal file about each student, including testing data of various kinds, anecdotal records, personality inventories, achievement samples, etc. The high school staff will assume responsibility for developing a summary of these personnel data for submission to college.

b. A basic curriculum study and evaluation of the purposes and program of secondary school.

c. Procedures for continuous follow-up of former pupils.

d. A continuous program of information and orientation throughout the high school course regarding the nature and requirements of certain occupations and specialized college courses. During the senior year, to devote special emphasis to the occupation or college of the pupil's choice.[7]

Personnel workers will be tempted to ask why such areas as heterosexual adjustment, or reading and study habits are not specifically included in these recommendations, especially for college-bound students. Despite this criticism, the latest Michigan Agreement Plan has dealt honestly with some of the issues raised by the *Eight-Year Study* and with some of the weaknesses of general admission under the former accreditation plan.

In 1948 the concept of equal opportunity for all at all levels of the educational ladder was reinforced by the President's Commission on Higher Education.[8] This has led to a lively discussion around the question, "Should everyone go to college?" This question points up the need to define purposes; purposes determine program and procedure. As higher education exists today, it is definitely not prepared to accept all who knock upon its door.

[7] *Questions and Answers About the Michigan Secondary School-College Agreement Plan*, pp. 3-4.
[8] President's Commission on Higher Education: *Higher Education for American Democracy*.

OBJECTIVITY

With the development of psychological testing during and after World War I, and with an apparent increase in the number of failures and drop-outs in the colleges, articulation moved into a seventh phase. There evolved an interest in the use of psychological tests for admissions purposes and for predicting success in college work. In 1928, for example, Dean Johnston of the University of Minnesota outlined the use of the College Aptitude Rating at his college and how it was determined:

First, we secure from the high school principal the individual rank of the pupil in his graduating class together with the size of the class. This rank is then converted into a percentile rank to facilitate comparison between those coming from schools of different sizes. . . . From the psychological test scores also each student is given his individual rank and this is converted into a percentile rank. The percentile ranks are then simply averaged to give the college aptitude rating.[9]

These objective data served to help parents and prospective college students to understand more clearly the chances of success in college. Other valuable data however, of a more subjective nature, such as high school teachers' comments, anecdotal records, and personality rating forms were not considered in arriving at the college aptitude rating.

The Present

A comprehensive review of trends in admissions procedures, perhaps the most important aspect of articulation, is provided in a chapter prepared by Smith.[10]

The most complete picture of the status of articulation today is found in a survey of 607 colleges and 1351 secondary schools recently undertaken by the Educational Records Bureau.[11] The survey revealed many encouraging trends as well as areas needing further study. For example, information about personal characteristics of applicants is given greater stress than formerly by almost 70 per cent of the colleges. It is interesting to note, however, that the majority of secondary

[9] J. B. Johnston: "The Articulation of Secondary Schools with Higher Education," p. 631.

[10] Margaret Ruth Smith: "Selection and Capabilities of Students," pp. 472-515.

[11] Committee on School and College Relations: *A Brief Report on College Admission: Fifth Report.*

schools furnish such qualitative data only when the college requests them.

Quantitative data from testing programs in the secondary schools are not generally accepted by the colleges. The varying norms, the different tests used, all add to the complexity of the picture and continue to make entrance tests desirable. There seems to be some question on the part of the colleges of the competence of high school personnel in this area. "If the colleges receive accurate, detailed test histories expressed in understandable terms, they may accelerate the trend to make the secondary school test records an integral part of the entrance procedure."[12]

The survey also devoted attention to the problem of recording secondary school progress. There is a trend away from percentage grades and toward letter marks, a trend of which colleges seem to approve. The general index of accomplishment most frequently used and receiving most attention from both secondary schools and colleges is rank in class. "However, most colleges are ready to consider rank in terms of quarters or some other fraction of the class, and are willing to consider substitutes for rank if the secondary school has no adequate basis for ranking pupils as a result of its own evaluation procedures."[13]

The Carnegie Unit is still used for course accounting by most schools and colleges, although one third of the colleges have given up the system. The move away from the Carnegie Unit is distinctly more pronounced in the western part of the country than it is in the East.[14]

On the question of curricular requirements, high schools tend to support their new courses as worthy of consideration by the colleges and the colleges seem to be reacting with favor to this stand on the part of the secondary schools.[15]

It is interesting to note that while high schools have up to now felt dominated by the colleges, the colleges are currently very receptive to suggestions from the schools. Actually, there is the danger that schools may be hiding behind imaginary difficulties in the form of fancied opposition from the colleges. The way is definitely open to those schools that are sincerely desirous of trying out new ideas, and

[12] *Ibid.*, p. 25.
[13] *Ibid.*, p. 34.
[14] *Ibid.*, p. 34.
[15] *Ibid.*, p. 42.

this is a most hopeful sign in the whole picture of school-college relations.

A more recent, but much more limited, study of articulation has been conducted by members of the faculties of Andover, Exeter, Lawrenceville, Harvard, Princeton, and Yale.[16]

This study deals exclusively with students from the schools mentioned and is concerned with the problem of making the last two years of secondary school and the first two years of college a more meaningful experience, specifically with relation to the curriculum.

Looking Ahead

The problem of articulation has been defined as a problem in continuity. At the present time the transition between school and college is more often abrupt than not and may be presented diagrammatically as follows:

If articulation is to become a continuous process, this scheme of things must be altered to assume the character suggested by the following diagram:

The first diagram seems to support the notion that we must make our young people "stretch" from B to C. Those who cannot bridge the gap fall through. The second diagram likewise implies a stretch, in the nature of challenge, from B to C. But the difference is that the stretch in this case is part of a continuous process in which the individual student and his needs determine the degree of tension.

This latter approach to articulation goes much beyond the area of subject matter. Also, it implies that college freshmen are not fully matured individuals, but young people whose growth can be greatly

[16] *General Education in School and College*, op. cit.

enriched through sympathetic understanding at this particular stage in their development. This point of view was emphasized in the impressive study conducted by Lincoln Hale.[17]

A question that now arises is, "What can be done to achieve this desirable interpretation of articulation in actual practice?"

WHOSE JOB?

Articulation is a process which extends over a period of time, and includes at least two geographically distinct places. It therefore involves many people. But like many such jobs, no one person feels primarily responsible for carrying it out and the job does not get done. It might be more fruitful, then, to recognize at the outset that articulation is necessarily a cooperative and continuous enterprise whose aims may best be realized through joint effort. In this instance joint effort refers not only to high school counselors and college admissions officers but, and especially, to students. For articulation is not something to be done for students or to students, but with and by students. Articulation is a process, not a collection of facts about college or a bag of tricks on how to get along as a freshman. This is not meant to imply that information is not important or that a bag of tricks may not prove useful. But it means that articulation is more than these. It is a process in which students must inevitably be called upon to play the leading roles, with high school and college staffs serving as coaches from the sidelines. We must remember that it is the students who are making the transition to college. As matters stand now, however, the players are usually watching and the coaches are playing the game. A fundamental practical problem, then, is primarily one of getting students involved in the process of articulation.

STUDENT EXPECTATIONS

Students develop expectations of college life at almost any age and in countless ways. An outstanding athletic team, for example, gives many a youth his first contact with and initial impression of a particular college. Aunt Sue's stories of her college days may intrigue her niece, while Uncle Fred's tales of life in the old fraternity house may thrill his nephew. Visiting debating teams, touring glee clubs or dramatic groups, especially if written up in the local press, make indelible impressions upon the youth of a community. A college

[17] Lincoln Hale: *From School to College.*

professor speaking before a group of parents of high school students may not see himself as a recruitment officer (or his negative counterpart), but he is definitely shaping an expectation of his college. Whatever expectations are developed, and however they are arrived at, they are probably inaccurate and misleading. It is these expectations, nevertheless, that constitute a student's first contact with college. They therefore form the initial step in the process of articulation. It is the level of perception at which a systematic approach to the problem is most naturally initiated.

A Starting Point

These expectations form an excellent basis for group discussions while the students are still in high school. Out of these discussions will come a realization of the need for more reliable information and the many available resources may at this point be suggested by the high school guidance staff.

The college catalogue is perhaps the most readily available resource for all high school students, regardless of geographical location. Its potential role in the articulation process has never been fully explored, however. For example, a section could be included on the problems faced by the members of the present freshman class. This section could contain the results of a survey conducted by the freshmen and written by them. It would deal with expectations, problems arising from them, and recommendations to the prospective entering class.

Some colleges, for a variety of reasons, and despite the added cost, may find it more appropriate to include this sort of information in a student handbook. The problem here is to make sure that the handbook gets to the high schools at least as early as the catalogues now do.

Such a catalogue or handbook, while an improvement over many in current use, would have limited value, however, unless it were used in connection with problem-solving discussion groups in the high schools. A college catalogue or handbook is much like a museum: it contains the answers, but not the questions. Unless questions are formulated before a visit to a museum, one is apt to emerge with little more than vague impressions and aching feet. Likewise, reading through a college catalogue or handbook may be an unprofitable exercise unless one is motivated by a desire to get answers to definite problems.

In addition to a more profitable study of college catalogues and handbooks, high school discussion groups could engage in a number of other worthwhile projects. They could contact recent high school graduates who have gone to college and learn from them directly some of the problems of adjustment to college. This could become part of the regular yearly follow-up study of graduates made by the guidance staff.

The fact that vacation periods in the high school and college calendars do not usually coincide presents opportunities for visits to the high school by recent graduates. A team of four or five college students could form a panel to launch a discussion around the general question, "What is it like to be in college?" At this meeting, a college admissions officer could be present to serve as a resource person. Also, parents would be invited to attend so that their perceptions of college life might be clarified. The general session could then give way to smaller group discussions, with a college student assuming the role of group leader. A variation of this idea is discussed in an earlier article by the author.[18]

In some instances it might be advisable to allow the high school seniors to meet in the small groups without their parents. If this procedure seemed appropriate, parents could profitably meet with the college representative and the high school guidance staff. When college admissions officers function as outlined here, the emphasis is one of service to the community as opposed to selling and recruitment. Some colleges may decide to use student panels on a more organized basis outside of vacation periods and as a regular part of the articulation process as opposed to more extensive use of recruiters. However, a college representative could profitably accompany these student panels to serve as a resource person.

The differing vacation periods likewise make it possible for high school seniors to visit colleges and see them in action. This suggests that the "big brother" and "big sister" plans might be adapted for use before high school graduation time. The knowledge of just how to get to the campus from the railroad station, for example, is most reassuring information. Knowing which dormitory freshmen live in, where the campus store is, or where the locker room is—all of these give the prospective freshman much needed reassurance. The boys will learn, for example, that you do not arrive on a college campus sporting your high school football sweater. The girls on the other

[18] Raymond Patouillet: "College Students Conduct School's College-life Program."

hand, will learn that if they are smart they will not buy any clothes until they see just what college custom dictates. This kind of information, although superficial from the point of view of college faculty, is of extreme importance to adolescents who want to arrive on the campus in the fall with a certain degree of sophistication and *savoir faire.*

Behind the Scenes

All of this student-centered activity, however, cannot take place unless high school guidance staffs and college admissions officers are able to visit each other and meet regularly to discuss mutual problems.

Colleges and schools need to work together on the problem of students' records, for example. If the high school faculty finds a cumulative folder confusing, how much more so will it be to the college! How can more information about candidates for admission be forwarded to colleges in meaningful form? Up to now, college representatives have done most of the traveling. Perhaps boards of education will see the value of allowing their guidance personnel, as well as their principals and superintendents, to visit college campuses and attend meetings of school-college committees.

High schools should be interested in learning how their graduates are faring in college. Colleges should be reporting back to high schools. This again is a task that would be greatly facilitated through regular meetings of representatives from both types of institutions, perhaps on a regional basis.

Some colleges, such as Alleghany and DePauw, have conducted educational conferences for high school seniors, especially those from areas with limited guidance services. Others, such as Hofstra on Long Island, conduct special orientation sessions during the summer for those students who have been provisionally admitted.

The growing literature on the topic of orientation is an encouraging sign that colleges recognize this area as worthy of serious study.

Conclusion

The problem of articulation is complicated by the fact that high schools and colleges are inspired by different philosophies of education. These are reflected in different purposes and procedures. Despite this basic difficulty, a historical survey reveals many emerging trends that point to the development of a more meaningful process of articulation. In the last analysis, however, articulation will become part of a continuous educational process to the degree that it involves students and meets their needs.

BIBLIOGRAPHY

Aiken, Wilford M.: *The Story of the Eight-Year Study.* New York, Harper & Brothers, 1942, 157 pp.

Butts, R. Freeman, and Cremin, Lawrence A.: *A History of Education in American Culture.* New York, Henry Holt & Company, 1953, 628 pp.

Educational Records Bureau, Committee on School and College Relations: *A Brief Report on College Admission: Fifth Report.* New York, Educational Records Bureau, 1951, 61 pp.

Fuess, Claude M.: *The College Board, Its First Fifty Years.* New York, Columbia University Press, 1950, 222 pp.

General Education in School and College. A Committee Report by Members of the Faculties of Andover, Exeter, Lawrenceville, Harvard, Princeton and Yale. Cambridge, Harvard University Press, 1952, 142 pp.

Hale, Lincoln: *From School to College.* New Haven, Yale University Press, 1939, 446 pp.

Harvard University Committee on the Objectives of General Education in a Free Society: *General Education in a Free Society.* Cambridge, Harvard University Press, 1945, 267 pp.

Hinsdale, Burke A.: *History of the University of Michigan.* Ann Arbor, University of Michigan Press, 1906, 376 pp.

Johnston, J. B.: "The Articulation of Secondary Schools with Higher Education." National Education Association: *Proceedings,* 1928. Sixty-sixth Annual Meeting. Washington, D. C., the Association, 1928, 1205 pp.

Patouillet, Raymond: "College Students Conduct School's College-Life Program," *Clearing House* 24:369-370, Feb., 1950.

President's Commission on Higher Education: *Higher Education for American Democracy.* New York, Harper & Brothers, 1948.

Questions and Answers About the Michigan Secondary School-College Agreement Plan. Lansing, Michigan, Published by Lee M. Thurston, Superintendent of Public Instruction, 1953, 14 pp.

Smith, Margaret Ruth: "Selection and Capabilities of Students." In P. F. Valentine (ed): *The American College.* New York, Philosophical Library, 1949, pp. 472-515.

Taylor, Harold: "The Philosophical Foundations of General Education." National Society for the Study of Education. *General Education.* Fifty-first Yearbook, Part I. Chicago, the University of Chicago Press, 1952, 337 pp.

Traxler, Arthur E., and Townsend, Agatha (eds.): *Improving Transition from School to College.* New York, Harper & Brothers, 1953, 165 pp.

4. The New Student Arrives at College

DANIEL J. GRIER

CONSIDER the emotions of the immigrant as he debarks in New York clutching his few personal possessions, with a few vague notions as to what this new country is all about, but full of hope, courage, and plans. So also are the emotions of the new student first setting foot on the campus of the college. Before him lies a great educational adventure in a new environment. If he is to make the most of the opportunities available in college he must learn a great many things both in and out of class. How he can help himself and be helped by others to become a well adjusted part of this new environment is the subject of this chapter.

The adjustment of the new student involves three inseparably related areas—emotional, material, and academic. His emotional problems center around himself as a personality in contact with the college environment. His material problems center around the physical factors of everyday living. And his academic problems center around a series of specific knowledges or skills he has undertaken to master. In the home town environment the student had home and family, school and friends, and he felt secure in that situation as one who belonged. He would be hardly human if the loss of support given by those attachments did not leave him ill at ease and bewildered. He yearns for the familiar and the lack of it brings a lump to his throat and a sinking feeling to his stomach. With whom is he now to share his troubles, his hopes, and his fun?

A new student has material problems that must be faced immediately. He must be satisfactorily housed, he must make arrangements for handling his finances, and perhaps he needs part-time work or a scholarship. He needs to know where to cash a check, buy books, get laundry done, where to get medical care, where his classes are held, and a thousand other small but important details.

Yet, adjustment to the academic area is often even more difficult. The process of registration and the academic regulations are usually perplexing. The student may have some choice of courses and he usually has classes in several different departments and buildings. He finds that he is expected to absorb more difficult material in larger doses at a higher rate of speed than ever before and he is often dismayed to find that his old slapdash methods of study are inadequate to this new situation.

While it may be convenient to categorize the adjustment problems of the new student into the three areas stated, they cannot be considered as mutually exclusive. They continually overlap and interweave throughout the fabric of his college experience and any attempt to divide them operationally would be like trying to make the student a trinity—one but yet three persons—an impossibility in all but theory or faith as theologians will testify. Adjustment or lack of adjustment in one area has a direct bearing on the other areas for they constitute the total experience in which the student learns as a whole person.

The Concern of Educators with the Student As a Whole Person

The concept of orientation as a learning process must be based on a philosophy of education which recognizes the student as a whole being, not as a mind and a body joined together. Not all current theories in American educational philosophy agree with this point of view. As pointed out in Chapter I, the three main philosophical systems as described by Taylor are the rationalist, neo-humanist, and instrumentalist.

The rationalist theory is obviously not conducive to the acceptance of orientation as a function of deeper teaching. In fact the rationalists probably would not regard it as a function of education at all. On the other hand, the neo-humanists do accept it as an educational function, but with their dualistic point of view they consider it of secondary importance. It becomes a purely administrative area designed to put the student in good adjustment so he can perform at his maximum ability in academic areas. They consider it a useful, nay even a necessary, preparatory or conditioning exercise for the really important things to come. Is this not, however, mere lip service to the concept of the student as a whole person?

The instrumentalists, however, since they do not accept the duality of mind and body, see the student as a total organism and place personnel work at the same level of importance in learning as any of the subject matter disciplines. They do not see orientation as a purely administrative function to be dealt with by a body of specially trained technicians only, but as an area of learning underlying the whole educative process. It becomes an integral part of that process rather than a mere side show. It is indeed important as a conditioning process but it goes deeper than that. It is a learning process which is continually at work whether the educator recognizes it or not. It goes on as much in the classroom as outside it, as Cantor readily recognizes.[1] The student learns by experimentation and experience how to arrive at certain standards which enable him to adjust to the environment as surely as he learns by experiment in the chemistry laboratory or in the sociology classroom to accept or reject certain theories in terms of setting standards by which he can progress in science, philosophy, or personal living. Corey points out that learning has been studied from two points of view; one of the learner himself, and the other of the observer.[2] Higher education today has largely devoted its research into learning processes from the observer point of view, on which findings most current programs are based. This seems consistent with the philosophies of both the rationalists and the neo-humanists. In recent years, however, a move has developed toward investigating learning from the standpoint of the learner. This is more consistent with the instrumentalist philosophy for it turns attention to expressed needs of the students themselves. Psychologists tell us that the satisfaction of needs is fundamental in human behavior. The individual will seek the satisfaction of his needs through experimentation and will have a thirst for knowledge which will answer his questions.

The fact that a young person comes to college indicates that he has a desire to learn something. He has a dissatisfaction with the *status quo* which places him in a position to learn. "Whether learning is intentional or otherwise, it is initiated by some tension or imbalance or dissatisfaction on the part of the learner. . . . This disequilibrium, or dissatisfaction, initiates not only learning but all

---

[1] Nathaniel Cantor: *The Dynamics of Learning.*

[2] Stephen Corey: "Psychological Foundations of Education." *General Education,* Fifty-first Yearbook of the National Society for the Study of Education, Part I. Chicago, the University of Chicago Press, 1952, p. 48.

behavior."[3] Orientation as a learning function must provide the means for satisfying a desire for change or improvement not necessarily provided in the classroom but in conjunction with that in the classroom since much of what the student learns is outside any purely academic curricular planning. Perhaps the concern of educators is to see that those learnings which have heretofore been considered outside the curriculum are made a part of it.

Orientation As a Function of a Dualistic Philosophy

Before proceeding to a discussion of orientation as a function of deeper teaching it would be valuable to review briefly current orientation techniques and the philosophy behind them. The literature of student personnel work during the last thirty years has discussed these techniques in detail and it is interesting to note that in that period of time, with a few exceptions, there has been little fundamental change in either the techniques or their use. To be sure many writers have advocated change but most of the changes have been variations on a familiar theme. Personnel workers have been largely concerned with the development of the whole personnel program, a development which was facilitated by a relatively wide acceptance of the neo-humanist philosophy. As Esther Lloyd-Jones[4] has pointed out, personnel work as a special domain has made its greatest strides in colleges and universities based on a neo-humanist philosophy. The dualistic concepts of this philosophy have greatly facilitated the establishment of programs concerned solely with the extra-class activities of students, which may contribute to the welfare of the student but are not concerned with the cultivation of his intelligence. Many personnel workers in this situation, while giving lip service to the consideration of the student as a whole person, have fostered what might be called a cult of ultra-realism which in part is based on insecurity. This is understandable for in many colleges and universities the ideas behind the instrumentalist-oriented personnel point of view have been fighting an uphill battle against rationalist ideas. In many cases this battle has been resolved in neo-humanist compromise. It is relatively easy in those circumstances for the student personnel administrator to establish a small empire without disturbing the academic faculty or being disturbed by them. It is unlikely

[3] Stephen M. Corey: Op. cit., p. 51.
[4] Esther Lloyd-Jones: "Personnel Work and General Education." General Education, Fifty-first Yearbook of the National Society for the Study of Education, Part I. Chicago, the University of Chicago Press, 1952, p. 216.

that fundamental changes in orientation techniques would be made in such a situation.

The impact of the instrumentalist philosophy on education early in the twentieth century gave rise to the establishment of what is now commonly called student personnel work. As part of that movement personnel-minded educators became aware of the need to help the student become a part of the college as one of the important factors in his over-all adjustment. During the third decade of the century orientation techniques, along with other personnel techniques, began to crystallize rather generally into the methods which, with variations, are now widely used. The techniques reported in 1948 by Bookman[5] do not differ widely from those discussed by Doermann[6] in 1926 and Gardner[7] in 1936. The criticisms found by Bookman are similar to those stated by Gardner. Most of the techniques used are based on observed student needs and some on their expressed needs. Most institutions as part of their general orientation program make some sort of pre-entrance contact with the new student through bulletins or informational literature and visits to high schools by admissions officers. Older students often establish a relationship with the entering students through what are commonly called "big brother" or "big sister" programs, which are frequently tied in with the efforts of the college housing administrators to aid the new students in gaining a feeling of belongingness. A formal program usually referred to as freshman days or orientation week carried on in the first few days immediately preceding the beginning of classes is also a widely used technique. This program usually includes informational lectures, testing, physical orientation to the campus, registration, social mixers, and counseling. Some colleges have informal freshmen orientation camps in a recreational spot not far from the campus. While most orientation programs concentrate on freshman week, some colleges have continuation programs which usually consist of orientation courses or counseling.

Critical evaluation of these techniques indicates that while many of them are theoretically planned to be of lasting value as functions of deeper teaching, the practice is frequently at variance with the theory. One of the essential weaknesses is that for the most part they

[5] Gladys Bookman: "Freshman Orientation Techniques in Colleges and Universities."

[6] Henry J. Doermann: The Orientation of College Freshmen.

[7] Donfred H. Gardner: Student Personnel Service. The Evaluation of Higher Institutions.

concentrate on the first few days and except for some counseling or continuation courses the student is then almost entirely on his own. This of course is consistent with dualistic theory for it does not interfere with the academic program. Much of the information given out during freshman week is in lecture form and the student is on the receiving end of a one-way line with little opportunity to relate the information to his personal adjustment. At the same time the period is often one of considerable confusion, much of the program serves only to further confuse the student, and it is probable that the results are the opposite of those intended. What seems to be ignored is the fact that many adjustment problems of the students do not become real to them until students are well along in college and that adjustment to the academic program is often the most difficult problem the student faces. Even the continuation programs are largely ineffective, according to Bookman, since many of the orientation courses are lectures and again the student is at the receiving end only.[8]

Furthermore, the lectures are often brought in from various departments or services and the course content becomes an unrelated hodge-podge. While there is no question of the positive value of counseling on an individual basis, limitation of time and personnel in all but the most personnel-minded colleges means that counseling becomes mainly therapeutic rather than developmental. Only the students with the most acute adjustment problems receive attention while the majority who seem to be making some sort of adjustment must be left to their own devices. In many colleges where elaborate programs using academic advisers are set up the counseling is ineffective because the advisers are either unskilled in personnel techniques or have no interest in the student except as an intellect. The advising consequently becomes a mere clerical routine of program planning.

Much can be done and has been done to aid the adjustment of the student through the use of residence hall counselors, but in all too many cases college residence halls are operated as business enterprises and the counselors are disciplinary flunkies. As such the residence hall is merely a hotel and the counselor the house detective. The extracurricular program at most colleges offers tremendous possibilities in genuine learning experiences for the students and it should be a fundamental part of the continuing orientation pro-

[8] Gladys Bookman: *Op. cit.*

gram, but this area of all the areas relegated by the dualists outside the pale is often considered the least important.

The failure of many current orientation techniques adequately to accomplish the purposes for which they are intended appears to be the result of operating in a neo-humanist atmosphere rather than in one which is genuinely committed to the total learning of the whole person. Certainly the new student needs pre-entrance conditioning to the new environment. He needs counseling and continuation programs and any other specific techniques based on both observed and expressed needs. There is no need to toss out current practices if they are used with the idea that they are part of the total learning process in college, not the student personnel administration side show. It is difficult for personnel workers who have been operating on a dualistic basis to make an abrupt shift to the concept that a sound orientation program is not the sole prerogative of a specialized personnel empire, but the function of the whole college—students, faculty, and administration.

Orientation As Deeper Teaching

Under a dualistic philosophy of education, orientation has been set apart as a conditioning function to be handled by the personnel workers and a few interested faculty members, and where it has operated as a part of the total learning process it has often been more by accident than intent or as something not usually considered part of the orientation program. Yet, in cases where the entire college cooperates in contributing to the learning process, the very essence of a genuinely effective program of helping students become a part of the college is implemented. Two examples which recently occurred in a large midwestern university illustrate this point. A student who had never had a similar experience was appointed to serve as convention chairman for the annual national convention of a large student organization. She was responsible for all the physical arrangements, speakers, selection of discussion topics, convention literature, finances, and the housing of over four hundred delegates. She effectively enlisted the cooperation and assistance of other students, members of the personnel staff, the student union, residence halls, physical plant, university editor, public relations director, and many others in accomplishing her task. When it was all over she remarked that she felt she had learned more about how to get things done and how to work with people than she had from all her other college experience during the preceding three and a half years.

At the same institution, prior to the national political conventions of 1952, about five hundred students actively participated in a mock political convention. To accomplish this they enlisted the aid of the whole university including administrative and service staff and members of the speech, government, and English departments. Many of the students involved were quick to point out that this experience drew together and made real the classroom training they were having in the three subject matter departments which cooperated, as well as affording considerable insight into our national political system. These were experiences in which the whole institution cooperated in a process of deeper teaching through the integrated efforts of a variety of student, faculty, and administrative facilities and departments. Although neither of the examples cited were considered part of the orientation program at that university, they illustrate the kind of approach that is needed to make orientation programs a part of the deeper teaching process, and they actually are a part of the total learning which helps to orient the student toward a more effective life both in and after college. In short, the objectives of orientation are precisely those of any other teaching function of the college which is interested in the education of the whole person.

If helping students become a part of the college is to be an important factor in the deeper teaching of students there are three points that must be considered in the establishment of a sound program: Student needs must be ascertained and met; students must be considered as whole persons and must be worked with as individuals; and orientation must be made a function of the whole college. With respect to the first point, student needs must be met, but they must be understood before they can be met. General needs as discovered over the years are widely discussed in the literature but every college has its own individuality which may give rise to learning problems peculiar to students in that institution, and personnel workers and the faculty must be aware of these needs. Second, the deeper teaching of the student as a whole person means that orientation must deal with all his needs and problems as an individual in spite of the fact that many of his needs may fall into certain general categories. Third, since orientation must be emphasized as a function of the whole college, the program should operate within a general framework of educational philosophy conducive to total learning of the whole student. This cannot be done effectively under a dualistic philosophy.

With these three points in mind it would appear that the most effective program designed to make students a part of the college would involve their concurrent orientation through both group and individual means throughout their entire college experience. In recent years more and more colleges have begun to realize this and a considerable amount of experimentation has been going on in methods of developing more effective programs. The remainder of this chapter will be concerned with some of the newer methods and adaptations of the older methods which are being used in an effort to make orientation a true function of deeper teaching.

In the initial contacts between the college and the prospective students, many colleges are turning away from the old sales techniques, which tend to mislead students, to programs which are more informative and educational. Advance literature in the form of bulletins and pamphlets which concentrate on answering the questions of prospective students are more and more in use, and these are being supplemented by both group and individual interviews between college representatives and students where a genuine effort is made to help the student come to an intelligent decision about which college to attend. Besides visits by the college representatives to high schools, many colleges have set aside days in which groups of students from the high schools may come to the campus and obtain better personal and physical knowledge of the college.

The "big brother" technique used by a number of colleges remains a valuable part of orientation for it aids in the deeper teaching of both the new student and the upper-class student counselor. It is desirable, however, that an attempt be made to continue the relationship between the two students beyond the first week or two of school, which has not always been the case. A variation of this technique is the use of the upper-class students as counselors in freshman camps. Both freshman and upper-class students have voiced their approval of the use of student counselors; the freshmen from the point of view that they feel much more comfortable in discussing most of their general problems with a well-informed and more experienced student who is much closer to their situation than are most faculty members, and the older students from the point of view that in training for the job they have an opportunity to draw together the varied information they have acquired both in and out of class into a much more meaningful pattern.

Freshman week also remains a valuable technique if care is taken to see that the student has some time in which to draw his breath and that he is not exclusively on the receiving end. Various changes are being made which should help to reduce the confusion of this period. Some colleges, particularly those whose students come primarily from an area closely surrounding the campus, are experimenting with advance registration during the summer preceding the students' entrance. Other schools which formerly required a complete physical examination during freshman week are experimenting with postponing the examination until after school starts in order to derive as much learning as possible from the experience, and with requiring a much more complete medical report from the student's home physician to use as the basis for his admission and subsequent health examination and counseling. Colleges are also examining their testing programs to make sure they are not giving tests just for the sake of testing, that only those tests which are necessary are given during freshman week, and that counseling use is made of test results. Such areas as reading improvement, extracurricular informational programs, and how to study programs are in some cases being handled through group discussions, in the residence halls, for example, or through enabling courses, rather than during the first few days. Most of these changes are for the purpose of spreading out the various parts of the program so that new students can derive deeper learnings and to effect a wider use of college facilities and personnel in the orientation of new students.

Efforts are also being made to take the individual general counseling of both new and old students out of the specialized areas of the Dean's office and the psychological clinic and to place more responsibility for it in the hands of faculty members and housing supervisors so as to make the counseling more developmental in nature and available to more students than is usually possible under the highly specialized system where counseling is mainly therapeutic and reaches an extremely limited number of students.

The use of teaching staff, upper-class students, and housing personnel has brought about the institution of in-service training programs designed to educate these persons in the value of counseling and to acquaint them with information and techniques which will aid them in contributing to the orientation of the new student. Counseling by members of the instructional staff is not new in personnel work but in many institutions this counseling has been limited to advice on programs and academic matters. Potentially it is one of the most valuable adjuncts of an orientation program concerned with the education of the whole person, but it is at this point that the vicious aspects of the dualistic philosophy are revealed. If the instructor or departmental adviser restricts his relationship with the student to merely approving courses or initialling a schedule card and he has no concern with any other aspect of the student's college experience, he is ignoring all the other factors which have so much bearing on whether or not that program of courses has any real educational meaning for the student. The adviser or instructor who sees his student as a human being like himself and regards his teaching as counseling, or vice versa, can through his knowledge and experience integrate the curricular program into the pattern of total learning the student is seeking to build. The trend toward this latter point of view appears to be continually growing, particularly with respect to the handling of freshman students.

By and large the use of student counselors appears to be restricted to general counseling, sometimes in group situations, on relatively superficial problems. It is generally agreed that their closeness to the younger student which is of such value in general counseling establishes natural lines of communication and understanding, but also makes it inadvisable for them to attempt to deal with anything else than relatively superficial problems of campus adjustment. Most colleges are making effective use of counseling in the residence halls and living units. This is a particularly helpful type of orientation counseling since the housing counselor is in most cases the only supervisory person who is likely to be in very close contact with the student when he is not in class. He is thus able to do much in helping the new student gain a feeling of belonging and to adjust to the total environment.

Extra-class activities are also important in the continuing orientation of the student. In spite of the evident value of such activities in the total education of the student, this part of the college experience has perhaps suffered from the dualistic point of view more than any other single aspect. Over the passive, and sometimes active, resistance on the part of more rationalist-minded faculty members, students have increasingly shown a great need for some sort of organized participation in activities outside of class, and they are likely to become involved in them whether or not provisions are made for constructive programs. If the activities are carried on without the approval or cooperation of the college they are potential sources for learning of an undesirable nature. With the kind of cooperation and integration indicated, however, by the two examples previously given, the extra-class activities become a co-curriculum of good and lasting value.

A number of colleges have experimented with various types of small group orientation with some success and this appears to be one of the more promising trends among orientation techniques. Wayne University has experimented with such a program and for a number of years Colgate University has had a preceptorial counseling program using small groups of students.* Also for several years a group program has been conducted at the Ohio State University Teachers College for orientation of new students with special emphasis toward preparing them for teaching.†

There are a number of advantages to an orientation program based on small groups. Only through the small group of ten to fifteen members can students actively participate in the orientation process through group discussion. Furthermore, they interact with one another in a manner which stimulates thinking and makes the process one of genuine learning rather than the mere absorbing of information. It is also possible to work with the students on a more nearly individual basis and to observe their behavior in terms of any possible severe maladjustment which can then be handled on a referral basis by the specialist. Grier[9] has suggested a program based on the democratic group process in which each incoming class would be divided into groups of not more than fifteen individuals with an orientation counselor or leader assigned to each group. Where it is possible to use upper-class students as counselors or where available faculty members are limited, it might not only be practical but desirable to assign a student leader to each group with a faculty counselor for each four or five groups. The program should be considered part of the curriculum, meetings should be at regular intervals for at least the full first semester, and credit should be given for them. Meetings should be conducted through the democratic group process with the leader acting primarily as a catalytic agent and resource person. The content may be mildly structured in terms of observed needs of students but it should be loose enough so that there is ample opportunity to discuss the expressed needs of the student.

* See Howard L. Jones in the bibliography for a more complete description.
† See Leston L. Love, and Lyle L. Miller and Alice Z. Seeman in the bibliography for a more complete description.
[9] Daniel J. Grier: *Orienting Students Through Group Counseling in a College Setting.*

Probably the greatest use of the group technique in orientation practice is in the informal kinds of meetings found in housing units and student organizations. Potentially these are ideal situations for deeper teaching but in the organization meeting, unless there is an experienced leader or source person involved, the learning is apt to be rather slow and laborious.

In a number of colleges the realization that some sort of orientation beyond freshman week is needed has led to the establishment of various continuation programs. Many of these have been the kind of orientation course that has been considered inadequate but there has been a trend toward developing less generalized courses, frequently called enabling courses. For example, Purdue University, among others, has established a course in developmental reading. This was begun as an experimental non-credit course and when its beneficial results were seen it became a regular credit course in the English department. Areas in which enabling courses have been more commonly established in addition to reading are personal development, educational and vocational guidance, personal and mental hygiene, and in educational areas such as agriculture, education, and engineering. An example of a specialized enabling course is another one at Purdue in the operation of the slide rule, proficiency in the use of which is of considerable importance to engineering students. In some colleges, often under the sponsorship of the student council, short courses in leadership techniques have been set up primarily for the benefit of students who are active in the organizational program. All of these courses are designed to meet some specific need of students in a particular situation or environment and indications are that they are likely to be far more effective than the old information-lecture type of course.

The success of an orientation program as a function of deeper teaching depends largely upon the philosophy, attitudes, and involvement of the whole college. The involvement of the whole college in the process will not take place automatically but as the result of a planned program designed to bring each segment of the college into a position where it can most effectively contribute its resources to the task of teaching the whole student. In-service training courses for faculty members are admittedly difficult to establish except in areas adaptable for enabling courses. In at least two areas, however, progress is being made toward bringing more of the college personnel into the picture. A number of colleges have established orientation programs for new faculty members in order to assist them in more quickly becoming a part of the college and thus, in addition to helping themselves, enable them to work more effectively with students. These programs are usually rather brief and they are often supplemented by handbooks explaining academic regulations and policies, services available to faculty, etc. Some schools, including the University of Wisconsin and Michigan State College, publish two handbooks, one for the faculty and one for the service personnel. Many of these handbooks would undoubtedly be more useful in terms of helping the staff member work more effectively with students if more stress were placed on staff-student relationships. In the area of student organizational work there appears to be an increased sensitivity on the part of the older students to their responsibility in helping the newer students become a part of the college. The decline in hazing as a student orientation technique and the development of more constructive programs such as responsible government by students, tutoring sessions by departmental or honorary student groups, leadership programs, etc., are all indicative of the trend toward involvement of the students themselves in orientation as an important learning process. Encouragement of such techniques by personnel-minded staff members is important in the over-all orientation program.

Summary

This chapter has been concerned with a broad view of orientation as an important factor in all the day-to-day experiences of the student in college. Actual techniques were discussed less than might be desired, but most current techniques are well covered in the literature listed in the bibliography. Furthermore, no program, however good it looks on paper, is worth the work and planning if it is not based on a sound philosophy. Certain formal aspects of orientation expressed in programs such as freshman week, group programs, and enabling courses have been discussed. In a larger sense helping a student become a part of the college involves both his formal and informal experiences. Thus a fundamentally sound orientation program must be based on an educational philosophy which without reservation accepts the student as a total organism and which facilitates the involvement of the entire college in the process. The orientation programs of most colleges are based on a dualistic philosophy which is not conducive to this type of program, and only by a program actively directed toward making orientation a function of deeper teaching can the student really be helped to become a part of the college.

BIBLIOGRAPHY

Arbuckle, Donald S.: "A College Experiment in Orientation." *Occupations* 28:112-117, Nov., 1949.

Association for Supervision and Curriculum Development: *Group Processes in Supervision.* Washington, National Education Association, 1948, 130 pp.

Bookman, Gladys: "Freshman Orientation Techniques in Colleges and Universities." *Occupations* 27:163-166, Dec., 1948.

Bookman, Gladys: *Freshman Orientation Techniques in Colleges and Universities.* Unpublished doctoral dissertation, University of Wyoming, August, 1948, 136 pp.

Brouwer, Paul J.: *Student Personnel Services in General Education.* Washington, American Council on Education, 1949, 317 pp.

Cantor, Nathaniel: *The Dynamics of Learning.* Buffalo, N. Y., Foster and Stewart, 1946, 282 pp.

Chamberlin, Dean, and Chamberlin, Enid, et al.: *Did They Succeed in College?* In *Adventures in Education.* New York, Harper & Brothers, 1942, Vol. IV, 291 pp.

de Huszar, George B.: *Practical Applications of Democracy.* New York, Harper & Brothers, 1945.

Doermann, Henry J.: *The Orientation of College Freshmen.* Baltimore, Williams and Wilkins Company, 1926, 162 pp.

Foster, Robert G., and Wilson, Pauline P.: *Women After College: A Study of the Effectiveness of Their Education.* New York, Columbia University Press, 1942, 305 pp.

Gardner, Donfred H.: *Student Personnel Service. The Evaluation of Higher Institutions.* Chicago, The University of Chicago Press, 1936, Vol. V., 235 pp.

Grier, Daniel J.: *Orienting Students Through Group Counseling in a College Setting.* Unpublished doctoral dissertation, Teachers College, Columbia University, 1951, 151 pp.

Jones, Howard, L.: "Preceptorial Counseling at Colgate University." *Occupations* 28:453-454, Apr., 1950.

Kelley, Janet L.: *College Life and the Mores.* New York, Bureau of Publications, Teachers College, Columbia University, 1949, 308 pp.

Lloyd-Jones, Esther: *Social Competence and College Students.* Washington, D. C., American Council on Education, 1940, 89 pp.

Lloyd-Jones, Esther, and Smith, Margaret Ruth: *A Student Personnel Program for Higher Education.* New York, McGraw-Hill Book Company, 1938, 322 pp.

Love, Leston L.: *Student Planning in College*. Columbus, Ohio, The Ohio State University Press, 1941, 156 pp.

Miller, Lyle L., and Seeman, Alice Z.: *Guidebook for Prospective Teachers*. Columbus, Ohio, The Ohio State University Press, 1948, 205 pp.

Mursell, James L.: *Developmental Teaching*. New York, McGraw-Hill Book Company, 1949, 374 pp.

National Society for the Study of Education. *General Education*, Fifty-first Yearbook. Chicago, Ill., University of Chicago Press, 1952, Part I, 377 pp.

Shimburg, Benjamin: "The Needs and Problems of Youth as Told by Themselves." Proceedings of the Fourteenth Annual Guidance Conference Held at Purdue University, April, 1949. *Studies in Higher Education LXIX* (H. H. Remmers, ed.). Lafayette, Indiana, Purdue University, 1949, pp. 74-88.

Slavson, S. R.: *Creative Group Education*. New York, Association Press, 1945, 247 pp.

Strang, Ruth: *Educational Guidance: Its Principles and Practice*. New York, The Macmillan Company, 1947, 268 pp.

Wharton, Mildred M. (compiler): *Orientation of Freshmen in Colleges and Universities*. Washington, National Association of Deans of Women, 1942, 27 pp.

Wrenn, C. Gilbert: *Student Personnel Work in College*. New York, Ronald Press Company, 1951, 589 pp.

5. How Records Contribute to Deeper Teaching

MARY I. OMER
EUGENE L. SHEPARD

The Purpose of Records

The college today is concerned with the total growth and development of the student. It recognizes that individuals differ in ability, interests, social and emotional maturity, and in terms of their socio-economic background. If a college is to plan educational experiences to meet the needs of its students and to counsel with them effectively, it must accumulate data and keep records on all aspects of the student's background, development, and educational experiences.

The personnel record provides the means for understanding individuals better so that effective counseling and education can occur. Through this the ultimate objectives of student guidance are achieved, namely, self-understanding, insight, and self-direction. Advisers, counselors, teachers, and administrators are able to help students learn only to the extent to which they possess an intelligent understanding of the individual. Records are the basis for this kind of understanding.

Students must be given the opportunity and the responsibility for observing their own needs, formulating their goals, noting their own progress, and evaluating their present accomplishment in relation to the objectives selected. Whenever a student is unable to make such significant and timely observations, he must be taught the procedure. It is the function of the staff to do this new kind of teaching. It is also the function of the staff to watch sensitively the state of the student's self-concept and the way his experiences and others' evaluations of him are affecting his motivations.

Records become increasingly important as the student sees their primary purpose is to help him (and his counselor) acquire a more thorough understanding, appreciation, and acceptance of himself. As the student views his record in this light it may become more than anything else the most concrete and significant revelation of his goals. Therefore, to the extent that student goals are important in personnel work, records are important.

Records also facilitate the communication of constructive understanding of a given student from one staff member to another. The more responsibility the student is asked to accept in collecting these data himself the less important this function becomes. Records and reports guarantee the preservation of important details, for in a program which emphasizes student responsibility for the observation, collection, and remembrance of significant details it is easy to neglect this aspect.

In addition to aiding the student in appraising himself, records of student needs, progress, and achievement are the basic facts essential to the continuous evaluation and revision of objectives, curriculum, and extra-curricular, instructional, and counseling procedures of an institution. Follow-up studies of the records of graduates, their activities, felt needs, and achievements provide data for evaluating the educational effectiveness of the institution, and whether or not the program is truly functional. Records can also serve as stimuli to teachers to consider and decide upon their course objectives, judge the effectiveness of their teaching, and the progress of the student in relation to the chosen course objectives.

Another purpose of records is that of furnishing transferable information for guidance. Education is a continuous process and should proceed smoothly over such transfer points as high school and college entrance, junior college to senior college, college to graduate school, and from any level of the educational system to employment in an occupation. Not only does keeping adequate records increase the likelihood of continuity in dealing with the student, but it supplies evidence concerning an individual's readiness and suitability for subsequent experiences, such as a particular college, business, or industry. Records and reports facilitate the communication of helpful data from high school counselors to college admissions board, from teachers to students, from one staff member to another, from adviser to counseling specialist, and in many instances to employer.

Understanding students better, evaluating student progress and institutional effectiveness, and fostering continuity and transferability of personnel data are the purposes of records.

The Development of Records

The idea of the development of records is here broadly interpreted to mean not only the developing or building of record forms but also the actual process of developing and of channeling information to be recorded. In a practical situation it is impossible for an institution to dissociate the development of its records from its philosophy in regard to records.

It is said that science became science when man began to keep records. One realizes, however, that the keeping of records can never be justified as an end in itself. Instead, records can and should be used as a means for the scientific study of problems. In personnel work recording should be adapted to counseling—not counseling to record keeping. In counseling, as in science, records become a report of what has happened and serve as the basis for important follow-up, evaluation, and problem-solving.

In developing personnel records it is important to consider what the individuals who are actually working with students need to know. For example, what has significance and usefulness for the teacher, the faculty adviser, the residence counselor, the medical and other specialists as they all try to counsel with the student about his growth and development? And of equal importance, what does the student need to know about himself?

Since the personnel record is about the student he should have a major part in building, maintaining, and evaluating it. Hahn and McLean state that "The more the student actively takes part in the collection and analysis of the information about himself, the more he may be expected to grow in self-understanding."[1]

The student should be introduced to the process of building his own record even before his matriculation at the college. This structuring may be initiated prior to admission by requesting him to fill out a comprehensive personal sheet. In an early counseling conference with his adviser he can be given the responsibility for keeping his own personal file up to date by recording his current scholastic achievements, social activities, extra-curricular participations, work experiences, and other evidences of his growth or progress. When he has completed this he arranges an appointment with his faculty counselor for purposes of discussion, interpretation, and evaluation

[1] Milton E. Hahn and Malcolm S. McLean: *General Clinical Counseling*, p. 98.

of these data. Each succeeding quarter he repeats this process. He knows that his record is open both to him and to his adviser and that he is free to examine his growth at any time. These periodic conferences with his counselor provide the student opportunities to inquire into each aspect of his own development. Together they consult the record for clues and answers to such questions as: Am I learning to make intelligent decisions? Am I honest with myself in appraising success or failure in an undertaking? What do I want to get out of this course or that? To what extent am I achieving my objectives? The student, learning during the first semester that his records are actually his own, that his adviser is there to counsel rather than direct him, will acquire the habit for self-direction. As he becomes a full partner in his growth process the student, instead of expecting the counselor or the teacher to supply the answers to his problems, is in a position to take the major responsibility for his own decisions and personal development.

When approached from the point of view just described, the development of personnel records becomes a cooperative venture and a continuous process which involves the student and all those who work with him in a personnel relationship. In gathering data about a student it is important to include information which will be helpful to him as he seeks to increase his understanding of himself and as he formulates his educational objectives and plans for realizing them. Wrenn points out that for counseling purposes, the information gathered and recorded "should be in a form to indicate its consecutive nature, how the student's program, health, plans, activity participation, have changed from term to term. In other words the record should be *comprehensive* as to areas of living and *cumulative* as to time."[2] Furthermore, the personnel records should reveal the problems a student has faced and how he has met them at various stages of his growth.

In considering types of records to be included in a record system and their relative usefulness one might consider the question raised by Strang. "What types of records do you think would be most likely to throw light upon desirable changes in student behavior?" She says further, "The word *desirable* implies reference to education objectives; the word *changes* implies growth. These are extremely important concepts which are basic to good personnel records."[3]

[2] Gilbert C. Wrenn: *Student Personnel Work in College*, p. 438.
[3] Ruth Strang: *Counseling Technics in College and Secondary School*, p. 181.

Again, as pointed out by Traxler,[4] a system of personnel records must not be static; it should be revised frequently as an institution's theory of education changes.

Today many sources are available for securing the record data needed in a college counseling program. For example, there is the pre-admission interview with prospective and entering students, autobiographies, questionnaires to be filled out by students, parents, and high school officials, student plan sheets, transcriptions of counseling interviews, test data, grades, extra-class participation reports, case histories, anecdotal records, and progress reports of various kinds.

More and more educational institutions are giving serious consideration to pre-college contacts with students, and counseling. This means that an increasingly large number of institutions are sending out admissions counselors to interview prospective students and their parents and high school principals or guidance directors. Usually special record forms are devised for use by the admissions counselors in making their reports to the board of admissions. These forms usually include, in addition to routine information such as age, address, birthplace and parents' name, significant comments about scholarship and citizenship, post-college plans, occupational interests, class attendance, extra-class participation, needs, home life, and social background. This information becomes a part of the record and supplements the student's statement of his needs and interests. It is also useful to the adviser as he counsels with the student in his selection of courses and out-of-class activities and as he seeks to stimulate the student in developing, throughout his college course, his capacity for self-direction. In an institution in which records are well integrated, for counseling use, copies of such records by admissions counselors are duplicated and sent to faculty and residence counselors and other personnel staff members.

As records are built or developed consultation with others who may contribute toward or use the records is extremely important for two reasons. First, those who are concerned with the records are in a position to make significant contributions as to the items needed in their work with students. Second, participation in record building provides excellent developmental training for those who work with students but who are not likely to be specialists in personnel work. Once a new record form has been tentatively set up, it should be tried out by representative individuals who will be using the form

[4] Arthur E. Traxler: *Techniques of Guidance*, p. 208.

or who will be in a position to observe the reaction of others in using it.

Again, when developing records, the objectives for which they are to be used must be kept in mind. There should be a definite relation between the finished record and the original objectives. In an institution where an entire system of records is to be developed, it is better practice to develop one record at a time, try it out and revise it, than to develop the whole series at once. Naturally all records in a system must dovetail, but often while experimenting with one record, observations will be made which will be of great value in the development of the additional records. It is well to study periodically the actual use made of records and to make revisions as needed.

In all record building, keeping, and interpretation, as well as in classroom instruction, the student should be the focus of attention. One way to help bring this about is to solicit the cooperation of students in developing and maintaining their own personnel records. Thus students, by collecting and learning to interpret information about themselves, gain insights and understandings which are invaluable to them. In this connection Hahn and McLean state:

A review of most cumulative record forms reveals that the following items are usually best drawn from, and recorded by, the students: Name, Place of birth, Age, Stated interests, Vocational preference, Work experience, Support of self or dependents, Earnings, Educational plans, Home-study conditions, Time budget, Hours devoted to study, Hours consumed by commuting, Extra-curricular experiences, Clubs and offices held, Notable accomplishments, Father's or guardian's name, age, occupation, and education, Mother's name, age, occupation, and education, Brothers and sisters.

In addition it is found to be helpful if the counselee records items from other sources, such as his school grades, yearly class program, and results of achievement, interest, aptitude, and ability tests. Those that, in the interest of accuracy or because they are the business of a medical or other specialist, should be recorded by someone other than the counselees, include: Physical disabilities (physician or nurse), Health, physical (physician or nurse), Health, mental (physician, psychiatric social worker), Personality ratings (counselor), Academic intelligence tests (counselor), Discipline (administrator), Number of days absent (clerk), Date and reason for leaving school (clerk).[5]

In a well-developed personnel program, classroom teachers have important contributions to make in the building of records. Tradi-

[5] Milton E. Hahn and Malcolm S. McLean: *Op cit.*, p. 98-99.

tionally, semester grades are considered a part of the student's total record and these only have been associated with the classroom teacher's contribution to records. A newer concept of the classroom teacher's role in record building recognizes that individualized progress reports may make a significant contribution to student learning by making him aware, at periodic intervals of his progress to date. The IPR* is definitely a counseling device. Its importance in this respect lies in the stimulation it can give the student through a periodic appraisal of the quality and quantity of his work, his growth, and his assumption of responsibility in terms of his immediate and long-range objectives. It is the responsibility of the student to clarify differences between his own appraisals and those on the IPR. Frequently this results in a conference between student and teacher and provides an opportunity for counseling.

In one institution, Stephens College,† where this type of progress reporting is in operation, the IPR system has been adapted for use by residence counselors, sponsors of extra-class activities, librarians and work supervisors, as well as by classroom teachers. In this way the student has an opportunity to gain insights regarding her progress in several different areas of her development. Thus she is in a better position, because of the periodic reports, to decide where to direct her energies in order to attain the desired balance in her total growth.

In understanding the IPR system one should keep in mind that reports usually are made to a student only when his work is at one of the extremes, either above or below average. No notation is made for average work and in the absence of a report the student may assume that there is no notable variation in his progress since the previous report. When an institution uses the individualized method to report progress, it is important that each student be adequately oriented to the plan. At Stephens College this orientation is included in the instructional program in the class in Communication Skills, required of first-year students. This classroom presentation is supplemented by an informal interpretation to each student by her senior sister. In addition, each classroom teacher or other faculty member who reports to students by means of the IPR is responsible for explaining to them the general bases on which his estimate of progress has been made.

---

* Throughout this discussion the letters IPR refer to individualized progress reports.

† See *Workbook for Advisers*, p. 90, for a copy of the IPR used at Stephens.

Another important factor to be considered in the use of the IPR is the time required by faculty members to prepare the reports. By use of symbols and an IBM form the routine work is reduced to a minimum. A simple system of symbols may be used to indicate to the student his progress from one reporting period to another. Four or five such reports each semester are sufficient to keep students informed. A range of symbols may include notations on strength, weaknesses, and needs and may be used to refer to both quality and quantity of work since the last reporting period as well as to the student's acceptance of responsibility and his growth in relation to estimated ability. Both failing and honors work may be recognized by such reports.

Although the term does not have the same connotation in all educational institutions, most college personnel programs do include the services of "faculty advisers." These individuals are in a strategic position to participate in the development of student records. The "adviser" is usually the coordinator of all available data and information concerning his "advisee" and he also furnishes other personnel workers, teachers, administrators, and parents with pertinent information. In some institutions the advisers send periodic reports to parents. At Stephens College* reports on course selection and initial progress are sent out during the early weeks of each semester and a letter commenting on the advisee's total progress to date is sent to parents soon after the middle of each semester. These letters contain, in addition to mid-semester grades, comments regarding the advisee's adjustment to group living, participation in extra-class activities, educational goals and plans, and any other significant information which should be shared with the parents. The student is not only aware of these communications but has the opportunity to make suggestions as to content.

Prior to the writing of these mid-semester letters the adviser receives, in addition to the mid-term grades of each of his advisees, a note from the residence counselor of each advisee containing significant objective data and pertinent comments regarding the student's needs and adjustments as revealed through life in the residence hall. The student, in conference with her adviser, compiles on a sheet prepared for this purpose an up-to-date record of her extra-class participation. The record includes such items as campus or hall

* See Workbook for Advisers, "Advising Letters and Reports to Parents," pp. 15-16 and 49-58, for detailed suggestions and sample letters.

offices held; committee membership; organization membership; religious activities; social activities; attendance at or participation in concerts, plays, lectures, exhibits, athletic contests, or sports; trips; and student employment.

Another type of record developed in some colleges is the confidential summary for each student, prepared by the adviser at the end of each school year. This report usually is both subjective and objective in nature and may include comments and ratings on personal characteristics, such as adaptability, appearance, consideration for others, cooperation, industry, initiative, etc.; attitudes and behavior in regard to student government and college regulations; attitude and behavior of others toward him; emotional stability; self-confidence; punctuality; attendance record; need for financial assistance while in college; special abilities, talents, and achievements; handicaps or limitations; extra-class participation; recommendations regarding further schooling, employment, etc.

The trend during the last five years toward increased emphasis on residence hall living as an educational experience places the residence counselor in a key position both to use and to contribute to the building of personnel records. Since he or she observes and works with individual students in their daily living experience, the residence counselor has an opportunity to become familiar with student needs and adjustments in everyday group living situations. Periodic reports by residence counselors on individual students add significant data to the student's personnel record.

At Stephens College, residence counselors send mid-semester reports to advisers with carbon copies to admissions counselors. These reports may include comments in regard to: (1) Personality traits such as friendliness, tolerance, consideration for others, objectivity, patience, poise, and self-confidence; (2) personal appearance including neatness, cleanliness, good grooming; (3) use of time; (4) citizenship; (5) health habits; (6) social activities; and (7) acceptance of hall responsibilities. At the end of the year the residence counselor prepares a confidential summary on each student who has lived in her residence hall during the year. This report is similar to the confidential summary referred to above as prepared by the adviser but places the major emphasis on attitudes and behavior in group living situations, personal relationships, acceptance of responsibility, and reaction to and participation in those experiences which have been provided by the college for the growth and development of students.

Recommendations are also made as to the student's strengths, weaknesses, and needs and as to her plans for next year. Although it is realized that reports of this type have their limitations because of the subjective element of the counselor's appraisal and interpretation, they are of considerable value in rounding out the picture of the "whole student."

Parents should not be overlooked as an additional source of information of value in record development. When they are encouraged to take part in furnishing, for counseling purposes, information regarding student needs, interests, limitations, successes, and goals, another step is taken in the development of integrated records. Special inquiry forms for use by parents usually make it easier to secure specific and pertinent information than when a general request is sent to them.

Administrators, both general and personnel, should play a major role in the development of records. Administrators, like all others who participate in the cooperative effort of the development and use of records, not only receive data about individual students but are in a position to channel significant information to faculty engaged in personnel functions. Administrators also are in a position to see how records from many different sources dovetail and are coordinated. Theirs is an over-all responsibility for the functioning of records and they may well be the springboard or motivating factor in getting attention focused on developing a functioning record system.

Finally, simplicity should be the keynote of a good record system. Records may be used by busy teachers and lay counselors who are not trained in interpreting records. A clear statement of detailed directions should accompany personnel records and is helpful to persons who fill out or use the forms. Records should demand a minimum of clerical time by the counseling staff.

Students and Others Learn Through Records

Self-direction and self-guidance are the ultimate objectives which counselors and personnel workers are striving to help students achieve. Records can and should be used for these purposes. But all too frequently we fail to make the student a full-fledged partner in the learning process. In many personnel programs we have developed elaborate procedures for gathering extensive data about students. They are given numerous tests, asked to fill out personal history blanks, write the story of their lives to date, engage in a series of interviews with a counselor who makes a record of the conversation. Various other methods are employed to acquire information concerning our students. As was indicated previously, the personnel record belongs to the student. He not only should have a part in the building of it but he should have access to the data (since it is about him) in order to be able to use it in the solution of his life problems. McDaniel[6] urges that we share our records with the student, and provide him with the material that has been collected concerning him before we discuss with him what he is going to do about his problems of scholastic improvement, occupational choice, or human relations.

. . . He [the student] must be a full partner in the process. All data that are gathered for counseling purposes are as much the property of the counselees as of the counselor, and can only become operative in terms of our objectives when they are effectively shared with the counselee. This is not to say that there are not data that should be used with discretion, largely because of the danger of being misunderstood and some data are valuable for research purposes. But on the whole, the files of the counselor should be open to the student concerned. Pupils should be encouraged at any time they meet a problem situation involving a change in their plans and activities, to go to the records and examine them, search them for clues before making a decision. These personnel records should represent longitudinal sections of the individual and should definitely be a part of the content of his education.[7]

If records are used by all who deal with the student as a means of helping him discover his needs, formulate his objectives, and evaluate his progress in relation to his past performance, then the goal of "self-guidance" becomes more of a reality. If education is not to cease at the end of formal schooling, students must learn (be taught) effective self-evaluation. Records are an indispensable part of this process.

In the teacher-student relationship learning through the use of records should be utilized to the greatest extent possible. Beginning with such a routine matter as the attendance report each student may be asked to be responsible for recording his own class attendance on a sheet posted in the room, or the class roll may be passed around the class. Group pressures have been found to be quite effective at one institution* in preventing falsification or inaccuracies in report-

---

[6] H. B. McDaniel: *Clearing House.*

[7] *Ibid*, p. 354.

* Stephens College, Columbia, Missouri.

ing. The use of a self-appraisal sheet at periodic intervals during the term is another technique for increasing student participation in evaluation. This self-appraisal might include what work has been done, and how thoroughly; also a statement of the student's own opinion about his general standing in relation to his classmates; effort expended; and progress made. This record provides the teacher with an excellent "springboard" for an individual conference with the student through which he is helped to readjust his evaluation in the light of his instructor's appraisal and the comparative accomplishments of his fellows.

Classroom teachers should have or be provided with information concerning each individual student's educational and occupational background, his current academic schedule, expressed career interests, and selected and carefully interpreted test results. Additional data regarding special limitations of a student which might affect his classwork such as impaired vision or hearing, or a reading or speech difficulty, are useful to the teacher in his work with the student as he establishes rapport in the early stages of the relationship, individualizes instruction, and builds motivation for learning. These data also enable the instructor to understand better why a student behaves as he does. Whether the institution is large or small the securing of the above information does not need to present a problem. If records are a cooperative venture and truly shared with a student, if he has been responsible for building and maintaining his own record and has full access to it, a teacher needs only to ask his students to provide him with the desired data.

As Brouwer[8] points out, the behavior of a student can be best understood when it is viewed in a context of information and understanding of the total personality. Consequently, all teachers are increasingly interested in all types of personnel data about students. The music teacher may have as much need to know about the family background or a current health problem as the student's adviser or the college physician. That a student is having difficulty getting along with his roommate is important information for the mathematics teacher as well as for the student's residence counselor. "Theoretically, everything that we could know about each student would, to one degree or another, have value to our understanding of him and would increase our effectiveness in teaching him."[9]

[8] Paul J. Brouwer: *Student Personnel Services in General Education*, p. 150.
[9] *Ibid.*, p. 150.

The trained residence counselor has an excellent opportunity for teaching. In assisting students to understand their needs, develop their interests, and realize their goals in their general human relations or social adjustment experiences, the residence counselor takes his or her place along with classroom teachers in sharing with them the education of the whole person. Residence counselors, in performing their teaching function, must be able to interpret data as these become significant in their work with students. Therefore it is important that the residence counselor have access to and use personnel records which will increase his effectiveness in his role as teacher.

At Stephens College,* the residence counselor makes extensive use of records in her work with students. In this institution each residence counselor has on file in her office a personnel folder for each student which contains the student's picture, pre-college data, the student's cumulative extra-class record, information regarding referral to special counseling services, the student's citizenship record, notes made by the counselor herself as a result of observations or of conferences with the student, admissions counselor, adviser, instructors, administrators or parents, and finally, copies of confidential summaries written at the end of each year by both the student's faculty adviser and residence counselor.

Frequently, because of the picture, the counselor is able to recognize the student upon her arrival. This immediately conveys to the student a feeling that someone is personally interested in her and helps in establishing rapport from the beginning. In any event the pictures facilitate the ease with which a residence counselor comes to recognize and know the students in her hall. The pre-college data are especially helpful to the residence counselor in learning to know the background, personality, interests, and needs of each girl. This information is also used in assigning new students to "senior sisters." Lists may be made of birthdays and various means may be used to recognize girls whose birthdays fall in the same month. The extra-class record is concerned with off-campus permissions, attendance at social and cultural programs, social and honorary sororities, hobby groups and clubs, offices held, hall responsibilities, and notable achievements. The residence counselor uses these data in counseling individual students as to use of time and a balanced program of out-of-class activities.

* See Mary I. Omer: *A Handbook for Residence Counselors*, pp. 34-38 and 83-85, for a detailed interpretation of the use of records by residence counselors.

Another record which the student herself compiles and which is extremely useful in residence hall programs is an "interest sheet." This includes up-to-date information regarding name of adviser, admissions counselor, senior sister, roommate, the student's activities during the preceding summer, offices held the preceding year (in the case of students beyond the first year), goals for the present year, check lists of hall committees so the student may indicate those on which she would like to serve, and check lists of possible hall activities to be checked and used as a guide in planning the hall program. The residence counselor finds many occasions to refer to and make use of information from this type of interest sheet both in her work with individual students and in planning the educational program for her hall.

Some residence counselors have found an anecdotal record notebook helpful. They use it for the daily recording of significant observations of student behavior and notes of student conferences.

Another use made of records by residence counselors is for purposes of recommendations. The residence counselor receives many requests from student organizations for recommendations for candidates for various offices connected with student government and college activities. Administrators seek recommendations and other information from residence counselors regarding the retention of students or regarding students who may be having academic or emotional difficulties. Frequently residence counselors are asked to fill in information blanks recommending students for advanced college work or for employment.

Records may help faculty advisers write letters and reports to parents on the progress being made and the problems encountered by the student. Conversely, many parents in response to the adviser's letters, provide him and the college with some expression of their thinking with regard to their son or daughter's proposed plans. When parents visit the college the up-to-date cumulative record is invaluable for making the student's achievements or lack of such more understandable to them. Trends in development may be seen and facts presented which are basic to realistic planning of the student's future education and occupation. Periodic reports of progress to parents, written cooperatively by the student and adviser, along with an occasional individual conference, are excellent avenues for helping them understand the nature of the needs, abilities, aptitudes, and attitudes of their son or daughter.

The counseling specialist whether it be in the area of reading, speech, psychology, health, or religion makes extensive use of records. These clinical records are usually more detailed in the one aspect (health, reading, etc.) than those kept by the adviser or residence counselor and describe more intimately those conditions causing maladjustment or defect in the particular case. In counseling students with deep-seated emotional problems Rogers[10] advocates that complete notes be taken during the interview so that both the counselor and counselee's statements are a matter of record. Although such complete record-keeping may not be necessary in all types of cases, in every instance the counseling specialist will recognize the importance of making a systematic recorded summary of all interviews with students in order that significant details are recorded and not lost due to his inability to recall them when needed at a later date. This detailed written summary of the content of each interview should not become a part of the permanent record of a student as it is "privileged" information. Only the fact that a student has been receiving specialized counseling should be noted in the record and this should be done with the student's knowledge and permission.

The administrative use of records in schools and colleges antedates their use for guidance purposes. Records entered the school system to facilitate teacher-principal cooperation in securing data for such routine but necessary purposes as the preparation of various types of reports to state, county, and local authorities, and as bases for the promotion and transfer of students.[11] Although administrators still need records for these purposes, in recent years the primary function of personnel records has become that of helping solve student problems and guiding student development. Today personnel officers and other administrative officers make daily use of the integrated cumulative student record, and are particularly dependent upon such records in counseling students and their parents, for conducting case conferences, supervising in-service training of counselors and faculty advisers, coordinating the special counseling services, and dealing with problems of curriculum planning, instruction, and evaluation.

Personnel officers in most institutions have occasion to interview students (and sometimes counsel them on a short-term basis) in regard to problems of almost every sort. On any given day the personnel staff may be conferring with a student about the frequency of his absences from classes, with another about his lack of motivation

[10] Carl R. Rogers: *Counseling and Psychotherapy*, p. 242.
[11] Anna Y. Reed: *Guidance and Personnel Services in Education*, p. 206.

for academic work, and with a third concerning his indecision about leaving school to enter another college, or to go to work. When a crisis has arisen in a student's life, when a student has been involved in a violation of the social or moral code, or when scholastic failure is imminent the administrator has need to acquire an understanding of the student as quickly as possible, and to search for clues as to the causes of the difficulty. A study of the cumulative record indicates those in the college who know the student best and what all their data show as to the conditions leading up to this failure, crisis, or misbehavior; also the dean is enabled to get a broader view of the student in various situations. With this background material as a beginning the administrator is better able to counsel the student, develop a plan, or arrive at a decision on the matter.

In conferences with parents or in correspondence with them concerning the student the information contained in the cumulative record is used extensively by the personnel officer as well as by the faculty adviser. In fact, the administrator more frequently has to rely on the record for an understanding of the student and his problem than does the adviser as the latter usually has had more opportunity to become acquainted personally with the student. A written summary of each conference with parents should be prepared and copies sent to all those directly concerned with the student's progress such as the adviser, residence counselor, admissions counselor, as well as the central records office. Copies of all correspondence between the personnel officer and the parents should also be sent to the above-named persons.

In most student personnel programs the personnel head is charged with the responsibility of improving, coordinating, and supervising the counseling being done in the institution. Coordination of the efforts of the various specialists with whom the student may be working, prevention of duplication of counseling and "clinic-hopping," and prompt referral of students to appropriate sources of help are possible only when there is a central cumulative personnel folder for each student easily accessible to the coordinator.

In training faculty members to perform guidance functions and helping them acquire "the personnel point of view," the case conference has proved to be an effective procedure. As Strang[12] points out, cumulative records serve as a starting point for the case conference. Such a conference may be arranged at the request of the

---

[12] Ruth Strang: *Op. cit.*, p. 195.

student's adviser, counselor, dean, or any instructor, whenever, in his opinion, a pooling of information will be useful to him or to others who are working in some capacity with the student in question. In Allen's opinion, the "case conference is perhaps the most effective means of helping teachers to understand the many problems involved in the interpretation of record data and student behavior."[18] Those invited to participate in such a conference may be the student's adviser, residence counselor, teachers, the college physician, a representative from the occupational counseling service, a psychologist, and the personnel head or other staff members. For all of those present the case conference should prove a valuable learning experience. Following the reports made by the members of the conference group, the data are analyzed and discussed in an effort to gain a clearer understanding of the student's specific problems and their underlying causes. While the primary objective of the conference is the consideration of a particular student's development and present adjustment, indirectly the faculty member is provided practice and training in interpreting test results and other personnel record data, and an opportunity to acquire desirable techniques in working with students. He also engages in a creative process of group thinking resulting in formulating recommendations designed to aid the student in making a more successful adjustment. The final step is the preparation of a written summary by the group chairman. The summary includes a statement of the interpretations agreed upon and a clarification of the part each participant is to play in the development of the student. This report is sent to all participants and becomes an addition to the student's cumulative record.

Although records should be built, maintained, and used by the student and those most closely connected with him at the various points in his development, it is necessary to provide a central place where copies of all pertinent data are assembled and integrated. Information gained from every source must be effectively gathered together and communicated to others who are working with the student, with provisions set up for sharing data which ethically may be shared and keeping privileged information from reaching those to whom it would not have meaning or who might use it in a manner detrimental to the student. This philosophy implies a continuous two-way flow of information from the original sources to the centralization point, and from the central location back to the various

[18] Wendell C. Allen: *Cumulative Pupil Records*, p. 59.

points of origin so that the new, additional information is reintegrated and used in the counseling or learning of the student.

Care should be taken not to include in the student's official, permanent record any information that could damage him at a later date. Hahn and McLean[14] and Williamson and Foley[15] have expressed this point of view in their recent writings.

This caution does not mean that certain items are omitted from the personnel record. It does mean that care must be taken not to make all items gathered a part of the student's *permanent* record. The personnel point of view holds that if a counselor comes into possession of certain confidential information by virtue of his counseling relationship he, like the doctor or lawyer, is obligated to protect the counselee from disclosure of this information without the student's permission. Hahn and McLean comment in the above reference that, "Records listing, perhaps, a minor theft during adolescence, a temporary emotional upset in college, denial of admission to college, refusal of a job, or unfounded suspicion can invoke unmerited penalties years after the event occurred."

Each item recorded on the permanent record should be considered from the standpoint of the circumstances surrounding it and of its relative significance. The philosophy represented in the point of view expressed above does not relieve the student from accepting reasonable consequences for his behavior. Indeed, as a part of the maturing process of developing insights and understanding, students should be helped to recognize that they are responsible individuals who accept the consequences of their actions. The important point is that once, through counseling and perhaps appropriate temporary consequences, students have learned from their mistakes, they do not deserve to be penalized again at some future date by having their permanent record refer to these incidents. Instead, the record should indicate that learning has occurred (if it has) and what values were acquired as a result.

The location of records and their administration is directly related to the basic educational philosophy of the institution. A record system must be developed from the bottom up by the individuals who are working with the student (teachers, counselors, residence hall personnel, faculty advisers, etc.) and used by these people if deeper teaching and significant learning are to occur. Record building

[14] Milton E. Hahn and Malcolm S. McLean: *Op. cit.*, p. 94.
[15] E. G. Williamson and John D. Foley: *Counseling and Discipline*, pp. 82-83.

and record sharing are cooperative undertakings and bear a reciprocal relationship to each other. Wrenn's[16] solution to the problem of record location and administration involves a system whereby each personnel office, dormitory, adviser, and counseling service devise and keep their own records of some phase of student life with provision made for duplication of widely used records. He suggests that a cumulative personnel folder for each student be on file in the most accessible personnel office, and for records which are not duplicated "a plan for cross reference from each office record to the central personnel file can be worked out at small expense in time."

The use of records in deeper teaching necessitates record integration. This involves coordination of data secured from the secondary school, from parents, admissions counselors, and from students themselves with the periodic reports from residence counselors, classroom teachers, counseling specialists, sponsors of extra-class activities, work supervisors, and administrators. With the new mechanical devices for duplicating records the task of integration may be somewhat simplified. Even so, each institution should experiment in this area until it finds a workable and reasonably satisfactory solution to its own problem.

One institution (Stephens College) has worked out a detailed and comprehensive plan for integrating its records.*

These suggestions may serve to guide others in the problem of the integration of records: First, a central committee should be established to develop records in keeping with the educational philosophy and emphases of the institution. Any record proposed for use by any personnel service or agency should be reviewed by this committee which should also be responsible for seeing that all records dovetail and for approving any necessary revision of records. Second, a cumulative personnel folder should be on file in the most accessible personnel office. Ideally, original records, duplicates, or cross-references of every student record which ethically may be shared should be filed in this folder. Third, a professionally trained person, preferably a personnel officer, should be responsible for an in-service training program for all those who contribute to and make use of the integrated records. This administrator also should see that the plan agreed upon for the

---

[16] C. Gilbert Wrenn: *Op. cit.*, pp. 438-440.

* See *Workbook for Advisers*, "Working Relationships Between Advisers and All Others Concerned with the Individual Student," pp. 76-86, for a description of this plan.

integration of records operates in accordance with the institution's basic philosophy in regard to records. Finally, periodic evaluations should provide the basis for needed changes or revisions in the plan.

Summary

This chapter approaches the question of how records can help in learning to know and understand students by considering three major points: first, the purpose of records; second, the development of records; and third, the use of records.

Records justify their existence if they fulfill their major purposes, which are: helping students to grow in self-understanding and self-direction; evaluating student progress and institutional effectiveness; and fostering group effort in stimulating and supporting continuous health, growth and learning.

In developing personnel records it is important to consider what the student needs to know about himself and what the individuals who are working with him need to know. The objectives for which the records are to be used need to be clearly defined and there should be a definite relation between the finished record and the original objectives.

The development of personnel records should be a cooperative venture and a continuous process, involving the student and all those who work with him in a personnel relationship. Among the many sources available today for securing the record data needed in a college counseling program are the student himself, parents, admissions counselors, advisers, residence counselors, classroom teachers, counseling specialists, and administrators.

Simplicity should be the keynote of a good record system. Records should demand a minimum of clerical time by the counseling staff. In all record building, keeping, and interpretation, as well as in classroom instruction, the student should be the focus of attention.

In the use of records as well as in the development of them, we should consider the student as a full-fledged partner and share with him and with others who work with him whatever data will help in teaching him self-direction and self-guidance.

It is necessary to provide a central place where copies of all pertinent data are assembled and integrated. Extreme care, however, should be taken against including in the students' official, permanent record information which can damage a student at a later date.

The use of records in deeper teaching also necessitates record integration. This involves not only coordination of data secured from all sources but dissemination of appropriate data to the student and to those individuals who are counseling with the student in his learning process. The new mechanical devices for duplicating records simplify the duplication and distribution of data which should be shared.

The following may serve as a guide in solving the problems of the integration of records: a central committee to develop records in keeping with the educational philosophy of the institution; a cumulative personnel folder on file in the most accessible personnel office; a professionally trained person responsible for a training program for those who contribute to and use personnel records; periodic evaluations to discover needed changes or revisions in the record system.

BIBLIOGRAPHY

Allen, Wendell C.: *Cumulative Pupil Records*. New York, Bureau of Publications, Teachers College, Columbia University, 1943, p. 59.

Brouwer, Paul J.: *Student Personnel Services in General Education*. Washington, D. C., American Council on Education, 1949, p. 150.

Cantor, Nathaniel F.: *The Dynamics of Learning*. Buffalo, N. Y., Foster and Stewart Publishing Co., 1946, pp. 13-30, 251-253.

Hahn, Milton E., and McLean, Malcolm S.: *General Clinical Counseling*. New York, McGraw-Hill Book Co., Inc., 1950, p. 94; pp. 98-99.

Lloyd-Jones, Esther, and Smith, Margaret Ruth: *A Student Personnel Program for Higher Education*. New York, McGraw-Hill Book Co., Inc., 1938, pp. 247-277.

McDaniel, H. B.: *Clearing House* 17:354-56, 1943.

Omer, Mary I.: *A Handbook for Residence Counselors*. Columbia, Mo., Stephens College, 1949, pp. 34-38; 83-85.

Reed, Anna Y.: *Guidance and Personnel Services in Education*. Ithaca, N. Y., Cornell University Press, 1944, p. 206.

Rogers, Carl R.: *Counseling and Psychotherapy*. Boston, Houghton Mifflin Co., 1942, p. 242.

Segel, David: *Nature and Use of the Cumulative Record*. Washington, D. C., U. S. Department of the Interior, Office of Education, Bulletin 3, 1938.

Smith, Eugene R., Tyler, Ralph W., and the Evaluation Staff: *Appraising and Recording Student Progress*. New York, Harper & Brothers, 1942.

Strang, Ruth: *Counseling Technics in College and Secondary School*. New York, Harper & Brothers, 1949 (rev. ed.), p. 181; p. 195.

Traxler, Arthur E.: *Techniques of Guidance*. New York, Harper & Brothers, 1945, pp. 202-214.

Williamson, E. G., and Foley, John D.: *Counseling and Discipline*. New York, McGraw-Hill Book Co., Inc., 1949, pp. 82-83.

Workbook for Advisers. Columbia, Mo., Stephens College, 1951, pp. 15-16; 49-58; 76-86; 90.

Wrenn, C. Gilbert: *Student Personnel Work in College*. New York, The Ronald Press Co., 1951, pp. 438-440.

6. Helping the Student to Gain Self-understanding

RUTH STRANG

"KNOW thyself," "be thyself," and "to thine own self be true" are ancient precepts. Recently they have received increasing attention in psychology. Such titles as *Man for Himself, Self-Consistency—A Theory of Personality,* and *In Search of Self* reflect this emphasis. From the first year of life the student is trying to develop a realistic and acceptable idea of himself.

Nature of Self-understanding

The self concept has three dimensions: (1) the self as viewed by the individual—his own idea of himself, or his ego; (2) his social self—how he thinks others view him, or his "social stimulus value"; and (3) the self that he would like to be, or his ideal self.

The self concept is the central core of personality. It is a persistent and pervasive pattern of ideas, attitudes, values. It permeates the person's inner world of thinking and meaning.

The self concept, however, is also dependent upon the outer world. Although physical characteristics, such as weight, height, and body conformation may be only slightly related to certain personality traits, the body image may have a marked influence on one's conception of himself. Adolescents tend to overemphasize undesirable physical characteristics. They are also greatly influenced by their past performance and by people's expectations of them. From the earliest years, the person sees himself through others' eyes; his self-appraisal reflects what others think and feel about him.

Origin and Development of the Self Concept

Many maladjustments that occur during college years have their roots in early childhood experiences. The infant who is uncomfortable, cold, hungry, unloved, who cries and no one ever comes to help him, is likely to become apathetic and to develop feelings of hopelessness about himself. If subsequent preschool and school experiences reinforce his feeling of inadequacy, the individual may arrive at college anticipating failure. Many retarded readers in both high school and college show this defeatist pattern, which prevents them from using their energy to good advantage.

The child whose every desire is granted by oversolicitous parents may misinterpret the parents' motivation, and develop a feeling of omnipotence. He may think of himself as able to bend others to his will and to get what he wants when he wants it. Sooner or later he must learn that the world, unlike his parents, is indifferent to him and sometimes cruel. If he is able to dominate others during preschool and school years, he is likely to arrive at college still maintaining this concept of himself.

If, during his second or third year of life, the child solves his dependence-independence conflict by choosing the dependency of infancy rather than the self-reliance of increasing maturity, and if he gains satisfaction from his dependency during school years, he will be poorly prepared for the responsibilities of college life. He has bartered submission for security. But it is only a superficial security, for underneath he feels a loss of self-respect.

If a child is rejected by his parents, wholly or in part, because he is not of the desired sex or is not as pretty or bright or responsive as they had hoped, he may accept his parents' appraisal of him, or he may try in devious ways to hurt his parents. If, in addition, there is a more attractive younger or older sister or brother in the family, the feelings of the less favored child usually are intensified. He may come to college without expecting to succeed. Indeed, if his resentment is turned against his parents, he may unconsciously want to fail. This was the case with Patricia, a college sophomore referred to a reading center because of failure in her college subjects. Interviews with her revealed her hostility toward her mother. Since her mother would feel disgraced to have a daughter flunk out of college, Patricia was rapidly achieving that end. When her hostility was brought out in the open, she was able to handle it on a conscious level.

From the earliest years, an individual's self concept evolves from his experiences—from restraints on his freedom, from expressions of approval or disapproval, from being helped or hindered in expressing himself. If the persons who count most in his life disapprove of him, he is likely to take a derogatory attitude toward himself. He is also likely to have a depreciative attitude toward others. The development of his self concept is largely in the hands of parents, teachers, and others whose love and respect he values most.

Of great importance also are opportunities for the individual to succeed through his own efforts. One way in which a person learns about himself is by facing the consequences of his actions. The child who solves his daily problems with only enough adult help to prevent failure and frustration will begin to think of himself as a competent person. The methods of problem solving which he acquires and tests through experiences will serve him well in meeting the new responsibilities and difficulties of college.

Probably the individual's peers exert the most potent influence on his self concept during pre-adolescent and adolescent years. Others of his own age now become the most important persons in his life. Their values, their approval or disapproval, their experiences, modify, for better or for worse, his idea of himself. The instability of early adolescence offers an opportunity to help the individual sort out childish ways of thinking and feeling and substitute a more mature self concept.

The expanding world in which adolescents live offers them infinite opportunities to learn. They become "a part of all that they have met." In responding to nature—the night sky, sunlight on autumn leaves, the spring—to friendships, to a variety of human personalities, to the consequences of their own and others' behavior, they live and learn and grow in self-understanding. As Emerson said, "The things taught in colleges . . . are not an education, but the means of education"—the means of increasing one's self-understanding.

A unified and harmonious self concept is an achievement. The building of the self—the image of who, what, and why one is—is a major task of adolescence. Young people have more capacity for finding themselves, for realizing themselves, for facing life and its emotions than we give them credit for. A realistic self-acceptance is a manifestation of maturity. During post-adolescence, changes are less likely to occur, and are harder to achieve.

The Self Concept and Life Adjustment

The self concept is important because it guides conduct. Insofar as it determines how the person perceives a situation, it limits his ability to learn from his environment. An individual's behavior is greatly influenced by his subjective picture of himself.

Of a number of factors that might be related to children's later adjustment, the best predictor was found to be self-insight. Next best was social experience. A realistic self concept contributes to mental health by preventing both the feelings of unfulfillment that arise from underachievement and the tension and strain that result from striving for impossible goals. A unified self helps students to integrate their life experiences.

The self concept is a most important factor in mental health. Failure to integrate the values in one's life may lead to inner conflicts, to indulgence in excessive day dreaming and fantasies, to escape into substitute activities—with consequent psychological problems. A person may try to defend his self concept, whether true or false, by means of all the mental mechanisms in his repertory. It is painful for him to give up his illusions and view himself more realistically.

The self concept also affects students' learning. According to the results of one experiment, the intensity of a student's need for achievement seems to be related to the goal he sets for himself. Students who were already successful and had the least need for achievement looked forward to the most success. Those who had failed and consequently had the strongest need for achievement saw the least success in store for them. Low self-esteem may find expression in many forms of failure. Today, ego-involvement is recognized as an important factor in learning. A person feels happy and successful in any socially useful activity that furthers his self-realization.

Attitude toward oneself is often reflected in attitude toward others. Self-deprecating persons tend to take a negative, critical attitude toward others. Low self-esteem seems to be associated with lack of appreciation of others. According to data furnished by one experiment, respect for oneself went hand in hand with respect for others.

The late James S. Plant said that one achieves integration of personality not only by finding common ground for agreement between oneself and others, but also by shutting out part of the environment pressing against the personality.

In many important ways the student's self concept is related to his total development—to personality integration, to mental health, to learning, to human relations.

Methods of Studying the Self Concept

A student's self concept may be studied in at least seven ways—through introspective freely written responses, self-evaluative questionnaires, attitude scales, projective techniques, interviews, group discussion, and sociodrama. Each of these methods has possible therapeutic as well as diagnostic value. Each should be interpreted and used along with all the other information available about the individual student. None of these methods is an end in itself; each is a means of helping the student gain a better understanding of his most acceptable self.

THE FREELY WRITTEN RESPONSE

The most direct way of getting information about the self concept is to question students with whom a constructive, accepting relation has been established. Two investigators[1], used the W.A.Y. Technic to study the self concept. As a stimulus, the question, "Who are You?" was introduced as follows:

The subject is given a plain piece of paper and is told: "I am going to ask you a question and I want you to write three answers to the question on this paper. Your answer may be anything you wish: words, phrases, sentences, or anything at all, so long as you feel satisfied that you have answered the question. Remember you are to give three answers. The question is: Who are You?"

The question allows a free field for responses, which permit analysis of what the subject says about himself. Some subjects merely identify themselves as to age, sex, and occupation; some give family status, some social status; others mention merely nationality or race or give other "non-individualizing" responses as if the person were denying his uniqueness. Some responses have emotional tones, either positive or negative, as in the following:

"I see myself a little inferior to others."
"I am a nobody."
"I am a small speck on this earth."
"I am a person not progressing as rapidly as desired."
"I am getting a lot of fun out of life."

Against the background of common responses, the unique and the bizarre stand out clearly.

[1] James F. T. Bugental and Seymour L. Zelen: "Investigations into the 'Self-Concept'—the W.A.Y. Technic."

Since the W.A.Y. Technic evoked such a large proportion of factual responses, the author tried out two other questions, which seemed to elicit more significant material. These questions were as follows:

1. What kind of person do you really think you are?
2. What kind of person do you want other people to think you are?

The following are the responses of four college students to these two questions:

Girl, Aged 18:
1. The kind of person that I really think I am.

I don't consider myself perfect, I know I have many bad points. Though I have good ones. I think I'm considerate of others and I like to help people in need. I'm not too loud, but sometimes silly and when I start talking to someone if the conversation interests me I talk too much; that's because I like discussion, say like in history or political questions. I'm lazy at times, though I try not to be. I'm usually friendly with those who are friendly, otherwise I keep by myself. I want to succeed in something but I'm quite mixed up and can't understand really why I keep thinking about this question a lot. Besides I do a lot of thinking if I feel disgusted with something. Otherwise I'm very happy if people make me happy and everything is O.K.

2. The kind of person that I want other people to think I am.

I would really like people to like me and know that I'm really a friendly person and easy to get along with. I know that at many times when I've gone some place new I feel as if some people don't like me and look at me funny. But I wish they didn't do this; I also wish they knew I wanted to really help those who need help. I want them to know that I'm kind and considerate of them. And that my bad points are being corrected with their help.

Boy, Aged 19:

1. The kind of person that I really think I am.

I think I am the sort of person who someone else can depend on in a pinch. I seem to be willing to do favors for people thereby attaining more friends. I am very carefree at the present time, and the only (maybe) thing that is wrong with me is the fact that I can't keep my mouth shut when an opportunity for a wisecrack arrives.

2. The kind of person that I want other people to think I am.

I want other people to think I am a "good Joe." Also, because I have an inferiority complex about my build, I want people to recognize the fact that I am a good athlete, and that's why I'm loud and boisterous.

Boy, Aged 18½:

1. The kind of person that I really think I am.

I believe that I am a person who has a fair and honorable attitude toward other people. I think that I have a pleasing personality, not all the time. Somehow or other I believe that I'm slightly on the excitable side and always seem to get involved emotionally in an argument. I also think a lot of myself, which I suppose you call conceited, but I believe that people should be the first to believe in themselves.

2. The kind of person that I want other people to think I am.

I want other people to think I am exactly what I am. Not the most generous individual in the world or the most sympathetic, but just a guy who has many good qualities, and some that are bad. Of course, I don't *want* people to just talk about my faults, but rather I would like them to emphasize my best.

Boy, Aged 18½:

1. The kind of person that I really think I am.

I think that I'm an unfriendly sort of person who thinks very poorly of people upon first impressions. My attitude in life is somewhat cynical and people who do not know me very well think that I am a very unfriendly person. Although I never bully people, I like to brag about myself. I have a nasty temper and often find myself in trouble because of it.

2. The kind of person that I want other people to think I am.

I want people to think that I am friendly and warm. I should like people to think of me as an honest, even-tempered individual. I should like to change my cynical attitude to that of a friendly one. My ambition is to make people say, "There goes the nicest guy I know!"

Many other responses were equally fascinating and unique.

These responses reveal many facets of students' thinking about themselves. They may be analyzed (a) for content, (b) for discrepancies between the kind of person the student really thinks he is and the kind of person he wants others to think he is, and (c) in comparison with all the objective data about the individual.

The college students from whom the responses were obtained recognized in themselves both good and poor qualities. On the positive side they pictured themselves as considerate of others, dependable, friendly, respected. They wanted to help people, though sometimes they did favors merely to gain friends. Most of all, they wanted to "succeed in something," and they wanted people to like them and emphasize their good qualities—to think of them as "a good Joe," a good athlete, warm and friendly—to say, "He's the nicest guy I know," "What a guy, he's sure got courage and not only that he's intelligent."

Among their faults, they mentioned being "lazy sometimes," being moody, sensitive, cynical, immature, sometimes silly, excitable, and too talkative. Some admitted conceit but one added, "I believe people should be the first to believe in themselves."

Only a few referred to conditions outside themselves—"the neurotic personality of our times"—as affecting their self concept. One girl, 18½ years old, expressed the intensity of her feeling about the state of the world as follows:

I hate the things that are happening in the world today, and time and again I wish I could do something, anything to help stop hate, war, etc. I try to help in my own way by thinking of other people—any way—anyhow—like doing a good deed or more a day. I only hope that I have no sons that I can raise to manhood only to have them taught how to kill.

In many instances, these students did not accept themselves. One, who described herself as immature, wanted people to think her very mature. The girl who was so deeply concerned with the state of the world said, "I can't show these feelings, so I cover them over by acting as though I hadn't a care in the world—and knew and thought even less about the world." A boy who was outwardly an extrovert, was inwardly an introvert. This apparent lack of self-acceptance has implications for the individual's mental health and for the importance of counselors' recognition of students' feelings.

It is possible, of course, that some of the students presented a somewhat idealized self concept. Offering each student the opportunity to describe both the kind of person he thought he was and the kind of person he wanted others to consider him, reduced the chances of evoking idealized images, however.

This technique may also be used by counselors and group leaders to clarify their professional self concepts. For example, some group leaders were asked, "How do you think of yourself as a leader?" One response will illustrate the value of this technique in understanding oneself as a professional worker:

I feel that I am only a fair leader. In discussions relating to material with which I am very familiar, I feel much more at ease. With material with which I am not too familiar, I feel the constant pressure of leadership responsibility and I am conscious of my inability to keep the discussion moving. I have a constant fear that the discussion will come to a momentary halt and I will be at a loss for doing anything. In a group involving action I feel more at ease.

This brief description highlights a common feeling of insecurity among leaders. Would they have this feeling of insecurity if they were able to realize more effectively the creative energy of the group and use school and community resources?

The unstructured autobiography is of value in showing the relation of the self-concept to specific influences. It shows how the student views both himself and his world.

Self-evaluative Questionnaires

The efficacy of self-rating questionnaires may be improved if the answers are interpreted as reflections of feeling rather than as statements of fact about personality. In other words, the responses on self-evaluative questionnaires may be treated by projective methods. To see if predictable personality projection could be so elicited, Maslow's security-insecurity inventory and a self-rating true-false health questionnaire were given to several hundred college students.[2] Those who were insecure tended to rate themselves more often as being ill, and to mark more items "false," than did those who were secure. It was also noted that the less structured items, such as "Do you consider yourself a rather nervous person?" differentiated more clearly between secure and insecure students than the definitely structured items such as "Can you sit still without fidgeting?" If questionnaire responses are interpreted as reflections of feeling and behavior, this much-maligned technique may acquire new vitality and value.

Attitude Scales

Attitude scales have been used to study students' attitudes toward themselves and others. For example, one five-point scale, described by Phillips,[3] consisted of twenty-five items referring to self-attitudes

[2] Gabriel Elias: "Self-Evaluative Questionnaires as Projective Measures of Personality."
[3] Lakin E. Phillips: "Attitudes Toward Self and Others."

and twenty-five referring to attitudes towards others. This investigator reported a substantial correlation between college students' attitudes toward themselves and their attitudes toward others. The correlation coefficient for older college students was + .74 and for college freshmen + .54. For high school groups, it was + .67. All these correlations are well above a chance relationship.

PROJECTIVE TECHNIQUES

Projective techniques are another promising means of understanding the individual's ideas about himself and his relation to others. The two most fully developed projective techniques—the Rorschach and the TAT—reveal much about personality organization. Qualitative study of the responses by a clinically trained person reveals not only indications of frustration, anxiety, and other emotions, but also the subject's reaction to these feelings.

The incomplete sentence technique can be used by teachers and counselors as well as by clinicians, though on a different diagnostic level. The following are examples:

I like_____
I feel hurt when_____
I want_____
I am afraid_____
I make believe_____
I hate_____
I am happy_____
I worry_____
I love_____
My most important wishes are_____

Such incomplete sentences guide the student in his own self-analysis.

In nonstructured or unstructured procedures, the individual can give the stimulus situation almost any meaning that he wishes. To the trained clinician, projective techniques reveal unconscious thoughts and desires.

INTERVIEWS

In the presence of a sympathetic, understanding, trusted person, the student is encouraged to gain an understanding of himself. He not only clarifies his self concept, but also reduces the intensity of his fears and anxieties by bringing them out in an atmosphere of security.

GROUP DISCUSSION AND GROUP THERAPY

Students often reveal themselves in the nondirective type of discussion. Stimulated by the group and a permissive adult leader, students often achieve insights over and beyond those elicited by other methods. As one student said, "One of the most important things for a person to do is to get to know himself."

The possible contribution of group psychotherapy to the understanding of oneself and others is being widely recognized. It is a method which, when conducted by experts, has the following features: a friendly and releasing atmosphere; a social situation in which persons can work out more satisfactory modes of adjustment for themselves and relate themselves to others; a reassuring recognition that others are struggling with the same problems; opportunity to be of service to others as well as to gain help for themselves (treatment is *by* the group as well as *in* the group and *for* the group); and assistance in interpretation of feelings leading to insight.

SOCIODRAMA

One of the values of the sociodrama or role-playing is to gain understanding of oneself and others. One student who had participated in role-playing sessions said:

I can truthfully say that I was able to iron out some of my personal conflicts while observing role-playing and doing the reading for the course as a whole. Who I am and who I want to be has always bothered me. The role-playing demonstrated techniques of helping individuals to find themselves.

None of these techniques should be used singly. All the information about a student should be studied in the same way that a painter first sketches the picture as a whole and then paints in more detail as his understanding grows.

These and other techniques contribute to one end—to help the individual understand himself and move toward the realization of his most acceptable social self.

Contribution of Groups to the Student's Self-understanding

In classes, in organized and unorganized student groups, through social life in the residence hall and other informal groups, the individual gains understanding of himself. He sees his achievement in relation to that of others and in relation to the requirements of certain subjects and jobs. When he has accepted responsibility and successfully fulfilled an obligation, he knows more definitely what he can do.

In classes there are many ways in which the teacher can foster the student's desire to discover and develop potentialities. In any class there are many covert tensions. For example, one gifted college girl, in describing her high school experience, said, "I just got by without doing any real work. But I felt an underlying uneasiness and unhappiness because I was not using my abilities and talents." These dissatisfactions about personal development may be brought out in subjective compositions; in discussions growing out of the study of literature or current problems; or in the short personal contacts friendly teachers have with individual students.

In class discussions and individual interviews the obstacles to understanding oneself and one's world can be brought out in the open, faced, and analyzed. This is a necessary first step to overcoming them. The more carefully these obstacles are defined and ways of overcoming them are suggested, the better the chance of success. Success in meeting obstacles to self-realization reinforces the student's purpose and effort; failure often leads to his giving up the struggle. Even seeing the obstacle in a new and more hopeful light favorably influences behavior. A successful experience in overcoming obstacles is one of the most potent means of modifying the self concept.

Consequently, teachers have a grave responsibility in their classes for setting the stage for success—for providing experiences in which every student can learn and grow. The "spur fallacy" implies that students are automatically stimulated by difficulty. This is true only when the difficulty is within their power to handle. When it is beyond their ability, it becomes a destructive force, often intensifying their idea of themselves as "failures."

Within the classroom situation the teacher must in some way integrate the student's needs with society's demands, and offer the appropriate experiences which will enable the student to perceive this relationship. The teacher has the task of discovering the student's ideas about himself, the values he holds, the attitudes he has developed. This is a truly creative process; it is the basis of effective teaching.

Belonging to informal groups enables the student to feel accepted and valued as a person who can be of service to others. The young person today identifies himself with many different groups whose values are often conflicting. He strives to integrate the divergent ideas among which he lives. He may begin to do this by finding common ground or agreement between his own descriptions of himself and those by other people, thus learning to accept the diverse realities around him. According to Menninger, "ultimately education is more important than therapy, not only because it can be applied to more people, but because in effect it is prophylactic."[4] Since other chapters will be dealing specifically with the group aspect, further detail is unnecessary here.

Contribution of Counseling to Self-understanding

Self-understanding is facilitated by a combination of methods— the techniques of study already described, beneficial interaction in groups, and individual counseling.

RELATION OF COUNSELING TO THE SELF CONCEPT

The counseling process may have a potent influence, for good or bad, on the student's concept of himself. At the most detrimental extreme is the instance of the registrar who told a student she was the worst failure they had ever had.

Perhaps equally devastating are such statements as, "Your intelligence is not high enough to succeed in college," or "This vocation you've chosen requires a higher level of intelligence." To most people, intelligence means a general prerequisite for success, not merely what the intelligence test measures.

In more subtle ways the counselor may, unintentionally, attack the student's ego. In some instances, for example, giving reassurance may make the counselee doubt the genuineness of his own feelings—was he foolish to be worried about this matter which the counselor seems to think is unimportant? Sometimes advice given with the best intentions has the effect of making the counselee feel that he lacks the resources within himself to think through his own problems.

Too frequently two-way communication between counselor and student is not established. It is difficult, indeed, to choose the right words. The safest procedure is for the counselor to follow the counselee's leads—to use, in general, the symbols he uses to express his

[4] Karl A. Menninger: "Present Trends in Psychoanalytic Theory and Practice," pp. 14-17.

feelings and motives. Then the counselor is more likely to say the words that have the intended emotional tones.

At the most beneficial end of the scale is developmental counseling, in which the student discovers his resources and abilities. This may be an exciting experience; it accentuates the positive—what the student can do, not what he cannot do.

Every school of counseling is concerned with the development of self-understanding. The counselor-centered approach emphasizes analysis, synthesis, diagnosis, and prognosis by the counselor, as well as "cooperatively advising with the student," and follow-up. The "middle-of-the-road" point of view stresses the need to adjust the method to the counselee; it holds that a counselor can use a variety of methods successfully. Persons who accept this point of view believe that "maladjusted normal people" need to learn (1) the causes of their difficulty and (2) better techniques of living. Carl Rogers' philosophy emphasizes the acceptance of the individual, and seeks insights by the counselee himself leading to "a more realistic and satisfactory control of his actions."

Students' Need for Counseling

Bernard Shaw once said that his happiness began when he realized that there were certain things he could not do, and directed his attention to doing the things he could do. Many college students feel the same way. Several studies showed that about three-fourths of the adolescents questioned were eager for self-improvement and self-understanding. They felt ready to take more responsibility than had been given them. Almost half said that they wanted to talk with someone about their personal problems. One-third felt the need for guidance, as they understood it. They frequently mentioned their desire for more affection and their concern about disagreements among their parents. About one-fourth felt that they were failures. Investigations of this kind, using questionnaires, sociometric methods, and nondirective or "open-end" interviews, show how much students need to get a realistic and acceptable idea of themselves.

The Faculty Adviser

The freshman comes to college expecting new experiences, ready for a reappraisal of his abilities, frequently unclear as to his purposes and values. This is a strategic time for counseling of a positive and developmental kind. A skilled faculty adviser who has a relatively small number of counselees and who maintains contact with them for at least a year—this would be the ideal situation.

Unfortunately, these desirable conditions do not often prevail in colleges. The work of faculty advisers is extremely uneven. Some have only one perfunctory interview with their counselees; others find time to give them substantial help.

When a freshman comes to a faculty adviser or counselor as David did, saying, "This business of going to college is a waste of time. None of the subjects I'm taking interests me. I don't see the point of studying since I'm not getting anything out of it. I might just as well quit now and go to work," what should the faculty adviser say? His possible replies might cover a range from the most directive and threatening to the most permissive:

"That would be a very stupid thing to do."

"You know your parents would never permit you to drop out of college now."

"I told you during freshman week that this would happen."

"It can't be as bad as you think; you'll begin to like college soon. Every freshman feels the way you do at first. I once felt that way myself."

"I think I can change your program so you will have more interesting teachers."

"Have you really tried to become interested in your subjects?"

"You shouldn't make a quick decision now that you'll be sorry for later. Let's talk it over first."

"Very well. Let's see what kind of work you can do."

"You're disappointed in college and feel it's a waste of time."

"It's up to you, whether you stay in college or drop out. Suppose you go on thinking it through a little more and telling just how you feel about it."

What would be the possible effects of each of these different approaches? Although different students would respond differently to the same approach, it seems obvious that the acceptance of the boy's feelings and encouragement to think it through and tell how he feels would be better than the reprimanding, advising, or reassuring approaches often used by faculty advisers.

Since the student's immediate concern is to succeed in his college program, and since his social and athletic activities are often contingent on that, the faculty adviser might well conduct an exploratory interview in which he and the student would both gain an understanding of the student's potentialities, interests, purposes, and values. The following excerpts from a verbatim interview illustrate a kind of developmental guidance which a faculty adviser can offer.

The student, a freshman girl, was a member of the orientation class which the interviewer was teaching. The following are excerpts from this initial interview:

Counselor: This is your hour, Jeanne; you can use it in any way you like. Suppose you begin by telling me about yourself.

Student: Well, I graduated from ———— High School and I've come to ———— College to major in education. I would have liked to have gone away to ———— State Teachers College, but it was one of those arguments at home that I should stay at home and go to school. I find it very interesting at this school and the people around me are interesting, but I have one difficulty that I would like to find out about so that I could help myself to overcome it and that is in English, in my vocabulary. When I'm talking to the other students I find it hard to express myself, and to use the words that I want to show what I really mean; some words that you use don't actually mean what you want them to mean. And I find other students have a very unique way of using words—some words I never heard of, never saw before, and especially in English when the professor uses some words I can't understand what he's talking about due to the words he uses. And I would like to know some way that I could through my reading increase my vocabulary and use the words in everyday living. And I'd like to know what books to read and on what level. I've read some books, but the books I've read haven't increased my vocabulary even though they're said to be good books. So that's what I'd like you to help me with—my vocabulary. . . .

Counselor: Well, one of the best ways of developing vocabulary is through wide reading. Do you do much reading, Jeanne?

Student: Now I do; I mean I don't read constantly, but I do pick up a book once in a while and try to increase my vocabulary through my reading. I never did read before even in high school, and when we were given a reading assignment, I would look it over, find out what it's about and then I could answer some of the questions, but other than that I never did any reading at all—it was just once in a while when I wanted to entertain myself—when I had nothing to do, some free time.

Counselor: When you say to entertain yourself, what sort of books did you read then, Jeanne?

Student: Well, I just finished Somerset Maugham's *Catalina* which I found very interesting—the unique way that he writes. I enjoy reading his books an awful lot. And I also read *Gentleman's Agreement*, but I didn't really enjoy this book because it didn't seem as good as it could have been. Some of the books were in relation to history—books that I had to have reports on; that was my only reading. I don't read the Book-of-the-Month Club's selections—we never get any of those at home because my father is the only one who ever reads; my mother doesn't care to read much; my sister is still in high school and she's studying music so she doesn't find much time to read either. So I'm the only one who can pick up a book once in a while.

Counselor: So you and your Dad are the only two readers in the house.

Student: Yes [laughs]. You see, he's the only one who really is behind me to go to school and get to be really observant, because he feels that he didn't have an opportunity for an education and that we should get one—I mean that he's the one who would like me to increase my vocabulary and my knowledge and he's very interesting to talk to, too.

Counselor: You talk things over a lot with your Dad?

Student: Oh yeah, he's a great talker and you just sit and listen a lot of the time. . . . He never went to school much, but through experience he's learned different things and so I don't have to learn the hard way; I can just learn from him and his experiences. He reads to increase his knowledge—where a lot of people read mysteries and things like that—he doesn't like to do that.

Counselor: I notice your reading is much like your Dad's.

Student: Well, I like to read books like that because I feel the same way he does about learning something. I feel it's silly to waste your time to pick up a book just because you get a charge out of it.

Counselor: You don't like to waste time. You read with purpose, you do things with purpose.

Student: Mmm. When I do something, I like to do it and get it done. I don't like to spend a lot of time on nothing. I'm very impatient [laughs]. My sister's the same way. We all are in my family. We don't waste time [laughs]. We get it done [laughing]. And we do it our way or we don't do it at all. . . . [Student talks at length about her sister and her sister's vocational plans. Counselor gives information about a possible scholarship in music.]

Counselor: And what are your plans in college? I only know the degree toward which you are working.

Student: I want to major in education—elementary education. I'd like to be a teacher. I feel I like children a lot. Oh, I don't know, a lot of people feel there's no money in the profession, but I feel I could help society by teaching little children and that's why I am interested in it. That's why I majored in elementary education.

Counselor: You seem to be very much interested in people.

Student: Oh yes, but it all depends on the person because I like people that I can get along with. Either I like the person or I don't. I'm not the type of person to put on—to be nice to his face and as soon as he turns around show that I can't stand him. I tell persons if I don't like them and I tell them why I don't like them. Then we can get along better; they understand me and I understand them. In that way I make more friends.

Counselor: You like an above-board, on-the-level relationship.

Student: Yes, I don't like the sneaky sort of people. . . . I'm nervous, you can see that now. 'Cause I'm not used to talking about myself, 'cause I feel there is not much to talk about.

Counselor: We all feel kind of funny when we start thinking or talking about ourselves to other people. But—you're an interesting person.

Student: [laughs] I could imagine I am quite a specimen. [Both counselor and student laugh.] I feel I'm different from everyone else. I mean— I'm not unconventional, but I mean—I usually try to get along with people others can't be bothered with.

Counselor: Just how do you see yourself as different, Jeanne?

Student: Well, uh—I don't know really. Some people will say about a person, "Oh, she's this and she's that," and I feel I'll find out why she's like that, you know, and maybe she's really not like that. I feel that I'm different because other people just let that other person go while I like to make friends with her and find out why she's like that. Other than that, I don't feel that I'm very much different from every-one else. I like to eat [laughing], sleep, go to basketball games, and things like that.

Counselor: How do you spend your free time, Jeanne? You've mentioned friends and so on.

Student: Now that I go to college [laughs], I don't have any free time. [Both counselor and student laugh.] Well, I like to participate in activities. When I get out at twelve o'clock on Tuesdays and Thursdays, I want to go to the different activities like today, the girls' tug of war. So really I don't have any spare time—unless to read, I like to read good plays or a good story, and other than that I like to knit and I like to play baseball with the kids out in the street. These are my three main interests. And, too, I enjoy listening to good music.

Counselor: From what you've told me, at one time you didn't like to read, Jeanne, but now you do a little more reading, but you also have hobbies and interests such as knitting, friends, games, and so on—so that you have a pretty well-balanced program. [pause] How about your high school, Jeanne, what were your experiences there?

Student: Well, my grades were always average and my counselor said I could do better if I put my mind on it. I used to fool around a lot; I had a good time. My marks could have been better if I knuckled down to it and did my homework when I was supposed to. . . . [Goes into detail about this.] And now that I'm in college I feel I've lost out because I have to study to make up the work I missed in high school. So I really regret not studying as much, but I had a good time so I really didn't lose out that way.

Counselor: You listened well in class and found you could learn that way.

Student: Yeah, I—uh—I made up my mind I wouldn't fool around in class. That's how I passed a lot of times without studying. My mother used to holler at me, "Jeanne, you're having a test tomorrow, pick up a book and start studying." "Oh, Mom, I know the stuff already." Then I'd go out wherever I was going. So that's why I got average grades. . . . [Continues talking about her high school marks and classes.] There's another thing I find, you're more on your own in college. There's no two ways about it. Nobody's going to tell you, "You're not doing too well." . . . The high school counselor would often tell me that it's up to me to get on the ball. He said I'd just have to read and study a little more. It's just that I'm lazy—a lot of times I've been told that—even in my music. I wouldn't practice— and therefore couldn't play as well as kids who were taking it for the same amount of time I was. It isn't that I couldn't learn it; it was just that I was lazy. . . . But when I had homework in math. I enjoyed doing the homework 'cause I enjoyed doing math.

Counselor: Now how about the elementary school, Jeanne? Do you remember much about it? That's a long time ago, I know.

Student: For some reason or other, in elementary school I was always the teacher's pet. . . . And I really didn't have to work. I fooled around as in high school and the teachers let me get away with it a lot of times [laughs]. I don't remember too much about elementary school.

[In reply to the counselor's question: Did you miss school at all? the student tells about her absence from high school for a month because of an injury to her arm, then goes on to tell about her work experience.]

That work experience made a big impression on me. I missed school because the people where I worked were much older than I—there were a few young girls, but they didn't somehow seem to suit me— they weren't the type of people I'd enjoy being with—that's the time I realized the difference between people who get an education—people who stay in school even though they can't afford it—and people who figure, "Oh, I'll quit school and go to work."

Counselor: So that really made you want to go to college.

Student: Yes. I think it's worth it to go four years to college, but I enjoy going to school anyway. [pause] I guess that's all there is about me to know—really.

Counselor: Well, I see the time is just about up, Jeanne. We'll have our next interview in two weeks. As you know, the time is yours. If you have something else to do in the interview hour, you can do it, but if you would like to come up and talk to me here, we could go over some of the things that are important to you. In the meantime, we'll be working on vocabulary in orientation class. One of the best ways to improve your vocabulary, as you've found out, is through wide reading on any subject, but there are other ways such as practice with key words on drill cards, or learning the basic Latin roots, prefixes, and suffixes, and so on.

Student: I found one thing very interesting in talking with you. Some of the things that come to light you don't realize when you start talking and telling about yourself—the different things that are really wrong with you. You understand yourself a little better, and get to know yourself better by talking to someone like this.

Counselor: You do learn a lot by talking to someone else at times.

Student: Things that you never realized before.

Counselor: Like what, Jeanne?

Student: Oh, I don't know. [pause] I just can't think of anything at the moment, but it's really impressed me—talking about myself—I never realized I could talk about myself to anybody. [laughs]

Counselor: [laughs] Right—I'll be seeing you later on, Jeanne.

Student: O. K. 'Bye.

What did the faculty adviser accomplish in this initial interview? First of all, he created a counseling relation in which the student felt free and stimulated to think about herself. The counselor was accepting, attentive, friendly. Without seeming inquisitive, he helped her, through occasional comments and questions, to explore conditions that might affect her college success—vocabulary, reading and study efficiency, interests, leisure activities, family attitudes and relations, relations with other people, ideas about herself, her elementary and high school experiences, absence due to illness, work experience. Near the end of the interview he came back to the problem of vocabulary which she had raised at the beginning of the interview. This interview was a personal continuation of the orientation course which he was teaching. His objective was to help her get off to a good start in her college subjects.

If the counselor's objective had been to help this student gain a deeper understanding of herself, he would have conducted the interview somewhat differently. For example, he would have been more alert to the dynamics of her behavior and have picked up important clues. At the very beginning Jeanne gave an important lead to understanding family relations, when she said, "I would like to have gone away to college, but it was one of those arguments at home that I should stay at home and go to school." This clue the counselor never picked up. Instead, he introduced the subject of football games. Later on in the interview the counselor again abruptly changed the subject when it might have been more profitable to ask, "How did you feel about giving up your music?"

The counselor made this kind of response a number of times in this interview. Perhaps he did not recognize the potential significance of the student's remarks; perhaps he was overanxious to reassure, to put the student at ease, to avoid emotional material; perhaps he himself had a need to be liked. It would be well for the counselor to examine why he thinks a counselee needs so much to be put at ease. In this kind of attempt to create a relationship, the counselor keeps sidetracking the student from the things that are most vital to her.

To accomplish the deeper purpose of the interview, the counselor would have had to reflect more accurately the girl's true feelings, rather than her self-deceptive evaluation of her personality. For example, the counselor reinforces Jeanne's need to make reading serious and purposeful when he says, "You don't like to waste time. You read with purpose, you do things with purpose." Some students take reading too seriously. Actually a good deal of reading should be fun. Moreover, in this case, the counselor does not know whether this emphasis on serious reading stems from the girl's excessive identification with her father—her desire to live for her father. Often, quite unwittingly, counselors reinforce a trend that is undesirable from the standpoint of the individual's total personality development.

Similarly, the counselor's response to Jeanne's comments about her sister assumes that she wants her sister in the same college with her. But other remarks hint at an underlying competitiveness. Until the counselor knows how Jeanne really feels about her sister, he should not assume that she wants to help her. If he does assume this, Jeanne may feel guilty at not feeling enthusiastic about the proposed plan. She may be afraid later to talk about her rivalry with her sister, for fear the counselor will think badly of her.

After Jeanne tells why she wanted to major in education, the counselor said, "You have a good reason." Here, again, the counselor accepted and reinforced a feeling without knowing enough about it. In some cases the desire to help others grows out of the individual's own needs and drives. Under these conditions, she will be jealous of their success, not rejoice in it. If, on the other hand, she works with others out of the abundance of her own self-affirmation and security she can then truly help them and rejoice in their success. The point is that in this first interview, the counselor does not know enough about the case safely to reinforce the feelings which the student at this time is free to express.

Reassurance often does not have the desired effect, as in the part of the interview in which Jeanne is self-disparaging and says, ". . . I feel there is not much to talk about." The counselor might have said something like this: "You don't feel you are worth talking about?" Instead, he reassured her that she was an interesting person, which evoked the more self-derogatory statement, "I could imagine I am quite a specimen." The counselor follows this comment with more reassurance.

Throughout the interview, the client wants to talk, and pours out a great deal of information. She is eager for insights and says near the end of the interview, "When you start telling and talking about yourself . . . you understand yourself a little better." But by handling the interview on a surface level, the counselor does not help Jeanne to develop new insights. Instead, she pours forth self-accusing thoughts. She calls herself "lazy," "not interesting," "a specimen," "not as industrious as my sister," etc. If she continues doing only this and nothing more really clarifying in continuing interviews, she will receive little or no help in clearing up her problems. She may get some relief through "talking it out." She may be flattered by the counselor's attention, but may begin to wonder if he does not have the same criticism of her that she feels for herself, since he seems to accept everything she says. If she does not improve in her work, she may feel further burdened by her failure to succeed for his sake. What she seems to want most is not only to talk about herself but also to find clarification of her self-defeating tendencies. This is counseling on the deepest level.

In a permissive, but not undirected interview, the faculty adviser can help the student understand himself in relation to his college environment, choose a suitable program of study and recreation, and make optimum progress in it. In the course of this counseling, he may deal to some extent with financial matters, health, family relations, and social problems.

The General Counselor

For help on some of the more complex cases, the faculty adviser may refer the student to other members of the college staff, such as the dean of students, dean of men, dean of women, and others holding similar positions who have more time and more preparation for counseling and psychotherapy. One college student, in looking back over her high school years, gave credit for her growth in self-understanding to her dean of girls:

As an adolescent, I wanted to develop a mature attitude toward an understanding of myself, my fellow beings and my world. I wanted to grow up to be a happy and useful person and to become the "me that ought to be." To attain this I was helped to profit by my past, to prepare for my future, and to live the present well. I was shown these things, not told. My dean helped me develop a philosophy of life by living it herself.[5]

The role of the dean is (1) to help faculty advisers become more effective as counselors, (2) to work more intensively with individuals, (3) to suggest modifications of policies and procedures in the light of student needs, and (4) to discover and use all the resources of the college and the community for helping students achieve an understanding of themselves and their environment.

The Educational and Vocational Counselor

If such a counselor is employed in a college, he can do much, directly and indirectly, to help students recognize and realize their vocational potentialities. As part of the orientation course he can open up to them possibilities in the world of work. He can prepare up-to-date booklets, as some colleges have done, showing the vocations and avocations for which each subject field prepares. Since a vocational goal is often an effective motivation for study, this information can be used to good advantage in subject classes.

In two or three interviews, with the assistance of appropriate tests, the educational and vocational counselor can help the student explore his strengths and weaknesses, his experiences, his satisfactions and dissatisfactions, and his personality trends in relation to certain vocations and the preparation needed for them. The educational and vocational counselor may also have responsibility for placement; at least, he will work closely with the placement office to help students carry out their sound vocational plans.

[5] Shirley Humfeld: "Students Look at Their High School Deans."

The Counseling Psychologist

The psychologist is equipped to help the student gain deeper insight into his personality. He is concerned with discovering the causes of the student's behavior as well as with appraising his abilities. His role is more diagnostic than that of the other counselors who have been mentioned. He may use projective methods as well as the usual psychometric tests of intelligence, achievement, and special aptitudes.

At the University of New Hampshire, well over half of the 119 students who visited the psychological clinic (7 per cent of the undergraduate enrollment) came to the clinic on their own initiative. About half of these problems were classified as educational and vocational maladjustment; about one third, emotional; a little less than one fifth, social; 14 per cent psychoneurotic; and 5 per cent, psychotic.

The psychologist has more responsibility than the general counselor and the vocational counselor for the psychotherapeutic type of interview. He focuses more attention on helping the student to change habits of thinking and feeling that may be preventing him from using his energy fully. By achieving a new orientation to himself, the student is able to handle life situations more competently.

The Psychiatrist

When deeper unconscious forces are interfering with a student's present adjustment, he may be helped by a series of intensive psychiatric interviews. The student must have a desire to change, and the worker must have time and specialized skill to gain this deeper understanding of hidden springs of action.

The psychiatrist employed by the college may also carry a number of short contact cases. In an hour's interview he may encourage a student to speak freely about himself; help him to relate and interpret the thoughts and feelings he expresses; and plan with him the next steps he can take on his own.

Like the counseling psychologist and general counselor, the psychiatrist works with and through teachers and faculty advisers, thus greatly extending his influence through preventive work. On the basis of his understanding of student needs, he is able to suggest administrative, instructional, and curricular changes that will help students to put their newly acquired insights to work.

Concluding Statement

The student's concept of himself is a dynamic thing. It influences his perception and consequently his conduct. He strives to maintain his self concept, whether it is true or false, constructive or destructive.

His understanding of himself has been growing since his earliest years. Although early childhood experiences set a certain pattern which is often persistent and stubborn, the group experiences of childhood and the instability of adolescence offer many opportunities to modify the initial self concept.

Life itself changes the individual's outlook. Through group experiences, he sees himself through others' eyes, incorporates some of their ideas into his thinking, tests his capacities through participation. His horizon widens through knowledge; his self-confidence grows through successful guided experiences.

In addition to experiencing the discipline of the group and gaining understanding through interpersonal relations, he needs occasionally to appraise himself. This can be done best in a counseling situation. With the faculty adviser, educational and vocational counselor, or general counselor, the student may have the exhilarating experience of discovering his potentialities and planning a total college program that will help him to realize them. When inner conflicts and unconscious motivations are holding him back, he may seek psychological or psychiatric aid in resolving these conflicts and releasing his creative energy.

The proof of a realistic concept of one's most acceptable self is good adjustment to college and to life.

BIBLIOGRAPHY

Bugenthal, James F. T., and Zelen, Seymour L.: "Investigations into the 'Self-Concept'—the W.A.Y. Technic." *Journal of Personality XVIII*: June, 1950, pp. 483-498.

Elias, Gabriel: "Self-Evaluative Questionnaires as Projective Measures of Personality." *Journal of Consulting Psychology XV*: Dec., 1951, pp. 496-500.

Humfeld, Shirley: "Students Look at Their High School Deans." *Journal of the National Association of Deans of Women XVI*: Oct., 1952, p. 36.

Menninger, Karl A.: "Present Trends in Psychoanalytic Theory and Practice." *Bulletin of the Menninger Clinic VIII*: Jan., 1944, pp. 14-17.

Phillips, Lakin E.: "Attitudes Toward Self and Others." *Journal of Consulting Psychology XV*: Feb., 1951, pp. 79-81.

7. Life Outside the Classroom

JOHN L. BERGSTRESSER
DOROTHY E. WELLS

E FFECTIVE application of the concept of "deeper teaching" in the life of the college outside the classroom calls for critical reexamination and clarification of objectives, imagination and creativeness in planning, willingness to experiment with new methods and activities, and persistent effort to improve the program through continuous appraisal. The "molding of whole persons" in terms of "individual purpose, character, and values," which is the aim of deeper teaching, also demands determined searching for ways to establish more direct and more vital interrelationships between activities outside the classroom and the academic program. The latter can be made more real to students, can result in deeper and more permanent learning, if experiences outside the classroom are deliberately planned to provide opportunities for the immediate application of academic learnings in the affairs of campus life.

College activities outside the classroom can, however, do something more than supplement, enrich, and provide a testing ground for classroom learnings. They can offer a variety of social and cultural experiences and other opportunities for the development of social growth, sound values, appreciations, and insights. Such possibilities are inherent in the unique nature of the college community. These unique contributions need not be in conflict with the valid aims of the academic program. Rather they can be planned to serve as ways of broadening and supporting these same purposes by the use of methods and activities which differ from those of the classroom.

The Objectives of Life Outside the Classroom Related to Deeper Learning; and Ways of Attaining These Objectives

The major thesis of this book—that all phases of student personnel work should make a telling contribution to "deeper teaching" and "deeper learning"—requires a restatement of objectives in terms of this basic assumption. The challenge may be expressed in the form of this question: In the light of this special concept of the function of college activities outside the classroom, what are the objectives that should give direction in planning and implementing the program and serve as the essential criteria for its continuous evaluation and improvement?

If "life outside the classroom" is to realize fully its potential for assisting in the achievement of "deeper teaching" and "deeper learning," it should be planned and appraised in terms of special emphasis upon the following objectives:

1. Supporting and Supplementing Academic Learnings Through Planned Opportunities for Their Effective Application in the Immediate Out-of-class Environment of the Students

Students often complain that much of the content of their academic courses is too abstract and theoretical for them to see in it any relevance to the "realities" of life. To some extent this apparent lack of relationship between learning and living is attributable to the students' youth and limited experience. There are, of course, a number of instructional techniques (e.g., laboratory experiments, field trips, internships, cooperative work-study plans, etc.) which often can be used effectually to help students bridge this gap. Many times, however, restrictions of the classroom situation severely limit the opportunities for the empirical testing out of the principles, hypotheses, generalizations, and methods of analysis which are indispensable elements of learning. The creation of such opportunities is educationally desirable in relation to the expected benefits of deeper understanding, better retention, and increased skill in intellectualizing. Several types of college activities outside the classroom can be deliberately used to help extend such opportunities.

An illustration is provided in the way one college dealt with a real and immediate problem in a student cooperative house where there was serious conflict over a cooperative food plan. The conflict involved basic issues of house government, responsibility and authority, food selection and preparation, and financial management and accounting. When the student officers of the house sought help from personnel staff members, the latter enlisted the active participation of a social science instructor in analyzing the existing house government. Many references were made to the principles and methods of democratic government which most of the students had studied. The effort to apply these concepts and techniques in the analysis of their own problem helped greatly in checking emotionality and producing objectivity. The end result was a revised house constitution, clear definition of powers and duties, and a striking improvement in morale and in the management of all house activities. In a similar way, assistance was obtained from an instructor and advanced students in accounting to determine sound and feasible methods of financial management and record keeping. A home economics teacher and one of her students gave informal instruction in food buying and menu planning. Thus in three instructional areas there was a direct application of academic learning to the out-of-class experiences of a fairly large group of students. The outcomes went beyond the observable benefits to the house organization. For many of the individual members, a significant kind of "deeper learning" was realized, and in this process the academic disciplines involved took on new meaning and relevance to life experience.

Equally good opportunities exist in the field of the fine and applied arts. Many courses in music, the graphic arts, etc., stress theory, historical development, form, and method, but provide scant "exposure" to the actual end products, and even less to the creative experiences, of the artist. Furthermore, many college students are not required and do not elect to enroll in these courses. And yet most colleges profess the hope that their graduates will carry over into their post-college life esthetic appreciations which will influence their artistic attitudes, interests, and behavior. "Life outside the classroom" can contribute at this point by offering enticing daily opportunities for students to look at worthy art objects, listen to good music, and try their hands (however amateurishly) at creative effort in the field of applied or fine arts.

The college union building can play an important role. In the Wisconsin Union, for instance, there are a large and well-equipped arts and crafts workshop, music listening rooms, an art exhibit room, hallways outside a magnificent theater for the display of art products, a photographic laboratory, etc. Residence halls can also contribute by providing facilities and activities which emphasize esthetic values. Even the simple step of providing good prints, loaned out by the library for use in dormitory rooms, has value. To achieve the best results in any specific college, however, the active collaboration of students and faculty members who are especially interested in the arts should be obtained. This action in itself can do much to bring about a more vital relationship between learning and living in this area of man's knowledge.

2. Providing Opportunity and Incentive for Participation by Every Student (With Due Regard for Individual Differences) in a Variety of Activities Conducive to Well-balanced Development

Out-of-class activities must be sufficiently varied to be appealing to many kinds of individuals, if they are to invite participation by all. Such a varied program will also offer opportunity and incentive for all-around rather than lopsided development. Participation by all can be stimulated by a favorable college-wide attitude toward community activities, but it should not be obtained by compulsory measures. This point of view is based on the assumption that such participation, when kept within reasonable limits of time and energy, has potential values for growth both in social maturity and concern for the common good.

An example of varied and well-balanced participation is shown in the experience of one student who belonged to a fraternity, the interest club in his major field, and the International Relations Club. He was a leader in his dormitory and in student government. These out-of-class activities made it possible for him to find social satisfaction, to apply classroom learnings in the field of recreation, and to experience warm personal relationships which cut across the stratified lines of social life on the campus. In his college it was fortunately possible to mingle with fraternity brothers, dormitory friends, students from other lands, and many others, with no fear of losing group status or offending campus mores and traditions.

The individual differences of students should be recognized and respected; and vigilance is necessary to avoid pushing students into sterile conformity. That is why it is so important to reject compulsion, or even the appearance of it, to induce participation. Students rather should be encouraged and helped to think critically about the potential values to them of participation in one or more of the available activities. Critical appraisal of these values by students can be greatly stimulated by making sure that they are themselves directly involved, along with staff members, in the processes of planning, policy making, and evaluation. Students, as well as staff members, should, if possible, be led to accept as a goal a program of activities that will give opportunities to all to grow in social competence—whether through specifically social affairs such as teas and dances or, more indirectly, through relationships which are by-products of hobby interests like photography and sculpture.

Surprisingly few colleges keep adequate records of what each of its students has done in student activities; and it is recognized that this is an expensive and time-consuming job if it is performed by making notations on each student's personnel record. A useful and fairly adequate record can be obtained, however, quite simply and inexpensively, if all students are asked to fill in a form summarizing their participation for the past semester or year at registration or at some other time of the year. At the same time they can be invited to make evaluative statements about the program; and the nonparticipants can be asked to indicate their reasons for not taking part in activities. Analysis of the results of this survey may suggest faults that can be remedied or gaps that can be filled. Then the form filled out by each student can be filed in his personnel record folder for subsequent use in counseling and advising. Both student personnel workers and faculty advisers should be urged to talk with students about the extent and quality of their participation in campus affairs. Especially in the case of the nonparticipant will it be of value to encourage the student to express his feelings, judgments, and attitudes. In many such instances, problems of shyness, finances, health, etc., will emerge through sympathetic and skillful counseling; and ways may be found to assist in their solution. At times it will be possible for the counselor or adviser by suggestion, referral, or direct action to remove a real or imagined barrier to participation.

Campus mores, customs, and traditions exercise compelling, and not always desirable, influences upon the nature and degree of participation in various kinds of activities. The attitudes of faculty members and student personnel workers are also influential although, unfortunately, not always in complete harmony. These two important influences should be brought into the open and dealt with honestly and intelligently. With respect to the attitudes of the instructional staff, personnel workers should acknowledge frankly that faculty colleagues have a legitimate stake in the out-of-class life of the college. Unless faculty members are drawn into a close partnership with student personnel workers and help to give leadership in this aspect of the college program, the desired goal cannot be reached.

3. FACILITATING THE SUCCESSFUL ACHIEVEMENT OF THE DEVELOP-
MENTAL TASKS WHICH ARE BIOLOGICALLY AND CULTURALLY IMPOSED

The program of campus activities should take into account the
developmental tasks which college students must deal with successfully to achieve healthy and satisfying growth in our culture. Havighurst, who defines a developmental task as being "midway between an
individual need and a societal demand," has described these tasks
concretely and has pointed up the importance of "timing" in the educational program. An understanding of these tasks would help to
provide activities which are appropriate for groups of students at
various stages of development. It would also direct attention to individual differences so as to avoid poor timing, especially in terms of
biological development, and consequent frustration and peer conflict.[1] The preceding chapter has treated this subject in some detail,
particularly as related to group experience.

It will be helpful to obtain detailed information about the characteristics and background of the student body. What are the key
interests, physical attributes, social backgrounds, standards of behavior, attitudes, and values of the students in a particular college?
These factors must be known and considered if the activities provided are to assist, and not impede, the learning of developmental
tasks and orderly growth toward maturity.

Students often have urgent and difficult choices to make in the
areas of religion, occupations, interpersonal relationships, sex, etc. For
example, some college students who are keenly concerned with questions of life values become terribly confused by what appears to be
an irreconcilable conflict between science and religion. This confusion
often manifests itself through disturbing conflicts with parents and
other adults, accompanied by opposing and frustrating feelings of
guilt and rebellion which may hinder progress toward mature and
nonhostile independence. Other students experience a tough problem
in how to make friends in college or how to deal with their first experience of falling in love. One student, with a shy and rigid personality, the product of a doting mother and a domineering father, made
many superficial acquaintances in classes among the male students
because he was bright and willing to help his classmates, yet he failed
to win complete acceptance as one of "the gang." His contacts with
women students were no more successful. When one girl did become

[1] Robert J. Havighurst: *Developmental Tasks and Education.*

interested enough in him to try to help him meet other women students, he quickly "ran for cover"—apparently because he unconsciously identified her with his mother from whose influence he was trying to escape. In situations such as these, a counselor or personnel worker engaged in group activities who has skill and insight can often assist students to work out solutions to their problems. The resolution of such dilemmas is what is required to deal successfully with developmental tasks.

4. STIMULATING SINCERE, ENJOYABLE, AND PROFITABLE SHARING OF COLLEGE COMMUNITY EXPERIENCES AND RESPONSIBILITIES BY BOTH STUDENTS AND FACULTY

"Deeper learning" through participation in out-of-class activities can best be achieved when there is a friendly community atmosphere which encourages students and faculty to enjoy relationships outside the classroom in addition to formal academic relationships. In situations which are free from pressures of grades, assignments, and the like, students and instructors often come to see each other as "real people" for the first time. That students want such opportunities to meet and know instructors is accepted as fact by most student personnel workers. Convincing evidence on this from the students themselves was reported by the Cooperative Study in General Education as the result of a survey in some twenty colleges.[2]

Some colleges have gone so far as to include students even in such groups as college curriculum committees and the committee on evaluation of teaching. Other institutions emphasize such faculty-student collaboration very little or not at all. Somewhere in between are many colleges where students and faculty share responsibility for various aspects of the college activity program. One instance is a student-faculty committee on orientation for new students. This kind of project can benefit from the ideas and experiences of students, as well as from the guidance and knowledge of the faculty; and joint student-faculty thinking will help assure a balanced program which will be enjoyable and socially successful, as well as academically helpful and informative. Another example is a student-faculty committee on scholarships, where both groups share in evaluating the worth and need of the applicants.

The value of such experiences for both groups depends on the

[2] Paul J. Brouwer: *Student Personnel Services in General Education*, pp. 213-214.

appropriateness and tone of the situation. The chances for success are enhanced when there is genuine and natural mutuality of interests. The strain of an inappropriate and unnatural social relationship was expressed by one professor's retort when students complained that many faculty members were completely disinterested in participating in student dances. He protested strongly that he did not lack interest in social contacts with students, but pointed out that he had long since "done his dancing" and was no longer interested in that kind of social activity. Instead he preferred other ways of meeting students socially, ways in which he could be "comfortably involved." Faculty members should be frank about such matters; but they should also be willing to suggest more appropriate alternatives. Only where there is "comfortable involvement" on both sides can there be a relationship of mutual enjoyment and an atmosphere of equal partnership, in place of paternalism or condescension on the part of the faculty and of submissiveness or apple-polishing on the part of students.

Tead has pointed out that students need and can benefit from "deft, mature leadership," and that the faculty has a responsibility for helping students learn and uphold "standards of decency and morality." Such leadership, he feels, cannot be assigned to any particular group such as the personnel staff, but must come from the entire adult population of the college. His contention is that where the faculty accept these responsibilities and offer "friendly guidance" to students, the benefits derived from activities outside the classroom are higher standards of behavior, better coordination with classroom learnings, and powerful motivation for student achievement.[3] In harmony with this point of view are the actions of faculty advisers of student groups who attend rather than chaperone social affairs, guide rather than direct students in their efforts, laugh at themselves and with students rather than assume a dour and superior air, and who win and retain student respect by virtue of behavior instead of position.

5. Adhering Uncompromisingly to Democratic Principles, Values, and Standards

Adherence to democratic principles should be a strong guiding force in all aspects of life in an American college, and democratic standards should be upheld and insisted upon by college authorities

[3] Ordway Tead: *Trustees, Teachers, Students.*

from top to bottom. Campus activities conducted in accordance with this kind of college policy would be open to everyone on the basis of qualification in terms of interests, skills, abilities, and achievements—and not denied for reasons of creed, color, etc. Student participation would be extended in those areas of policy formation and procedural decision in which they can assume real responsibility commensurate with increased authority. In this way, and many others, emphasis would be placed on the duties of democratic citizenship, the other side of the bright coin of democratic rights and liberties. Opportunity and instruction would be provided for frequent practice in the use of the specific techniques of democratic procedure in debate, legislation, and execution of majority decisions. Consistent application of democratic theory in campus affairs would lead to "deeper learning"—in terms of respect for the opinions of others, the duties and rights of both the majority and the minority, and the practical skills and "know-how" needed for the successful functioning of a democratic society, etc.

Democratic procedures will also help students resolve many problems related to adult authority. Where student and adult tackle issues of campus life in honest collaboration, there is much less fear on the part of the student of an unreasonable or arbitrary imposition of regulations and policies. Mutual respect of each for the other, and the sharing of common responsibilities, will lead to sounder student-faculty relationships, and will ease, if not eliminate, the pressures arising from youth's natural tendency to rebel against the authority of parents and of faculty who are often their substitutes in the college environment. Student-faculty committees in which each member has an equal voice and vote are functioning successfully in many colleges. The deliberations of such committees and the mutual sharing of responsibility for their action are usually beneficial to students and faculty members alike. They often come to have new faith in each other. Students may gain greater respect for the perspective and experience of their adult colleagues, while the latter may become more sensitive to the potentialities of seemingly "immature adolescents" for responsible and intelligent behavior when they are treated as young adults.

In the chapter which follows special attention will be given to learning democracy through participation in campus government. Virtually all areas of campus activity, however, can contribute to this aspect of "deeper learning." Student publications, for example, offer an excellent opportunity for democratic learnings. Not only can the student learn proper layout and journalistic techniques, but he can also be taught to be truthful and fair in reporting and to balance freedom of expression with responsibility. There are great learning possibilities in a situation where students are asked to share in setting editorial, news, and advertising policy for the college newspaper. One college, for instance, has in successful operation a plan that places this responsibility on a joint student-faculty board of publications, on which there is representation from the student body at large, the student government organization, as well as from the newspaper staff. This board does not engage in any prepublication censorship of the student newspaper. At the same time, the editor and staff are held accountable for the contents of the paper in terms of the basic policies which the board determines and makes as explicit as possible for the guidance of the staff.

6. Fostering Understanding of the Role and Acquisition of the Techniques of Leadership in a Democratic Society

The obligations as well as the opportunities and rewards of leaders in a democratic society are strikingly different from those of leaders in an autocratic society. This contrast has been vividly portrayed in the United Nations through the actions of representatives from democratic and autocratic states. These differences have educational significance and should be made clear to students who aspire to leadership in the college. Students who understand the qualities of democratic leadership will not only be more effective in discharging their immediate responsibilities, but also, in terms of future obligations in the community at large, will help to fill the need for increasingly skillful leadership in our society. Colleges should be energetic and resourceful in stimulating "deeper learning" for leadership through out-of-class activities.

The program of activities for life outside the classroom is rich in opportunities for leadership experience through student clubs and organizations and campus affairs. Extracurricular activities also afford an equally important kind of opportunity for students—that of learning the appropriate role of a follower in democratically organized groups and how to find satisfaction by making substantial contributions in whatever roles they are called upon to perform in particular situations. One young man who was majoring in speech achieved outstanding success as the president of the forensics club of his college. He was instrumental in greatly increasing the membership

and status of the club and in leading the debate team to many vic-
tories. At the same time he was able, as a member of the music club,
to adapt himself easily and cheerfully to a very modest role. He gladly
accepted minor committee assignments, helped arrange furniture
and address envelopes for programs and parties, and attended meetings regularly. Instead of losing status by assuming the role of loyal
follower in this second activity, he became increasingly respected and
liked by the members of both organizations.

Students should learn to select leaders for qualities which will
further group or college aims rather than selfish interests. Moreover,
those selected should accept leadership with a willingness to assume
the responsibilities entailed and not for prestige values alone. In a
student body election a strong student newspaper can help in this
regard by presenting valid aims and objectives to be achieved and
describing the qualifications necessary in a person who is to assume
leadership. News stories on the candidates for leadership positions
can analyze the individuals' experience, training, interests, and personal qualifications in order that students may select more wisely.

7. OFFERING INSTRUCTION IN SPECIFIC SKILLS AND PROMOTING DEEPER UNDERSTANDING OF SOCIAL RELATIONSHIPS WHICH WILL FOSTER GROWTH AND MATURITY IN SOCIAL COMPETENCE

Social competence is more effectively achieved when students learn
social skills both in the classroom and through extracurricular activities. Many classroom activities permit an easy give and take of
ideas which is akin to the conversational activities of a social event.
The art of conversation is important for all students to learn, particularly for the shy student who needs to know how to hold his own
and for the loud-mouthed one who needs to socialize his aggressions
in order to win acceptance by his peers. All students can benefit by
learning to listen and to respect the views and opinions of others.
Faculty can be instrumental in helping students acquire social skills,
especially if they have a high degree of social competence themselves and set a good example. Even the common courtesies are important, though often neglected, learnings which college students
need to respect and practice to attain a high degree of social facility,
ease, and enjoyment.

Often progress in acquiring skill and ease in social relationships is
most rapid if the learning situation starts with the student as he is
and permits him to "catch on" without being subjected to painful
embarrassment and invidious comparisons. The emphasis will then

be on the student as a person and his relationship with others rather than on making a fetish of etiquette. Some students, it is true, will be ready for specific training in such things as how to behave at formal functions, how to introduce people, how to dress appropriately for specific occasions. For other students, who are excessively shy and uncomfortable in purely social situations, social "manners" and social growth may better come by less direct means. Such young people frequently develop socially through participation in crafts, sports, music, chess, photography, and similar activities, where a by-product of their interest in learning or perfecting a skill is social learning through natural contacts with others who share these specialized interests. Sensitivity to and respect for individual differences is of supreme importance here.

One college attempted by systematic observation of individuals in various kinds of group meetings and in other situations to identify shy students who did not "belong" in any social group. The next step was an effort to discover any active or potential hobbies they possessed. Then friendly, tactful, and persistent efforts were made to draw them into small group activities related to their hobbies. The result was that many of these students not only enjoyed the activity itself, but also gradually made new acquaintances and achieved a sense of belonging. Increased self-assurance and pronounced growth in social competence was noted at the end of the year in an encouraging number of instances.

In some college residence halls there is a plan for rotating student host and hostess responsibilities at the dinner hour. Students learn to carve and to serve, to be attentive to the needs of their friends, and to encourage a pleasant flow of conversation at the table. Dress is informal, but neatness and cleanliness are emphasized, and the atmosphere is relaxed as in a home where a small group of friends might be entertained.

The foregoing examples of techniques for teaching social skills by direct and indirect means are merely suggestive of the many ways by which this objective may be achieved.

8. UNDERSTANDING THE SOCIAL AND CULTURAL FORCES THAT EXERT PRESSURES ON THE ATTITUDES, VALUES, AND ACTIONS OF INDIVIDUALS AND GROUPS IN THE COLLEGE COMMUNITY

Personnel workers, and other members of the college family as well, can profit from studying the findings of the cultural anthropologists who in recent years have thrown a spotlight upon the social structure and dynamics of American communities. What these researchers have discovered about the impact of the mores, caste and class, and the clash of opposing cultural interests upon the individual and the community has vital significance for campus life. Especially is this true if the college is to continue to be one of our society's chief instruments for facilitating social mobility—that is, to phrase it in terms of the democratic ideal, for assuring opportunity for persons to progress and "succeed" on the basis of ability, regardless of race, class, color, creed, or economic background. Accurate knowledge of the potent, yet often subtle and concealed, cultural forces that act upon the individuals and diversified groups on the campus can lead to realistic, wiser, and more skillful manipulation of college community life. This thesis is elaborated in some detail in Kelley's[4] book and in a brochure by Sutherland and others.[5]

A determined attempt should be made to persuade social psychologists and cultural anthropologists on the faculty to apply their methods of analysis in research projects focused on the college community itself. These studies could throw new light on social pressures operating on all the composite elements—students, faculty, administrators, clerks, maintenance staffs, and even trustees! Disregard of these pressures can result in a naive and superficial explanation both of individual attitudes and conduct and of group actions and interactions. Valid data and insight will make possible more accurate "diagnosis" and hence more intelligent "treatment." Although such research will be useful in any college, its potential value is most apparent in colleges where social conflicts are brought into sharp focus by their cultural settings—for example, certain metropolitan institutions, often called "streetcar" or "subway" colleges, where all or most students live off the campus, where many of them work part time, and where the pressures resulting from urban life, minority group status, etc., are keenly felt.

The faculty specialists referred to can also give valuable aid if they are induced to participate in discussion and spot analysis of various campus issues—the issue of restrictive membership in fraternities and sororities, to cite one "hot" and timely example. One college, in attempting to anticipate the problems stemming from a shift from a downtown to a high-class residential location, found it very profitable

[4] Janet Agnes Kelley: College Life and the Mores.
[5] Robert L. Sutherland, et al.: Students and Staff in a Social Context.

to get such faculty members to discuss the probable implications of this move with personnel workers and student leaders. Besides helping the students to plan with foresight for desirable adjustments of campus activities. these discussions stimulated them to examine critically and with increased objectivity the mores, traditions, and standards in vogue on the "old campus."

9. STRENGTHENING THE UNIFICATION OF THE CAMPUS COMMUNITY BY SPONSORSHIP OF ACTIVITIES THAT WILL RELATE THE INDIVIDUAL AND THE GROUP TO THE COLLEGE AS A WHOLE

If the college is to prepare students for effective participation in community living after college, ample opportunities should be provided in the campus environment for them to identify with the college community as a whole and to have the experience of contributing frequently to the common good. Unless this is achieved the college may never attain the characteristics of a unified community. Instead it will tend to be a mere collection of buildings housing a number of fragmented subgroups. To combat extreme fragmentation of the college community, especially in the very large universities, at least some activities and events are needed which will involve large numbers of students drawn from all segments of the population. The existence of physical facilities which are adequate to serve the purpose of a true community center can aid tremendously to promote unification.

A college union building can serve this purpose admirably, providing it is constructed and equipped to accommodate large group events, as well as to cater to the interests of individuals and small groups. A keen sense of identification with and pride in the college can stem from being one of many who experience an inspired dramatic or musical performance, a large banquet, a successful prom, and so on—and it is surely good to have a number of these kinds of campus-wide activities, instead of relying solely upon King Football to provide the only focus for community loyalty and unity.

The college union should, however, also be planned and equipped to foster the development of a rich variety of small group and individual activities. The ideal community center would even provide equipment and serve as a "home base" for numerous outing activities, such as hikes, picnics, and ski trips. It would contain such facilities as music listening rooms, a photographic darkroom, a library for leisure-time reading, a hobby workshop, rooms for chess and bridge, combination dining and meeting rooms for small gatherings. The existence of such facilities makes possible the creation of a program of activities that will draw virtually all members of the college community—faculty as well as students—into frequent contact with the hub of community activity. The presence on the campus of such a vital nerve center need not be in any sense a restrictive or narrowing influence. Nor does the existence of a center for community activity deny the unique merit and need for the development of many similar individual and small group activities in decentralized units, such as dormitories, student religious houses, and other natural centers of student life. On the contrary, with imaginative leadership, these two equally valuable and complementary approaches can both serve to extend the circumference of group life, leisure-time interests, and relationships with the community outside the college.

10. AFFORDING FREQUENT AND PLANNED OPPORTUNITIES FOR FRIENDLY CONTACTS AMONG THE DIVERSIFIED ELEMENTS OF THE COLLEGE COMMUNITY, INCLUDING MINORITY GROUPS, FOREIGN STUDENTS, MARRIED STUDENTS, VETERANS, ETC.

The democratic theory of human relations and the powerful forces that are creating crises in world affairs demand that our society— above all our educational institutions—make rapid advances in breaking down prejudices based on race, color, creed, and cultural differences. Any college enrolling a diversified student population has on its doorstep a laboratory for experimentation in the improvement of understanding, cordiality, and mutual respect among differing cultural groups. Too often members of minority groups, while not subjected to discourtesy or obvious discrimination, experience only the superficialities of politeness and tolerance and are denied genuinely friendly social contacts. Segregation in housing and restricted membership in campus groups, for example, foster such superficialities and hinder the attainment of genuine communication and human relationships that have real personal and social values.

Campus-wide and smaller group activities in which many kinds of students can work together as equal partners in a common cause facilitate the growth of candid communication, appreciation of unique individual worth, and respect for the distinctive contributions from many peoples to the mosaic of national and world culture. An example is found in colleges where international relations clubs and collegiate councils of the United Nations are vigorous and strongly supported and whose membership cuts across all lines of social cleavage on the campus.

There are, unfortunately, innumerable instances of conscious and unconscious prejudiced behavior on the part of both students and faculty. For example, the professor who unthinkingly but obviously singles out the Negro students in a class by calling on all of them in turn; the fraternities which discriminate openly or secretly against Negroes, Jews, foreign students, and so on; the instructor who always seats women in the back of the class and then either ignores or embarrasses them; the students who are politely condescending to their brethren from overseas because of an assumed superiority based upon the foreigner's limited mastery of English; the younger students in control of student body funds and activities who are unsympathetic to the differing social interests and needs of older students and married students. Honest self-criticism, especially on the part of the more favored members of the campus social complex, is necessary to identify and then to eliminate both the obvious and the subtle forms of prejudiced behavior.

Sometimes minority groups have a telling effect on the college and its mores. Such was frequently the case when veterans appeared on campuses in appreciable numbers, expressed by speech and action their aversion to activities of a "rah-rah," adolescent nature, and eventually brought about the dropping of certain childish traditions and the substitution of more mature patterns of behavior. In one college a group of young teachers from Germany, brought to the United States by the State Department to study the American educational system, made their presence on the campus felt in many ways. Their spontaneous and expert group singing, their ability to get good "mileage" from every dollar they spent, their artistic skills and good taste, their command of English as a foreign language, their self-reliance and resourcefulness in exploring the city and state—all these made strong impact upon the American students, inducing imitation at some points, respect and even envy at others. The good fruits of the mingling of native and German students were, however, experienced also by the latter. Above all, they gained a knowledge—perhaps even an awe—of democracy at work that could not have been duplicated by the reading of a ton of books.

11. Planning and Operating the Program in Such a Way That It Will Harmonize and "Mesh Gears" With All the Basic Objectives of the College

That disharmony often does exist between out-of-class activities and the basic aims of the college is evident in recent exposes of bribery, "pay-for-play," and proselytism in intercollegiate athletics. Equally subversive practices are found in unscrupulous manipulation of student elections and in "graft" with respect to the financial operation of the student newspaper, the junior prom, or the college yearbook. To tolerate these practices, or to dismiss them as being the responsibility of "someone else," is to ignore the potent influence of such out-of-class practices upon the present and future conduct and moral values of students. It is also to be blind or indifferent to the fact that the extracurriculum in such instances is working in direct opposition to the aims for which society has created and supports the college.

Surely it is not too idealistic to assert that an institution of higher learning has the responsibility to stand uncompromisingly for sound ethical principles—both in its instructional program and its extra-curriculum. Such a stand does not rule out fun and spirited activity, but it does require that high standards of integrity, decency, and good taste be used in judging what is desirable and appropriate for the college community. "Humor" magazines that depend upon mere smut and obscenity for sales appeal do not measure up, nor does a dramatic program that never rises above adolescent farce and imitation of night club acts. Dances that degenerate into drunken brawls are not social activities which are in harmony with the basic aims of higher education. If opportunities for enjoying music outside the classroom are limited to dance bands playing songs from the current "hit parade," the extracurriculum is falling short of its maximum possibilities for enriching the musical experiences of students.

The unique values of growth in critical thinking and civilized maturity for which the college exists must be learned by practice as well as by preachment. There is no better time or place to begin the process of living up to these excellent ideals than in the present and in the immediate environment of the college community itself.

12. Strengthening the Unification of the Campus Community by Sponsorship of Activities That Will Relate the Individual and the Group to the Community in Which the College or University Is Located

If the college is to prepare students for effective participation in community living after college, ample opportunities should be provided while they are students for them to identify themselves with the larger community and to have the experience of contributing frequently to the larger civic good. This type of activity can again combat extreme fragmentation within the college community by involving numbers of students drawn from all segments of the campus population and often the faculty as well. Such experiences may often be directly related to curricular goals, may be voluntary or on a paid basis; but whatever the motivation, this kind of service offers excellent training for leadership in civic affairs and can make the community a better place in which to live.

There are opportunities in almost any community for students to contribute their services to philanthropic camps, welfare agencies, youth programs in churches, Y.M.C.A.'s, Boy and Girl Scouts, Camp Fire Girls, hospitals, etc. Participating in civic projects such as the Red Feather drives, even merely stuffing envelopes for "T.B." drives, assisting with community surveys, singing in a church choir, teaching a Sunday School class, or developing an active campus chapter of the League of Women Voters, closely related to the activities of the community chapter—all can provide for the immediate application of academic and outside-the-classroom learnings in the affairs of the community at large. Such "off-campus" experiences can also contribute significantly to the deeper learnings with which this book is concerned.

13. Adapting to New Opportunities and Needs Arising from Shifts in the Composition of the Student Population, Economic Conditions, and Other Factors of Social Change

Personnel work which is concerned with "deeper learning" must be imaginative, creative, and experimental. As the composition and characteristics of the student body change, the activity program should be adapted to new needs and conditions. Often, when these changes occur, the methods best suited to accomplish the aims of life outside the classroom are not obvious or predictable on the basis of past experience. What has proved successful in the past may no longer be appropriate or most effective. Better solutions of problems may arise out of experimenting with a new approach and initiating new activities.

In one large university, when veterans and their families moved into the housing facilities provided by the college, the personnel staff began to plan activities for the wives. Bridge groups, get-together teas, and dancing parties were set up. Interest and participation were so meager, however, that an investigation was made, and it was discovered that these women were more interested in their homes and families than in these kinds of social affairs. Consequently a plan was devised for a child psychologist from the faculty to donate his time and meet with the women for discussion of the problems of childhood care and development. The home economics department helped with discussions on home furnishing, budgets, and diet. Soon the husbands became interested and joined the sessions. These stimulating meetings were followed by a coffee hour, and this group of young people with limited income, energies, and time found both profit and enjoyment in their out-of-class activities.

The recent threats to academic freedom in many colleges have had a direct impact on activities both in and out of the classroom. These threats, resulting from domestic and world-wide pressures, create a problem which should be approached with wisdom, imagination, and courage on the part of the whole college. As these problems relate to life outside the classroom, what should be the attitude toward student groups which are or are suspected of being Communist-influenced? Are members of these groups to be passively accepted, guided, ostracized, or kicked out of college? What student activities can offset the influence of such groups, and also help in the reeducation of their misguided members? Is it possible to channel ultraconservative behavior patterns which are born out of fear into ways of doing things which will be constructive and positive, rather than stultifying, narrow, and superficial? Faculty and students must experience more "deeper learning" than ever before, if such challenges are to be met in ways that will develop "individual purpose, character, and values" through the activities of life outside the classroom.

The Evaluation of Life Outside the Classroom

Life outside the classroom, because it encompasses a wide variety of activities and a large number of people, imposes special difficulties in evaluation—particularly in obtaining an over-all appraisal that will give a Gestalt picture of the program rather than merely separate and unrelated appraisals of its several aspects. In the light of this dilemma and the limitations of time and staff, it would appear justifiable at times to substitute for highly objective techniques of evaluation other methods that are reasonably valid, though less exact, and which are more economical. This more subjective approach often affords practical assistance in the assessment both of some parts of the program and of the program as a whole. Even in the ideal situation, with unlimited funds for evaluative research at hand, it is doubtful that the most advanced statistical and scientific techniques now available would be adequate for the task.* Many changes in student behavior, however, which either cannot be measured scientifically or require prohibitive expenditures of time and effort to do so can nevertheless be systematically and fairly accurately observed. If these behavioral observations are followed up by repeated "diagnoses" and comparison of these results, the process will produce an evaluation of considerable merit.

In appraising activities in the student personnel program there is much worth in the attempt, however subjective, to ascertain the values gained by the group and the individuals who participated. What kind of judgment did the students use in planning and conducting the activity? Where did they do well, and where were mistakes made? Was the thinking of the students critical or biased and shallow? Consideration of such questions as these is a part of "deeper learning" for students in that self-evaluation will help them to become more honest in appraising themselves and their activities. In such evaluation there is again a potential relationship to the classroom teaching of critical thinking. If it is important to apply critical thought to a problem in philosophy or science, is it not equally so for young people to be critical and straightforward in facing the consequences of their own conduct and activities?

If students are to appraise critically and develop mature judgment, they should take an active part in the planning and promoting of evaluation projects for extracurricular activities, and in the interpretation of the data. They need to feel that their participation in evaluation means they are cooperating in an important part of the college program. Their ideas are often fresh and fruitful and their assistance of genuine value. They learn to criticize their activities in

* See Chapter 20 for further elaboration.

terms of values to the individual, values to the group and its objectives, and values to the college community. Properly directed, the give and take of criticism can become an honest and forthright, yet kindly, adventure in appraisal.

This is not to say that the use of subjective or "rule-of-thumb" types of appraisal should eliminate the use of more technical or scientific methods. Just as in painting the artist makes use of new oils, new media, new tools resulting from scientific discoveries, so the educator as practitioner of the art of "deeper learning" should avail himself of the scientific tools at his command. There are testing, survey, research, and evaluation techniques which may well be useful in critical assessment of the program. Moreover, personnel workers can often draw upon the logic, steps, and methods of scientific evaluation even when using a more subjective approach. Many college personnel staffs cannot be expanded to include specialists to perform expert and scientific evaluations. Where the "generalist" takes all the time required for such evaluations, other important phases of the program usually suffer. If a more subjective approach can be practically useful in revealing trends, weaknesses and strengths, can point the way to improved programs, can keep objectives in tune with changing times and student needs, then perhaps a good portion of our effort and money should be spent on this approach to evaluation.

BIBLIOGRAPHY

Bergstresser, John: "Education Outside the Classroom, Part I: Its Functions." In Fowlkes, John Guy (ed.): *Higher Education for American Society*. Papers delivered at the National Educational Conference, Madison, 1948. Madison, The University of Wisconsin Press, 1949.

Brouwer, Paul J.: *Student Personnel Services in General Education*. Washington, D. C., The Cooperative Study in General Education, American Council on Education, 1949.

Deutsch, Monroe E.: *The College From Within*. Berkeley, Cal., The University of California Press, 1952.

Falvey, Frances E.: *Student Participation in College Administration*. New York, Bureau of Publications, Teachers College, Columbia University, 1952.

Havighurst, Robert J.: *Developmental Tasks and Education*. Chicago, The University of Chicago Press, 1948.

Kelley, Janet Agnes: *College Life and the Mores*. New York, Bureau of Publications, Teachers College, Columbia University, 1949.

Lloyd-Jones, Esther: *Social Competence and College Students*. Washington, D. C., American Council on Education Studies, Series VI, *Student Personnel Work*, Vol. IV, No. 3, 1940.

Sutherland, Robert L., et al.: *Students and Staff in a Social Context.* Washington, D. C. American Council on Education Studies, Series VI, *Student Personnel Work*, Vol. XVII, No. 18, 1953.

Tead, Ordway: *Trustees, Teachers, Students.* Salt Lake City, University of Utah Press, 1951.

8. Student Participation in Campus Government

LUCILE ALLEN,
FRANK BALDWIN,
MARK BARLOW, Jr.,
and ISABELLE J. PEARD

CAMPUS government depends on the nature of the educational institution in which it functions, the nature of the student body, and the extent to which the campus lives up to the ideals of democratic government.

The nature of the institution, its purpose and goals, and the appropriate methods for their attainment are seen differently by those associated with any given campus. Within any single institution the various groups—that is, the faculty, students, and administration —see their role in carrying out the commitment of the university from different points of view. It is therefore their right and responsibility to seek clarification of purposes and methods that are mutually understood and accepted.

The nature of any student body includes differences in motivations; from exclusive concentration on intellectual development to the most esoteric hopes for human perfection, differences in capacities to handle responsibilities, differences in backgrounds, and differences in concepts of good government are bound to exist.

The institution must provide the opportunity for education, but education is not domination or authoritarian control. It is not carried out in artificial settings or under pressures. There must be freedom to make mistakes. Its success depends on a willingness of the student to learn and the capacity of the staff to teach.

The nature and practice of democracy and the desirable directions of its development are subject to wide differences in interpretation, whatever the social institution. Conflicts regarding the "American way of life" versus the "new social order," concern for the individual versus concern for the group, and status quo versus revolutionary changes are constant sources of stress. Certain difficulties in operation plague democracy at all levels. In the practice of democracy, not only the campus, but the nation itself is weakened to the extent that each may lack representatives of real stature, to the degree that each has governmental representatives who are content to use shoddy means for "good" ends. Furthermore, in both nation and campus a large number affected by a decision are lethargic about the issues. To some extent the moderates have abdicated on our campuses, as well as in the larger community.

There is also confusion about authority in a democracy. One faculty member said seriously, in speaking of a student, "I didn't know whether to tell him he had to, or to be democratic and let him do as he pleased." Democracy does not mean the absence of authority. The difference between democracy and totalitarianism is not in the degree of authority, but in its source and use. For example, democracy delegates authority and gives the delegate some freedom to use it. Government is, in the last analysis, control—and control by authority, which in a democracy is delegated control, the exerciser of which is responsible to some person or aggregate of persons.

Here confusion exists on our campuses. In the national government, authority is delegated by the people to their governing officials, and the officials are then responsible to the people. In college government, however, authority is delegated by the trustees to the president of the college or university, which authority the president then delegates to the faculty, other administrators, and the students. Thus, unlike other communities, the president and faculty of a college are not responsible to the students as a constituency. Governmentally, the president is responsible through the trustees to a group or groups outside the campus. The responsibility of the institution to the student is to provide the means for his intellectual, civic, and social development. An important area where this development may occur is in student participation in campus government.

Student Participation in Campus Government

Since all government is concerned with the exercise of, responses to, and responsibility for authority, it may be appropriate to consider the student's maturity regarding authority. The student attends college when he is in the process of gaining "independence." That is, he is making new adjustments to the idea of authority by substituting for the old parental authority the authority of society in general and of his immediate society, the authority of the situation, and "internalized authority" where his controls are within himself. If his earlier experience with authority has been unfortunate, his new freedom may cause him to react blindly against any kind of control or restriction, including student-administered control. A normal campus in normal times can help such students and absorb their rebellious feelings and behavior without loss of stability. With a preponderance of such students, especially if they dominate student government, their influence may be a threat to stable government, whatever its structure. It follows that college staff members concerned with campus government must interest themselves in the clarification of university goals, in the structure and function of the campus government, and in the growth of the student in insight, maturity, responsibility, and stature. Perhaps the campus, which has been said by many to be an ideal laboratory for teaching democracy, need not simply reflect the conflicts of national government, but can also be used to train able civic leaders and work out new methods worthy of democracy's high ideals.

Student participation in campus government, then, has two major purposes: first, to serve as a laboratory for student development in the skills, attitudes, and methods of democratic citizenship; and second, to carry whatever responsibilities have been delegated to the students in the functioning of the university. In the second-named purpose their responsibilities include, in the large part, providing the social environment and setting the social standards of the student community. Once they have assumed these far-reaching responsibilities, no other division of the university can carry the students' part in it. The whole climate of a campus educates the student body, and all students should be guaranteed relatively stable social education in their campus society. The degree to which a university can expose the campus climate to risks in order to provide a laboratory of learning is a moot point. In the interests of true education, it cannot afford to risk a chaotic or shoddy social environment; neither can it afford to eliminate true student responsibility if students are to grow. Sometimes presidents or trustees lay down rigid requirements, either directly or through the adviser, that stifle growth. Sometimes the adviser cannot or will not risk errors on the part of students. Some margin of error where inexperience is operating must be counted in as a part of the learning experience.

The first-named purpose of student participation in government, that of serving as a laboratory for student development in the skills, attitudes, and methods of democratic government, is strongly emphasized in the thinking and writing of educators.

For example, the President's Commission on "Higher Education for American Democracy" states:

If our colleges and universities are to graduate individuals who have learned how to be free, they will have to concern themselves with the development of self-discipline and self-reliance, of ethical principles as a guide for conduct, of sensitivity to injustice and inequality, of insight into human motives and aspirations, of discriminating appreciation of a wide range of human values, of the spirit of democratic compromise and cooperation.

Responsibility for the development of these personal qualities cannot be left as heretofore to some courses or a few departments or scattered extracurricular organizations; it must become a part of every phase of college life.[1]

To educate our citizens only in the structure and processes of the American Government, therefore, is to fall far short of what is needed for the fuller realization of the democratic ideal. It is the responsibility of higher education to devise programs and methods which will make clear the ethical values and the concept of human relations upon which our political system rests. Otherwise we are likely to cling to the letter of democracy and lose its spirit, to hold fast to its procedures and follow undemocratic courses of action in the very name of democracy.[2]

The crux of the difficulty is not in comprehending the truth of these statements, but in implementing them. How does one go about helping students develop a matured understanding of democracy's problems and methods and integrating democratic principles into their lives?

The authors suggest that this may be approached by listing some of the specific skills and attitudes essential in a democracy, by considering means existing on a campus for teaching students these skills and attitudes, and by considering the functions and patterns of campus government. The discussion will of necessity be indicative rather than complete.

[1] President's Commission on Higher Education: *Higher Education for American Democracy*, Vol. 1, "Establishing the Goals," p. 10.
[2] *Ibid.*, p. 12.

Some of the Specific Skills and Attitudes in Democracy

Some of the essential attributes of a democratic citizen are:

1. *Straight dealing.* A corollary of personal freedom is that the individual says what he means to all persons concerned, that his goals as well as his methods be as open, consistent and honest as he can make them.

2. *Predictability.* People should be able to count on a person to keep his commitments, to carry responsibility that he has agreed to carry, and to serve his contracted purpose.

3. *Good judgment.* A democratic citizen should be free to see a situation as it is, uncolored by personal needs or his pet crusade; he should be free to see people and issues in terms of themselves without prejudgment on the basis of race, religion, or position.

4. *A comprehensive loyalty.* His loyalty must be to principles. He must refer his personal urge to "fix a ticket for a friend," so to speak, or his interest in a special group, to the framework of the total good.

5. *An understanding of communication.* Many of our difficulties stem from a lack of effective communication.

6. *Cooperation.* Cooperation is not a trading of support (if you back me in this, I'll back you in that) or going along with a predetermined plan. It is operating jointly toward a common end. It involves an equality of status in the discussion, an equal freedom to contribute at an early stage of the planning, and an absence of implied threat or reward, apart from the reward of achievement.

7. *Ability to understand the responsibilities of leadership and followership.* The situation and one's responsibility should dictate whether he leads or follows, not his compulsion either to be out in front or to avoid the limelight.

8. *Ability to see a problem in its context of time and place.* A democratic citizen must take into account long-term goals, the background and history of an issue, as well as the immediate pressure.

9. *Creative and constructive thinking.* Specifically, one must learn how to see more than one way of dealing with a situation, and how to choose the best of many alternatives.

Means Existing on a Campus for Teaching Democratic Skills and Attitudes

How can we teach students to learn these specific skills and attitudes essential in a democracy? The student can learn these skills and attitudes in three ways: (1) by example, through the way the university personnel operates in relation to students and student government, (2) through governmental experiences with peers, and (3) through contacts with the advisers of student government.

THE UNIVERSITY

The nature and functioning of the university itself contributes much to the important teaching of these skills and attitudes. In its general structure and in the mood of its out-of-class relations with students, it should so operate that it sets a good example before students. The president, the deans of men and women, and the faculty do well to treat students as responsible participants in the academic community. University personnel must try to keep their individual limitations and the institutional pressures under enough control so that they offer demonstrations of the kinds of skills and attitudes already mentioned: straight dealing, predictability, comprehensive loyalty, cooperation, and good communication. Much of the students' most valuable learning can be in imitation of the methods of the university personnel. An indulgent or arbitrary administration can misuse this function at either extreme. If it does, the laboratory of democracy becomes totalitarian or laissez-faire.

STUDENTS WITH STUDENTS

A second source of education in these skills and attributes is through the student's experience with his peers.

The association of a student with his fellows while participating in student government contributes to his development as an individual and to his present and future usefulness as a citizen.

While facing mutual problems with other students, he can learn to appreciate another's worth and dignity while at the same time taking inventory of his own stature. If an idea or an issue about which he feels strongly is rejected by the group, he must learn to take it in his stride and interpret it not as a rejection of him but as a rejection of his ideas. As he can learn to accept defeat unflinchingly, so must he also accept victory with genuine humility.

The nature of the elections of student government officers determines the future relationships of students. Elections by coalitions of established groups forces the student government into the direction of partial commitments. This association of the student with the coalition that sponsored him may weaken his sense of responsibility to the total group whom he should be serving. It also affects the working government organization when pawns of vested interest groups cannot focus their attention equally on all important issues; their objectivity is clouded by feelings of prior commitment and obligation.

Continuity of a student government organization from year to year is a difficult thing to preserve. The student executive, in assuming the maximum amount of responsibility within the least possible time, requires a clear picture of his job. This is a responsibility of the outgoing officers. It should become a part of the yearly function of a student government organization, with the cooperation of the whole college, to plan and administer a program of training for the incoming officers.

This training program should impress the incoming student officer with the desirability of waiting until he gets his bearings, and understands the campus situation and the relation of the student government to it before initiating major legislative changes. Outgoing officers should pass on sources of valuable information and guidance to be used throughout the tenure of office. Training then becomes a continuing process.

A training program in which the current officers participate to a large extent gives a needed opportunity for the officers to discuss the over-all program. It should be a part of each officer's function to prepare a written report of his activities throughout the year. This should include programs completed (with an analysis of the unsuccessful ones), programs in process, and future programs worthy of consideration. This report should be written with a view to passing it on to future officers.

It is wise that student officers discuss with each other as well as the adviser an agenda previous to a meeting. Such prior discussions soon teach the student to seek important facts that may be needed before further discussions and before decisions. An issue suddenly brought up for the first time in a meeting of the student government organization often does not have the necessary facts to accompany it. Some students are quick to comment even though they have little background information; other students are quick to recognize the lack of adequate information. The student, therefore, can learn not to form opinions when he has little information and to speak only in areas where he has background. To postpone a decision until the facts are in is hard for anyone to learn, but it is wise procedure, and an important learning. As the discussion of an issue proceeds, an alert student will see that there is a place for both intelligent conservatism as well as thoughtful liberalism.

Student leaders are always faced with the problem of bringing the rest of the student body along with them. Leaders soon learn that a hasty decision can be as disruptive as no decision. If a decision is to be soundly made, it must be based on pertinent information carefully gathered, collated, and presented, fully debated, and carefully weighed. A wise decision is not reached by rabble-rousing, coercion, and pressure. Real growth can follow if students are forced to think through an entire problem as best they can, arrive at a solution, and live with the solution until such time as new factors may call for reconsideration.

With adult guidance, students can learn that a satisfactory compromise solution often can be reached, not by bringing pressure against one group or another, but by seeking all pertinent information available. Student government leaders, if they properly represent their constituencies, must establish and follow certain communications procedures. Students not directly within the framework of the government are quick to censure when their student leaders have assumed prerogatives or have made a decision without seeking the opinion of the groups they represent.

ADVISERS TO STUDENT GOVERNMENT OFFICERS

A third source of education in the skills and attributes of civic responsibility is through the students' relations with the adviser to student government officers. The adviser is a key person in the development and stability of good campus government. The adviser must be able to represent the students' point of view with faculty and with administration. The adviser should also be able to interpret with knowledge and accuracy the administration's position to students—particularly in a large institution. He or she has a responsibility (1) to help effect and clarify the climate and context in which student government works both in general outline and specific detail, (2) to educate student officers in the methods and procedures of democratic government, and (3) to help students grow as they work.

The usual methods of working together are unproductive unless there is also a readiness for cooperation, a desire on the part of everyone concerned to think objectively and constructively, an effort to understand the feelings and ideas of others and to work through with them to an acceptable solution. Rapport must be built as a cushion for the inevitable bumps. It cannot be commanded—it must grow, experience by experience, by mutual effort, and through a substantiated confidence that neither adviser nor student is using the other for concealed ends.

Both student and faculty, to be effective, must remain in their own roles. Students who compulsively curry favor with adults or categorically object to any opinion of any adult on the one hand, and advisers who have to be one of the boys or fear "trouble" on the other are alike not free to work on the matter at hand. Both student and adviser are valuable precisely because of their positions. They should avoid cutting themselves off from the groups they represent by making a closed combine; they must not isolate themselves. Their strength is in the blending of their combined perspectives. The corollary of this is that neither adviser nor student should use the pressure of his position or of his following to force the other into line. The good situation is never one of domination on either side. Their cooperation must be built on their freedom to discuss honestly. The adviser and the student should focus on the job to be done, mutually respecting each other's responsibilities and commitments.

It is essential that the relationships and responsibilities of student government regarding separate student organizations, faculty committees, student-faculty committees, and administrative committees be discussed by the adviser with each succeeding group of government officers. The students should be helped here by contact and interpretation to see faculty and administrators as individuals like themselves who are subject to the same kinds of pressures, uncertainties, and differences of opinion in carrying out their responsibilities, and not as stereotypes of authority.

The adviser and former student officers together have a responsibility to educate student officers in democratic procedures and skills. The training should include the essentials of parliamentary procedure, the use of committees where aspects of a problem can be studied and discussed and then returned to the larger group with recommendations, and the like.

It is important for students to learn and use adequate means for gathering information on which to base a decision. Often officers are assailed by verbal minorities, or pushed into unpremeditated action by the school paper, or overly impressed by a petition. Students must learn ways to assess and evaluate the ideas and opinions of their peers. All students have a right to be heard—minorities as well as majorities. Minorities may be a source of ill-considered and partial plans, but they also may be a source of creative and valuable ideas. The officers must learn to consider all proposals and to blend and combine many points of view in one solution. Appropriate use of polls, wide group discussions, advice from students experienced in the area under discussion, methods and solutions of comparable problems on other campuses—all these contribute to the student officer's learning. The adviser can also suggest consultation with members of the faculty and administration who, by voicing varying ideas and points of view, can help to clarify the thinking of students. The adviser can point out the value of having discussion precede taking a stand, of having voting only after thorough discussion.

The adviser probably works most helpfully at the point of agenda— the prethinking where he or she raises questions, indicates further sources of information, helps to list alternatives, and helps the student to consider outcomes and to predict effects.

The adviser can provide continuity by turning to past years when a similar issue had arisen. Achievements and experiences of other years are thus not lost, and the same mistakes need not be repeated; with this continuity, affairs can spiral rather than circle. The adviser can further help the student not only to see the similarities between a given year and other years, but also to evaluate the mores and mood of the campus for the current year, the probable issues, and the probable effect of national affairs, such as the draft, on the campus population.

The adviser's relation to the student can be a supportive one, particularly in a time of pressure following an unwise or unpopular decision in student government. At all times, emphasis should be on the next steps to be taken—not on fixing the blame for the decision, but in learning from the experience what should be avoided next time. The statement that students learn from their mistakes is true enough, but the learning can be negative as well as positive. Unguided, a student can deduce from an unpleasant experience that it is simpler to work only with one's cronies, or that "you just can't trust anybody." The adviser can help the student with constructive evaluation, so that mistakes can be truly educative. The situation itself does the teaching where it can be correctly interpreted in the light of principle and procedure.

A discussion between adviser and student on government in general is often productive. There is much that is not generally considered "good" in national and international government, such as taking no stand by refraining from voting (the weak countries in the United Nations), filibuster, the grasping of power by unethical means for what is held to be good ends. On the other hand, the growing inclusiveness of much U. N. planning and discussion, and congressional use of committees rather than individuals for decision-making are worthy of emulation. A discussion of the theory of democratic government, and the use of recommended readings, such as Leighton's *Governing of Men* or Tead's *Art of Leadership*, will raise the student's sights and give him a broader context for thinking through campus problems.

Certain principles can evolve in the adviser-student discussions. For example, students are eager to demonstrate courage, but often unsure as to what it is. Sometimes it is defined for them as daring to "defy the administration," or to push the "college authorities" in a certain direction. It is pointed out often enough that courage sometimes involves taking a stand against one's peers. The perennial problems related to the control of drinking and social practices usually fall largely and rightly within student jurisdiction. If, after careful consideration, the regulations are believed by most responsible students and faculty members to be reasonable for that campus, then the student officers may demonstrate courage by risking unpopularity to stand by a decision.

The adviser should meet regularly not only with the student president, but also at regular times with him or her together with the other officers. Otherwise the one-to-one relationship of adviser and student president may place the latter in a less fortunate position with his fellows. The adviser's relationships with these officers should be open and aboveboard, never *sub rosa*.

In short, the emphasis in learning should be on cooperative, not divisive techniques and on open methods, not power politics. The best adviser-student relationships occur around positive programs and projects. Good relationships do not exist in a vacuum.

The adviser should foster student growth in capacity, understanding, stature, and active responsibility. The adviser should help the student to evaluate his own motivations away from undue satisfaction in personal recognition, paying back grudges, or use of scapegoats, and toward satisfaction in seeing a whole program progress, in encouraging other students to grow, in delegating responsibility and credit, and in providing training for good leadership in succeeding years.

Sometimes the demands of a student's position exceed his ability, his sense of obligation, or the amount of time he can spare from his primary personal and academic commitments. If he is heavily overloaded, both the student as an individual and the successful discharge of his responsibilities suffer. The ensuing physical and mental fatigue may be too great a strain on his judgment and even his integrity. It is the obligation of the adviser, the medical staff, and other students to see that no student allows himself to continue the duties of his office in such a case.

The adviser can help the student to extend his vision beyond the issue at hand, to foresee, to predict, to get a longer and broader sense of place and time. The year-long relationship should find the student growing more mature in judgment and attitude according to his capacity. Adviser and student must not expect perfection from each other; both have limitations, and these limitations are also part of the context.

Often, the advisers to government per se are the deans of men and deans of women or persons on their staffs. Faculty serve in important specialized capacities and as consultants and critics. It is important that advisers operate in a general framework of responsibility to the institution and not represent themselves. They should themselves have a margin for error and not be merely mouthpieces for a superior; otherwise they will not be able to transmit important freedoms to the students with whom they work. Creativity cannot flourish at any level without responsible persons who are also free. When the adviser sits on a joint student-staff board, whether or not he has a vote, he must guard both against dominating the meeting on the one hand and being a cipher on the other.

Obviously the adviser of student government must be a person of stature. He must be relatively secure, personally and professionally. As consistently as the students, he must evaluate his own motivations, study his own framework for operation if he is to function freely in it, and scrutinize his own methods of working. He must also be educable, able to profit from experience, to evaluate his mistakes, and to see his work in perspective so that a mistake does not unduly disturb him. The manner in which the adviser meets crises, makes decisions, and reacts to misunderstandings can give a positive example to the student. He must have sufficient scope and freedom to do these things—to be an educator, not a dictator.

There are on our campuses forces that tend to widen a dichotomy between staff and student—the natural ones of distance in age, position and background, plus any negative accumulation from past relationships, youth with age and age with youth—others artificially engendered, such as suspicion and distrust, automatic assigning of unworthy motives, and a desire to use any available weapon to pay off real or fancied injuries. When issues of serious import which involve emotion more readily than judgment arise on a campus, it is essential both to focus on the issue and to follow procedures as set up in calmer times rather than to focus on personal attack and discard constitutional procedures. Working together, student officers and advisers can demonstrate for the whole campus how this can be done.

Ideally, both adviser and student develop and express convictions of their own based on principle. They both grow in the capacity to comprehend another's ideas, irrespective of his position. The strength of any such relationship is an atmosphere where ideas can freely be discussed, not bowed to or automatically rejected. Directness, and greater maturity and experience can be the invaluable contribution of the adviser; freshness, responsiveness, and spirit can be that of the student.

Functions and Patterns of Campus Government

The structure of the government must demonstrate the principles of representation, communication, and participation by both students and faculty. This may be provided by student representatives on certain faculty committees and faculty advisers on student committees. It may be provided by equal membership on certain others, or by parallel committees coordinated by a joint steering committee. Whatever the method of providing for this communication, it must be explicit in the structure that it is student participation in government. Students do not "run" a campus and should not be deceived into thinking they do; they may carry sole responsibility for some decisions, share the responsibility for other decisions, and contribute ideas and information toward others. Where the serious error of a kind of labor versus management pressure is present in campus thinking (i.e., students should work to get "concessions" from a vested-interest administration), structure and method and climate must offer proof to the contrary. It is this interdependence which weaves the web of community life.

In general, the size of the campus and the diversity or homogeneity of its groups dictate the speed with which change in government structure should occur. Constant change in government ("We're doing over our Constitution again this year!") is unwise since it threatens stability and prevents a system from having a real trial; no change for long periods of time suggests a static and unresponsive government.

Although the aspect of government dealing with control is organizationally one of the most difficult problems, the service and co-ordinating aspect of government is also important. The areas of concern might be summarized thus:

Student Government

A. Standards and control of
  1. The individual
  2. Groups
B. Coordination
C. Services

The structure through which these areas of concern are administered varies, depending on the nature and goals of the college or university. Small men's colleges and small women's colleges often have a single structure (or council) which carries responsibility for all aspects of student life. Small colleges with specialized purposes, such as Antioch with its work-study program, may combine the functions of faculty and students in a single campus government. The large coeducational institution is required by its size and diversity to set up more complicated structures.

RESIDENCE COUNCIL

In institutions that are predominantly residential, that is, where most of the students live in college-owned or supervised residences, a form of residence council often carries direct responsibility for the standards and control of the individual, and delegates to committees under its jurisdiction responsibilities for services and coordination.

The smallest representative unit is usually the corridor (in a university dormitory), the fraternity, sorority, or cooperative house. From these units representatives are sent to a larger organizational unit, the dormitory, and, in turn, government among the dormitories is further coordinated by an over-all residence council. An interfraternity council, Panhellenic council, or cooperative association serves a similar function.

The residence council sets up regulations facilitating the residence life of dormitories, sororities, and fraternities in relation to orderly living and the use of residence facilities. Since the nature of the problems of men and women are different to some extent, the nature of the regulations and penalizations are different as a result. Therefore, men should handle the problems of men's residences, and women those of women's residences. The level of referral for the more serious infractions is usually a judiciary board made up of students representing all of the men's living units for men's problems, and a similar board of women for women's problems. Here the faculty and administration are usually represented. A third and final judiciary group handles the most serious problems referred by student government where expulsion of a student is a possibility. This group is predominantly faculty with small student membership.

Some problems concerning individual behavior should not be acted on by students alone. They are those that involve special legal, medical, and psychological problems. Stealing, for example, should not go immediately to a student court. A well-trained counselor or psychiatrist should talk with the student, should help him to appreciate his own position and the attitude of students. The highest student government officers should know the procedures and processes, but not usually the name of the student involved. Knowledge of the process takes away an aura of mystery and avoids rumor. It gives the officers another opportunity for growth in human relations. If the student shows progress as a result of this counseling, it is indeed possible that he should remain at the institution. If, on the other hand, after weeks of work there is no positive trend in the attitudes and behavior of the student, the college as a community can assume that the defect in personality cannot be corrected in his present environment. The final authority for dismissing a student is legally the responsibility of the administration.

Problems of sexual morals, even with mature faculty judgment, are difficult to solve and remedy. The purpose here should not be punishment or making an example of the student, but rather correction if that is possible, or quick removal of the student if it is not. When the student is a menace to the society in which he lives, he must necessarily be removed so that others will not be influenced.

In addition to providing for infractions of the mores, student participation in government should even more importantly concern itself with the developmental aspects of group life. In its service program, it may sponsor discussions, parties, educational meetings, lectures on study habits and careers, and countless other events which add to the student's sense of belonging, enjoyment, and education.

COUNCILS OF ORGANIZATIONS

Groups that are of sufficient cohesiveness to have a stake in their reputation as a group may and should assume responsibility for the standards of their activities. They should make and implement regulations for the control of their members to this end. They are often responsible to an over-all council or board made up of representatives from all groups who have assumed this kind of responsibility, plus representatives of the faculty. The responsibilities of the council, in addition to jurisdiction over such groups as fraternities, sororities, and independent council, might include campus dances, the scheduling for all student-sponsored campus events, "Spring Day," and the like.

Apart from control and jurisdiction, this board frequently provides records of past events, suggestions for constructive programs, and booklets on campus and community resources for programs.

Groups of a somewhat different nature such as special-interest groups, professional fraternities, and honoraries may also be served by such a board or council. Recognition of new clubs and avoidance of duplication in program and function may be an additional responsibility of the council. On large campuses, the disciplinary problems of groups may be handled by one board, and the recognition and coordination of special-interest groups by another board.

In practice, faculty representation on such boards or councils is from predominance to small representation.

STUDENT COUNCILS

The student council usually functions primarily in the areas of coordination and services. Its membership should be representative of all the students. The activities of the council can be varied. It may assess student opinion on all-campus questions and present it to the group that can use such opinion. It may, through its own committees, work with faculty and administration on such matters as orientation of freshmen, Parents Day, vocational conferences, and such publications as the freshman handbook. It may also assume responsibility for workshops, leadership conferences, student book exchanges, and foreign student programs. Student councils may also participate for the university in local, state, and national welfare organizations such as the Community Chest, the Red Cross, and the World Student Service Fund.

Other forms of shared participation should be mentioned. Many campuses have had success with a student-faculty administration committee composed of student leaders carrying major responsibility, chairmen of faculty committees on matters relating to student life, the advisers of student government (usually the deans of men and women), the president of the institution, and the public relations officer. This group discusses campus matters, but does not make policy. Its purpose is to exchange information in a broader context for the sake of greater common understanding. In this way, potential problems may be discussed before they become major campus issues and the facts be clouded with emotion.

Student government groups are often asked to send representatives to college and university administrative committees. This representation will be meaningful and not merely an idle gesture if (1) students are asked for opinions in areas that justly concern them and to which they can contribute a part of their experience, and (2) opinion is sought enough in advance of a decision so that its value can be weighed with other representative discussion. Areas of university administration to which students would contribute might be athletic policy, regulation of social conditions, registration of automobiles; but would not include the employment and tenure of faculty or the fiscal policies of the university.

In the interest of completeness, it is well to consider the effect of national groups on campus student groups. These include National Interfraternity Council, National Pan-Hellenic Council, National Independent Council, National Student Association, and a host of others. When local fraternity groups are considering discrimination clauses, for instance, the national groups usually present pressures in a single direction. The National Student Association, as any other group, may differ from year to year in its national and local leadership as well as in its stated objectives. In some years its influence may be strong and positive, in some years strong and negative, and in other years weak and ineffective. This is not to infer that national associations are always complicating in their influence on the local campus; they may serve to stimulate and broaden thinking, and press in a constructive direction. Campus groups, however, usually have more in common with each other, by virtue of their common environment, than with their national groups. The local situation should have priority and students should be able to think through the modifications or diversities necessary to their own local situation instead of accepting a blanket direction. They should also be permitted and feel an obligation to contribute to and influence the national stands taken by national organizations. To insure this ready exchange of opinion and information, budgets, minutes of all meetings, including executive committee minutes, and recordings of all acts, resolutions, speeches, and the like should be made available to the local group. The flow of opinion should be upwards, not simply downwards. It is important that campus organizations should feel greater loyalty to their own community and help to direct national groups toward "grass roots" thinking.

The following are a few general statements concerning student government.

1. All good government must have some conflict and permit expression by the nonconformist as well as the conformist. Conflict between ideas and values clarifies them. If there are too many conflicts, however, they may destroy campus morale. The mutuality of concern, the common ground, the eventual resolving of issues— these must be the major concern. The success of government is not measured by the number of issues that arise, but by the issues resolved and the general stability and dignity of its jurisdiction. Maintaining equilibrium in a forward moving society is a satisfactory accomplishment.

2. The framework of the government and the allocation of responsibilities may evolve in a more liberal or a more restrictive direction, but any specific decisions must be made within the framework as it exists. The rules of a football game are not revised at the time of the referee's decision. They must apply for that play and for that season, though they may fruitfully be modified at a later, more objective time. This procedure for handling any matter is especially applicable in times of stress.

3. Students are concerned with power and invariably ask early in each year, "What power do we have?" Power should not be deeded by a benevolent college president; power safely must follow responsi-

bility. When students, out of concern and readiness to assume responsibility, request the authority to undertake a certain project, three steps must be used as a procedure. They must offer a plan that promises wisely to serve a community need. They must have worked out details that show a comprehension of the task they have undertaken. They must consider possible consequences in an ongoing situation and the ways they have of dealing justly with the problem.

4. "Never take a strong stand on a weak position."[3]

5. Students may be dictators with other students. The mere fact that students are running something does not insure its democratic nature. Democratic education and behavior is essential on all levels.

6. Informal communication needs special consideration. Briefly, this type of communication should come early in any discussion of issues or plans. Surprises are not usually welcomed by students any more than by faculty or administration. The shock with which students learn of new plans in housing at the time the ground is broken, or administration learns of student action without consultation regarding the facts must be avoided. Early communication tends to avoid the spreading of rumors and the premature and often incorrect publication of the whole matter in the campus newspaper. Journalistic zeal for a scoop where no communication channels are respected can precipitate all kinds of crises. Before early communication can be realized on any campus, some provision for respecting confidences and the timing of release of the news must be agreed on by students and administration.

BIBLIOGRAPHY

Barnard, Chester: *Functions of the Executive.* Cambridge, Mass., Harvard University Press, 1938.

Benne, Kenneth: *A Conception of Authority.* New York, Bureau of Publications, Teachers College, Columbia University, 1943.

Day, Edmund Ezra: *Education for Freedom and Responsibility.* Ithaca, New York, Cornell University Press, 1952.

Donham, Wallace Brett: *Education for Responsible Living.* Cambridge, Mass., Harvard University Press, 1944.

Falvey, Frances E.: *Student Participation in College Administration.* New York, Teachers College Studies in Education, Columbia University Press, 1952.

[3] Alexander Leighton: *The Governing of Men,* p. 275.

Harvard University Committee: *General Education in a Free Society.* Cambridge, Mass., Harvard University Press, 1945.

Hollingshead, A. B.: *Guidance in Democratic Living.* New York, D. Appleton-Century Company, 1941.

Hynes, Dorothy: *A Study of the Range of Student Government Functions at Seventy Co-Educational Colleges and Universities.* Unpublished thesis. Ithaca, New York, Cornell University Press, 1951.

Kelley, Janet: *College Life and the Mores.* New York, Bureau of Publications, Teachers College, Columbia University, 1947.

Leighton, Alexander: *The Governing of Men.* Princeton, N. J., Princeton University Press, 1946.

Mead, Margaret: "Administrative Contributions to Democratic Character on the Adolescent Level." *Journal of National Association of Deans of Women,* Vol. LV, No. 2, Jan., 1941, pp. 51-7.

Overstreet, H. A.: *The Mature Mind.* New York, W. W. Norton & Company, 1949.

President's Commission on Higher Education: *Higher Education for American Democracy.* Vol. I, "Establishing the Goals." Washington, D. C., Superintendent of Documents, United States Printing Office, 1948.

Seeley, R. S. K.: *The Functions of the University.* Toronto, Oxford University Press, 1948.

Strang, Ruth: "Contributions of Research to Discipline and Control." *National Society for the Study of Education.* Thirty-seventh Yearbook, Part II, 1938.

Tead, Ordway: *The Art of Leadership.* New York, McGraw-Hill Book Company, 1935.

9. Learning to Live Healthfully

ELIZABETH McHOSE

THE health of the student is inseparably associated with the most effective application of the personnel point of view. The currently accepted concept of health as a "state of complete physical, mental and social well-being"[1] coincides in every respect with the personnel worker's concern for the whole student. In harmony with the accepted aim of personnel work as striving "to help every student through his own efforts, to discover and develop his potentialities,"[2] the health worker seeks to help the student recognize his own health problems and to continue the process begun in early childhood of gradually assuming more and more responsibility for his own health practices.

Actually, the college is concerned with the total health of the total student in the total situation. Total health of the student implies physical, mental, emotional, and social phases inextricably intermeshed. The "total situation" encompasses many ramifications which may involve the home and various off-campus circumstances as well as the college. Obviously, ways and means of helping students solve their complex health problems will be as varied as the range of problems. Attempts at solution need to be the joint responsibility of the student himself, his family, and the entire college community. Often the best approach to solution calls for a coordinated plan which involves all of these forces combined.

The Freshman Arrives at College

From the health point of view, we see the newly arrived freshman as a unique individual who possesses a certain fund of information and understanding concerning health, and indulges habitually in

[1] *Handbook of the United Nations and the Specialized Agencies*, p. 162.
[2] Ruth Strang: "Student Personnel Services for Graduate Students in Education," p. 89.

151

specific health practices some of which may be peculiar to himself, his family, and his community. Most important of all, he brings with him a sizeable store of attitudes toward health and health matters. Thus, he is the sum total of his past experiences as they involved his home, his friends, his school life, and the cultural patterns and value systems of his neighborhood and community. These practices and attitudes, it must be remembered, include not only positive but negative ones such as fears, prejudices, and resistances to certain health ways and teachings.

Many of the immediate problem situations that confront the freshman have to do with health. First, the student is faced with the need to plan his entire day. An uncharted block of time contrasts strangely with the completely rostered day of the modern high school. He remembers vividly that in high school or prep school life flowed along serenely just as long as one stayed within the prescribed schedule. Within this new, uncharted block of time it is necessary to secure a reasonable amount of sleep and rest. But perhaps the presence of a roommate with totally different habit patterns may present complications. Or perhaps commuting time gnaws disastrously into the evening study hours, so that sleep must be woefully curtailed.

The campus cafeteria and snack bars involve budgetary problems as well as the wise selection of energy-building meals. Even cleanliness and good grooming can present new problems, for accepted campus standards may be strangely at variance with home customs. An inviting sports program calls for choices commensurate with the student's physical abilities and his total work load. Often the freshman has not the slightest idea as to how great a load he can handle competently. Even the class assignments sound different. The college faculty appears to expect capabilities for self-help which the student may or may not have acquired at the lower level. The lack of sound study habits may start the freshman immediately on the road to academic failure.

A cold in the head, constipation, or other slight symptoms which heretofore have been handled in competent fashion by a watchful mother, are now overlooked as too unimportant to be worth a trip to the health service office. Besides, an imminent test might be jeopardized if he were detained in the infirmary and he does not wish to risk his grade. Thus, a simple cold may lead to a more serious respiratory involvement, or mild constipation to the laxative habit.

These are but a sampling of common problems as reported by residence hall and health service staff. Obviously, none of these problems is simple in structure. Most of them are interrelated with the deeper problems of adjustment to college.

Adjustment to college involves problems of mental and emotional health. The impact of a completely new environment calls for tremendous adaptability. The student's immediate need for status may be so urgent as to lead to the temporary abandonment of nearly all the rules of healthful living. For the time being, to be one of the crowd is all that matters.

Dormitory or fraternity life may prove overstimulating to the student accustomed to a quiet home life. Emotional stability is needed to cope effectively with loneliness and homesickness. Frequent tests of one's values may prove unsettling especially if some values are none too firmly established.

Financial insecurity or inability to manage finances sometimes results in serious undermining of health through insufficient food or the wrong choice of food. On the other hand, the extreme urge for status may lead to extravagant expenditures which make devastating inroads into the total budget. Actually, preoccupation with any one or any combination of these problems may lead to serious inroads on physical health.

Closely integrated with the situations just mentioned are problems of social health. The college campus offers situational tests of the ability to get along harmoniously with all kinds of people regardless of nationality, race, creed, religion, or beliefs. The student may need help in dealing with feelings and prejudices of which he has never before been conscious. He may need help in finding a congenial social group, choosing new intimate friends, in being accepted, and in learning how to participate with satisfaction and success as a member of the group. The maintenance of happy relationships with faculty and fellow students may call for special skills which he has never developed. Certainly the student needs to know as quickly as possible what helpful resources exist in the college and in the community and to learn to make the best use of such resources.

It is important, too, from the health point of view, that the student during his years in college maintain understanding relations with his family and does not grow too far away from them. He needs to adjust to the changed relations which physical absence from home entails, but he may need to learn to re-evaluate the worth of the permanent family ties and plan not to lose contact under the stress and stimulation of campus life.

Finally, he may need help in the development of a feeling of social responsibility for the total health of his fellow students and others with whom he comes in contact. He needs to become aware of the implications of his physical health habits and the need to live so that his practices will help positively toward the maintenance of safety and health on the campus and in the community. He must realize, too, that it is a sign of maturity to make consistent and continuous efforts in this direction.

What the College Can Do

As a first step in a positive program, the college needs to foster on the part of faculty and staff, as basic to the philosophy of the institution, the encouragement of each student to attain and to maintain an optimal degree of health as being fundamental to the accomplishment and attainment of life goals. The crux of the problem in health education is to influence what the student *does*, not merely what he *knows*. Motivation in health education has long been the subject of research. Recent efforts point out clearly that if undesirable health habits are to be changed or new ones initiated, the motivation needs to be tied up with life goals. These goals, in other words, must be of sufficient critical importance to the person concerned in order to influence him to make the required changes. It is the task of the personnel worker, the faculty adviser, the health education teacher, the health service staff members, and others closely associated with the individual student to help him clarify his goals for himself. He needs to see his own health in relation to the attainment of the larger goal of success in college: friends, sports, academic achievement, and the greatest degree of self-development of which he is capable. He needs to see health as the means to an enjoyment of a rich and full life, as the way to the greatest degree of self-realization as a person, as a responsible citizen carrying out his obligations to the community, and as a future homemaker and parent. This philosophy needs to so permeate the entire faculty and administrative staff as to ensure its impact on the student in learning and teaching situations.

The college needs to make the most of the situations offered by the two constants in the freshman health or hygiene course.

THE HEALTH EXAMINATION

Most colleges offer a health examination to every freshman at the beginning of the first semester. Since this is his first contact with the college health service, his experiences usually color his future attitude toward the department and even toward health matters. Hence, it is most important that this first contact be a satisfying and meaningful experience.

There is need to create a wholesome attitude toward the medical examination, not only among the students but among faculty members as well. Because of his past experiences with health examinations at school or with physicians in general, the student may have a completely negative attitude. There may be deep-seated fears and resistances to overcome.

It is important that the student receive careful preparation for the health examination. The responsibility for this preparation might well be shared by the health education teacher, the personnel staff, including the residence counselor and faculty adviser as well as the members of the health service staff. The student needs to be made aware of the significance of the health examination in relation to his immediate and long-range life goals. He should understand the procedures to be used and the reasons underlying the use of these procedures. He should be made aware of the advantages of willing and intelligent cooperation on his part during the examination and in any follow-up measures that might be recommended. Any long-term program of correction begun in previous years and which needs to be continued through college should be given careful attention and cooperation by the college personnel concerned.

Each contact with the health service department should be an educative experience for the student. The center itself should be a cheerful, attractive place. There should be up-to-date educational material in the waiting room and on the bulletin board. The infirmary section too should be as attractive as possible. A calm, unhurried atmosphere should pervade.

Punctuality on the part of the staff members will do much to encourage it on the part of students. Office hours should be arranged so that it will not be too difficult for the majority of students to secure appointments at convenient times. Well-trained personnel with the student point of view in mind should hold regular appointments as members of the college staff.

In the eyes of the student, the importance of the examination is greatly enhanced by the dignity of a personal appointment. He may need to be impressed with the obligation implied by a personal appointment and the necessity of keeping it faithfully.

The examination should be as complete and thorough as possible.

It should embody the best accepted standards and practices.[3] At the close of the examination, there should be an unhurried review of the findings by the physician for the student.

Provision should be made for immediate follow-up by means of collaboration with the student's family and with the family physician, if possible. Available referral services on the campus and in the community should be utilized to the fullest extent.

Accepted standards include recheck examinations for the following:

1. Students readmitted to college after temporary withdrawal for reasons concerning either scholarship or illness.

2. Students who plan to undertake intensive study schedules, activity programs, or jobs requiring undue time, in addition to their studies.

3. Students who request examinations.

4. Students who are engaged in organized and competitive sports. The health service should have the authority to determine the physical qualifications of any candidate for organized team sports.[4]

Provision should be made for subsequent opportunities for health counseling in privacy. Students will need to be informed as to the proper procedures for arranging for such counseling.

The members of the health service staff should cooperate with the college administrators and the personnel staff in pointing out to students, particularly to the freshmen, the importance of giving consideration to any protective group insurance plans made available to them by the college or university. Complete details of such plans should be presented to students and parents at the time of admission so that they will have time to acquaint themselves fully with the merits of the respective plans before college opens. It is possible to budget in advance with a reasonable degree of accuracy for the usual college expenses such as tuition, board, room, etc. However, if the student or parent is not prepared for unexpected expenses due to illness or accident, the effect of such an occurrence might be so devastating financially as to necessitate complete changes in the individual's educational plans. The peace of mind to be gained through insurance coverage is well worth the relatively small additional expenditure.

The most satisfactory college insurance policy appears to result from an on-the-spot study of the institution's individual situation and needs. Such a study should be made by a competent insurance broker

[3] *A Health Program for Colleges*, pp. 29-31.
[4] *Ibid.*, p. 31.

with the cooperation of the administrative staff. The two types of students' medical reimbursement insurance plans in widest use at present are (1) accident reimbursement and (2) accident and sickness reimbursement. The annual cost to the student or parent is nominal, ranging from approximately $5.00 for accident reimbursement for women to approximately $20 for accident and sickness reimbursement. In most plans there is a stipulated maximum for accident reimbursements. In sickness benefits, the "allocated" plan of coverage appears to be more practical, with definite amounts listed for each type of service required. Coverage should be arranged to include participation in all forms of college activities including those held prior to the beginning of classes, such as freshman orientation. It should be clearly understood by staff, students, and parents that any insurance plan made available by the college operates entirely outside the usual services offered by the health service department.

Members of the health service staff, the personnel staff, residence hall counselors, and the health education teachers should be well informed as to the details of the institution's student insurance plans, so that they may be able to interpret them correctly to the students and to assist them in following proper procedures in filing claims.

Certainly it is essential that at all times the relationships of the health service personnel with students should be such as will tend to keep the channel open for future visits to the center.

THE FRESHMAN HEALTH EDUCATION COURSE

In most colleges it has been the custom to assign all freshmen to a required health education course known traditionally as "freshman hygiene." To offset the rather negative student attitude which has come to be associated with this course, a number of colleges and universities during recent years have revamped the content in terms of current problems of students and changed the title accordingly to *Personal and Community Health, Modern Living, Effective Living, Contemporary Health Problems, Social Living,* etc. The implication is a trend toward a broader and more functional type of course in line with the current concept of health as a way of living. Since all college students are usually enrolled in this course and since it is the last formal health instruction many of them will receive, certainly it is important that this course should be a truly significant experience for all. Courses can be made more functional and meaningful through such means as the following:

1. Cooperative planning by teacher and students;

2. Building the course content and experiences around the needs and interests of the students;

3. Relating the health instruction to the individual and group health needs as shown by the medical examination, the observation of the health practices of the students, the current problems of campus life, etc.;

4. Helping the student to gain an acceptable concept of self, to set up his own individual health goals, and, through counseling, to devise practical plans and initiate steps for approaching these goals, thus solving his own health problems;

5. Including opportunities for group experience in solving problems of healthful living as they may arise (a) in the residence hall, fraternity or sorority house, or dormitory, (b) in the cafeteria, dining hall, or snack bars, (c) in the locker room, gymnasium, playfield, or swimming pool, (d) in varsity or intramural sports situations, (e) in commuting, (f) in relations with compeers, (g) in connection with participation in extracurricular activity, (h) within the family situation, (i) in social situations, (j) in the community, and (k) in connection with the armed services;

6. Including units on education for family living and health problems of adults;

7. Helping the student to face objectively controversial issues pertaining to health matters, such as drinking, smoking, etc., and in the light of scientific knowledge and a sound value system, to make his own decisions concerning them;

8. Fortifying the student with correct information so that he may properly evaluate for himself the forceful health appeals which constantly confront him by way of the various mass media;

9. Offering frequent opportunities for self-evaluations and evaluations of course experiences; and

10. Striving to relate health instruction with (a) the health units or implications contained in other courses, and (b) with health activities on the campus and in the community, and on state, national, and international levels.

HEALTH PROBLEMS IN HOUSING

Whether the student chooses to live in a college residence hall, a fraternity or sorority house, or in an off-campus room with a private family, the housing of students is a serious matter which involves health problems for which the college or university must assume the major responsibility.

The daily routine of the residence hall should be based upon a careful consideration of the safest ways of meeting problems incidental to group living. Full cooperation should be given to local and state health authorities in all matters affecting environmental sanitation, and at all times the best standards for health and safety must be upheld. Close liaison with the student deans and the health service department must be maintained. The residence hall counselors should strive to secure the students' willing cooperation based upon their appreciation and understanding of the conditions and hazards involved. Whenever possible, the students themselves should be given the opportunity to participate in the solution of the problems of living healthfully. Many problems of group living can be handled adequately through group counseling. An alert residence hall counselor will be constantly on the watch for opportunities for tactful individual counseling about personal habits or practices which are not in accord with accepted standards or which imperil the health or safety of others.

Supervision should be extended to the students living in fraternity and sorority houses or under other cooperative plans. Certainly no student should occupy an off-campus room unless conditions have been thoroughly investigated by a university housing director and found to meet the university standards in every respect.

The matter of proper lighting merits special attention because its importance is so often overlooked. Needless to say, adequate lighting for study should be provided in student rooms, classrooms, study halls, and libraries and it should be checked periodically by a member of the health or maintenance staff.

College administrators and local health authorities need to work together in the maintenance of safe and sanitary college dining halls, but they need to be concerned, also, about all restaurants and eating places frequented by students. In the case of the student in the off-campus rooming house, perhaps the student's counselor is the most logical person to take the responsibility for encouraging him to maintain desirable food habits and helping him cope with the problem of finding safe and sanitary places in which to eat.

The physical education and athletic program should be carefully scrutinized to determine whether there is full utilization of the many opportunities for emphasis upon healthful living. If the student's counselor is familiar with the program and organization of this department, he may assist the student in the selection of elective activities commensurate with his capabilities and in the light of his total load. Poor reactions or unhealthful effects upon the student may be noted by the counselor. This information should be passed on to the physical education department or to the health service department. On the other hand, through the cooperation of the counselor and the physical education teacher, there can be more effective utilization of the many natural opportunities offered by the activity program for speeding the process of adjustment to college by helping the student find status in a group situation, form congenial friendships, and find satisfying fun and recreation.

It is important, too, that the same high standards of healthful living be maintained in connection with the use of facilities such as showers, locker rooms, swimming pool, etc. Here, too, there needs to be full and complete cooperation among college administrators and the local and state health authorities.

SERVICES FOR UPPER CLASSMEN

Upper classmen have health problems, too! Throughout the student's entire college career there is need for health appraisal and health counseling. Problems remaining unsolved at the end of the freshman year usually snowball into larger ones. Cumulative health records must be kept up to date and the student needs to be encouraged to note objectively his own progress in the correction of remediable defects. From time to time he needs to examine his own personal health goals and accomplishments and, if need be, helped to set up new goals and to redirect his efforts in the light of his changing life goals apace with his own maturation. The student with a special handicap may need help in adjusting to varying conditions each semester. Frequently the upper classman needs assistance in the interpretation of health emphases which appear to be at variance with his past experiences. Where and how to live present perennial problems to some students. The graduating senior may need help in solving placement problems which bear upon his individual health assets. Channels must be provided whereby all students may be constantly reminded as to the current resources for health service and health information on the campus and in the community. Obviously, the college should strive to utilize every possible means to meet the health needs common to most students throughout their four years at college.

Over-all Planning for Healthful Living

Since problems involving health concern all students and permeate every phase of college life, efforts toward helping students live more healthfully must stem from every part of the institution and at every level. In order to be truly effective, these efforts must be integrated wisely. Ways of accomplishing desirable and necessary cooperation will vary according to the basic plan or organization within the institution.

The following suggestions are possible plans which might be tailored to fit the needs of almost any individual college or university situation:

1. Establishment of an all-college or all-university health council: This council would include in its membership representatives from all segments of the institution and serve as a clearing house for health matters, study ways to improve existing health efforts, initiate new ones, and seek to work out the most effective means for the coordination of health efforts within the institution and the community;

2. For functional purposes, the organization of various subcommittees within the health council, each to focus upon a particular phase of health or a health problem: Membership of each subcommittee would consist of faculty and students and cut across all departments and divisions varying in representation according to the scope and responsibilities of the subcommittee. Subcommittees on safety, nutrition, and family life education would be particularly valuable because of the extent of the problems included;

3. Involvement of student groups and organizations in the solution of special health problems which concern campus living, such as the student government association, student senate, women's athletic association, science club, etc.;

4. Furtherance of a desirable emotional climate throughout the entire college by the encouragement of democratic administrator-teacher-student relations;

5. Interdepartmental planning of health and related courses through faculty-student committees, thus making the courses more functional;

6. Closer relationships of college health activities with community health affairs, thus extending to students opportunities for wider experiences;

7. Selection of emotionally stable faculty and staff personnel (par-

ticularly those in close contact with student activities and in key positions for leadership and counseling);

8. Wise use of student records, including health records;

9. Effective use of mass media on campus as applied to health matters and health activities;

10. Meeting of specific needs of students through the formation of interest groups, such as married students' forums, radio groups, film forum, etc.;

11. Constant emphasis upon opportunities for co-recreational activities in wholesome, satisfying situations which foster good heterosexual relationships, such as co-recreational sports, dramatics, outing clubs, etc.;

12. Maintenance of close and understanding relationships among personnel workers, health service staff, physical education staff, faculty advisers, etc., in order to provide students with more effective help in solving their problems;

13. Provision for in-service opportunities for faculty refreshers on various phases of health education, such as problems of adult life, recent advances in science and medicine, etc.;

14. Attempts to meet the health education needs of alumni by means of refresher courses and workshops on such topics as may be selected by the participants themselves through pre-workshop involvement;

15. Sponsorship of timely health exhibits, forums, film forums, etc.;

16. Maintenance of adequate up-to-date library resources in health literature, audio-visual aids, and materials;

17. Participation by the university in research projects in health education when possible or feasible;

18. Participation by the college or university in worthy community health projects and activities;

19. Provision for an adequate health budget, which will permit the maintenance of the best standards of health service, healthful living, protective measures, and instructional materials in health education;

20. Pooling of resources in the way of supplementary health materials located in the various departments and community agencies and making them available for the enrichment of teaching and service;

21. Occasional interdepartmental sharing of staff members who possess special knowledge and skills in the area of health education;

22. Establishment of an adequate emergency fund for assisting the needy student for whom prescribed, immediate, remedial health measures may be vital to the solution of some deep personal adjustment problem or preprofessional problem;

23. Inclusion of adequate plans for group insurance for students, with a policy arranged to fit the needs of the individual college or institution, and the cooperation of informed personnel in the uniform interpretation of such plans to students;

24. Provision for the education of parents of college students through exhibits, conferences, films, etc., in order to secure more intelligent cooperation and to increase their appreciation of the health program;

25. Provision for the effective articulation of health service and health teaching with the physical education department so that the student may become increasingly aware of this integration through his practical experiences;

26. Provision for the continuous evaluation of the health program and its effectiveness, including health service, healthful environment, safety, health teaching, physical education, and recreation; and

27. Appointment of a health coordinator whose task would be the coordination of the various aspects of health as set forth in the above suggestions (the health coordinator would be a person who has a background in education and in health education).

The best interests of the college student are most effectively served through the deeper integration of the efforts of health and personnel workers. Many of the suggestions offered here are not new. But how many of them have been given a fair trial on a college or university campus? The full import and the optimal possibilities for accomplishment through cooperative endeavor have neither been realized nor even imagined. Tradition has made it difficult to hurdle the rigid invisible departmental and divisional lines which exist in many colleges and universities. To storm these lines in dramatic fashion is neither wise nor feasible if lasting results are to be attained. Beginnings are slow and inconspicuous but there are countless opportunities for them.

Perhaps the most vital immediate need on the part of the college personnel is a greater sensitivity to these opportunities when they do arise. This means the earlier identification of health problems which may be intertwined with behavior patterns of the individual and of the group.

Along with this increased awareness on the part of college personnel, there must be nurtured an ever-deepening faith in the value and power of a cooperative approach toward problem-solving, and the patience and determination to follow through. With a sufficient understanding of the potentialities of continuing group planning and group thinking, a satisfactory degree of success is virtually assured. Obviously, cooperative effort on the part of all concerned is necessary if maximum results are to ensue.

BIBLIOGRAPHY

American Association for Health, Physical Education and Recreation: Yearbook, 1951: *Developing Democratic Human Relations Through Health, Physical Education and Recreation.* Washington, D. C., National Education Association, 1951.

Boynton, Ruth: "Student Personnel Work, XI. Student Health Services." In Walter S. Monroe (ed.): *Encyclopedia of Educational Research* (rev. ed.). New York, The Macmillan Company, 1950, pp. 1335-39.

Diehl, Harold S., and Shepherd, C. E.: *The Health of College Students,* a report to the Youth Commission. Washington, D. C., American Council on Education, 1939.

Handbook of the United Nations and the Specialized Agencies. New York, Department of Public Information, United Nations, May, 1946.

Strang, Ruth: "Personnel Services for Graduate Students in Education." National Society for the Study of Education, *Graduate Study in Education,* the Fiftieth Yearbook, Part I. Chicago, Illinois, University of Chicago Press, 1951.

Third National Conference on Health in Colleges: *A Health Program for Colleges.* Report, National Tuberculosis Association, New York, 1948.

10. The Physical Education Program

WILLIAM L. HUGHES

IN FORMER days when education was viewed as a "discipline," learning through participation in physical activities was given little or no consideration. Education consisted of book learning, and brain and brawn were thought to exist in inverse ratio. The placing of philosophy on a high level and skills on a low one was a fourteenth-century concept. Little did people realize at that time that doing is followed by considerable knowing. Skill and body were associated. The latter had appetites; it was subject to disease. The academic mind looked down its nose at muscle even though muscle was required in the looking.

Today science has rejected the dichotomy of mind and body. Biology, physiology, psychology, sociology and philosophy recognize the fact of organismic unity. Not only is the individual a whole but he is a part of his environment with which he reacts and interacts in a total situation. This concept of the education of the whole person necessarily includes physical education and is the heart of the personnel point of view.

In their desire to be intellectual, educators may forget that man is an organism; a feeling, behaving, playing person as well as a reading, writing, and reciting individual. Physical education dates back to the primitive man who first taught the young to jump, climb, and throw. Even though the need to throw spears and climb trees has passed, the biological patterns of the organism remain with the same basic demands. The concept of the dual aspect of mind and body resulted, to be sure, both in a training of the mind and a training of the body. As a part of the concept of the wholeness of the organisms, however, physical education becomes education *through* the physical. This means that physical education, like all education, is concerned with social, emotional, ethical, and intellectual as well as with physical outcomes. Education through the physical seeks the associated and concomitant as well as the technical learnings of a physical experience.

Even though the education of the whole person is professed in theory there is the ever-present danger, in a modern industrialized society filled with labor-saving devices, that the physical will be neglected. Recognition of the wholeness of man should not relegate the physical to a minor role, neither should it be stressed unduly. The book worm and the "dumb" athlete are both social monstrosities.

Physical educators, therefore, share with all other educators a common concern for the developing person in all of his aspects. They share the same goals although they use different materials and methods and a wide variety of experiences to attain them. Thus, they have allied themselves strongly with all workers in the educational scene, and especially with counseling and guidance personnel.

The Student Looks at Physical Education

Each student in a college or university is a unique individual possessing certain interests, attitudes, skills, and understandings with respect to physical education. Interest may be centered only in basketball or dance or it may be lacking altogether. Attitudes may have been colored by success or failure as an athlete, by the type of program, by the inconvenience of dressing, or by many other factors. An entering freshman may have been the best boy or girl athlete in the high school with rather distorted values regarding education. If these same individuals are relatively unknown in college the effect on egos may be devastating. On the other hand, the entering freshman may have been nonathletic with a feeling of inferiority on that account and a cynical attitude toward physical education and athletics.

Even though many schools and colleges have reorganized their programs to meet the needs and interests of young people, there remain a number of factors which may cause a distaste for physical education. The girl, for example, may believe that participation in physical activities will develop her into a mannish, muscular type. Insufficient time for dressing or the inconvenience of it may have left her with a feeling of untidiness. The boy's experience with physical education may have been largely a deadening routine of calisthenics, which he learned to detest, or he may view it as a program of highly competitive athletics which he considers beyond his attainment. The secondary school program may have failed to develop beyond the novice stage the physical skills of the boys and girls. Students may have a feeling of antagonism against a requirement, or a particular type of program, or large classes. In spite of the time devoted to physical education in high schools and colleges many students are still graduating from the latter ignorant of the means of health maintenance, physically inadequate for modern high-pressure living, seriously lacking in recreational skills, and unable to make friends easily or to feel at ease in a group. Whatever their physical education interests and attitudes, they are the sum total of their past experiences with sports and dance activities as they involved their home, their school, and their community.

College men and women are confronted with many problems. Some of them are concerned with physical education. Is there a requirement? What is its nature? Is there opportunity for choice of activities? Shall he or she participate in intramural sports and/or intercollegiate athletics? What opportunities are there for co-recreation? In view of the large blocks of available time in college, as contrasted with the completely rostered day of the secondary school, how much of each day or week may justifiably be spent in physical recreation? These and many similar questions need to be given careful consideration. Obviously, they should be answered by the student in the light of his academic load, his social and other extracurricular activities, his travel or commuting requirements, his work schedule, and the habits of his roommate and other associates.

Why Physical Education

Regardless of his likes and dislikes, his interests and skills, his academic load and extracurricular activities, the college student wants to know why he should participate in organized sports and dance activities and what he may expect to get out of them.

Physical education can make a number of contributions to the complete development and education of college students.

1. The unique, although by no means the only, contribution which physical education can make to college students is to their organic development. This remains one of the basic needs of man. In spite of profound changes in his environment, man's biological organism down through the years has remained essentially the same. College students today have the same kind of vital organs and the same

arrangement of vital systems that have existed in man over the centuries. It is a fact of real significance that a rapidly changing society has no counterpart in the biological mechanism. The tempo of life has stepped up tremendously in the last decade so that man's organism has been catapulted ahead thousands of years overnight. It is a sedentary world in which college students are now living. They are surrounded by labor-saving gadgets. Machines have largely eliminated all heavy hand work and hard physical labor so that such experience is almost unknown to modern youth. The automobile and other forms of transportation have seriously reduced walking and running. No one wishes to revert to the physical labor of primitive man, but as civilization gradually removes the necessity of physical work the total result of sedentary living may, and often does, have a deteriorating effect on organic development and indirectly on healthful, happy, and effective living.

There is no way for the youth of today to avoid the demands for big-muscle activity, since muscles are as much a source of man's vitality in a machine world as they were in the days of the cave man. Biology teaches us the importance of *large* muscles, meaning those of the trunk, hips, legs, shoulder-girdle and arms. Because of the way the vital organs of the body arose and developed, man is able most effectively to influence the processes of these organs through the action of the skeletal muscles. The sound development of the circulatory, nervous, and other systems must come about indirectly through large-muscle activities. The college student who has not learned this basic fact is missing an important part of his education. Modern distractions and stimulating influences, together with sedentary living and the reduction in time devoted to physical activities, cause some scientists to wonder whether man can survive the civilization he has built.

These facts will give a clue to the college student as to the importance of organic development by means of participation in physical education activities. There is no alternate route or short cut and there should be no delay. The strategic time is during childhood and youth. Granting the importance of the objective of organic development young people should remember, however, that there is no virtue, per se, in bulging biceps and that strength and endurance are valuable only when there is a cause to serve.

2. Physical education also can contribute to the education of college young people by providing opportunities for all to acquire

recreational skills, and to experience the satisfaction of performing efficiently in the racially old natural activities of running, jumping, throwing, climbing, and striking. There is ample evidence of the high correlation between skill in an activity and participation in it. People do things they enjoy and they enjoy the things they do well.

Satisfaction in skillful performance is valuable mental hygiene and contributes much to the development of the personality. The obligation of education to develop play skills also is clear, since youth are likely to use these skills rather than undesirable types of amusements in their leisure time. While many skills involving coordination are possible, they contribute little or nothing to the education or development of young men and women unless they can be used vocationally or avocationally.

Educators, and particularly physical educators and coaches, need to understand that motor skills are highly specific, and the college athlete who learns only the skills of the so-called major sports has only a partial physical education. In fact, it is quite possible for an All-American football player, or other sport star, to be a "physical illiterate" if he has developed skills in only one position in only one sport. Colleges that permit this are doing an injustice to the athlete. A broad program of required activities, intramural sports, intercollegiate athletics, and co-recreation will provide opportunities for all students to acquire a variety of recreational skills. Such a program is the best guarantee that the athlete, as well as those less talented, will be better prepared for a wholesome and happy use of leisure time. Individuals possessing varied recreational skills will be more self-sufficient and less dependent upon other persons or on commercial amusements for entertainment. A college graduate thus equipped also is more likely to return to his home community determined to improve the recreational opportunities there.

3. Closely related to the acquisition of recreational skills is the development, through participation in sports and rhythmic activities, of a play attitude and an abiding interest in recreation that will function in leisure time throughout life. Too many college students, who merely are exposed to the program of physical education, backslide after graduation and fail to continue to participate. The play spirit, the urge to continue to play, may not be strong enough to keep the graduate active when the compulsion of a requirement and the convenience of play and dressing facilities are removed. But as was pointed out above, proficiency and participation are highly cor-

related. It is important, therefore, if they are to benefit most through participation in physical activities, for students to get out of the dub class in some activities and into the enjoyment and satisfaction level of proficiency while they are in college.

Unlike health, recreation is an end unto itself. It is really an attitude, a psychological reaction, a way of life. In this sense there is no such thing as a recreation activity. Any activity becomes recreational if the student chooses to do it voluntarily, on his own time, in his own way, and for his own satisfaction. For all-around development this recreation should not be all physical, or all mental, or all social. The institution should provide many forms of wholesome recreation.

Institutions of higher learning can do much to promote recreation by: (a) developing wholesome recreational interests, attitudes, and skills, (b) providing a variety of recreational opportunities for students, (c) serving the community by means of leadership and facilities, and (d) carrying on research in recreation.

4. Physical education can contribute to the relief of emotional strains and tensions. Overcrowded cities with the resulting noise and confusion; the tempo of college life with the pressure of studies, social affairs, extracurricular activities, work, rapid eating, and inadequate lighting; radio, motion pictures, and television—these and hundreds of other distractions and stimulating influences with the resulting reduction in time for active recreation cause strains and tensions. Participation in sports and dance can do much to relieve them, or, if these activities are overemphasized, to increase them. Moreover, under the stress of competition the participant may be tempted to antisocial behavior. In an atmosphere charged with emotion basic desires are present and there is an interplay and possibly a clash of personalities. In such a situation the whole organism is involved; but under proper leadership the participant learns the wholesome and accepted behavior.

5. Physical education can help college students develop their social relationships by offering many opportunities to practice desirable citizenship traits through participating harmoniously and cooperatively in group activities. Probably no other area of education provides such varied opportunities to practice cooperation, loyalty, tolerance, understanding, and respect for personality. The informality and gaiety of the physical education situations in sports and dance, the pressure to win, the anger and frustration when one strikes out or is tackled behind the line of scrimmage, the temptation to retaliate

against an unsportsmanlike adversary—out of these situations, under proper leadership, may come such learnings as honesty, friendliness, generosity, and tolerance. When the crisis comes in sports, as in battle, participants are not concerned with such artificial matters as racial and national origin or religious belief. They function as a team fighting for a common cause.

Physical education is the great common denominator which is needed alike by white and colored, rich and poor, high and low I.Q., Yankee and Southerner, American and Russian. The standards, ideas, and ideals learned through participation in physical education activities may be just as influential in character formation as the sum total of the classroom lectures.

6. Finally, physical education provides opportunities for creative self-expression. The concept of physical education as an art form is being emphasized increasingly. Of all the many activities in the program, dance movement in all its forms offers the widest opportunity for creativeness. Here, much as in painting and sculpturing, man may reflect his thoughts and feelings through movement. The dancer may express himself in response to mood or music or convey his ideas in rhythm or in some other motor pattern. Sports, too, may be viewed as art forms for in these activities one may find the setting for the creation of mood or figure.

Why, then, should the college student take physical education? What learnings are possible through participation in physical activities? Outcomes from participation should include organic development, wholesome recreational interests and skills, relief from emotional strains and tensions, growth in social relationships, and creative self-expression.

The college graduate who backslides on his participation and allows himself to deteriorate physically and who fails to carry-over into his home and business or professional life the principles of sportsmanship and fair play has tragically missed the important lessons which he should have learned through participation in sports and dance.

What the College Can Provide

The students enrolled in most institutions of higher learning today represent a normal cross section of a complex democratic society. In admitting students with such diverse backgrounds each institution assumes the responsibility to provide the various services necessary for their welfare and education. Many of these services and problems are related to the health and physical education of the students.

College physical education consists of four main phases: required classes, co-recreational activities, intramural sports, and intercollegiate athletics. An acceptable program includes a wide variety of activities and experiences that are adapted to individual capacities, interests, and needs. These include athletics, aquatics, camping and outing, corrective exercises, gymnastics, stunts and tumbling, recreational activities, rhythmics, including folk, square, social and modern dance, and sports of an individual and dual type.

THE REQUIRED PROGRAM

Before the last war some college educators questioned the desirability or justification of any requirement in health and physical education. But the fact that nine million young men were rejected for health reasons as physically unfit for any form of military service is a powerful argument in favor of adequate health services and health education. The further fact that countless thousands of young men who were accepted for military service were so underdeveloped physically that they could not swim, climb a rope, leap out of a trench chest deep, or jump across a four-foot ditch caused many educators to change their views regarding a requirement. It became clear that this phase of the complete education of a college student could not be left to chance.

The time allotted to physical education in colleges is of real importance if the objectives are to be attained. Organic development, recreational skills, and adequate growth in social relationships and emotional adjustment cannot be realized overnight. The physical education class period, after allowance for showering and dressing, leaves only approximately thirty minutes for instruction and activity. A requirement of two periods totals only one hour per week. Assuming a student sleeps 8 hours per night or 56 hours per week in a 168-hour week, he has 112 waking hours remaining for work and play. It is obvious that only one hour devoted to physical education out of a 112-hour work-play week is insufficient to attain the objectives sought unless, in this brief time for instruction, motivation, activity, and guidance, the desire to participate is firmly established. It becomes imperative for the physical education teacher to develop within the student a play attitude which will cause him voluntarily to choose activities on his own time, in his own way, and for his own satisfaction.

CO-RECREATION ACTIVITIES

The trend toward education for leisure brings with it an emphasis on co-recreation. This serves as an excellent laboratory to supplement the readings, classroom discussions, social events, and other forms of coeducation. Young men and women need to learn to play together so they may better work and live together.

Traditionally, physical education for boys and girls has been conducted separately. This has carried over into college. As a rule, college men prefer activities involving a high degree of strength, endurance, and skill. Women, on the other hand, are more interested in grace and rhythm of movement. Basically, however, the differences between the sexes in biological drives and urges are more in degree than in kind and while the programs for men and women should not be identical, neither should they be entirely separated. Studies show that a majority of college students favor co-recreation. Suitable activities are archery, badminton, boating, camping, dancing, fishing, golf, riding, shuffleboard, skating, skiing, swimming, and tennis.

There is some indication of a trend to provide a man and a woman as co-supervisors of recreation for college students. This is commendable and should be encouraged.

ATHLETICS

Competitive athletics occupy a prominent place in college physical education. Objectives and outcomes for this specialized phase of the program are the same as for all physical education. Some critics are opposed to athletic competition but the evils associated with athletics lie not so much in the competition itself as in the extreme emphasis placed on winning. Games and sports could not exist without competition since it is their very essence. In spite of the dangers of overemphasis, competition is desirable in the development of the personality. Every normal person, at various stages of his development, wishes to test himself against a standard and in relation to his contemporaries. This struggle to attain one's best adds fiber to one's being and makes life more interesting and worthwhile.

Both competition and cooperation are behavior traits that can be learned. They are not necessarily opposites but may supplement each other. It would be difficult if not impossible to eliminate them without destroying individuality. Where more than one person is involved, cooperation is usually essential for successful competition. Moreover, such behavior patterns reflect the ideas and customs of the society of which they are a part. The problem in athletics is to control rather than eliminate competition. Whether practices of the jungle or a sound educational program eventually will prevail will depend, in large measure, upon a leadership which is more interested in the education of young men and women than in the mere winning of games.

INTRAMURAL SPORTS

The intramural sports phase of physical education has developed and expanded to such an extent that no college program is considered complete without a wide variety of such voluntary recreational activities for both men and women.

The common practice is to provide a man supervisor for the men's program and a woman supervisor for the women's program although a recent trend is to name a man and a woman as co-supervisors of recreation. The organization usually provides an intramural council for men, made up of representatives of the competing units, which serves as the policy- and rule-making body. The Women's Recreation Association Board has about the same purpose and functions. Activities connected with officiating, managing, playing, and serving as policy-maker provide many opportunities for student participation. Intramural programs can be and usually are among the most democratically operated activities on the campus.

INTERCOLLEGIATE ATHLETICS

Many educators today still believe that students may derive important benefits through properly conducted intercollegiate athletics. The outcomes to be realized through participation in this specialized phase of the program are the same as those claimed for physical education as a whole, that is, organic development, recreational skills, and growth in social relationships and emotional adjustment. This is particularly true in the colleges where no effort is made to recruit and subsidize athletes. On the other hand, in institutions which promote high-pressure athletics the program is likely to be conducted as a business rather than as an educational enterprise. In such cases it is to be expected, if deplored, that business principles and policies will guide since "big-time" athletics are an aspect of our culture which reflects the social scene in a system of free enterprise. So long as inter-collegiate athletics are financially dependent on gate receipts and until society generally acquires a different ethical point of view, just so long are they likely to be conducted as business rather than as educational enterprises.

This is not to imply that intercollegiate athletics cannot be and are not conducted in a sound and acceptable manner. Many institutions conduct a program with legitimate students who normally enroll without special recruiting or subsidizing.

Participation in intercollegiate athletics has some distinct advantages since it requires a high degree of competence in several important aspects. In the first place, the quality of competition on the varsity level calls for a high degree of fitness which represents the best in individual perfection. Intramural participants seldom, if ever, attain this perfection and usually they are unwilling to make the necessary sacrifices. Varsity training tends to develop an attitude favoring fine living and a self-discipline for athletic purposes. These are valuable substitutes for other and less worthy interests even if the student fails to extend or transfer them into other aspects of living. Young people who spend their time in wholesome sports are not using that time loafing in pool rooms and taverns. It should be pointed out, however, that for athletics to be more than a substitute measure, positive attitudes must be built toward leisure time, and toward the part which motor skills play in the personal and social development of women.

Even though participation in athletics may be beneficial to both sexes, this does not mean that the program of athletics for women should be similar to that of men. Due to sex differences the activities and their conduct need selection with reference to physiological functions, characteristic qualities of development, and psychological and emotional differences. Girls, for example, should not play football, but if certain fundamental principles are observed they may profitably compete in intercollegiate archery, badminton, golf, softball, swimming, and tennis, or even in basketball and hockey. These principles include: the leadership of professionally trained women; requirement of a health examination of all participants before, during, and after each season of participation; provision of a wide variety of sports to meet the needs of the different interests, levels of skill, and physical condition; and such restrictions on participation as short practice sessions, short seasonal schedules, minimum travel, liberal substitutions, and limitation of participation to only one sport per season and to only two sports per year.

Administration of Physical Education

Traditionally, health services, health education, required physical education, intramural sports, and intercollegiate athletics grew up independently. This separation had its advantages in helping each unit to establish itself. Some argue that this independence is still desirable if each phase of the program is to live and thrive. Advocates of this separation believe that objectives are different, that the personnel is highly specialized, that joint use of facilities results in friction, that financial support of the various units must necessarily come from separate sources, and that a single administrative unit is not feasible because of the extent and diversity of activities. Each of these arguments has merit and some of them are particularly convincing, but they do not always apply. Tradition, of course, is not a legitimate reason for keeping related units separate and independent. This is especially true if such an organization does not permit the best possible service and education for students. Separate staffs, programs, facilities, records, and budgets are not always the most effective or economical.

One of the best ways to attain maximum coordination of health services, health education, physical education, and athletic programs is to merge them into a single administrative unit. This facilitates administration since the president deals with only one rather than with several administrative officers.

From the personnel point of view physical education, including athletics, should have consideration in over-all college budgeting and should be financed in the same manner that funds are provided for books, for laboratory equipment, and for other supplies and services. While the abolition of all gate receipts is too revolutionary to be feasible at the present time, it is an objective which commends itself to all thoughtful educators.

RELATIONSHIP TO PERSONNEL AND OTHER DEPARTMENTS

Because of the diverse services offered students in institutions of higher learning, a coordinating council may be advisable for effective cooperation and coordination of matters pertaining to student welfare. Such a group serves as a policy-making, policy-reviewing, and coordinating body for the total physical welfare program for students.

It should consist of representatives from all departments and areas concerned: academic and student deans, administration, faculty, students, trustees, and alumni.

The personnel worker's concern for the whole student, and his aim to help the student discover and develop, through his own efforts, all of his potentialities makes close cooperation with physical education highly desirable. Since cooperation, however, is a two-way proposition physical educators, too, must seek every opportunity to integrate their efforts with those of the student deans if the best interests of the students are to be served. The physical educator, if he envisions his profession in its entirety, is a personnel worker himself.

PHYSICAL EDUCATION PERSONNEL

The physical education and athletic staff should consist of men and women who are professionally trained in health education, physical education, and recreation. It is never satisfactory to give the direction of and instruction in sports and dance to persons who are not professionally trained. The selection of a college coach whose only recommendation is the fact that he was a former athlete is indefensible. It is desirable that all these technically trained persons have the personnel point of view. One of the most severe indictments of college physical education is that undue staff time and energy is spent on the few athletes to the neglect of the great mass of students. Staff members need to be used equitably to serve the development of all the students.

Conclusion

The purpose of institutions of higher learning is to provide opportunities for each student to develop himself, through his own efforts, to the limit of his various capacities in the skills, knowledges, and appreciations which contribute to personal health and happiness and to civic usefulness. The modern college provides the means for exploring many fields or areas of activity, including physical education. To be of maximum effectiveness, this program must be closely coordinated with the general academic and personnel programs. If such cooperation exists desirable learnings should result through participation in physical activities.

BIBLIOGRAPHY

American Association for Health, Physical Education, and Recreation: Yearbook, 1951: *Developing Democratic Human Relations Through Health, Physical Education and Recreation.* Washington, D. C., National Education Association, 1951.

Brownell, C. L., and Hagman, E. Patricia: *Physical Education—Foundations and Principles.* New York, McGraw-Hill Book Company, Inc., 1951.

Hughes, W. L., and Williams, J. F.: *Sports, Their Organization and Administration.* New York, A. S. Barnes and Co., 1944.

Oberteuffer, Delbert: *Physical Education.* New York, Harper & Brothers, 1951.

Scott, H. A.: *Competitive Sports in Schools and Colleges.* New York, Harper & Brothers, 1951.

Williams, J. F.: *Principles of Physical Education.* Philadelphia, W. B. Saunders Company (5th ed), 1948.

11. Where and How Students Live

DOROTHY V. N. BROOKS

FOR a large segment of the college population, going to college has meant living away from home. The first colleges in America provided quarters for their students as an adaptation of the English universities that were their forebears.[1] Later only the smaller colleges continued to provide housing for all of their students. Historically the large state institutions that have cared for the greatest number of students in higher education made no provision for the housing of men and at best only partial provision for the women. In 1949 a survey conducted by the National Association of Deans of Men indicated that for each school that housed all of its men there were seven that housed none and that on the average those which did provide housing were able to accommodate only one-third of their students.[2]

Leacock speaks feelingly for many a student when he writes of his Canadian experience.

When I was a student at the University of Toronto thirty years ago, I lived, from start to finish, in seventeen different boarding houses. . . . There were hundreds of us drifting about in this fashion from one melancholy habitation to another. . . . In the life we led we had practically no association on a large scale, no common rooms, no reading rooms, nothing. . . . The real thing for the student is the life and environment that surrounds him. All that he really learns he learns, in a sense, by the active operation of his own intellect and not as the passive recipient of lectures. And for this active operation what he really needs most is the continued and intimate contact with his fellows. Students must live together and eat together, talk and smoke together. Experience shows that is how their minds really grow. And they must

[1] W. H. Cowley: "The History of Student Residential Housing."
[2] National Association of Deans and Advisors of Men: "Report on College Residence Halls Questionnaire."

live together in a rational and comfortable way. . . . If a student is to get from college what it ought to give him, rooms in college with the life in common that they bring, are his absolute right. A university that fails to give it to him is cheating him.[3]

With the increasing recognition that the educational process involves the whole student for his entire time on the campus, the educational values of adequate housing with a residence program have come to the fore. MacLeish summarized the changing thinking when he said that, prior to the House Plan,

. . . most of Harvard's undergraduates lived a highly individualistic, not to say atomistic, social life. . . . The system was defended as making for greater self-reliance and individuality, but the Administration has never counted the imaginary benefits as outweighing the obvious losses. The individualism of the Harvard undergraduate was too often the individualism of loneliness, and the sophistication was too frequently the sophistication of cultural ignorance. . . . To bring living men together by their own volition it is necessary that they find congenial meeting places and that these congenial meeting places be always available. The Harvard housing problem will not be written down as solved until all students in the University, graduates as well as undergraduates, are given the advantages which have proved themselves in the seven already built.[4]

It is unlikely, before the projected increase in enrollment is realized, that building programs can overtake the backlog of the student population for whom the colleges have made no housing provision. It is obvious, therefore, that many campuses will continue to rely in part on commercial ventures in the community. Furthermore, as urban campuses continue to enroll increasing numbers of commuting or day students, some attention needs to be given to ways of uniting them to the campus and to providing for them a modicum of the experiences other students find in residence. It is to all phases of student living as well as to the several categories of students it enrolls that a college needs to give its attention.

Residence Halls

The most obvious expression of the values attached to residence experience may be seen in the buildings a campus provides for dormitories, but the physical plant is only the skeleton about which must be molded the program that gives pulsing reality to life in residence. Much has been written and excellent handbooks are available con-

[3] Stephen Leacock: My Discovery of England, pp. 98-101.
[4] Archibald MacLeish: The Next Harvard, pp. 46, 49.

cerning the structural features and furnishings of residence halls.[5] This is not the place to review these standards except to reiterate that design tends to be one important determinant of program. No original building or remodeling of older structures should be undertaken without thorough agreement in advance among the personnel staff, the business office, and the architect as to what constitutes the basic essentials for all aspects of housing.

Business managers beset with the inescapable costs of amortization cast covetous eyes on nonincome-producing rooms, yet the personnel philosophy of the institution is expressed more cogently in the use of space than in pages on program in a catalogue. Fortunate is the campus whose financial officers see housing as more than food and shelter and who recognize the educational value of corridor lounges, recreation rooms, or libraries.

Organization patterns for the administration of housing vary widely from having complete responsibility lodged in the dean's office to full authority being under the business office, but neither extreme is likely to produce a satisfactory situation. Where responsibility is shared according to the respective interests there is more likely to be better coordination with the financial office on the one hand and a more satisfactory integration with the total personnel program of the institution on the other. While such divided administrative authority is fraught with complications, and the administrative unit that is locally the stronger is always tempted to demand sole responsibility, still difficulties can be successfully surmounted when there is clear-cut delineation of responsibilities as well as mutual skill in interpersonal relations among staff members.

Often he who controls the budget calls the tune. It becomes of paramount importance, therefore, that administrative principles governing income and assignment of funds recognize the personnel staff and personnel functions as central to any housing plan. Just as a residence hall program is handicapped if these factors are not borne in mind in space allocation, so is it handicapped if its needs are not borne in mind in annual budgeting. A careful evaluation of the total services to be expected from the fees charged for food and rent should include the personnel items. Budget making, therefore, goes hand in hand with program planning.

First, the salary and maintenance charges for personnel staff are as

[5] "College Residence Halls," *Bulletin of the American Institute of Architects.*

Harriet Hayes: *Planning Residence Halls for Undergraduate Students in American Colleges and Universities.*

legitimate charges upon the residence income as are those of the house director or the food manager. Moreover, the portion of the budget attributable to the personnel phase of residence life should be under the direction of the personnel dean to whom the staff is ultimately responsible, while the director of housing or the business manager assumes administration of the operational aspects.

Second, it is important that provision be made for a student supervised budget to cover student activities in the house. While this may be collected with the rental income, in some situations it may be better procedure to have it come as a separate house tax. Many houses have found it good policy to have those participating in special events, such as dances, pay a nominal charge rather than let the special events be a drain upon the treasury. It is also sound public relations policy for income from dormitory vending machines and student agencies to augment the house exchequer rather than to go into other funds of the university.

Last, above and beyond the funds directly under student control, there needs to be a fund for general house program at the disposition of the head resident, as a legitimate tax upon the income of the house.

The rates established for rooms are of importance to the personnel officer not only as the source of income for staff and program, but also because the policy on rates affects the social structure of the house. It is well not to have a "poor man's wing" or a "rich man's court" if a unified house is the objective. Moreover, the practice of assigning rooms by number drawing or date of application makes generally uniform rates more equable. Consideration needs to be given, also, to a form of scholarship policy which assigns rooms within a unit to students who work for their room or for whom the room assignment is a form of scholarship help.

Conflicting theories about the effect of location upon student adjustment, of segregated versus mixed classes, and of continuous versus annual occupancy are staunchly defended by exponents on both sides of each argument, but little research has yet been done to demonstrate the relative merits of various plans for occupancy. On campuses where emphasis is given to strong class spirit, value is seen in housing assigned by class units. It is believed by many that freshmen are oriented more satisfactorily when housed apart from other classes save for a responsible corps of selected upper-class student counselors. Others note that the plan of housing by classes fails to provide leaven for the sophomore slump or the senior apathy while they believe that immaturity is perpetuated when freshmen are isolated.

The argument for continuous residence within a given hall is exemplified in the Harvard House and the Smith College Residence plans.[6] Here the advantages of the class orientation of freshmen are combined with the later identification with a house group across class lines which then becomes the nucleus for the college experience. For many another campus the fraternity house may be a rough counterpart in providing the sense of a continuous home base throughout the college years. It is generally agreed that freshmen have priority when housing is limited. On campuses where it is not possible to offer college-supervised housing of equal merit to all students beyond the junior year there is little excuse for establishing the "squatters' rights" principle for a lucky few. It is well under such conditions to reassign space annually, selection being based on number drawing.

Procedures for room assignments differ widely. The admissions office may make the arrangements for freshmen; it may be seen as the function of the dean's office; or on larger campuses the director of housing may assume this responsibility. The important point is not so much who does the actual work as that room assignments be recognized as a personnel function and that there be cooperation among all offices involved.

The feeling of belonging and of acceptance begins for most college students with the roommate or on the corridor where he resides. For this reason, it is of utmost importance that the arrangement be a congenial one. Provision for changing rooms and roommates falls within the province of the personnel office, and where change is within a given house, the head of residence, who is sensitive to the many implications for student adjustment, should arrange the transfer.

The pressure of increased enrollment and of rising maintenance costs oftentimes leads to increasing the occupancy quota of a house. Where this pressure has resulted in overcrowding, the educational values of residential life and even the physical, emotional, and intellectual well-being of individuals has been jeopardized. The head of residence has a responsibility for making careful observations on the total adjustment of individuals living under crowded conditions, and upon that officer's judgment should rest the decision for the point at which the law of diminishing returns begins to operate in any situation.

[6] Elliott Perkins: "Interim Report on the Houses."

Head Residents

When it is agreed that housing of students is an appropriate college function because of its educational value, then the individual designated by whatever title as head of the house becomes an educational personnel officer who should be appointed by the personnel dean responsible for the housing program. The educational contribution of residence hall living should never be secondary to business efficiency. It is not a question of one or the other: both are needed and balance can be achieved if responsibility for the education of students as individuals and in groups is always kept as the focus. This requires the closest coordination at all echelons among those in charge of the operations of the physical plant, the dining services, and the personnel staff.

It is important that the head of residence be one of those engaged in carrying out the total personnel program in order that the living aspects of that program be fully integrated with all other aspects of personnel work. The residence unit should never be isolated from the other counseling, cultural, or social facilities of the campus, nor should the personnel resources of the residence hall ever be subordinated to the mechanics of operation.

There is no one pattern for the head of residence in a college-operated hall. The choice will depend in part on such factors in the local situation as the size of the unit or the salary as well as on whether the institution sees in that individual a key figure who is implementing its philosophy of personnel work as a form of deeper teaching. A faculty member relieved of some academic duties may be the answer for those colleges who accord equal prestige and reward to teaching, research, and counseling. An older woman who has successfully reared her own children may now turn the warmth of her personality and the wealth of her experience to the service of a larger group. A younger man or woman trained in student personnel administration may recognize in residence hall work the golden opportunity for the generalist.

From whatever diverse backgrounds they enter, all should have in common the sympathetic objectivity and the flexibility that bespeaks a personal stability anchored in deep spiritual philosophy and in rich personal resources. All need to have an intellectual vitality, cultural interests, and civic awareness that makes them worthy of responsibility for the higher education of youth. All need to know enough of sociology to employ, and if need be to alter, the pervasive and specific mores; enough of psychology to understand the meaning of adolescent behavior and the developmental tasks that confront young people; enough of group work to create a dynamic experience in shared responsibility; enough of counseling to understand the potential in each student for growth and the symptoms that make referral more appropriate; and enough of administration to work always in the context of team membership and through appropriate channels. None can possess all of these virtues in equal measure; all can hold them as aspirations to be striven for. This implies continuous in-service training in the fine art and science of human relations.

In-service training of staff is an important aspect of administration and supervision in any type or at any level of work. In the area of personnel work in residence units the in-service training program assumes paramount importance. By the very nature of the duties there is imposed upon head residents a certain isolation which makes the teamwork through training programs essential to *esprit de corps*. Trained personnel need the intellectual stimulus of fellow workers, while those who have not had any formal training benefit when theory and practice go hand in hand. Moreover, in the rapid turnover characteristic of this area of service, continuous training assures continuity of policy.

The content of such programs will vary widely with the needs, imagination, and leadership within the group. Obvious is the need for familiarity with an interpretation of the work of such cooperating services as health, academic advising, or remedial reading; obvious, too, is the value of lectures by specialists within the academic community or by outside consultants. More significant than these programs is the need to develop attitudes and skills through training in good observation and discussion techniques.[7] This means that the staff itself must participate in the formulation of its own program. Above and beyond any specific content, however, is the contiguous association with the personnel dean who by his or her attitude towards staff establishes the climate which either inhibits or promotes the best development of each individual in his own tasks.

Food Service

Throughout all cultures man has seen in the partaking of food a simple ritual that binds friends together, provides a sense of well-

[7] Ira J. Gordon: "Guidance Training for College Faculty."

being, and contributes to the flow of ideas. These comprehensive values taken in conjunction with the more obvious need of youth for an adequate and appetizing diet are arguments enough for dining service as an integral part of any residence plan.

With the increasing democratization of higher education many students are now being drawn from backgrounds of limited social experience. If they are to function effectively in the roles to which they aspire in post-college years, it is important that these young people learn from daily practice to be at ease in an environment that characterizes personal culture and gracious standards. It is therefore not enough that the nutritional needs be met; it is important that the full possibilities of the meal hours be tapped for the social education of individuals. Specific responsibility by the college for education in the simple amenities of gracious living cannot be ignored.

Dining within the house is the most desirable practice, for just as a family finds a pivot for family life around the table, so does a residence unit identify some of its most treasured customs with the dinner hour. Moreover, with the sense of rush and urgency that has come to characterize student routine there is great virtue in breaking the cycle by eating at least one leisurely meal a day in a calm setting. For these reasons preference is given to smaller, more intimate dining units and to table service at tables small enough to permit shared conversation. The pressure of numbers and the bogey of costs may make this an impractical recommendation in some situations and cafeteria service may have to be the pattern for many colleges. Even under such a plan much can be done to assure well-ventilated, well-lighted, acoustically treated, and attractively appointed dining halls, for modern functional design gives attention to the esthetic as well as to the utilitarian aspects of living.

Although food service appropriately belongs under the jurisdiction of the business manager, the relationship with the personnel staff and with students needs to be one of closest cooperation. On the one hand there is the great contribution that meals for special occasions can make to program, on the other is the fact that menus and food costs are an ever-vulnerable Achilles' heel for student discussion. A manager of food service who uses constructively the liaison with student committees and personnel staff to seek suggestions and to interpret his position has gone far toward solving one of his most vexing public relations problems.

It is common practice for the dining hall to serve the men and women in separate units, largely because men's and women's houses have not been built contiguously. The experience of a few institutions, however, indicates that the values of coeducational dining may not have been thoroughly explored. Exchange dinners at periodic intervals are warmly received on many campuses. Certainly the campus that has dining services as an integral part of residence has gone a long way toward fulfilling the program essentials of any house.

Residence Program and Government

Adolescents need opportunity to acquire the basic skills which are required for everyday social activity. Dormitory life should be so structured as to provide these experiences as well as to facilitate what the psychologists speak of as the developmental tasks of adolescence. In order that the halls may contribute to these ends, a program must emerge that is tailor-made to the pattern of the group life of the residents. The ideal program will supplement but not compete with all-campus or student union activities; it will fulfill cultural and recreational as well as the social needs of its members; and it will provide for small group interests as well as large events.

The customs, the traditions, the ceremonials that grow up around a house are constructive ways of achieving group cohesion and of encouraging that important sense of belongingness. The faculty coffee hour, the Christmas dinner, the house dances, the intramural games—all are events that give opportunity for the cultivation of social skills, for the carrying of responsibility, and the development of leadership. On the other hand, equally significant in providing centers about which house life can polarize are a music room, a house library, a spontaneous softball game, or informal discussions.

Provision for group life, whether formally structured or spontaneous, does not just happen. It is in part the result of good architectural planning that provides space and facilities; in part it is in the vision of the staff who permit and encourage student initiative; and in part it is the administrative planning that provides a budget for this important aspect of residence hall living. It is important, therefore, that the college define in detail what is seen as the purpose and function of residence hall life in the total educational experience. Social growth does not take place in a vacuum, nor by reading and thinking about it, nor even in the office of a skilled counselor. Development for the adolescent emerges from complex interactions with his peers of which those within the residence halls are among the best. Personnel work thus places new emphasis on facilitating many types of social learnings.

Each individual needs to learn to be one of a group, considerate of the needs, the desires, and the wishes of others and able to subject his own wants to the greater good of the greater number. The residence hall provides the most natural unit a campus affords for these learnings through student participation in government. It is here that the individual may learn democracy, not alone through reading, but also by direct experience in action and example. The grass-roots philosophy of democratic procedures will never find more fertile soil nor more wholesome climate than exists in a house organized to govern itself, express group opinion, and meet group needs. Here group solidarity is enhanced by a formal organizational structure.

Such an organization is not a device apart from the college administrative structure; the whole philosophy of administration recognizes differentiated responsibility of and mutual interaction among the various groups composing the college community. The areas of student authority should be defined and then freedom for action and freedom for mistakes within these limits should be respected.

Whether the government organization of the house is an entity in itself, is a unit in a federation of residence halls, or is a part of the over-all student government structure will depend upon the nature of the campus. In an institution which takes responsibility for housing the large majority of its students, the residence halls form natural units of representation. This pattern makes for uniformity and for integration of the house with other aspects of campus life but care must be exercised lest the sense of participation and the power of decision be too far removed from the individual resident.

Whenever people live in close proximity, common understandings are necessary. In a residence hall these are established as standards to facilitate living together which, on the one hand, may be thought of as a contract between the institution and the individual defining their mutual responsibility, and, on the other, may be seen as the rules and regulations the students formulate to govern themselves. In general, students respond favorably to standards they have a part in forming or evaluating.

Beyond the areas specifically allocated to student responsibility are broad aspects of residence hall or campus policies and procedures where students cannot and should not be expected to take responsibility but where their voices provide a two-way channel of information and interpretation. In these areas joint student-faculty-administrative committees and conferences can be most profitable. The value of such communication is increased in proportion to the ability to anticipate a topic of mutual concern rather than acting after the fact. For example, students cannot set rates, but they can understand general principles undergirding factors affecting rates, and the business office that prepares graphs and charts showing the expenditures of the student's dollar will enlist cooperation and support.

Cooperative Housing

Cooperative housing for students is a general term that may take on one of three different aspects on different campuses, but all have in common the object of reducing board and room cost. In some residential colleges it has been common practice to set aside one house accommodating fifteen to seventy-five women, which may or may not have been endowed, as a cooperative house in which girls under college supervision participate in the tasks of housekeeping and the food preparation. Another phase closely akin to the first is seen in those situations in which the institution itself, or an organization with a specific interest in college students, establishes and gives general supervision to a house which students then run by planning, buying, budgeting, and operating all aspects of the undertaking.

A third form is seen in the independent cooperatives which develop, often on the Rochedale principles, at the periphery of a campus as an answer to the search for low-cost student living. The hazards to both sound budget and sound personnel practice are greatest in this latter type of cooperative house because those attracted to the plan have the least financial backing. Houses tend to be purchased in poorer areas and are often inadequate for multiple residence. Economies may lead to overcrowding and the precarious financial structure creates an atmosphere of insecurity.

Experience indicates that a student-operated residence demands an average of an hour a day of student labor in addition to the time for the care of his own quarters; yet the economies effected may be as much as fifty per cent of the cost of commercial housing. The cooperative mode of residence can form an incomparable laboratory for democratic living in which a strong sense of belonging, the challenge of responsibility, the demand for new experience, and the zest for adventure all fuse.

Good outcomes cannot be left to chance, however; the personnel worker charged with the responsibility for supervising a cooperative endeavor whether as a resident counselor, as a member of an advisory board, or as a liaison officer needs to be well aware of the social forces at work to affect morale. He needs to know how group techniques, discussions, and ratings may all be used to develop objectivity among members that will ward off deleterious cliques or rumblings. The college has a responsibility, moreover, to insure high standards of housekeeping, of balanced, adequate diets, of good work habits, of sound financing, and of manners in conformity with good social practice.

A sense of group inferiority is an ever-present danger in a co-operative house, yet there is inherent within the structure of a cooperative unit the roots from which can stem sturdy pride, group loyalty, and wholesome independence. A balanced membership is the first step in the creation of a positive attitude. Being chosen for such a residence experience should be an honor. While financial need may well be a prerequisite, some evidence of a better-than-average scholar-ship and some leadership ability may also be important qualities. Attention should be given to diversity in backgrounds in order to enrich or broaden the group as a whole. Different races, different faiths, different geographical origins may achieve this objective. A balance among classes is almost a necessity if continuity from year to year is to be achieved.

Once selected, the second step is house organization with agree-ment on job analyses that will leave no question about the who, when, and how of procedures. Next, a carefully thought-through social program can do much to create pride in the house and to establish good public relations among varied groups on the campus. Faculty guests, an agreement for an exchange of guests with the dining halls, an informal buffet supper for dates in which all share the work—these are but some of the ways in which healthy self-esteem and good fellowship can be created. Properly administered, values beyond economy recommend cooperative housing as worthy of college support.

Fraternity and Sorority Housing

Housing as a function of fraternity life burgeoned during that period of expansion in higher education when impersonalized ad-ministration acknowledged only a lecture room responsibility for students.[8] Contemporary thinking would emphasize a cooperative relationship between those responsible for the student personnel program and the fraternities. This responsibility has three goals: to insure appropriately planned residence units that give due weight to study and sleeping quarters as well as social and recreational space; to insure sound financing of the original plant as well as fiscal integrity of current operation; to gear the fraternity experience into the total educational personnel program of the institution.

The pattern of fraternity life is a reflection of the philosophy of the institution and it is therefore probable that chapters of different groups on the same campus will have more in common than will members of the same group from different types of campuses. This means that the policies governing the groups must emerge from the local situation in cooperation with the college personnel staff and the respective national officers, rather than being determined solely by the national groups or the local chapters. The program for rushing, the time of pledging, the policy with respect to freshmen either dining or living in the house—all will be influenced by the personnel program outside the fraternity house.

Likewise the policies concerning residence staff within the chapter house reflect not only student mores but also institutional philosophy. The public's expectation for the "protection" of women students led to the standard employment of chaperones or house mothers in the sorority house. The practice, on the other hand, is by no means universal among the men's groups. The recent experience with graduate counselors or young instructors in both men's and women's groups has had good response. Strong alumni or faculty advisory boards cooperating with the college personnel staff and the student officers can do much to enhance the experiences within the fraternity residence unit, in which attitudes and environment are both conducive to good scholarship and high personal standards.

Whatever the solution may be for adult guidance within the fraternity residence unit, any designated resident should be considered as a member of the staff of the dean of men or dean of women, with that office participating in the appointments and conducting the same staff training program that is conducted for the university-operated residence halls staff. The payment of salary through the college treasurer makes tangible the tacit relationship,

[8] American Council on Education, Committee on Student Personnel Work: *Housing of Students*, p. 54.

even though the bulk of the sum is derived, as it should be, from the primary resident group. It is the responsibility of the personnel staff to so work with the fraternity as to minimize any weaknesses and to maximize the advantages which may accrue within a continuing small group for the cultural, social, and intellectual development of individuals.[9]

Off-campus Housing

Although there is a marked trend toward college or university residence halls, it is obvious that many campuses will continue to rely in part upon commercial ventures in the community. These will vary from the single student in a family domicile through the traditional boarding house to the absentee landlord's provision for a rooming house or even light housekeeping arrangements. The residents of the community should understand that when they receive students into their homes they become responsible to the college for the welfare of these young people. The minimum an institution owes its students is assurance that standards for safety, plumbing, space, and furnishings are maintained. This can only be done by inspection, with the requirement that students live only in approved quarters, but this is a supervisory service and not an educational function.

It is almost impossible to conduct a personnel program for these off-campus units. Some institutions have attempted partial solutions: on the one hand, there may be an association of approved landlords which meets with the personnel staff; on the other, there may be a student government structure based on geographical zoning that forms units for intramural sports or social programs and thus permits a sense of group identification. These are steps in the right direction, for although they are half measures as judged by residence hall programs, they may be the only out-of-class provisions for some students.[10]

The student who works for his room is in a special category of off-campus housing and should always be the special concern of someone in the personnel office. First of all, it is necessary to establish and interpret standards to prevent exploitation on the part of either party to such an arrangement. How much time on what type of chores is equivalent to the prevailing rate for room and board? No student new to a community nor a housewife new to this type of

[9] Burns Crookston: *Integrating the Fraternity With the College.*
[10] E. G. Williamson and Lynn Draper: "Where Shall the Students Live?"

service can answer the question unaided. The personnel office has a further obligation to see that the individual is not working to the detriment of his health or academic standing.

Foreign Students

Foreign students have come to this country in increasing numbers to avail themselves of special and technological education. One of the choice by-products of their experience should be the contacts they make with typical and broad segments of American life. On the other hand, one of their choice contributions to American students is the cultural interpretation of another people that can come from direct experience. The foreign student who comes as an undergraduate to a small campus usually has his housing needs well cared for as an institution policy as well as through the natural concern of staff and student for the adjustment of a stranger in their midst. Larger and particularly urban institutions have been less conscious of their obligations, and especially when the students have come as older or graduate students, little attention has been given to this important aspect of their American education. Here is a significant avenue for international understanding and good will which too often has been neglected.

Counselors to foreign students agree that the best orientation is achieved when a foreign student can live as a member of the family in a cultured American home, but, since such arrangements are rarely possible, they also recognize the advantages of a student from abroad rooming with an American or in proximity to Americans of his general educational level.[11] To be decried is the all-too-common practice of students from abroad congregating in isolation from American students in a cosmopolitan club or comparable group housing. Definitely last in order of desirability is the solitary living that comes in a privately operated rooming house.

Colleges and universities that accept students from abroad have a moral obligation for their induction and orientation into American life, which includes living arrangements with social and cultural opportunities as well as a responsibility for the intellectual and academic opportunities.

Graduate Students

Graduate students often constitute the forgotten members of a campus otherwise well aware of the needs of students. Personnel re-

[11] *Handbook for Counselors of Students from Abroad*, p. 48.

quirements of the individual do not stop with graduation, and housing may be as great a problem for the beginning graduate student coming to a new campus as it is to the neophyte freshman, and is even more likely to be complicated by his limited budget. The housing of the graduate men and women should, therefore, be within the purview of any long-range housing program for an institution.

On a large campus particularly, departmental clubs or other social units cannot replace the sense of a home base which a graduate residence can supply. In the graduate experience where emphasis is placed on specialization and the intensity of research, the normal contacts within the daily living routine take on special importance. Naturally the age, the experience, and the interest of this group will make a program somewhat different from that appropriate to the undergraduate but this does not detract from its relative significance for the well-being of this important segment of the college population.

Married Students

The married undergraduate was at one time almost unknown to the American campus. A young man was supposed to have "completed" his education and be prepared to support a wife before undertaking matrimony, while frequently a girl was not permitted to continue registration after her marriage. Even before World War II that pattern was changing as the number of young people undertaking long professional training increased and as the thinking relative to the desirability of early marriage for those ready to undertake it became more prevalent. The return of the veteran student with his wife and children nevertheless created for many campuses their first awareness of the need for married student facilities.

The veteran pattern in turn set the mode for many younger couples. Now on many campuses a small group of married undergraduates is a normal part of the enrollment pattern. The married graduate student has always faced a serious housing problem that has often necessitated makeshift quarters and disproportionately high rentals. Yet in these young couples society has a stake to assure conditions conducive to a constructive marriage.

The postwar temporary housing for married veterans, with all of its structural limitations, underscores the essential values for family living in the units of simple, low-cost, two- or three-room apartments. The leadership which sprang almost spontaneously to provide community organization, nursery schools, extension or adult education classes, hobby groups, and social programs revealed the needs of this group as well as the potential for leadership which resided in it. Married students, graduate or undergraduate, are as truly a responsibility of the personnel officer as any other segment of the college population.

While priority must always be given to the need for undergraduate and particularly freshmen housing, any long-range university planning will concern itself with a survey of married student residential needs and the concomitant personnel interest that will ascertain the community services available to supplement and enrich the home life of these young people while on the campus.[12] If group housing for married students were to be financed under the same plan used for self-amortizing dormitories for other students, adequate housing at substantial saving could be supplied to this minority. Very few campuses can rely upon the community to provide adequate housing for this group.

Living at Home

An increasing number of young people will find their higher education at city junior colleges or at the larger municipal universities while residing at home. A residence hall plan is not within the program of such institutions, yet the day student is in particular need of the advantages dormitory living provides those who live away from home during their college years. On the one hand, is the need for parents to understand the emancipation that must now be accomplished under the paternal roof; on the other is the need to give the student a sense of identification with a small group within the total college structure. Personnel officers of some of the larger municipal colleges have been unusually successful in working with students on a so-called house plan that permits just such centers for activities.

The situation of the day student on a predominantly resident campus can be approached several ways. Where the individual is affiliated with a social group, identification is easily cared for. Often social groups arrange to have local members reside in the house for brief periods of time. It is common practice to have local students live on the campus during orientation week and for the students thus inducted into the house to be nonresident members throughout

[12] George B. Bowers: *Housing for Married Students.*

the year. The inclusion of city students within the membership of residence hall groups cannot be counted on to happen automatically, but must be borne in mind by the head resident during planning sessions with the student officers.

Where the number of day students precludes this practice, it is sometimes possible to organize the group as a commuters' club, to establish a day students' lounge, or to have a luncheon club. Sometimes this group can sponsor specific projects or conduct their own social program. The important thing is that this group not be overlooked in preoccupation with the resident student and that all possible facilities be put at the service of the day student.

It matters not in which type of housing a student lives—a residence hall or dormitory, a cooperative house, fraternity or sorority, or in off-campus housing—it is here that the personnel program of the institution can really function. Here it can operate on a "grass-roots" level which permits a "natural" group where needs are easily recognized. It is here that deeper learnings result from the recognition that students in living units are whole persons who not only must have shelter and food while on the campus but also a full-rounded living experience which will develop them into better and more adequate persons. Discerning personnel officers are aware of the educational opportunities so readily available in housing units and make the most of them in the highest interests both of the students and of the institution.

BIBLIOGRAPHY

Albright, Preston B.: "The Place of Residence Hall Organization in the Student Personnel Program." *Educational and Psychological Measurement XI*: Winter, 1951, pp. 700-703.

American Association of University Women: *Housing College Students*. Washington, D. C., American Association of University Women, 1934.

American Council on Education, Committee on Student Personnel Work: *Housing of Students*. Washington, D. C., Volume XIV, Series VI, 1950.

Augustine, Grace M.: *Some Aspects of the Management of College Residence Halls for Women*. New York, Crofts, 1935.

Borreson, B. James: "The Application of Personnel Methods to University Housing Procedures." *Educational and Psychological Measurement VII*: Autumn, 1947, pp. 583-93.

Bowers, George B.: *Housing for Married Students*. Ed. D. project, Teachers College, Columbia University, New York, 1952.

Bryan, Mary D., and Handy, Etta H.: *Furnishing and Equipment for Residence Halls*. New York, Bureau of Publications, Teachers College, Columbia University, 1933.

"College Residence Halls," *Bulletin of American Institute of Architects*, Washington, D. C., 1948, 1949.

Cowley, W. H.: "The History of Student Residential Housing." *School and Society XL*, Dec. 1, 1934, pp. 705-12; Dec. 8, 1934, pp. 758-64.

Cowley, W. H.: "Significance of Student Traditions." *Higher Education and Society, A Symposium*. Norman, University of Oklahoma Press, 1936.

Crookston, Burns: *Integrating the Fraternity With the College*. Ed. D. project, Teachers College, Columbia University, New York, 1953.

Dana, Arthur: *Kitchen Planning for Quantity Food Service*. New York, Harper & Brothers, 1949.

Gibbs, Elizabeth: "Cross Educating the Residence Hall Staff." *Journal of Home Economics 34*: May, 1946, pp. 355-358.

Gordon, Ira J.: "Guidance Training for College Faculty." *Journal of National Association of Deans of Women XVI*: Jan., 1953, pp. 69-76.

Handbook for Counselors of Students From Abroad. New York, The National Association of Foreign Student Advisors, 1949, pp. 48-9.

Hartzfield, Freedo O.: *The College Residence a Laboratory for Living*. Unpublished Ed. D. project, Teachers College, Columbia University, New York, 1947.

Hayes, Harriet: *Planning Residence Halls for Undergraduate Students in American Colleges and Universities*. New York, Teachers College, Columbia University Press, 1932.

Hayes, Harriet: *College Operated Residence Halls for Women Students in 125 Colleges and Universities*. New York, Teachers College, Columbia University Press, 1932.

Hopwood, Kathryn L.: "A Training Program for Campus Leadership at Ohio State University." *Journal of the National Association of Deans of Women XI*: Jan., 1948, pp. 89-93.

Hopwood, Kathryn L. *The Student Assistant in the Women's Residence Halls of the Ohio State University*. Columbus, The Ohio State Press, 1950.

Labelle, Alta M., and Barton, Jane: *Administrative Housekeeping*. New York, G. P. Putnam's Sons, 1951.

Leacock, Stephen: *My Discovery of England*. London, John Lane, The Bodley Head Limited, 1922, pp. 98-101.

Louis, Broth: "The Role of Student Government in the Student Personnel Program." *Educational and Psychological Measurement X*: Autumn, 1950, pp. 569-76.

MacCready, Hazel F.: "Off-Campus Housing Program." *Journal of the*

National Association of Deans of Women IX: No. 3, March, 1946, p. 137.

MacLeish, Archibald: *The Next Harvard.* Cambridge, The Harvard University Press, 1943.

National Association of Deans and Advisors of Men: "Report on the College Residence Halls Questionnaire." Mimeographed committee report. Frank C. Baldwin, Committee Chairman, April, 1949.

National Association of Deans of Women: *Residence Halls for Women Students.* Washington, NADW of NEA, 1947.

Ohlsen, Merle M.: "Developments in Residence Hall Counseling." *Educational and Psychological Measurement* X: Autumn, 1950, pp. 455-63.

Orme, Rhoda, *Counseling in Residence Halls.* New York, Bureau of Publications, Teachers College, Columbia University, 1950.

Perkins, Elliott: "Interim Report on the Houses." *Harvard Alumni Bulletin* 53, Dec. 9, 1950, pp. 260-264.

Perkins, Elliott: "Evaluation of Dormitory Counselors." *Educational and Psychological Measurement* XI: Autumn, 1951, pp. 419-26.

"Proceedings of the Annual Conference of the National Association of College and University Housing Officers." 1949, 1950, 1951, 1952. Mimeographed.

Stewart, Helen Q.: *Some Social Aspects of Residence Halls for College Women.* Santa Monica, California Professional and Technical Press, 1942.

Thompson, Florence M.: "The Use of Dormitories for Social Education." *Educational and Psychological Measurement* VII: Autumn, 1947, pp. 648-54.

Thompson, Florence M.: "Residence Halls and the Educational Program." *The Educational Record* XXIX, Jan., 1948, pp. 64-71.

Vallery, H. F.: *Student Personnel Problems in Men's Residence Halls* (with particular reference to Louisiana State University). Unpublished Ed. D. project, Teachers College, Columbia University, New York, 1950.

Van Alstine, F. L.: "Relation Between Housing and Scholarship." *Journal of Higher Education* XIII: March, 1942, pp. 158-9.

Williamson, E. G., and Draper, Lynn: "Where Shall Students Live?" *The Educational Record* XXXII, Jan., 1951, pp. 29-44.

Wilson, Frances M.: "What Makes an Effective In-Service Training Program?" *Journal of the National Association of Deans of Women* XVI: Jan., 1953, pp. 51-6.

Wilson, Margaret M.: "Dynamics of a Residence Hall Program." *Occupations* 29: Nov., 1950, 116-22.

12. Learning With Students from Other Lands

NORMAN KIELL

IN THE ancient tradition of universities and colleges, centers of higher learning in the United States have always warmly welcomed students from beyond its borders. This has never been truer than today when more than 31,000 students from abroad are studying in 1404 colleges in all of our forty-eight states and the District of Columbia. A short decade ago (1942–1943), there were only a comparative handful of them—8075—in this country. This nearly fourfold growth is indicative of the value placed on having students from other lands in our colleges and universities.

That the exchange of students is an effective method of promoting international good will has seldom been doubted. Indeed, the basic philosophy of UNESCO is the belief that international understanding and cohesion can be advanced by practical assistance in bringing people of different national and cultural backgrounds together for purposes of education, training, and common programs of work and study. No part of the program of UNESCO has enjoyed more solid support or evoked wider interest and sympathy than that of the exchange of persons. The Fulbright and Smith-Mundt Acts have also fired the imagination of students and faculty by their potentialities. All of these agencies have for their primary objective the furthering of better understanding among nations by the exchange of persons.

The vital importance of this exchange cannot be measured by numbers alone. The investment in people in terms of such projects can be a practical way of affecting the world in which we live. "There is no guarantee that international education will save the world but it offers a practical, inexpensive means of bringing about better understanding and achieving long-range results out of all proportion to the money and time involved."[1] Students come from Africa, the Near and Far East, southern Asia, war-torn and reconstructed Europe, from the three-quarters of the world where spreading shadows of social revolution warn them that they must return to their homelands prepared to play some part. Theirs is still largely a middle world which has not chosen sides in the Atlantic-Soviet struggle. Their choice may depend upon our recognition of the vital stake with which they challenge us.

Of the 31,000 foreign students in the United States now, it has been estimated that some 60 per cent are engaged in the study of scientific and technical subjects and another 20 per cent in fields closely related to the economic and social development of their countries. These students are here for practical reasons: they require more specialized education and more "know-how," which American institutions are uniquely equipped to offer them. Their own governments look to them to bring back and apply for their own country's benefit the technical knowledge and skills which they have learned in the United States. But they will carry back something else: their impression of America and its democracy as they found it. How they weave their impressions into the fabric of their home country's social and economic ferment, political dissatisfactions, restlessness, and desire for change is critical for the survival of the democratic world.

Ideally, the exchange of students can become a formidable instrument for forging good will and promoting the democratic ethic. We have been too prone to regard students from other lands as "unofficial ambassadors," to believe that mere presence in a foreign country will increase a visitor's understanding, will help cross-fertilize cultures, will soften or destroy unfounded prejudice, and will multiply opportunities for the advancement of human welfare the world over.

Such is not always the case. Foreign students' visits are often productive of misunderstandings and even ill will. "America," says Myrdal, "is truly a shock to the stranger."[2] The transplanting of people from one culture to another is inherently a difficult thing. It involves, inevitably, shock and misapprehension; and this has wide implications for the whole effort of the international student program. The tremendous claim of wide benefits, along with the tremendous investment, is splendid in intent, but in terms of the whole problem of developing international understanding, we must see to

[1] Kenneth Holland: "The Foreign Student in the United States," p. 138.
[2] Gunnar Myrdal: An American Dilemma, p. 3.

it that international understanding does take place. "It is perfectly possible for an international fellowship to fail in its effect, indeed to do more harm than good, unless it is administered with care and intelligence."[3] The enterprise is difficult and demands a corresponding effort to do well.

The Needs of Foreign Students and How They Can Be Met

ORIENTATION

Perhaps the first effort that must be exerted is the orientation of the overseas student. This is a dual responsibility, to be borne by both the newcomer and personnel staff of United States institutions, since the continuous process of orientation involves the student from the time he first considers studying abroad to well after he has returned home. "Orientation in American customs and institutions," according to 352 German exchange students who were interviewed in August, 1950, after their initial orientation period and then again in May, 1951, just prior to leaving this country, "appeared as both the most important aspect of the orientation received and also as the greatest deficiency."[4]

The problem of orientation is a broad one, but its solution lies in specific and well-defined areas. Orientation means easing the sharp transition which occurs when the overseas student enters an entirely new world; it means that special efforts must be made to present the foreign student with the fullest opportunity to study, within the framework of a given curriculum, in the setting of this country, the things for which the United States stands. It means, simply, introducing the student to this new world and helping him to participate in it.

Before the student even reaches a United States port of entry, it is imperative that he be grounded in the different kind of educational experience he will encounter here, in the new culture, and the reality of American democracy. There are several avenues through which this can be achieved.

The student can obtain accurate information from United States information and education officers who are attached to many American embassies. Some universities, like Syracuse and Washington,

---

[3] Frank Aydelotte: *The 32nd Annual Report*, p. 11.
[4] Robert T. Bower, *et al.*: *An Analysis of Attitude Changes Among German Exchangees*, p. 27.

supply especially prepared pamphlets which inform the students of the particular conditions under which they will study and live. Until alumni associations are established abroad, individual students who have been in the United States and returned to their home countries can answer questions which bedevil the new applicant for admission to an American institution. Copies of *Meet the USA, Indians Going to America,* and *Living in the United States, A Guide for New Visitors,* as well as packaged libraries of Americana, ranging from Twain's *Huckleberry Finn* to Brogan's *The American Character,* along with representative high-caliber magazines, should be at the students' disposal. Proper and complete clearance of all the requisite forms and data necessary for admission—including specific appraisal of the prospective student's knowledge of spoken and written English*— should be obtained prior to the student's leaving his home country. And finally, a personal letter of welcome to the new student from the responsible university official is of vital importance.

Organizations exist which are prepared to meet the new student at the time of his first entry to this country. The United States State Department maintains a staff at the major port cities of New York, New Orleans, Miami, and San Francisco. The Committee on Friendly Relations Among Foreign Students arranges to meet new students arriving in New York or San Francisco, to assist them with customs clearance, to arrange temporary housing, to conduct tours of the two cities, and to facilitate their onward travel to the institution they are to attend or to an orientation center.

The orientation center has been a development since 1942. In that year, the United States State Department awarded a grant to Wilson Teachers College in Washington, D. C., for the establishment of an Orientation Center for Foreign Students and Trainees. Other institutions, among them Louisiana State and the University of Michigan, had developed their own orientation center programs independent of any outside aid. These programs, however, were primarily a matter of intense English courses to prepare the student for study in an American institution.

Orientation centers today differ from these earlier programs in that English language courses are incorporated in a fuller program which includes the study of American history, economics, literature, and government, and which is designed to prepare the student in many

---

* The Department of State has developed a standardized English proficiency examination for foreign students.

respects for his experience in the United States. Since 1949, the Institute of International Education has attempted to administer this kind of orientation program for the Department of State. The orientation centers are located on eighteen college campuses scattered throughout the country. Enrollment totaled 850 for the 1952 six-week summer course.

In assigning students to the centers, the Institute's objective is to establish a balance of nationalities, age, and sex on the assumption that the ideal center includes students from as many different national backgrounds as possible. The attempt is made to offer the student an experience which will be essentially different from the kind he will have at his academic institution. In general, the objective of the Institute program falls into three categories: (1) to introduce the student to American life and customs; (2) to prepare the student for academic and administrative procedures; and (3) to give the student facility and confidence in the English language.

Other agencies have sponsored orientation centers, but with a different emphasis. The International Service Seminars, operated under the auspices of the American Friends Service Committee, have proved very effective as summer projects. In a vacation setting, American and foreign students get to know each other as individuals, working, studying, and playing together. Thrown into close intimacy, where cooperation is necessary for optimal realization of the Seminar's goal, the students find it easier to understand differences and to build on common ground.

The Experiment in International Living of Putney, Vermont, centers its orientation program on bringing the foreign student into an American home as a guest for one month. In the summer of 1952, 183 German, Austrian, French, and Danish students lived with American families in communities all over the United States. This program is worked out with the cooperation of the Institute of International Education and community chairmen in many cities, who are responsible for securing interested families in having a foreign visitor during the summer.

Such programs are well worth the effort. The student is helped to make his adjustment to America and American democracy more quickly and with greater understanding; the foreign student adviser finds his burden lessened; the university has a student better equipped to handle the intricacies of the American educational system; and the general public has a person who can contribute to its fund of knowledge because of the student's participation in community activities.

The orientation process reaches its high point at the arrival of the student on the campus and in his integration to campus life. Even supposing the visiting student has been briefed while in his own land, and perhaps exposed to some currents in an orientation center, he is still bewildered by that peculiar American institution known as "campus life." Fortunately, most colleges and universities have provided "Foreign Student Counselors" to help facilitate the adjustment of the students to the local campus, to make their absorption into the student body as easy as possible, and to make the student aware of his value as a foreign student.

. . . The only way the student can accomplish his mission in this country is by participation in our life. He must work, play and think with us; he must see us at home, at school, and in our community activities; he must learn from first-hand experience about our problems, our fears, and our aspirations. Moreover, it is only through such participation that the student from abroad can share his culture—his problems, his fears, and his aspirations—with us. . . . Orientation, therefore, must aim to develop the motivation and the capacity for full participation as an equal in the corporate life of the institution and the community.[5]

The crux of the orientation process, then, is participation. For orientation requires participation, and participation bespeaks understanding; and without understanding, the student is incapable of sharing.

Many foreign student counselors have set up their own orientation course, much like the universally practised freshman week. Geared to information giving, to explaining the mechanics of the American higher educational system, to unfolding the mysteries of the true-false test (often a *bête-noire* inasmuch as this kind of examination is as American as a banana split), to dispelling the Alice-in-Wonderland-Hollywood attitude toward American life and culture, to meeting the students informally and in a personal ccounseling situation, this program, if well organized and operated, can do much to make the foreign student feel enough "at home" to begin to feel part of the dynamic community in which he now finds himself.

Some institutions, like Teachers College, Columbia University, make mandatory that all foreign students take a course in American

[5] *Handbook for Counselors of Students from Abroad*, p. 50.

culture and education supplemented by field visits to schools, industries, cultural centers, and social welfare agencies. Many universities provide diagnostic English tests for the new students and assign them to appropriate courses according to the level of proficiency demonstrated. On campuses where there are few students from abroad, the orientation process can be facilitated by intensive group and personal counseling throughout the student's first semester, at least.

COUNSELING

While American university administrators and officials have been generous in enrolling overseas students in their institutions, many have done little subsequent to this action. After the student has been accredited, he is let loose on his own recognizance, left to make the adjustment to a new educational system and culture as best he can. In many cases it has been too easy for the foreign student to gain admission and he has been given too much consideration in his classes and too little consideration outside his classes. The newcomer to the American campus needs a well-rounded and vigorous advisory program wherein he can secure the assistance he needs when he needs it.

Foreign students have to face all the problems students in general are confronted with, as well as a myriad of difficulties peculiar to their status as strangers in a strange land.

. . . Barriers to communication and genuine intercultural understanding. . . . laws and regulations of the Immigration and Naturalization Service, housing, inflation, . . . limitations on dollar exchange abroad, unfamiliarity with standards, methods of instruction, and academic procedures in the U.S.A., are all potential sources of insecurity and emotional disturbance to students from abroad, and, therefore, indicate the need for someone whose business it is to know these [students] . . . as persons, to know their personal problems, and to assist them in finding satisfactory solutions.[6]

The role a full-time, trained foreign student adviser can play in assisting the overseas visitor to meet his academic and personal adjustments while in this country may mean the difference in determining the student's basic attitudes toward the United States and American democracy. The counselor's personality, his understanding of the cultures from which the students come, his awareness of their

[6] *Ibid.*, p. 126.

problems, his alertness and ability to help them meet their needs, his channeling of their activities into a positive appreciation of the American scene whenever possible, will go a long way toward contributing effectively to international understanding.

SOCIAL ADJUSTMENT

Adequate and sympathetic counseling in their personal and academic problems is but one need of the foreign student. Complementary to this is the need to be brought into the social orbit of both campus and community. Ideally, this is also the function of the foreign student adviser. The student may garner only negative values until he is helped to live by participating in the American democratic life without losing his own cultural identity. The great problem is how to draw the student into this orbit. It cannot be a catch-as-catch-can affair.

Perhaps no single force can accomplish more toward removing the artificial barriers between men and nations than the university. In such a setting, we can help thoughtful students from other lands, particularly those from color-conscious Africa and Asia, to realize the dynamic qualities of American democracy as well as its imperfections; and we can assist our own students in developing into internationally minded citizens, so desperately needed for our century. The social integration of all students is as vital as their academic development.

. . . Realizing that his challenge is to give these potential leaders of the world an experience in the spirit and dynamics of democratic living necessary for genuine understanding, the counselor brings to bear the basic principles and techniques of effective human relations in working with students from abroad, and in getting other campus people (both students and faculty) to work and live with them. . . . Learning by doing is a sound principle of international education. The social needs of the students provide the greatest incentive for participation. Each student needs and wants, to some degree, to belong to and participate in a group. Moreover, a large portion of student life is spent in organized or informal group life. The counselor's problem therefore is threefold: (a) to organize appropriate intercultural activities; (b) to organize groups in such a way that students from abroad and U.S.A. students will do things together; and (c) to make these activities satisfying so that individuals will spontaneously regroup themselves for activities of their own choosing.[7]

[7] *Ibid.*, pp. 70, 73.

Campus activities can include folk and social dancing, field trips, an international film series, meaningful celebrations of national holidays, food festivals, informal picnics and outings, international clubs, and other affairs indigenous to the mores of the particular institution. Perhaps, however, the fostering of deep personal friendships with Americans is the most important facet in this social adjustment of the student from another land. The abiding impression of the United States that this student will take home with him will not be what he learned in Electronics 304, but the more intangible, residual feelings of friendship he feels toward individual Americans. If he is to learn the ways of democracy, *he must not be socially ostracized.* It is not that we deliberately keep the foreign students apart from us; it is that we do not deliberately seek their company. As a result, the tendency of the visiting or international student is to associate primarily with his own compatriots. The American student loses an enriching experience thereby, and the foreign student has a rather lonely, sterile, and inevitably distorted view of American mores and values.

If foreign students were brought often and regularly into the living rooms of American homes, they would have something with which to counter the statistics they read about divorce and morals in the United States. Now, many of the invitations they do receive are extended by those well-meaning citizens who are more concerned with introducing an exotic note into their home entertainment than with cultivating mutual regard. The result is too frequently a quiz program, with the visitor responding to curious questions, his "foreignness" thrown into sharp relief.

Recently a number of foreign students representing several countries were invited by a church group to meet its members and to speak with them about their home countries. The students were chagrined to discover that the circulars which had been printed for the occasion urged the members to "Come and See the Foreign Students in Their Native Costumes; Listen to Their Weird Music; Watch Their Strange Dances. . . ." This sort of demonstration of narrow understanding is, nevertheless, preferable to keeping our doors closed to the students. If we open them wider and more often, we will find, as with many new experiences, that hesitations and blunders give way to an enriching association which may be enjoyed by these students and by us.

Perhaps the really vital need to get close to the students from other lands becomes more apparent when we examine three surveys made within the past few years. In 1951, Bower, reporting on attitude changes of German exchangees, found that while the personal qualities of Americans appear to have made the greatest impression on them, Americans have not invariably made a favorable impression.[8] In 1952, a survey sponsored by the Evaluation Section of the Education Exchange Service of the United States Department of State reveals that European students were more likely than others to express unfavorable opinions about Americans and America.[9] And in 1949 the writer discovered, after interviewing 100 Indian and Pakistan students, that before arrival in the United States, 68 per cent had markedly favorable opinions of this country but that after living here for some time, only 22 per cent were still favorably inclined in their attitudes toward the United States. Fifty-seven per cent held decidedly unfavorable views![10]

Charged with the proper spirit, the counselor can tap, educate, and secure the resources of campus and community so that the visiting student will become more than an academic bowing acquaintance to his American neighbor, and so that the returning student will, by virtue of close intimacy with American friends, be more favorably disposed to the United States. The benefit campus and community can derive by sharing in the enterprise is no less real. Community organizations are usually seeking stimulating projects and program ideas. Libraries welcome exhibits of arts and crafts which foreign students can lend and which might otherwise be unobtainable. Local radio stations are pleased to present enriching foreign student programs. The American public is inveterately willing to contribute its effort, time, and funds to something worthwhile, and to learn. A main function of the counselor's office is to serve as a pump primer to start this mainstream of community interest moving.*

Without question, the most rewarding feature of a program in organizing the resources of a community is that of the successful home visit. If every student from abroad could have a second home in the

[8] Robert T. Bower, et al.: Op. cit., p. 123.

[9] Attitudes of Foreign Students in Ten Orientation Centers in the Summer of 1951, p. 4.

[10] Norman Kiell: A Study of Attitudes of Indian and Pakistani Students Towards America and American Democracy, p. 156.

* An indispensable frame of reference, which details many concrete skills and techniques for such programs, is the Handbook for Counselors of Students from Abroad. It is invaluable for the "how, what, where, when and why" of working with foreign students.

off-campus community, misunderstandings about American life, mores, and values would be largely dissipated and the effectiveness of the foreign student program would be greatly enhanced. The foreign student counselor has several agencies at his disposal which are already geared to this facet of activity. The Committee on Friendly Relations Among Foreign Students, Rotary and Kiwanis Clubs, student denominational groups, 4-H Clubs, and other service organizations are usually prepared to invite foreign students to members' homes for visits ranging from an evening's entertainment to Christmas and summer-long holidays.

Housing

Correlative to the problem of home visits for the foreign student is the concern for his housing. The creation of a healthy educational environment demands that the highest priority be given to the students' living quarters. Where they live and the conditions under which they live are of primary importance in determining and influencing their attitudes and opinions of this country.

Whether a student hails from Rome, New York or Rome, Italy, or Frankfort, Kentucky or Frankfurt, Germany, or Cairo, Illinois or Cairo, Egypt, he is faced with the need of a place to live; but the foreign student finds it doubly difficult to secure proper housing. Bewildered at the outset by the new culture in which he finds himself, the overseas student, and particularly the graduate foreign student, in all probability has to locate his own quarters. Knocking on prospective rooming house doors, he may be rebuffed by the landlady because of his accent or the color of his skin. Careful spadework by the foreign student adviser can perhaps eliminate such thoughtless prejudice. "Orientation" meetings with Landlady's Leagues and on an individual basis may be required.

The student from abroad who merely rents a room with an American family is not gaining the kind of experience we covet for him. In evaluating different types of housing facilities, the ideal arrangement is the one in which the foreign student lives with an American family and is accorded family participation privileges. Here again, the foreign student adviser must play a part, for the right student must be placed with the right family. The creation of understanding through living together is a delicate responsibility.

Where it is not feasible to place the student in a private home and enjoying the privileges of family life, the next most desirable arrangement is placement in a student dormitory with an American roommate, matched as carefully as possible according to age, level of scholastic attainment, and sympathetic vision. The happy results of such pairing can exert a profound influence in the foreign student's total adjustment while in this country.

The institution of the International House is a more dramatic way of accommodating foreign students. The three largest—at Berkeley, Chicago, and New York—house about five hundred each. Smaller units, such as the Cambridge International Student Association and Washington (Seattle) International House, accommodate about twenty-five students each. Their by-laws insist that a certain number of United States students be included in the housing unit. The International House is designed to provide a residential center for foreign and American students in which an on-going educational, social, and cultural program gives these students an opportunity for the exchange of ideas. While excellent in intent, in actual practice the desired results are not always achieved unless the program is very carefully administered. Racial and ethnic groups tend to keep to themselves, usually preventing any inroads into their self-imposed segregation. Contact with other International House members may degenerate into little more than the casual "Hi!" of the hurried and harried student neighbor.

There is no easy solution to the problem of housing the foreign student. Each campus must work within its own local frame of reference. Cooperative student housing, including foreign student residents, has been successful at the University of Michigan, the University of Southern California, and The Ohio State University. Many fraternities and sororities have taken over complete responsibility for sponsoring individual overseas students, electing them to membership, giving them their room and board, and paying their tuition and incidental expenses. The Hillel Foundation, since 1935, has also done this for hundreds of young Jewish escapees from Nazi Germany and from D.P. camps. And so, similarly, have the Student Christian Associations throughout the land. How each campus meets the housing situation for its foreign students depends largely on the stimulation and effective leadership of both the community and the campus.

FINANCIAL AID

In the academic year 1915–1916, the total foreign student enrollment in United States colleges and universities was 3790. In 1935–

1936, it had doubled to 6627, and in 1945–1946, nearly tripled to 9775. By 1949–1950 it had burgeoned to 27,717. But since 1950, the population has remained rather constant, somewhere between 30,000 and 31,000. Despite the fact that today's number of overseas students is the largest in history, it represents a progressive retrogression, for the rate of increase has not been maintained.

Two factors account for this unhappy phenomenon: the acute crises in dollar shortage abroad and ever-rising inflationary costs in the United States. The foreign student is caught in the middle and thus economic assistance becomes almost mandatory. The United States Advisory Commission on Educational Exchange, after an investigation of the situation, recommended, and the State Department adopted as a policy, that first financial responsibility devolves on the individual student or his sponsor; second on his government; third on American private resources; and finally on the United States Government.

The possibility that the educational exchange program may be curtailed—slowly but measurably—is a sore reality to face, particularly at a time when our institutions offer the greatest opportunity for specialized education and deeper learning, and when so many nations look to the United States for leadership. What, then, can the foreign student do to help himself financially, and what can be done to help him?

Certification by the university official responsible for foreign students and approval by the Immigration and Naturalization Service is required before the student can be gainfully employed, either part or full time. Certain conditions obtain for foreign student employment in each category. Only graduate students are permitted to work as laboratory assistants, tutors, fellows, or instructors—and they must maintain a full course of study while thus working part time. Others must show evidence that they have to meet the cost of study because parents are unable to send money or they are unable to obtain money from home. For full-time employment, government regulations provide that where practical training is required or recommended by an institution, the student may be authorized to accept such training for a period up to a maximum of eighteen months in six-month installments. Permission is given only when practical experience is designed to implement the theoretical training received in the college or university.

Financial help for individual students sometimes can be secured from citizens, civic organizations, and religious groups in the community, when the need is made clear. Although universities and colleges are themselves dependent on the generosity of benefactors or taxpayers for their survival, more and more reliance must be placed on them to waive tuition fees and to provide housing accommodations for the foreign student. The availability of established scholarships, fellowships, and loan funds should not be overlooked. UNESCO's *Study Abroad*[11] renders perhaps the most complete listing of study grant opportunities available and can be consulted advantageously.

Many of the students are sponsored by their own governments and thus incur minimal or no financial worry. The great majority, however, are not so fortunate. The United States Government has recognized the seriousness of the situation and in the last few years has carried the full costs of a substantial number of students who have come here under the specialized one-year programs for Germany, Japan, Austria, Finland, and Korea. Special funds have been set aside by the Government to provide for Chinese students stranded in this country at the time of the Chinese Communists' advent to power. Fulbright Travel Grants, covering the cost of ocean passage, have been a boon to qualified foreign students and scholars. Private foundations, such as the British Dominion Division of the Carnegie Corporation and the Phelps Stokes Fund, are assisting African students, while the Watumull Foundation gives grants-in-aid to Indian students. Here, too, in the final analysis, each campus community must be as ingenious as possible in finding ways and means of helping the foreign students complete their education.

Conclusion

"The American university has become an international university," a State Department official has recently stated, "but we are not yet fully aware of it."[12] Only recently scientific studies and adequate samplings have been initiated to evaluate this program in the United States. "In the United Kingdom and France, although these governments are also heavy investors, there has been less concern about establishing objectively the degree to which the programs approximate their stated goals. The absence of basic data in this field is noteworthy."[13]

[11] UNESCO: *Study Abroad*, International Handbook, Fellowships, Scholarships, Educational Exchange.
[12] Oliver J. Caldwell: Unpublished speech.
[13] Cora DuBois: "Cross-Cultural Education," p. 331.

Thus almost every ramification of the program of the international exchange of students needs to be developed, for like the democratic educative process itself, it is dynamic and ever-unfolding. The needs are manifold: for trained and skillful foreign student advisers; for appropriate orientation; for the social integration of the student into "town and gown" environments; for establishing campus and community relationships; for proper housing accommodations; for adequate financing; and for basic research into the problems involved. They are all necessary if the desired objectives of the international student program are to be realized.

We have always assumed the exchange of students worthwhile. We have had an unquestioning faith in the presence of foreign students on our campuses as a valid method of contributing to international understanding and creating an international conscience. The potentialities of such a program are great. When people really understand each other, peace must and will ensue. This is the larger aim of the international student program. This is the ultimate aim of the democratic ethic.

BIBLIOGRAPHY

Attitudes of Foreign Students in Ten Orientation Centers in the Summer of 1951. Washington, D. C., U. S. Department of State, June, 1952. Mimeographed, 14 pp.

Aydelotte, Frank: *32nd Annual Report.* New York, Institute of International Education, 1951. 72 pp.

Bower, Robert T., McKenzie, Berta, and Winograd, Burton: *An Analysis of Attitude Changes Among German Exchangees.* Final Report. Philadelphia and Washington, D. C., Bureau of Social Science Research, The American University Institute for Research in Human Relations, August, 1951. Mimeographed, 126 pp.

Caldwell, Oliver, J.: Unpublished speech delivered at The New School for Social Research, New York, Spring, 1952.

DuBois, Cora: "Cross-Cultural Education," *Psychiatry* 15: Aug., 1952, pp. 330-332.

Handbook for Counselors of Students from Abroad. Prepared by Members of the Practicum for Foreign Student Advisers. New York, The National Association of Foreign Student Advisers, 1949. Mimeographed, 214 pp.

Holland, Kenneth: "The Foreign Student in the United States." In Edwin, Mary (Ed.): *American Universities and Colleges.* Washington, D. C., American Council on Education, 1952 (6th ed.), 105 pp.

Myrdal, Gunnar: *An American Dilemma: The Negro Problem and Modern Democracy.* Vol. I. New York, Harper & Brothers, 1944, 705 pp.

Kiell, Norman: *A Study of Attitudes of Indian and Pakistani Students Towards America and American Democracy.* Unpublished doctoral thesis. New York, Teachers College, Columbia University, 1949, 189 pp.

UNESCO: *Study Abroad.* International Handbook, Fellowships, Scholarships, Educational Exchange. Vol. V. New York, Columbia University Press and UNESCO Publication, 1952, 436 pp.

13. Financial Realities and Resources

PAUL G. BULGER

THE first reality to be faced by college or university administration and also by consumers of higher education is the fact that it costs money to run a college. This has always been true, but it seems much more pointed in these days when all costs are increasing.

Even with the increased enrollments during the first few years following World War II, colleges were hard pressed financially because of the demands for more staff, more buildings, and more equipment. The brief leveling-off period and the now evident upswing in enrollments have not brought a lessening of the pressures of money shortages, nor does it seem likely that these pressures will be relieved by the number of potential freshmen who are beginning to descend on the colleges.

What does it cost to operate our colleges and universities? About two billion dollars (gross) in 1950. What are the sources of these dollars?

. . . In the cases of the 800-odd public institutions, 60% of their 1950 income came from government (state and local) appropriations; about 35% from student fees; about 2% from current operating gifts; and 3% from miscellaneous sources. During the same year, the average for over 1200 private institutions was 70% from student fees; 12% from endowment earnings; 12% from current operating gifts; and about 6% from miscellaneous sources.[1]

Student fees in the private institutions account for twice as much income as in public institutions.

Carnegie Institute of Technology reports the following history of tuition charges:

[1] John D. Millet: *The Manual of Corporate Giving*, p. 208

215

1918	$ 75. per year
1927	$320. per year
1940	$400. per year
1946	$450. per year
1950	$600. per year
1953	$680. per year

The Institute points out that the tuition paid by the student is only 50 per cent of what it costs the institution per student. These are some of the financial realities facing the colleges.

Are we going to raise college tuition to where it balances the real dollar cost of educating a student? If this is done, what is going to happen to the higher educational opportunities for the children of low-income families?

Even in 1936, a study of 30,000 boys and girls in Pennsylvania by the American Youth Commission showed that out of every 1000 high school graduates, 174 did not go to college because they could not afford it. If tuition prices continue to go up, colleges will price themselves "out of the market." Financial assistance to students may be one of the answers. Certainly, with more and more people going to college from all the different social and economic groups, the need for financial aid to students is becoming a major problem, both for students and for college administrations.

The Need for More Funds for Student Financial Aid

Many of the privately supported colleges and universities and some of the public institutions of the country have "development plans," the objectives of which are to secure gifts and grants to further their educational programs and to seek assistance from alumni, corporations, foundations, and friends for scholarships, fellowships, research assistantships, and loan funds for students. Most institutions will readily admit that their funds for student aid in these various forms are too limited.

Fortunately, there is a great deal of interest in the support of student financial aid programs. This is manifested by both labor and management. A certain union, for example, has created scholarships at Columbia College of Columbia University for the sons of members, while a large automobile manufacturing company has made available generous scholarships for the sons and daughters of its employees. Those responsible for or concerned with the financial aid program in an institution will encourage such interest and see to it that the "development officer" or public relations staff is sensitive to the details of students' financial needs and works at building up of scholarship and endowment funds.

It is generally accepted that the prime responsibility of the colleges and universities of America is to help develop good citizens and leaders. A well-operated financial aid program for students should help achieve these purposes.

Millett points out, however, that:

. . . Financial assistance to individual students is financial assistance to the institution only under three conditions: (1) if the tuition charge is approximately equal to the real cost of the instruction afforded; (2) if the student who is assisted would not otherwise have enrolled and paid tuition, and the addition of this student's income does not entail a corresponding outlay in educational cost; or (3) if the corporation making a fellowship or scholarship award to a student makes a corresponding contribution to the operating income of a university.[2]

This represents an important problem for our national economy: how to keep our institutions of higher education financially sound so that they can continue to be seed beds for the leadership of our country. More attention is being given to this problem recently than ever before, but it is not the problem with which we are directly concerned in this discussion. Here we are concerned with the problems of cost as these confront the students themselves.

Costs to Students

The student is interested in going to college to get an education. How it is to be paid for is a problem not only for each college, which must solve its own financial difficulties, but also for the student and his family. Neither the student nor his parents usually recognize the fact that tuition fees do not pay the total cost of an education. They figure their budgets on the basis of what the college says it will charge them for tuition, housing, food, various fees, and other items. Whether or not a student goes to college or to a particular college may depend on the point of view he or his family takes toward these cost items.

Their point of view may also be affected by all that is said and written about financial help in the form of scholarships and fellow-

[2] *Ibid.*, p. 212.

ships, loan funds, partial payment tuition plans, part-time employment, etc. This information may not reach the student and his family in a way that helps them think through the problem of financing his education. Consequently, it is a challenge to the institution to offer financial information not only about its own resources but also about outside sources, and guidance that will put a carefully planned financial base under each student needing aid and will encourage as many as possible of the potential leaders to plan for and to come to college.

At the same time, it does not benefit the institution or the students to distribute financial aid "on a silver platter" for there is great value in the American way of accomplishment through one's own efforts. A sound financial aid program is one of assisting students, not of underwriting them.

It becomes clear as we work with students over the years that many of their problems stem from financial worries. These, of course, reflect in their work in the classroom, in the laboratory, in their social adjustment, and may actually interfere with many of their deeper learnings from campus life.

Financial Counseling

It is readily conceded that there is need for a program of financial counseling in every college or university. The individual or individuals who undertake this type of deeper teaching should be clearly aware of the financial resources of the institution, should have a rich knowledge of finance, preferably a background in finance, and a deep concern for the student and his development. They must be cognizant of the relationship of sound finances and sound mental health. This type of counseling should not be done per se but rather as providing an opportunity for the student to know himself, to evaluate his situation and his potentialities. Such counselors should be good teachers, "socially inspired" men or women, skilled in the medium of human relationships.

How does the counselor operate in a financial aid program? What are the bases for decision-making? How much aid should be given and to whom? Unfortunately, there are limited monies and job opportunities in most of our colleges. Should someone holding a fellowship be eligible for a loan or for part-time employment? Should aid be distributed as widely as possible or should it more adequately finance a limited number who merit it? And how should "merit" be defined? Should those who receive scholarships and fellowships (if they maintain institutional standards) automatically be granted one the following year?* Does the counselor wait for students to apply for aid or does he search out students in need of aid? If the institutional program operates as it should, students, the entire personnel staff, and faculty will become increasingly aware of existing possibilities for meeting the needs of students and of the students who have financial needs. How does this become a reality?

A student having financial problems perhaps needs a loan; perhaps a part-time job that would give him sufficient time for study yet provide needed income. Perhaps he needs to be guided toward making an application for a scholarship or fellowship; perhaps he needs to consider the possibility of dropping out of college and working for a time, saving his money, and returning; perhaps he should cut down his academic load in order to take a part-time job. What is best for the student and what will best assist his growth and development at any given point? A faculty adviser, a housing counselor, or others in close contact with the student should be aware of these problems and interested in how they can be solved. A counselor concerned with deeper teaching will be able to help the student's adviser and the student discover how the pieces fit together for the greater benefit of the student.

Organization

There are those who feel that a centralized office of financial aid (including responsibility for part-time work) is the answer to many of the questions listed above. Such proponents would have the central staff interview, investigate, and collect all data regarding applicants for various types of aid. In some instances, the director or head will make all decisions regarding the rejection or acceptance of an applicant; in others these decisions would rest with a committee (except, of course, in the case of part-time work). The argument is that this type of administration cuts down on costs, overlapping, inefficiency, and duplication of effort. Some advocate that a centralized office of this sort is an essential in a large university; that it is an impossibility for every department or even for every school or college to have its own financial resources or to administer them according to its own policies or whims; that it is fairer and more democratic to maintain a central administration; that a central office prevents the

*The Ford Foundation continues the scholarship support of students they have started on four-year programs.

student from shopping from office to office; that it equalizes competition between the larger schools or departments and the smaller units; that the gifted student in Latin or Chemistry is thus as likely to receive a scholarship or loan or part-time job as is the athlete.

On the other hand, dangers in the centralized setup must be recognized. There is some evidence that only the more aggressive or desperate students reach the central office. If this office does not have active lines of communication with faculty counselors, with housing counselors, with the various other members of the personnel staff, with all those of the institution who perhaps know the whole student, it will function in a mechanical way with little concern for the values or philosophy advocated in this chapter. How can any central financial office undertake to know many students, their financial anxieties, their problems resulting from these anxieties? How can such an office know whether these students truly deserve assistance, whether they deserve it as much as some students who have not the nerve to ask, and just which type of financial aid will contribute best to each student's development? It is apt to be a faculty counselor, a housing counselor, a member of the personnel staff, another student, or all of these working together, who know the student best, who must do the initial financial counseling and enlist the aid of the financial aid expert or encourage the student to seek his aid.

Committees of faculty and staff are invaluable in developing policies and in making final decisions regarding students who shall receive aid, for such decisions should not be made by any one individual, no matter how well trained or how capable he may be. Not only does a committee make it possible to share these important decisions, but the committee also may bring to itself as a member or consultant the individual on the personnel staff or faculty who knows the student applicant best. Few institutions have as yet given thought to the values of student participation in this important phase of student personnel work. It has been suggested by those who have tried it that student members on such a committee are likely to represent most accurately the trials and tribulations of their fellow students and are likely to be sound in their judgments, to say nothing of the learnings they themselves may gain from such committee experience.

The University of Oslo in Norway goes even further in student participation. There student loan committees have been operating since 1947. The University makes available a certain sum of money; this is administered in part by several student committees which look at the needs and attitudes of the applicants and then make recommendations to a student-faculty committee.[3]

The committee administering loans or scholarships and fellowships will do a better job if it has access to the kind of records on the applicants that are discussed in Chapter 5, "How Records Contribute to Deeper Teaching." Records showing the student's background, development, educational experiences, educational goals, his self-understanding, insight, and self-direction will help immeasurably in making the right decisions.

A part of the record system which is not utilized to its greatest potentialities is the admission application. Traditionally, we look at almost every phase of the student's personality, character, and scholastic qualifications before admitting him. Yet few admission committees have done any thinking and planning with the student as to how he is going to finance his program of study and living. Why do we not include, as a part of our application form, a request for a statement of personal finances and financial plans? This would give faculty counselors and the student personnel staff immediate access to those in need of guidance and help, often before their problems become too acute.

Whatever the type of administration of student financial aid in the college or university, whether central office, departmental counseling, committee, or any combination of these, we cannot overemphasize how important it is for any institution to have a definite philosophy of student aid and to have clear and definite policies. These policies should be worked out in terms of the objectives of the college, its resources for aid, and the percentage of the student body who need and are worthy of assistance. There should also be a close relationship between financial counseling, the administration of aid, and the financial office of the institution. All three need a clear understanding of the policies and practices of the others. All should have a share in the setting and modification of these policies and practices.

Scholarships and Fellowships

Scholarships and fellowships are usually outright gifts awarded to students on the bases of scholastic ability and promise for the future as determined by reports, recommendations, and examinations. There is a tendency to weigh ability against need in the granting of this

[3] James A. Storing: "Student Aid in Norway."

type of aid. Competition is usually keen for awards offered by institutions, by corporations, foundations, and other groups. The financial personnel officer of the institution can do much to soften the refusal of applications for scholarships and fellowships, and to offer encouragement and frank advice where this is warranted. A rejection letter may well include an invitation to confer with the financial counselor whenever this is possible.*

Loans

Some feel that higher education is not an inherent right of the student of average intelligence to be paid for by society at large, but rather a valuable privilege that should be paid for by the individual himself. They therefore advocate more use of loan funds and fewer out-and-out grants. There is no doubt that some students place a higher value on a fund that must be returned, that loans can give valuable financial and business training to the student, and that the obligation of repayment eliminates the idea held by many students that society should "hand them" an education.

Lloyd-Jones and Smith state that:

Applicants for loans are usually considered on the bases of: (1) present need, determined by the analysis of application blank, containing budgets and a clear statement of present financial circumstances, and a personal conference; (2) future ability and willingness to repay the loan, estimated by intelligence and talent as judged by scholastic standing and examinations; (3) enterprise, which may be ascertained by what he is doing to help himself; (4) health, which is rated by a physical examination and the student's present record: (5) integrity and reliability, estimated by past performance in the home community and the college or university community. These are the usual criteria on which evidence and information are sought in the loan application blank. Past performances in the home and college community are evaluated through references. . . .[4]

Some institutions make it a policy to secure commercial credit agency reports on all applicants for loans, in fact on all applicants for any type of aid, except part-time jobs. These reports are relatively

* A discussion of scholarship and fellowship application blanks and the type of information needed is available in Lloyd-Jones and Smith's A Student Personnel Program for Higher Education, p. 152. Wrenn's Student Personnel Work in College, p. 362 calls attention to Feingold's sample application form: S. Norman Feingold: Scholarships, Fellowships and Loans. Boston, Bellman Publishing Co., Boston, 1949, pp. 19-21.

[4] Esther Lloyd-Jones and Margaret Ruth Smith: A Student Personnel Program for Higher Education, p. 153.

inexpensive and are usually sound in their analysis of the individual's financial status. This same source of information may well be used in determining what to do about delinquent loan accounts. At any rate, some form of follow-up on loan payments should be worked out to provide a system that is exact, precise, and prompt but at the same time takes into account the difficulties a former student may have in repaying.

Collegiate institutions are not banks in the sense that they are not dealing primarily with the financial picture. Modern banks use some methods, however, that colleges might well imitate. Anyone applying for a loan from a reputable loan agency will be impressed by the care and skill of the personnel handling loans. The same friendly yet business like procedure can operate on the collegiate level, initiating the student into procedures based on sound business policy. Often the student can be led to see the value in borrowing so that he will not have to work and thus delay, say, his graduation date; and he may come to recognize that he is making an investment in himself which should be a sound one. The securing of a loan can be a truly educational experience on the part of the student.

It is usually the practice to charge a low rate of interest while the student is in college and then to step it up upon graduation and maintain the increased rate during the period of repayment. The interest received from loans may offset to some degree the loans that are not repaid.

The total amount loaned to a student and the length of time for repayment must be considered in the light of the student's educational and occupational objectives. Each case should be considered individually even though hard-and-fast rules are much easier to administer.

Those who know and work with students will find that an emergency loan fund which involves no more than a bare minimum of "red-tape" is essential for solving certain student problems. A small loan may sometimes mean the difference between triumph and defeat. This type of fund should be available to all who work closely with students and should be so administered that the money may go into student hands with little or no delay.

Part-time Work

Part-time work offered by most colleges and universities has contributed its share to the belief that anyone of average ability and health can earn a college education. On the other hand, careful counseling will point out that there are health hazards involved, that excessive time devoted to self-support may produce a demoralizing effect on scholastic standing and social contacts, and that many of the fringe benefits of college life may have to be sacrificed. The institution itself may suffer if the number of self-supporting students is so great that the available means of assistance is spread too thinly, and if a disproportionately large number of self-supporting students (in a sense part-time students) tend to turn the college into a part-time institution. Too large a number of such students will jeopardize the outside-the-classroom and social life of the college. It is true also that an excessive number of students in competition for jobs makes it possible for employers to take advantage of the student market.

Part-time jobs are a part of the whole financial aid picture. They should be seen, however, not only as a form of financial aid, but also as a part of a student's total strategy for learning and strengthening himself. Counseling for part-time employment will include personal budget-making which will guide the student in deciding whether he should take a job. Often a loan, or a scholarship, or even staying out of school to earn may be a better answer to a student's problems, rather than a job which may handicap his best and most rapid development.

A wise financial aid counselor handling part-time employment must be a person of imagination who can understand people and create jobs; he must coordinate his work with the admission and placement policies of the institution, and wherever possible he should relate the employment to the student's educational and vocational objectives. He will recognize that department heads, faculty members, and others will frequently have calls for students to fill openings and that these staff individuals will often know the right students for the right jobs to a greater degree than he can.

Cooperative Housing

There are some who feel that a cooperative housing program is a distinct part of the financial aid picture, particularly in its educational or deeper teaching possibilities. It offers not only an opportunity to save money on living costs, but a grand experience in living and working together. The college that will assist students in maintaining a high standard program of cooperative housing will contribute not only to financial assistance but also to the growth of its students in a very real way.*

Conclusion

In a collegiate financial aid program the needs of students for financial counseling or teaching are an important and first consideration. All faculty and staff members should be sensitized to its educational potentialities and to its philosophy and policies. Student participation in reviewing its philosophy, policies, and operation will not only result in their gain in wisdom but also will contribute to the good of the institution. In order to derive the deeper learnings with which this book is concerned, financial aid becomes a counseling process rather than merely a service of appropriating money to students. Its philosophy, policies, and operation must be considered in terms of the individual student, his abilities, needs, and hopes, his life in college, his vocational future following graduation, and how such assistance may contribute to his development, as well as in the light of the objectives of the institution and its resources for financial aid.

BIBLIOGRAPHY

A *Partial Bibliography of Materials Related to: I References on Loans, Fellowships, Scholarships, and the Exchange of Persons Programs. II Materials on Counseling, Guidance, and Program Planning for Persons Working with Students, Teachers, Leaders, and Professors from Other Lands.* Prepared by Thomas E. Cotner, Chief, and John W. Grissom, Research Assistant, Educational Exchange Section, International Educational Programs Branch, Federal Security Agency, Office of Education, Washington, D. C., 1952.

Falvey, Frances E.: *Student Participation in College Administration.* New York, Bureau of Publications, Teachers College, Columbia University, 1952.

Hungate, Thad Lewis: *Financing the Future of Higher Education.* New York, Bureau of Publications, Teachers College, Columbia University, 1946.

Lloyd-Jones, Esther, and Smith, Margaret Ruth: *A Student Personnel Program for Higher Education.* New York, McGraw-Hill Book Co., 1938.

Millett, John D.: "Higher Education," in *The Manual of Corporate*

* See Chapter 11, "Where and How Students Live."

Giving. Kingsport, Tennessee, National Planning Association, 1952. Chapters 10 and 11.

Pollard, F. G., and Sharpe, Russell T.: "Student Financial Aid," in W. S. Monroe (ed.): *Encyclopedia of Educational Research.* New York, The Macmillan Co., 1950, pp. 1347-53.

Sharpe, Russell T., et. al.: *Financial Assistance for College Students.* Washington, D. C., American Council on Education Studies, Series VI, Student Personnel Work, No. 7, 1946.

Smith, Margaret Ruth: *Student Aid: Bases of Selection of Students to whom Loans, Scholarships and Fellowships Are Awarded in a Graduate School of Education.* New York, Bureau of Publications, Teachers College, Columbia University, 1937.

Storing, James A.: "Student Aid in Norway," in I. L. Kendel (ed.): *School and Society,* Lancaster, Pennsylvania, The Society for the Advancement of Education, Inc., Vol. 75, 1952, pp. 310-313.

Wilkins, Theresa Birch: *Scholarships and Fellowships Available at Institutions of Higher Education.* Washington, D. C., Federal Security Agency, Office of Education, Bulletin 1951, No. 16.

Wrenn, C. Gilbert: *Student Personnel Work in College.* New York, The Ronald Press Company, 1951.

14. Moving Toward Marriage and Family Living

MARY F. LANGMUIR

B Y THE time they reach college age, all students have moved far towards the kinds of marriage and family life they will create in their own homes. This is true because the attitudes and expectations, the needs and defenses, the hopes and fears which they will take into marriage and parenthood are already deeply rooted in their personalities. Even though students do change and become more mature during the college years, their basic character structures remain amazingly constant.

The "precept and deeper teaching" which can help college men and women achieve sound and good relationships in marriage and family will recognize this fact. Marriage is essentially a relationship. Education for marriage very literally begins at birth. Much that is learned and believed in childhood must be unlearned in maturity. This is particularly true as far as feelings about oneself, one's parents, one's brothers and sisters, and friends of the same and opposite sex are concerned. Unexamined and unconscious expectations of relationships and roles which all children carry out of childhood into maturity can seriously interfere with fulfillment and realistic satisfactions in marriage and family living. In a fundamental sense, preparation for marriage and family living at the college level is emotional re-education. This is essential for all students, not just for those who are having difficulties in adjustments and relationships in the immediate college environment.

Emphasis on the importance of relationships and experiences in childhood does not mean that little can be done to help students as they move closer to marriage—or begin their marriages—during their college years. What can be done, and what needs to be done, is crucial. It does mean, however, that colleges cannot depend primarily on lectures, textbooks, and traditional courses to meet the needs of students as they grow toward emotional maturity and self-understanding.

Fortunately for education at all levels—but particularly for college and professional education—we are learning at long last that there is no necessary correlation between academic success and competence in human relationships, between intellectual development and emotional maturity. In fact, knowing the "answers," mastering principles and theories can make it harder rather than easier to live wisely and generously in marriage, and to succeed in that closest and most complex of all human relationships. Impatience with the long, slow process of change in oneself, one's marriage partner, and one's children is a major source of difficulty in the family lives of many college graduates. College education is not, of course, solely responsible for such impatience. But liberal arts education fails in its most important obligation if and when it does not help students develop tolerance, understanding, insight—and patience.

How the college as a whole can assist students to move toward successful adjustments in marriage and family living is inevitably a complex and multidimensional problem. As has already been suggested, helping students achieve the self-understanding and emotional maturity which are essential to all good human relationships is not primarily a matter of courses in psychology, child development, and marriage and the family. Such courses can be useful and helpful, however, and should be included in all college and university curricula. To be most effective, they should be planned cooperatively, offered in several departments, and open to students with a minimum of prerequisites. Different approaches, different methods, and different materials are valuable and necessary.

Regardless of the method or the approach, however, all courses which are designed to help students understand themselves and the problems which are part of growing up and family living must be made relevant to the problems these students are facing, and the realities of their lives. There are special problems of adjustment before marriage, in marriage, and outside of marriage which belong uniquely to growing up and coming to maturity in mid-century America. If students are to be educated and re-educated effectively for emotional maturity there must be recognition on the part of faculty and administrative and personnel officers that patterns of growing up, of marriage and family life, have changed—and are still changing.

More Students Are Marrying Early

It is not possible to describe or evaluate all problems of the pre-marriage or the marriage relationships of today's college students. The data are not yet available. At the same time one trend is definite and unmistakable. It is certain that at least for the next decade an increasing number of students will marry before they complete their college courses. Women's colleges, men's colleges, and universities are currently reporting marriages of more undergraduate students than ever before. The draft, the inevitable delay in completing education or getting established in business or the professions, anxiety and uncertainty about war and the future are all factors contributing to the present trend toward earlier marriage among college students.

Two definite patterns of student marriage have already become clear. The *weekend marriage* is now a commonplace on campuses all over the country. Young husbands and wives continue in residence in their respective colleges but spend as many weekends together as distance, finances, and their studies permit. The second pattern, the *shared residence and study marriage*, finds the undergraduate wife combining housekeeping and a regular academic program. Her undergraduate or graduate student husband may or may not combine studying and part-time employment.

In marriages of both kinds the parents of the student husband and student wife usually continue to pay for tuition and board and room. Thus more and more parents are helping finance the beginning of a marriage at the same time that they are finishing paying for their son's or daughter's college education. It is also frequently a part of the same pattern that parents take care of a grandchild while a daughter completes a last term or year of college. There is, of course, nothing really new about the parent generation helping out the college generation in marriage or with grandchildren. What *is* new is that the patterns of marriage which have been considered "normal" for graduate students at least since World War I are now becoming "normal" for more and more undergraduate students. The problems of adjustment and relationship are again not new, but they are having to be met by young husbands and wives at an earlier age and in the face of a particularly uncertain future.

This trend toward earlier marriage obviously suggests that the more familiar, more leisurely pattern of getting acquainted while in college, of enjoying the companionship of many different students before becoming engaged to one, of longer engagements, of waiting for marriage until after graduation can no longer be taken for granted by parents or colleges. As long as military service must be reckoned with, the present trend will doubtless continue. Very possibly it is here to stay.

Emotional Maturity Is Essential in Marriage

In spite of earlier marriages and the changing patterns of undergraduate life, the important question with respect to marriage is not *how* soon or *when* but always *how ready* for the relationships and responsibilities of family living. Readiness for marriage at whatever age is essentially a matter of emotional maturity—of the capacity to give love and to receive love, the ability to establish a close, mutually satisfying, supporting and creative relationship. Some students are "ready" at twenty. Others will not be ready, unless they receive prolonged psychotherapy, at fifty.

It is in this aspect of personality development—the capacity to relate well to other people—that the experiences and relationships of childhood are so crucial. It is important for all faculty and all administrative officers—not just for counselors—to realize that students bring to college as part of their unique personalities what the late Karen Horney[1] has called a "basic strategy" or way of life. This strategy was gradually developed in the years of early childhood as each student learned to cope with the demands and requirements of an adult world which even at best was often difficult and frequently hostile. The three basic strategies which children in our culture develop, according to Dr. Horney, are to move *toward* people, or to move *against* people, or to move *from* people. All individuals, including children, inevitably find themselves moving now in one direction, now in another in the normal give-and-take of family life, college life, or social life generally. What Dr. Horney meant by basic strategy, however, was something quite definite and very significant. She meant that a child may become, essentially and characteristically, a *compliant* person (moving *toward*), an *aggressive* person (moving *against*), or a *detached* person (moving *from*) in all his or her relationships with other people. She also meant that a basic strategy once developed and intrenched, so to speak, in the personality can seriously

[1] Karen Horney: *Our Inner Conflicts.*

limit a person in his fullest development. Thus any inflexible way of relating can keep an individual from responding to people and events in terms of the actual realities of relationships and situations. It can condemn an adult to using, over and over again, even in his own marriage and family relationships, a strategy or defense that grew out of the dependence and helplessness of his childhood.

Another helpful way of describing general personality types which are to be found in the present generation of undergraduates grew out of an intensive study of adolescents in a typical midwestern city. Robert Havighurst and Hilda Taba,[2] in reporting on the individual adolescents studied, discuss the characteristics of the *adaptive person* and the *submissive person*. These appear to be two different aspects of Horney's "compliant personality." They also describe the *self-directive person* who is much like the "detached" personality who characteristically moves away from people. Horney's "aggressive personality" who moves against people is similar to the *defiant person* of the Havighurst and Taba study. Their fifth type is the *unadjusted person* who is familiar in every dormitory on every campus.

It is not necessary to be in complete agreement about these particular formulations of personality types to find them useful, helpful, and illuminating. While no individual is ever a "pure" type, all students and faculty alike do have characteristic ways of getting along or not getting along with people. Students are necessarily influenced by the emotional and social climates which are created in the total fabric of interpersonal relationships in any college or university. In general terms impersonal, strongly competitive, authoritarian environments are destructive of good interpersonal relationships. On the other hand objective, but friendly and cooperative, nonauthoritarian atmospheres can and do foster better interpersonal relationships. These quite different climates are to be found—in varying degrees—in classrooms, departments, dormitories, and administrative offices of every institution.

Attention has been called to the fact that students bring to college basically different ways of relating to other people because this fact is relevant to the whole problem of emotional maturity and emotional re-education. As a rule, for example, self-directive students prove to be "successful" in college. Such students have strong drives, high standards for achievement, and the need to excel. They already

[2] R. J. Havighurst and H. Taba.: *Adolescent Character and Personality*, Chapter 11.

have, or easily acquire, the important academic values of detachment, objectivity, and excellence. Their approach to life, including relationships, becomes characteristically intellectual and impersonal. They are considered very mature and they consider themselves mature. The fact that long ago in childhood they may have learned to move "away from" people in part because their early childhood needs for closeness and affection and acceptance were not met is overlooked.

All colleges today are being forced to deal with an increasing number of students who need psychiatric or counseling services because of these very unmet needs. One of the most important developments in terms of the total education of students is the gradual improvement of academic and personal counseling—not just for acutely "unadjusted" students but for all students. The increasing number, for example, whose parents have been divorced can be expected to have special adjustment problems in college. Other students who grew up in homes where there was "emotional divorce,"[3] if not actual divorce, often have even more acute difficulty in adjusting to the freedom and responsibilities of college life.

To return to self-directive students, college education all too often reinforces their childhood pattern of isolation and detachment instead of helping free them to become truly mature, both intellectually and emotionally. The successful, self-directive students—particularly women—usually have very special problems in relation both to marriage and emotional maturity. They may be women for whom marriage and family life must be postponed until they have "achieved." Or they may marry before they have reached their "goals," expecting quite confidently that it will be "easy" to combine housekeeping, marriage, children, and a career. With overconfidence in the intellectual and objective approach to life, they believe—and have been taught to believe—"that any intelligent woman can learn how to keep house or bring up children when she needs to." For many reasons self-directive students typically avoid counseling in college, or discussion of their personal relationships. They look down upon and avoid what on most campuses are still considered to be the "nonintellectual," "nonacademic" subjects of child study, personality development, marriage, and the family. They inevitably go into marriage emotionally unprepared and with impossible and unrealistic expectations.

[3] See J. Louise Despert, M.D.: *Children of Divorce.*

All students do not need "courses"—or counseling—in order to move successfully toward marriage and family living. Also, many courses in family relationships are not well taught, that is in ways which are relevant to the present and future needs of students. Yet whenever college women do successfully combine work and marriage we may be sure that they are emotionally mature, are "adaptive" as well as "self-directive" individuals. They were either students who through childhood and all their growing years were becoming emotionally mature, or they were students whose college experiences helped in their emotional re-education along with their intellectual training and development. Somehow, naturally or with special help, they developed the capacity to give love and to receive love, to establish close and creative relationships.

Married Students Have Special Needs

It is not yet known whether the students who marry in college are more likely to be "self-directive," "submissive," "aggressive," "adaptive," or "unadjusted" persons. Nor is it yet known how many of these early marriages will prove to be successful or unsuccessful. What evidence there is, however, suggests that marriages of students still in college are not essentially different from later marriages in the number of problems, the kinds of satisfactions, and the likelihood of success and failure.

For purposes of this discussion the important point about student marriages is that they provide college personnel officers and faculty with unprecedented opportunity to learn from students themselves what college education can and should contribute to preparation for marriage and family life. Both the married and the unmarried students are deeply concerned with problems of sexual adjustment, relationships between men and women, and continuing needs for individual fulfillment.

Before, as well as after graduation, they have many questions about the effectiveness of their college education in preparing them for personal, community, and family living. Because problems of adjustment and relationships are particularly acute in our modern world, students should be invited to help evaluate the strengths and weaknesses of college curricula, methods of teaching, extracurricular activities, counseling services, and all aspects of college life from the point of view of preparation for social and emotional maturity. Students know—even if faculty and administrators often do not seem to know—that the world in which they will finish their education, marry, bring up their children, and carry on their work is changing and has changed. They feel that their future is now and they mean to have it, whether they are prepared or not.

There is real evidence that the present generations of college students are both more realistic and more idealistic than their parents and teachers were at the same ages. By and large today's students are not afraid to take on family responsibilities early. They are willing to work hard and live frugally. They expect to do their own work and take care of their own children. They are prepared to move as often as the dictates of military service require. Obviously, in spite of their willingness, young husbands and wives cannot meet these responsibilities, and face these problems of adjustment and relationship, without more realistic help than is available in most colleges and universities today.

Since the problems of the married students are the problems most students will face sooner or later, the married students now in college should be invited to cooperate in a serious and thorough study of all aspects of their marriages. There can be no question about their readiness and willingness to cooperate.

As an example of student interest and concern, two seniors at Vassar College* made a study of what they call "the reasons for the apparently increasing number of 'young marrieds' in eastern women's liberal arts colleges." With the help of faculty and other students they prepared a comprehensive questionnaire which was sent to all married students in nine eastern women's colleges.

There was a total of 225 married girls in the following nine colleges: Barnard, 68; Bryn Mawr, 15; Connecticut, 7; Mount Holyoke, 2; Pembroke, 19; Radcliffe, 44; Smith, 20; Vassar, 24; Wellesley, 26.

These Vassar College seniors summarize the results of their study as follows:

Most of the girls were married either the summer before or during their senior year and planned to finish work for their Bachelor's degrees. Most of them were between 20 and 22 years of age, and the majority of the husbands were between 21 and 26 years of age. The majority of the girls had known their husbands from 1 to 3 years before marriage, and they were married in a church ceremony. In most cases the husband and wife agreed on religious preference. Love and the military services were the main factors influencing the girls to marry before finishing

*Jane Bollwinkel and Virginia Clark, Vassar '53.

college, and it was a desire for a degree that made most of them decide to return to college after their marriage. The majority of both sets of parents (the larger percentage in the boy's sets—probably because of their being older) definitely approved of the marriage plans. A very few of them reported that they eloped because of parental disapproval. Few of the girls were influenced by the example of others combining marriage and study in making their own decision, according to what they said.

The husbands' occupations were fairly evenly distributed in the categories of student, business, and military service, with the largest number being students, followed by businessmen. Nearly all of the husbands had attended college, and the majority plan to get graduate degrees. The majority of the girls are financed by combined husband and parental support or by total parental aid.

Most of the girls who are not married to service men live with their husbands. Only a few girls live in college residence.

Most of the girls' marks have either stayed the same or improved with marriage. Marriage has limited their extra-curricular participation, however. Not many of the girls mentioned academic problems that had arisen, and few felt that the faculty-administration and student attitude were different toward them.

Several have children and a few more are expecting them.

Most of the girls will be working or studying in the immediate future, and most of their plans for the distant future include keeping house and raising a family.

These girls report that they find their combination of marriage and study difficult and time consuming, but entirely worthwhile and rewarding.

Surely there is no better way to help college students as they move toward marriage and family living than to invite their active and responsible participation in formulating their problems and seeking better solutions.

BIBLIOGRAPHY

Despert, J. Louise: *Children of Divorce*. Garden City, N. Y., Doubleday, 1953.

Gruenberg, Sidonie M., and Krech, Hilda Sidney: *The Many Lives of Modern Woman*. Garden City, N. Y., Doubleday, 1952.

Havighurst, R. J., and Taba, H.: *Adolescent Character and Personality*. New York, J. Wiley, 1949.

Horney, Karen: *Our Inner Conflicts*. New York, Norton, 1945.

15. *Planning Vocationally and Finding a Job*

MARION J. CROSBY

IT IS the purpose of vocational guidance to help an individual understand himself in relation to the role he must fulfill in the world of work and to acquire information about the various occupations which may be open to him. Equipped with such knowledge he is better able to choose a vocation in which he can best use his particular talents, and make sound educational plans to secure the training essential for entrance into his chosen field. Ultimately, of course, the aim of vocational guidance is successful placement in a job which will give the individual an opportunity for growth, productivity, and advancement commensurate with his abilities.

When should an individual begin thinking about his choice of a vocation? In junior high school boys and girls must decide what courses to take in high school. This choice will determine to a great extent the vocational opportunities that will be open to them. It is desirable, therefore, if vocational guidance can be introduced at this level. It is too early then, of course, to make final decisions; rather, thinking should be in terms of broad fields rather than specific jobs. Each occupational field offers a variety of positions requiring different degrees of ability and training, and at almost every stage one can branch off into any one of several directions.

In high school vocational guidance and placement is still more important than in junior high school. Many students will discontinue their formal education and seek employment immediately after, or perhaps even before, graduation. Yet an increasing number of students now go on to institutions of higher learning for liberal arts, or specialized vocational and professional training. The individual who has started making vocational plans in high school is in a much better position to choose a college wisely and to profit by higher education.

Our economy is a complex one and vocational planning and training are no longer family affairs. Parents often lack realistic information about work opportunities and requirements essential for various occupations. Moreover, many young people want to enter "glamor" fields. They believe they possess certain talents which they do not in fact have. They assume the abilities and qualifications they desire and are often encouraged in this by relatives and amateur counselors. Statistics show that young people generally aspire to occupations in the middle and upper categories of the occupational scale. What is more significant, the majority of them do not achieve such goals, either because they do not have the ability to compete successfully in overcrowded fields, or because they find it impossible to secure the necessary training. Many times students have no conception of the duties to be performed on a job; nor do they know whether actual satisfactions to be derived from certain types of work are the satisfactions they hope to get out of life. Most individuals can succeed and be happy in any one of several vocations. But happiness and success do not automatically follow if the choice is left entirely to luck. Consequently, colleges have had to assume more and more responsibility for providing the information necessary to help individuals choose wisely and prepare adequately for their life work.

Placement service is also important, since an increasing number of well-educated young people become available for employment each year. A college education is no longer at a premium and a diploma is no guarantee of a job. Many find it necessary to get additional training in business or professional schools, or to accept positions they consider beneath them. Every placement director has heard the complaint, "I didn't go to college four years to do that!" Yet one has to face facts. Of the 60,000,000 workers in this country, four-fifths of them do work that does not require a college degree. This is bound to create problems for young people who have been taught to aim at the higher occupational levels. Furthermore, without guidance many graduates find the transition from college to work difficult. Some drift aimlessly and take the first job offered them. Others become disillusioned and ask, "What is wrong with me that I cannot find a job? Or with my college education that it did not prepare me to earn a living? Or with our economic structure that offers no outlet for my creative abilities?" It should be possible at the present time for everyone to find a job. Moreover, everyone should be able to find some satisfactions in socially useful work at whatever level. He must have, however, a realistic attitude toward what he can do and what there is to be done. It is the responsibility of the college through its vocational guidance program to help the individual develop this attitude.

Institutions offering graduate study have a similar obligation to their students. It is often assumed that guidance and placement service is no longer essential at this level but this is not always the case. Within every field of specialization, be it engineering, law, psychology, or chemistry, there are many different jobs to be done, some few opportunities for employment. Vocational choices tend to become narrower once the individual has chosen his major field. He needs to appraise his assets and liabilities even more carefully in relation to the requirements essential for success. Possession of a master's degree will not ensure employment or success, and unless the individual has developed fully as a person and has received adequate training and guidance he may still become a vocational misfit.

Coordination of Vocational Guidance and Placement Services

In the undergraduate college vocational guidance and placement can be handled most effectively through a bureau working in cooperation with the administration and major departments to serve the entire student body. The work is greatly facilitated if the administrative structure of the college allows for this special department of vocational guidance and placement services. If this is impossible, and in many cases it is very difficult, then functional coordination may be achieved by an informal organization of those doing various phases of this work. In either case, coordination of vocational guidance and placement is important both because it avoids unnecessary duplication of effort and, at the same time, allows the student to develop his vocational plans consistently through a well-organized four-year program. In the liberal arts college counselors must discuss opportunities and make placements in a wide variety of fields—advertising, merchandising, publishing, teaching, scientific research— with special emphasis on trainee positions for beginning students. Many institutions also maintain graduate placement service for alumni. The problems encountered at each level are similar and can usually be handled in the same bureau.

In the universities vocational guidance and placement services tend to become more specialized. At this level counselors need information about opportunities and positions available for professionally trained individuals—nurses, lawyers, engineers, librarians—many of whom often are mature persons with a great deal of experience as well as graduate training. No one centralized bureau could possibly do an equally good job in placing graduates from the various schools. Each major department or school of the university is usually best equipped to handle the guidance and placement of its own students. In many instances it is not a full-time job and can be handled by teachers or administrators on a part-time basis. It is important, however, that they not only be experts in their own field, but that they have the student personnel point of view in order to take adequate account of the needs of the individual as well as the demands of the profession. It is also important that these decentralized agents for vocational guidance and placement have the technical, advisory, and coordinating help that can be given them by one or more specialists in vocational guidance and placement.

The Liberal Arts College

Vocational guidance has an important role to play in the liberal arts college. This type of institution is better fitted than any other to develop the "whole person." But in many instances colleges have failed to keep pace with changing conditions. Intellectual and cultural traditions still prevail, as indeed they should, but not to the extent that vocational planning is excluded. Education should not be either cultural or vocational. It should be both. For if a choice has to be made, many practical young men and women know that they must be prepared to earn a living even if they do not acquire the cultural background, broad interests, and social conscience that the liberal arts education offers. Instead they choose a practical course of study leading to immediate employment. This might not be necessary if the college would take responsibility for providing adequate vocational guidance.

In the liberal arts college the vocational guidance counselor needs a broad understanding of human nature and behavior as well as specialized training in testing, interviewing, and counseling. He must also have a fund of information concerning occupational opportunities available to young people, and, if possible, business or industrial experience. His first responsibility is, of course, to the student, but every specialist must realize that the best interests of the student are served only when counselors, teachers, and administrators work together. Consequently, he must always be on the alert to avoid the dangers inherent in specialization and centralization of services, or he may find himself conducting a limited program isolated from other college activities. This is not likely to happen if he is clearly related to other aspects of the student personnel program through definite administrative arrangements. There should, of course, be functional coordination among personnel officers, and regular and full cooperation of those in charge of admissions, educational counseling, psychological testing, curriculum planning, social activities, public relations, alumni programs, and of course faculty members. This is a big assignment, but each staff member has information which is invaluable to the others. Each must see his own job as an integral part of an educational program whose broader aim is to assist the individual to develop all his potentialities for successful living.

Students benefit immeasurably when there is close cooperation between vocational counselors and faculty members, particularly those who do educational counseling. It is extremely important that each understand the point of view of the other. Vocational counselors should realize that educational counselors are quite right in advising students to choose courses in which they are genuinely interested and which will give them a broad background. If vocational planning at the liberal arts level is essential, educational counselors should realize their responsibility also for advising students to take courses which will be of practical value in securing employment immediately following graduation. Vocational counselors can be very helpful to members of the curriculum committee by suggesting courses that should be offered to give the students the best possible vocational preparation at this level. It is not the function of the liberal arts college to offer specialized vocational training. However, some practical courses may be included and regular courses taught in such a way that the vocational implications are stressed.

The Faculty Member's Contribution

Faculty members in their turn have much to contribute to the counselor's understanding of the student. They see him in the classroom, observe what use he makes of his intelligence, discover special abilities and skills, note his work habits, his attitudes toward criticism, his relationship to other members of the group. Much of this information cannot be obtained from tests, individual interviews, or the counseling situation. Instructors can also be of help to the placement office by passing on the names of employers in their special fields who may have positions available. Usually the best interests of all are served if all information about students and jobs is assembled by the placement officer. He should get in touch with the employers in order to get an accurate picture of the job requirements and then refer the students who are best qualified for the position.

Use of Records

Specialized vocational counselors and placement officers should, of course, become the beneficiaries of whatever personnel record system the college has developed. Records that grow out of the kind of plan which Shepard and Omer describe in Chapter 5 are of great value to the vocational expert as he tries to contribute further to a student's understanding and planning. The person with adequate professional training for his responsibilities in vocational guidance will understand how to interpret and use constructively, both for the student and for society as represented by prospective employers, the accumulative information in the students' personnel records. Furthermore, the vocational officer, from his relationships with students and employers, will accumulate further experience and information which he will organize as meaningfully as possible in further record entries.

The Alumni Secretary

In many small colleges the jobs of placement director and alumni secretary are one and the same; and if not, there should be a close relationship between the two. To offer continuing guidance and placement service to alumni is one of the best ways to maintain an active alumni association, which can be a great asset to the college as a whole and to the placement office in particular. Some of the most worthwhile career conferences are run by alumni associations. Successful alumni have much to contribute in the way of advice to beginning students, and are many times potential employers.

Public Relations

Vocational guidance, particularly through its placement work, offers one of the best means, and often one of the least used, for the furtherance of good public relations between the college and the community. There is a big job to be done in bringing about better understanding between colleges and industry. Colleges too often become "ivory towers" and fail to understand the employer's point of view; while some employers, in their insistence upon securing employees who have been technically trained, may fail to understand the broader function of education, which aims at developing all the potentialities of the individual, not just his vocational aptitudes. College placement bureaus, as most employment managers know, offer one of the best sources for generally excellent recruits. It is the responsibility of the placement director to bring the "right" person and the "right" job together, so that individuals who are socially and economically of great potential value may be utilized in the most productive way for the benefit of the individual, the employer, and also of the community.

Vocational Guidance Courses and Counseling

If these ideals are to be realized, long-term planning is essential. Vocational guidance should begin in the freshman year and continue through college. It is desirable if it can be designed as a regular course with students meeting once a week, with attendance required, at least until the individual has demonstrated that he is capable of making wise vocational plans and carrying them out. Work during the first two years should include a general introduction to the field, a survey of the various occupations of interest to college graduates, problems involved in self-analysis, and finally a comparison of both subjective and objective factors considered important in choosing a vocation. During the last two years students should concentrate on preparation for placement, first in a general way by exploring employment possibilities, studying company policies, job requirements and duties, salary scales, and promotional opportunities. By the senior year students should register for placement, assemble references, write letters of application, prepare for interviews, and ultimately choose the job which seems to offer the greatest number of satisfactions as well as the best opportunity for personal growth.

While self-analysis and occupational analysis are fundamentally inseparable, it is perhaps helpful for the student to look first at himself and attempt to discover his own abilities, interests, and values before beginning the study of vocations. This part of the program should be conducted by a person qualified to handle personality problems, perhaps a professor from the psychology department or the person in charge of psychological counseling. Much of the introductory material can be presented effectively through lectures and classroom discussions, supplemented by reading assignments and term papers presenting autobiographical data. Of course, in the final analysis personality adjustment is an individual matter and each student should be given an opportunity to discuss his own particular problems with a counselor. In the beginning, however, group discussions can be very valuable. Students are often surprised and relieved to find their problems shared by others.

Group tests may be administered provided the college is adequately staffed to handle such an extensive program. However, unless these can be interpreted individually they are relatively useless from the guidance standpoint. If the results are used by the student's counselor they may, of course, prove of value in alerting him to possible strengths and weaknesses, interests, and anxieties of which he might well be aware as he attempts to counsel with the student. If a program of group tests is not feasible, it may be left to the discretion of the counselor to decide after talking with the student whether special tests should be given. If so, there are many types of personality, intelligence, interest, and aptitude tests to choose from, depending on the individual's need. If used wisely the results of these tests may be helpful to the individual in his self-analysis. The presence or absence of certain traits and attitudes is sometimes significant in suggesting the kind of satisfactions he may find in various of the vocations. Correlations found to date, however, are not sufficiently high to warrant prediction of success or failure in any given vocation. If personality tests reveal evidence of serious neurosis or emotional instability, individuals should be referred to a psychologist or psychiatrist, for disturbance at a deep level may make it difficult to choose wisely or succeed in any vocation.

In analyzing personality the individual should realize that it is not simply the sum total of a number of isolated traits, but rather a "dynamic whole" made up of interrelated parts. So it is not the trait itself, be it good or bad, that is all important but rather the role it plays in the total personality structure. Since personality is dynamic it will change as the student assimilates the new experiences that college is bound to bring. He must learn not only to see himself as he is at the moment, but also to discover his potentialities for future development. Vocational choice should, therefore, be flexible, since latent potentialities may be developed and obstacles to success overcome during the years ahead. However, vocational choice based on potentialities alone may be unwise unless the individual faces the fact that he will have to work hard to develop these latent aspects of his personality. We are realizing increasingly how important motivation is, and individuals who seemingly lack some of the characteristics essential for success in certain vocations may, if strongly motivated, become very successful.

In order better to understand himself each individual needs to examine his relationship to his family. Has he without thinking adopted their attitudes and values? Or if his relationship is negative, is he throwing over attitudes and values which are really meaningful to him? Before he can know whether his vocational choice is the right one for him he must understand the attitude of his parents toward his vocational aims, whether they are allowing him to develop his own interests and abilities, or whether they are imposing on him their own unfulfilled ambitions. It is likewise important to distinguish between personal and collective values. They may be identical; if not, there may be deep conflict before he can honestly decide on the relative importance of these in his own life. In an age which prizes highly the financial success and prestige that business and industry offer their executives, a young man may find it difficult to choose a life of service as a teacher or minister. Real success and happiness will depend on his making the decision that is right for him as a person.

Self-analysis is a continuous process, which should go on throughout college—in fact, throughout life. Through it one learns to see himself as he really is and eventually to become the person he is capable of being. A counselor who has a broad understanding of human nature and values, as well as a knowledge of occupations, can help the young man or woman to see vocation as one means, though not the only one, of fulfilling himself and achieving wholeness. The assurance that he is making the best use of his talents for his own development as well as for the benefit of society should bring happiness and success, which is the ultimate aim of vocational guidance.

After being introduced to the problems of self-analysis the student should begin his study of vocations so that he may compare his interests, abilities, and values with the actual demands and satisfactions of the various occupations. The first year's work should include a general survey of broad occupational fields and descriptions of typical jobs, particularly at the beginning level. If too much emphasis is placed on atypical or top positions, the student may build false hopes which can result only in disillusionment when he starts looking for his first job. Furthermore, it makes it difficult for the placement counselor who may have to tell him that the job he wants requires a Ph.D., or twenty years of experience, and that only one person in a thousand may ever hope to have such a position anyway. He may eventually be that person, but not unless he gets off to a good start in his first job.

Vocational information may be presented in a variety of forms. The counselor in charge will probably start with a series of general lectures. Later, career conferences may be arranged to bring in outside speakers who can contribute much of interest as a result of actual work experience. Film presentations are popular with students provided really good material can be obtained on occupations at the college level. Much information is available in book and pamphlet form. The counselor should work in close cooperation with the librarian to see that the latest vocational material is readily accessible in a special section of the library. Field trips give the student an opportunity to acquire practical information about jobs and companies. After being introduced to the various sources of information each student should be given a project to work on involving the analysis of one or more vocations of special interest to him.

When some progress has been made in both self- and occupational-analysis, each student should begin the preparation of two profiles, one portraying his own interests, abilities, values, and limitations; the other showing the demands, satisfactions, and disadvantages of each vocation of interest to him. These profiles must be individually worked out, but there are certain basic factors which must be considered by everyone. There is the question of health, for example. For some this must be a primary consideration, but the individual who can accept his limitations and learn to live within them may have a normal, happy, and productive life. On the personal side of the profile the individual must list his physical assets and liabilities, then compare these with the demands of the vocation under consideration. If he has poor eyesight, scientific research involving microscopic blood analysis would probably prove a great strain and in the long run force him to give up the occupation for which he had prepared.

The question of general intelligence is also important to everyone. With the expansion of educational opportunities, academic standards have been lowered in some institutions to accommodate students of average intelligence. Many are quite capable of finishing college with satisfactory grades but lack the ability to do graduate work which is essential for entrance into some occupations. There are many jobs, however, which do not require a high degree of academic intelligence. Anyone who is willing to work hard may achieve a degree of success commensurate with his ability. If he does this the chances are that he will be happy and productive, provided he has accepted his own abilities and limitations. Some individuals enjoy a routine job in a general field that interests them; others may be happy only at the top and should be advised either that they will have to compete constantly with other very able, highly motivated people or else that they should attempt to get into a field which is not highly competitive.

On the practical side money is an extremely important item to be considered in making vocational plans. First, how much is available for graduate school preparation or for investment in business? Does the individual have sufficient talent to warrant scholarship aid? Is he equipped with skills which will enable him to earn a living while he continues his graduate study on a part-time basis? Funds may have to be available to assure the necessary training so that the individual may "prepare for" and "enter into" his chosen field. Salary is also an important consideration. Students have a right to assume that work will provide sufficient remuneration for the necessities as well as some of the luxuries of life. For some, money will be the deciding factor in vocational selection. For it they are willing to work hard and make great sacrifices. Others prefer to do work that interests them even though it does not pay as well. Some feel a real call to serve mankind regardless of financial return. For others opportunity for advancement in an occupation is paramount. A few outstanding individuals in every college class will reach the top in their chosen fields. For them work will be almost synonymous with life itself and no sacrifice will be too great to pay for success. But there is not room for everyone at the top, so it is fortunate that not everyone has the ambition or desire to get there. There are other values in life more important to them—leisure-time activities, for example. They may not want to spend more than seven or eight hours a day at work since for them life really begins after five o'clock. They find enjoyment in family life, reading, gardening, attending concerts, or doing volunteer work in the community. All these pursuits may offer satisfactions which far outweigh financial compensation or success.

Individuals to whom these values are important will not want a job that involves travel or requires too much overtime work.

So each individual must go on working out his own scale of values and checking these against the demands and satisfactions of the various vocations. To assist an individual to explore these far-reaching implications involved in vocational choice is much more than just good vocational guidance. It is a contribution to "deeper teaching" in that it helps the individual to work out his total philosophy of life and at the same time see his job in relation to it. This is an important part of the educational process which aims to develop the "whole person."

Vocational guidance begun in a general way during the freshman year should be continued during the sophomore year with more emphasis on specialization as the individual becomes more aware of himself as a person and narrows his sphere of vocational interest. By the junior year most students will be working with a fairly definitely defined purpose and may well begin to plan for placement or a program of graduate study. Individual counseling becomes increasingly important, but some groups of students majoring in related fields should continue to meet together to discuss basic problems of interest to them all.

The development of a healthy attitude toward work will do a great deal to make the transition from college to the job easy and pleasant. Work should be approached as a challenge toward further self-development. Since the first job is rarely the last, it should not be an end in itself. If seen in relation to a future goal it becomes much more meaningful. It may be the beginning job in one's chosen field and eventually lead to a better position in the same field. It may, on the other hand, be a temporary job not directly related to the goal, but one which will provide the money necessary for professional or business training. A graduate degree is indispensable even for the beginning jobs in some occupations. Business skills are a great help in getting an entree into fields otherwise closed to beginners. A job has meaning when seen in relationship to the end it serves. If this is understood it may help the individual make a good adjustment on the first job and also avoid that period of aimless drifting from one job to another, which is the experience of many young graduates who have not made vocational plans.

Most young people, particularly college graduates, approach the world of work with high ideals. The future belongs to them and it is important that these ideals be kept and realized. This too requires sound vocational planning; otherwise individuals of great potential value to society may become disillusioned when they find no immediate outlet for their abilities. It is perhaps a sad commentary on our economic system that so few jobs require either creative ability or social conscience. High ideals, if not seen in the right perspective, may even be a disadvantage in making the adjustment on one's first job. Failure at this level may destroy the chances of promotion and so deprive one of future opportunities for the realization of these ideals. Attitudes which are stressed in college may not be the same as those which make for success on the job. Both are important and must be understood in relation to each other. Ambition is prized highly in college and will be a great asset in business, but not if it makes the individual unwilling to start at the bottom and work up in his chosen field. Intellectual attainments, all-important in college, would prove an asset in all areas of life, but not if they give the individual a feeling of superiority over co-workers who are not college graduates. Nor is creativity always an asset if it prevents one from doing routine work and doing it well. So, while college may have developed ambition, intelligence, and creative ability, the job may require patience, perseverance, tolerance, and adjustment to a different set of values, each of which is important to success.

A great deal of unhappiness may be avoided if the individual knows what he has a right to expect from his job. No job will enable him to live fully in all areas of his life. Nor should it. That is one reason why a general education, which aims at wholeness and well-rounded personality adjustment, is so important. What if the first job does not give one an adequate chance to express his ambition, intelligence, and creativity? It is his responsibility to see that these values are kept alive, if not on the job, then outside of working hours. If he can do this the time will come when he does have a job which will use all his abilities, for there are always such jobs waiting for the individuals who have real ability and determination.

Early in the senior year each individual should register with the placement office. There will be some who do not plan to work immediately and others may have definite jobs in mind. Nonetheless, registration is desirable. Records should be completed at this time and references assembled for possible future use. Cards may be marked "inactive" for the present and registration reopened at any time desired.

Lectures and group discussions dealing with such topics as letter writing, preparation for the interview, and personal appearance and grooming should be continued during the last year. Ample opportunity should be allowed for individual counseling to help each student plan his own particular job campaign. Up to this point each individual has been thinking primarily in terms of what he wants and expects from his job. Soon he must learn that his prospective employer has a right to expect certain things from him. Employers are in business to make money or to give service. Each employee has a job to do that, at least from the company point of view, is important. Whether or not it has meaning in relation to the individual's vocational plans is not the responsibility of the employer. Employees have a right to expect to earn more money than the salary offered and to receive increases automatically and indefinitely, while realizing that every job carries a maximum salary beyond which it is difficult to advance. A young woman in Washington or New York City may start a secretarial position at $55 or $60 a week, yet few such positions are worth more than $80 or $85 even after years of experience. The individual may be worth more but the job is not.

After four years of college many individuals feel they are qualified to take on administrative responsibility without realizing that it will take years of experience before they are qualified to do this. Employers cannot be expected to let beginners handle their public relations program or negotiations with unions. Frequently, young people say they are willing to start at the bottom without any clear notion of where the bottom is. It often means doing a routine job for quite a long time. However, most companies have policies whereby employees are promoted within the organization as opportunities occur. Young people who have ability and ambition plus perseverance and the willingness to work hard and do well every task assigned to them may be sure of advancement. This takes time and each employee must wait his turn. Employers cannot discharge perfectly satisfactory workers in order to promote newcomers even though they might be capable of filling positions at higher levels. Some young people are so anxious to get ahead that they are unwilling to wait for promotions. They become discouraged and drift from one job to another, building up poor employment records. Good placement counseling should prepare the individual to appraise his first job realistically. If it does seem wise to leave he should make constructive plans for a second job that will mean either an increase in salary or broader experience in line with his vocational plans.

Preparation for placement should include a study of specific companies. All big companies and many small ones publish booklets setting forth policies, benefits, insurance and pension plans, as well as many items of interest to new workers. Personnel managers are more than willing to send this material to placement officers. While some companies may try to oversell themselves, these pamphlets if interpreted wisely can be very valuable in helping students acquire factual information. When the time comes to apply for a job each applicant should be armed with as much information as possible about positions in his chosen field. An employer is always favorably impressed by applicants who have taken the trouble to inform themselves about opportunities in general and about his company in particular. Furthermore, such information is essential if an individual is to make a wise decision about accepting or rejecting positions that may be offered to him.

In the final analysis getting a job depends on an individual's ability to sell himself. He must know his product, namely himself, and the market in which his abilities can be sold to advantage. Then he must present his qualifications in a manner that will convince some employer that he will be an asset to his organization. The first impression is all important, for if it is not good there never will be a second. It may be made by a letter and accompanying résumé, an application form, or in a personal interview. If applying for a position out of town, answering ads in newspapers, or exploring possibilities in one's chosen field, the first step will be to write a letter. It is surprising that many college graduates do not know how to write a good business letter. Any course in vocational guidance should include many letter-writing assignments so that the individual may learn not only the rudiments but develop a style that expresses his own personality. He should know that good-quality, plain typing paper is correct, that personal stationery or note paper is not; that typewritten letters are usually preferred, though legible handwriting may be acceptable. He should know the name of the person to whom his letter is to be addressed, and be sure to spell it correctly. The letter should be businesslike, get to the point quickly, and state the type of position applied for. Employers are not interested in autobiographical data but there are certain vital statistics they do want, e.g., name, address, age, education, college major, special skills, extracurricular interests, job aims, employment record, and references. These facts may be included in the body of the letter, particularly if it is exploratory, or if the applicant is a beginner without an impressive record of training or experience. Some companies prefer that this information be presented separately in the form of a résumé. This is always desirable if the individual has outstanding ability or work experience.

If companies are recruiting personnel all applicants will be asked to fill in application forms. The individual should read instructions carefully and think about what he intends to say before he starts to write. When he has finished he should look over the form to see that information is complete and accurate, that the handwriting is legible, that the general appearance is neat. An applicant who writes his name in the wrong place, who cannot remember the date of his last job, who has a leaky fountain pen should not be surprised if told the company has no opening for him.

If his letter and application form have made a good impression the applicant will be called for an interview and again the first impression is extremely important. The first thing the employer will notice is personal appearance. Whether he should or not, he is going to assume that an individual's appearance and grooming are a reflection of his personality and an indication of the way he will handle a job. A careless and slovenly appearance may mean careless and slovenly work. A girl is believed to be smart if she looks the part. Many young people who are well groomed according to college standards need advice about the suitability of clothing to be worn at the interview. Juvenile dress indicates immaturity, while party clothes show poor judgment and a wrong attitude toward work. Business clothes should be chosen in good taste with emphasis on good grooming and on sensible and conservative style and color. During the junior and senior years students should be required to attend lectures in grooming and given an opportunity to present themselves for interviews in which they are asked to "dress the part." The knowledge that one is well groomed and properly dressed will increase the poise and self-confidence necessary for handling an interview successfully.

To students who have been adequately prepared for placement the interview will not be a frightening experience. In fact, they should have had many practice interviews during the last two years of college. The interviewer is a human being just as much interested in making a good impression for his company as the individual is for himself, and the interview is simply a conversation between two people interested in securing information from each other. The individual who has made sound vocational plans knows himself and his goal and what he can expect from an employer. He has readily available all information that the interviewer is likely to want and also has in mind a number of questions he will want to ask about the company. The knowledge that he is well prepared will enable him to relax, yet remain alert and responsive as the interviewer takes the lead. His questions and answers will reflect courtesy, and when the interviewer indicates that the interview is finished he will express his appreciation for the opportunity to discuss employment possibilities with him. It is not usual to have a definite job offer following the first interview. Employers may want to make further inquiries about the applicant and talk with other candidates. The applicant himself will want to make further inquiries about the company, discuss the matter with his counselor, and perhaps apply for other positions before making his final decision.

When the individual receives an offer he should think it over carefully to determine whether or not it fits in with his vocational plans. If it does, fine; if not, he should let the employer know at once and express his appreciation even though he does not wish to accept the position. As he continues job-hunting he will realize that this is an important learning period. Each interview gives him an opportunity to meet new people and to discuss the different kinds of jobs available with different companies. Gradually his aims become more clearly crystallized. When he does decide on his first job he should feel that he has taken a step in the right direction, which will lead eventually to the goal he has set for himself. If he has made the right decision he will want to stay on his first job at least a year, which will be his "freshman year" in the world of work. After this he should reappraise his abilities and plans in the light of his work experience. He may wish to remain with the same company and wait for his promotional opportunity, or he may prefer to transfer to another company. He may even wish to get into an entirely new field of work which offers possibilities he has not dreamed would interest him when in college.

This is about as far as one can go in planning the initial job campaign. Its ultimate aim is successful placement and when this has been achieved the formal vocational guidance program may be said to be finished in the same sense that formal education may be said to be completed upon graduation from college. However, if education and guidance have been really successful the processes which have been initiated will continue throughout life. Each individual will from time to time analyze himself, reappraise his abilities, interests, and values in the light of each new experience. He may follow closely the plans he made in college or he may shift his direction many times before achieving fulfillment in his life and in his work.

Follow-up

The work of the placement office, however, is not yet finished. Within a month or two after graduation follow-up letters and questionnaires should be sent to each student. If he is having a difficult time in adjusting to the new job, or if he has doubts about the wisdom of his decision or about his outlook for the future, he should feel that there is someone at the college to whom he can turn for further guidance. For it must be remembered that the ultimate aim of guidance is not just placement, but *successful* placement. Since most institutions continue to offer placement service to their alumni, each graduate should indicate whether or not he wishes to remain on the active list for replacement if opportunities occur. If he is happily placed for the present he should be invited to reopen registration if at any time in the future he wishes to change his position.

Questionnaires should request information relative to placement: How did the individual get his position? What is the name of the company and of his immediate supervisor? What is the title of his position? His duties? Salary? This much is essential for the records and should be reported to department chairmen, other college officers, and instructors who have participated in the guidance and placement program.

Additional data may be gathered from research studies to determine the types of positions held by college graduates, placement in fields related to areas of specialization, and other topics that may be of particular interest to different institutions at different times. Since no program is perfect, guidance officers should also welcome suggestions regarding the effectiveness of their services. Constant revision is necessary and will be most helpful if it grows out of the actual experience and needs of the graduates themselves.

Another letter and questionnaire should be sent to each employer who has hired a recent graduate. This in itself is good public relations for the placement office and the college. It can serve as the basis for a harmonious working relationship between the guidance officers and the various personnel managers during the years ahead. The information which they can furnish regarding the employee's adjustment on the job, his work habits, future potentialities, etc., is important for the records and invaluable in counseling the individual should he return for further guidance and replacement. It is a source of great satisfaction to the placement officer to know that a student is happily placed and that the employer is pleased with his choice. However, if things are not working out too well it is important that all three work together in order to get matters straightened out to the mutual satisfaction of everyone.

Throughout this chapter, ways and means of vocational guidance have been suggested in order ultimately to assist the student to successful placement on a job which will give him an opportunity for continuing growth, productivity, and satisfaction.

BIBLIOGRAPHY

Allport, Gordon W.: *Personality: A Psychological Interpretation.* New York, Henry Holt, 1937.

Bennett, M. E.: *College and Life.* New York, McGraw-Hill Book Co., 1941.

Boynton, P. W.: *Six Ways to Get a Job.* New York, Harper & Brothers, 1945.

Brooke, Esther E.: *Guide to Career Success.* New York, Harper & Brothers, 1947.

Calvert, Robert, Jr.: *A College Placement Program.* New York, Ed. D. project, Teachers College, Columbia University, 1952.

Forrester, Gertrude: *Occupations: A Selected List of Pamphlets.* New York, H. W. Wilson Company, 1949.

Gerth, Josephine H.: *Highways to Jobs for Women.* New York, The Woman's Press, 1948.

Hilton, M. Eunice: *Guide to Guidance.* Syracuse, Syracuse University Press, 1947.

Hoppock, Robert: *Group Guidance.* New York, McGraw-Hill Book Co., 1949.

McKinney, Fred: *Psychology of Personal Adjustment.* New York, John Wiley & Sons, Inc., 1941.

Moore, Robert Foster: *Blueprint Your Career*. New York, Stackpole & Heck, Inc., 1949.

New York University Occupational Index. New York, Occupational Index, Inc., 1946.

Occupations for Girls and Women. Selected References. Washington, D. C., U. S. Department of Labor, Women's Bureau, June, 1948, Bulletin No. 229.

Placement Guidance Manual. Washington, D. C., Graduate School of Business Administration, Howard University, June, 1948.

Rosengarten, William: *Choosing Your Life Work*. New York, McGraw-Hill Book Co., 1936.

Shartle, C. L.: *Occupational Information: Its Development and Application*. New York, Prentice-Hall, Inc., 1942.

Strang, Ruth: *Counseling Technics in College and Secondary School*. New York, Harper & Brothers, 1949.

Super, Donald E.: *The Dynamics of Vocational Adjustment*. New York, Harper & Brothers, 1942.

Super, Donald E.: *Appraising Vocational Fitness*. New York, Harper & Brothers, 1949.

Traxler, Arthur E.: *Techniques of Guidance*. New York, Harper & Brothers, 1945.

Williamson, E. G.: *Students and Occupations*. New York, Henry Holt, 1937.

Williamson, E. G.: *How to Counsel Students*. New York, McGraw-Hill Book Co., 1939.

16. Learning More About Purpose-Formation and Self-Control

ANNA L. ROSE HAWKES

THE purpose of the college is to educate. Any discussion of discipline or, to use the newer term, student control, should start from this statement, which points up sharply the modern attitude toward this ever-present educational problem. At no time in recent years has the source of authority for personal conduct been a more vital topic than it is just now.

Some people seem to feel that the college should not have to consider this matter. Character, they say, is or should be formed by the time a student enters college. Attitudes are developed, standards of ethics and morals have been set, and habits are formed. This, of course, is true. All students have learned attitudes, standards, and morals of some sort at home and/or in Sunday School before they come to college. But many homes, churches, and lower schools have not been successful in developing sufficiently fine qualities of character in individuals. In any case, none of us has ever formed his character perfectly. There is always more to be learned. The college must accept continuing responsibility in this area.

This being so, the point of view from which the college administers discipline or student control is of paramount importance. Time was, and not so long ago, when discipline was considered to be only punitive. A misdemeanor has been committed, a punishment is meted out, justice is done, and the matter is closed. This action assumed that the punishment assigned would awaken the student to a better way of conduct. This conception of discipline implies that an external stimulus can not only insure conformity to the accepted code, but can also bring about a radical change in attitudes and deportment which will prevent the recurrence of the antisocial conduct. It is based on the theory that fear of punishment will prevent unsatisfactory behavior.

It is doubtful, however, if fear has ever produced maturity, or if external force has resulted in desirable activity.

Discipline, to be successful, must produce in an individual the desire to choose, on his own initiative, the higher levels of human behavior instead of the lower. It must develop an inner stimulus which will result in the right response to whatever situations in which the individual finds himself. The end result may be the same, but a reasoned discovery about one's impulses and actions is much more apt to result in self-control than is an unreasoning fear of some outside authority.

We all meet this question of authority, not only in our relations with our students if we are teachers; with our children, if we are parents; but with ourselves, most intimately of all. At one extreme is authority, a code of rules from some outside source, a superimposed will. At the other extreme is absolute freedom of action by the individual, without reference to any person or any regulation. In between these two extremes of rigid rules and complete freedom is an internal regulation of personal conduct, which is not an authority at all, but that highest of human responses, a voluntary, uncoerced, spontaneous loyalty to the ideals and values of human relationships, what Lord Moulton over thirty years ago called "obedience to the unenforceable."[1] Obedience to a dictum or law under pain of punishment does not contribute to deeper learnings as does obedience to a principle consciously adopted and freely accepted as a method of living understandingly and happily with others and with one's self.

Conditions of present-day college living present many new and different social pressures. Every student of college age has much to learn in terms of his own purposes and self-control. When a student is accepted by a college, it is assumed that he has reached a certain level of mental and physical development. It is likewise assumed that he has reached a comparable level in his moral and ethical development. Academic achievement can be measured by entrance examinations, school records, and various other devices available to admissions officers. Moral and ethical development is much more difficult to measure. It cannot be determined with anything like the same precision as can academic accomplishment. Letters of recommendation, however flattering, fail to reveal the student's sense

[1] John Fletcher Moulton, "Three Domains of Human Action."

of ethical values. No one but the individual himself knows his own strengths and weaknesses. Directors of admissions, with all kinds of measurable data, make mistakes in appraising a student's readiness for college work. It is not surprising that they also make mistakes in estimating the same individual's readiness for group living.

What resources does the college have to assist a student to achieve his optimum development in the face of the many conflicting opportunities which are open to him in his new environment and which necessitate a choice? How can a college help a student to develop personal standards and values and give him remedial help when he fails to do well in meeting problem situations?

Discipline as Deeper Teaching

According to Funk and Wagnall's *College Standard Dictionary*, discipline is not punishment but "systematic training," especially "the training of the mental, moral, and physical powers by instruction and exercise." Webster defines it as "the treatment suited to a disciple or a learner." These definitions clearly define an educational process, not a causative result. Education means progress and development; it is active, it necessitates a change that comes from within, it is not a product of authority arbitrarily applied. If rules and regulations are laid down which do not require students to develop self-reliance and responsibility; if the disciplinary measures adopted result in continued immaturity and childishness, then such a program has no educational value.

The first obligation of any college which professes the personnel point of view, therefore, is to see to it that its students are presented with challenging opportunities to develop their moral and spiritual potentialities as well as their academic possibilities. Discipline, properly managed, results in a gradual but progressive growth from the inexpert to the accomplished, from immaturity to maturity, from external authority to self-discipline.

The second characteristic of personnel-centered discipline is that, in order to be effective or intelligent, it must be adapted to the point which the individual student has reached in his moral development. The whole process of growing up involves a series of awakenings to ethical values. Frequently, the individual is not cognizant of the areas in which he is insensitive to these standards. He has not yet become aware of the accepted code.

The young child is not conscious of the standards of conduct which are acceptable in any community. He does not realize the distinction between social behavior and a completely self-centered attitude. It is not immoral for a three-year-old to use his imagination in a manner which in an adult would be called lying; it is merely nonmoral. He has not yet awakened to the difference between lying and the truth, and he has no idea of the social results of his actions. It is equally true that he is not yet sensible of the meaning of the ownership of property. Anything that he sees and can get belongs to him as much as to anyone else, and until he is awakened to the meaning of such action, an appropriation of toys or books or money has none of the attributes of an unsocial act.

Anyone not intimately connected with a college is frequently surprised to find that many a college student has never really been aroused to the importance of some of the most vital ethical questions. There is little doubt that much of the socially unacceptable behavior on the part of grown men and women is due to the fact that, mature though they may be in years, they are still children as far as standards of conduct are concerned.

If a director of admissions could have known exactly the qualities of character that the applicants to his college had developed, doubtless some of them would have been rejected. To disqualify a student for his first social or moral misdemeanor would be as unwise as to disqualify him for failing his first examination in Chemistry. Such a regulation requires no judgment on the part of anyone, and does not fit every case.

Progress through college cannot and should not be completely standardized. The variety and confusions of the possible responses to the college environment cannot be settled in a mechanical manner. The college is obligated to discover just what is behind the disturbing behavior. The easier way would be to impose an appropriate punishment for every misdemeanor. A wise college dean used to say that this conception of discipline requires only a book of rules, a police officer in academic costume, a guilty youth, and an inexorable penalty. Of course, this attitude toward discipline requires no analysis of motives, assumes no intelligence on the part of the administrator, and no discretion.

But the effort to analyze motives, to understand the human situation involved, to discover the point which an individual student has reached in his moral and ethical development, requires intelligence of a high order, keen judgment, and a real and sincere belief in the educative value of learning reasoned self-control. Thus, although two students may be guilty of identical misconduct, a discerning study of the two cases, revealing the differences in ethical values between the two, will result in very different treatment, if each individual is to benefit by the experience.

A direct corollary of this study of the difference in levels of development attained by students, is the fact that every case should be treated on its individual merits. Punishment as punishment is rarely regenerative. But if it provides an awakening to one's responsibilities, it can be of the greatest significance. In developing an effective program of education in the area of morals and standards, it is essential to know the individual student as completely and intimately as is possible. How will this youth react in this situation? What will be the effect of this experience on this student? What will challenge this individual, young, inexperienced and immature, to face his problem squarely and make a wise and intelligent decision?

It is likewise essential to make known the individual to himself. He should be made aware of his uniqueness as a person, with all of his particular inherited tendencies and traits. He should be helped to analyze his motives, to study his impulses, and to discover the limits of his freedom, as determined by the rights of others and by his position as a member of a social group.

This limit of freedom is often difficult to present to a young person. Absolute freedom of speech, or action, or even of thought is an absurdity in any society of human beings. The relation of freedom, absolute and relative, to the idea of "obedience to the unenforceable," presupposes an awareness of self and one's place in society which few adolescents have attained. They see even necessary rules and regulations as limiting their freedom, never realizing that freedom without law becomes license, but that freedom within the law becomes liberty.

We need rules for one or both of two reasons: lack of judgment, and lack of knowledge. If the child has mature social judgment he would know that, for the comfort of the household, he had better hang up his coat. If he had adequate knowledge he would be aware of the danger of playing with matches. At a different level of development the same conditions hold for the judgment and knowledge of adolescents and adults. Those who have worked with young people know the countless hours spent in attempting to cultivate judgment and increase knowledge in order that rules will be unnecessary.

Of course, it is much easier to rely on authority than to depend on one's own knowledge or judgment. But the more laws are needed, the further the individual and society are from independence. No one can achieve real maturity until he has learned his own limitations and potentialities, and has arrived at the point where he can take charge of himself. Individuals can rarely do this unless they are treated as individuals, and not merely as one of a class.

Such individual treatment of misbehavior has one serious danger. Because such a procedure sometimes allows a student to remain in college whose record does not seem to commend him as a desirable member of the college community, the report may become current among the other students that it is easy to "get by" and that the authorities are lenient, if not unconcerned, with any irregularity of conduct. The constructive elements, however, in such individual treatment should soon win the respect and appreciation of both students and faculty.

It should not be inferred that this approach implies that academic or moral delinquency should be taken lightly. The idea is to place the emphasis on the way in which the facts are made known to the individual. The technique should leave the student aware of his weakness, determined to remedy it, and convinced that this can best be accomplished under the conditions proposed.

Methods of Administering Discipline

The spirit in which discipline is administered and the methods used are important factors in the development of moral and ethical maturity among students. These range all the way from complete faculty control vested in the whole faculty, to complete student control.

Institutions have been known to discuss cases of discipline in full faculty meeting, in some instances after the culprit has appeared for questioning. Nothing more grotesque than such a discussion can be imagined. Neither intimacies of background, attitude, and provocation nor any extenuating circumstances have any force when recited to a body whose members find it almost impossible to bridge the gap between their own experience and the immaturity, inexperience, and lack of judgment shown by an adolescent student. In addition, few on the faculty may have known him, certainly not better than as a member of a class. Few faculty members have the time, or will take it, necessary for the tactful understanding of even the least evidence of misbehavior. If the end to be achieved is anything more than a recital of the evidence and an imposition of a penalty, such a procedure is hopelessly ineffective.

Another system is the appointment or election of a faculty committee on discipline. The function of such a committee and its mode of operation differ widely in different institutions. In many places it is merely a fact-finding committee, which is expected to levy the appropriate punishment on the basis of the evidence presented. It is possible for such a committee to have a really human and understanding concept of its responsibilities. Service on a committee of this kind, however, leads one to suspect that such is not generally the case. If the committee is appointed and if the appointing officer, usually the president of the institution, has a discerning attitude toward student problems, there is a better chance of a considerate and perceptive committee than if the group is elected by the faculty at large. Such a method is only as effective as the temperament and interests of the members of the committee make it possible to be.

In many institutions, one officer is delegated as the officer of discipline. Any disadvantages resulting from this method seem to be more than made up for by at least two advantages. In the first place, a uniformity of procedure is assured which can be attained by no other method. If each instructor, for example, believes himself to be a disciplinary officer responsible for the adjustment of academic dishonesty in his classes, the result to the student depends on the individual instructor's attitude toward such dishonesty in academic work. Thus, the whole question of academic integrity becomes merely a gamble between instructor and student, depending on the personal popularity of the faculty member and the opinion prevalent on the campus regarding his forbearance. This does not imply that an instructor should not be allowed to discuss with his students any dilemma in which they may be involved. If desirable relations between instructor and student obtain, it is not only natural but helpful for such a conference to take place. But when a decision must be made as to the disciplinary action which should be taken, the instructor does not properly enter the picture.

Where one officer is responsible, he can call in any instructor or consult with any other officer, as he wishes. It ensures a different committee for each case, and makes it possible to get assistance from those on a college campus who know the student best. It likewise affords continuity of treatment in the follow-up measures so often vital to the proper solution of a problem.

The centralization of discipline offers a second advantage. It is of supreme importance that all the information and records concerning a student be in one place. A record concerning every action of a disciplinary character should be in the confidential file of each student. To expect every instructor to furnish such reports for each of his students involved in such action would be quite out of the question. There would be no uniformity in reporting to a central office the information regarding any student action which might be criticized. If there is a central confidential file for each student, where information of this sort can be found, then the disposition of a case will be very different from the sum of the independent actions of the various people who might have dealt with it. When one officer knows the whole history, he will see that while the first offence may have been an accident and the second a coincidence, the third strongly suggests a habit! The compilation of cumulative information on student attitudes, behavior, and conduct cannot be complete unless it is kept in a centralized file, for which one person is responsible.*

With such a confidential file the question always arises, how long should such material be kept? It seems evident that such items should certainly be retained as long as the student is in college. One college dean was in the habit of telling students that he was making a note of the antisocial behavior which would be placed in the individual's personal file. Then he would add, "When you graduate, if you would like to ask me for this bit of information, I should be glad to give it to you." When a student shows by subsequent behavior that he has learned by the experience, the record should by all means be cleared. If it is a situation in which the individual is asked to leave college, then probably the supporting evidence for this action should be retained. Possibly the "statute of limitations" for college disciplinary information should be graduation. A college which has finally placed its seal of approval on an individual would scarcely care to remember adolescent indiscretions.

It is frequently assumed that the personnel officer cannot be a disciplinary officer and be effective. Again, this depends on the spirit with which discipline is administered. If the attitude is merely that a crime has been committed and the offender must be punished, then the picture the student would have of such a person would be that of a wrathful and avenging judge, and not that of a friendly and under-

---

* See suggestion on use of personnel records, who should contribute to them, their location, and their use in Chapter 5.

standing adviser. But if the person responsible for discipline believes his duty is to discover what weakness or habit, what immaturity of judgment or lack of knowledge, was the cause of the action under criticism, and to help the student help himself, then it is reasonable to assume that the person who knows him best can help him most. There are few young people who do not really desire to become persons worthy of the respect of their fellows. Whatever they may say to cover up their feelings, they are grateful in their hearts to anyone who will help them find the way. To separate counseling and discipline function means inevitably not only that the counselor need not discipline, but also that disciplinarians need not counsel. The latter is clearly intolerable in any educational situation.

The development in a number of institutions of an "honor system" has led to the assumption of the responsibility for discipline on the part of the students in all matters except academic disqualification, probation, etc. This is accomplished in various ways. In some instances there is a faculty-student committee which handles all affairs of a disciplinary nature. Unless this is very carefully handled, and unless there is excellent rapport and mutual confidence between students and faculty, the usual result is that the faculty votes together and the students vote together. If the chairman is a faculty member, the students are apt to feel that such a committee is of no avail.

Where student government is highly developed and has its authority from the trustees of an institution, there is apt to be a responsible attitude on the part of the students that is healthy and heartening. There is no question but that in many cases students can get to the bottom of a case better than can faculty members or administrative officers. Certainly student opinion can do far more in controlling cheating and matters of social conduct on a campus than can any other group. Student government, where it is effective, can be a vital force in developing an understanding of authority, which results in a conscious self-control in the interests of the social group.

There are two disadvantages, which at times seem to outweigh the many advantages, of such a form of government. Student officers change each year. One year the leadership may be mature, intelligent, and sincere in the discharge of duties. Next year, this may not be so. Therefore, there is great fluctuation in the effectiveness of the program.

In the second place, the short-range view which students perforce have does not give them the experience or the insight to deal with the perplexities of their peers. To determine just what the human situation really is, to leave the offender in a better rather than a worse position, to encourage him to set his sights high, and to develop a set of guiding principles for ethical and social behavior require experience and discrimination which few student committees possess.

In cases where student boards work closely with a dean or other administrative officers, where all information from all sources is brought to bear on the problem, where discussion is free and respect and confidence is shared, the recommendation of the student group is likely to be sound and considered. Such a combination can be successful. It depends on the tact and equanimity of the administrative officer and his or her belief in and respect for student opinion and responsibility.

A discussion of student responsibility for discipline is not complete without some analysis of the meaning of an honor system. Unless an honor system applies to the social areas of student life as well as the academic, it will fall of its own weight. Students cannot assume responsibility for honor in examinations unless they also profess honor in their actions outside the classroom. No man can live half slave and half free. To shift responsibility for one's social actions to an outside authority, while controlling academic exercises by inner stimulus is to operate under a false premise. Further, for an honor system to be really effective, the faculty must cooperate wholeheartedly with the students. This does not mean lip service to the ideals the students have set for themselves. It does mean sincere belief in the ability and right of the students to control their own actions.

It has happened in some institutions that the code itself has become more important than the individual. When this appears to be the case, the institution might as well hand over discipline to the police officer in academic garb with his book of rules and penalties. No regeneration can come to the student who is dismissed on the mere evidence of wrongdoing, with no investigation of causes or individual circumstances.

This conception of an honor system and the individual approach to discipline does not preclude punishment. It should be obvious to anyone that unless some action follows improper behavior, whether one is on one's honor or not, the student body would infer that such behavior was negligible and, even when known to the responsible students or college officers, was regarded lightly or entirely overlooked. This attitude is equally bad for the individual and the group. Just requittal of the action involved usually results in a greater sense of social responsibility.

A case of discipline may properly be regarded as a work of art. Even if it means elimination from college, it is not well done unless the student understands the reason for the action, agrees that no other course is possible, and feels that it will probably have a constructive effect on his future behavior. All would agree that the only real education is self-education. So, too, the only successful discipline is self-discipline.

A college is an educational institution, educational not only in the domain of the mind, but also in the realm of the spirit. The stimulus and challenge may come from without, but the change is within. For after all, neither parents, nor teachers, nor his own friends can educate a person. The conditions can only be made as favorable as possible for the individual to grow in mind, body, and spirit to the full stature of which he is capable.*

BIBLIOGRAPHY

Crow, Lester D., and Crow, Alice: *Mental Hygiene in School and Home Life.* New York, McGraw-Hill Book Co., 1942.

Hawkes, Herbert E., and Hawkes, Anna L. Rose: *Through a Dean's Open Door.* New York, McGraw-Hill Book Co., 1945.

Hymes, James L., Jr.: *Discipline.* New York, Bureau of Publications, Teachers College, Columbia University, 1949.

Moulton, John Fletcher, (1st Baron): "Three Domains of Human Action," *Atlantic Monthly.* 134: July, 1924, pp. 1-5.

Redl, Fritz: *Mental Hygiene in Teaching.* New York, Harcourt Brace and Co., 1951.

Sheviakov, George V., and Redl, Fritz: *Discipline for Today's Children and Youth.* Washington, D. C., N.E.A., 1944.

Wickham, E. K.: *Children's Behavior and Teachers' Attitudes.* New York, The Commonwealth Fund, 1928.

Yeager, William A: *Administration and the Pupil.* New York, Harper & Brothers, 1949.

* Much of the material in this chapter appears also in Herbert E. Hawkes and Anna L. Rose Hawkes: *Through A Dean's Open Door.*

17. Developing Spiritual Insights

ORDWAY TEAD

"I believe everyone always acts from selfish reasons."

"There are no definite standards of moral conduct to which we can refer for guidance."

"The behavior of those who renounce and suffer as do martyrs and saints is pathological and compensatory."

"There is no room for God to account for our grasp of reality and no need of a God to help our effort to lead a decent life."

"Scientific knowledge is the only real knowledge we have."

Everyone who works with young people in college today hears these sentiments or others like them reiterated dogmatically by students both in class and out. We accept sympathetically the rightful mood of free and sceptical inquiry which is thus indicated as the privilege and duty of those alert college students who are eager to examine the basic preconceptions of life. We are not disturbed by honest doubts. The disconcerting fact is rather that such statements are a far too accurate reflection of the climate of sentiment and conviction (or lack of conviction) which is widespread in the older community. That this prevalent sentiment has much to do with the spiritual unrest and moral confusion of the younger generation seems a reasonable conclusion.

We should, therefore, characterize briefly the nature of the present spiritual dilemma. What have we lost? What can we retain and move forward to affirm about insights into spiritual realities? What, if anything, can the college do in terms of policy, program, and procedure which may be educationally constructive in the light of the spiritual difficulties now encountered?

A word of warning is first in order. This entire book is designed to address itself to the total outlooks and needs of college students. The basic historic aims of the college are correctly weighted on the side of the life of the mind, the life of reason, and the clarification of understanding and wisdom at the deepest level of human comprehension. It is, indeed, a valid premise that every phase of the student's life in college should minister to and strengthen his realization of the college's purpose for him in terms at once intellectual and spiritual. This is not to say, however, that richness of rewarding spiritual insight is primarily the product of education. The great founders of the world's religions—those acknowledged, superior human spirits who have been noble, saintly, and spiritually wise, along equally with those unidentified men and women of integrity in all ages and places who have walked humbly with their God—all of these are now honored without reference to the degree to which they were "educated" in the conventional sense. They have been turned to for heartening support as exemplars in the human situation because they are realized to be in possession of some Reality which brought love, dignity, holiness, purity of purpose to the ordering of their lives.

"The wisdom of this world is foolishness with God."

On the other hand, I do not belittle the indispensable value of education nor do I advocate any obscurantist approach to its purpose and conduct. The historically persistent effort of mankind has been to become more and more rational and better and better informed about the nature of the world in which we live and move and have our being as integral in its functioning.

If in some way present education seems to "take us away from God," if it leads to a denial or subordinating of "the reasons of the heart which the reason knows not of" (Pascal), that is so much the worse for education. And this dubiety as to clear purpose is one of higher education's basic difficulties today.

What Is the Dilemma?

The dilemma of the modern mind—vividly exemplified in too much college instruction—is the confusion between the seeming implications of scientific points of view as an approach to all the reality we confront as contrasted with a religious point of view which embraces a God, a moral order, a sense of profound spiritual meaning and purpose in human experience—all of which may not necessarily be susceptible of actual proof but which for those who will take the leap to faith adds a new dimension to living. The situation is helpfully summarized in a recent volume, *Religion and the Modern Mind*, as follows:

The truth is that the ultimately moral character of the universe, whether it is personified in the form of a righteous and transcendent God or is conceived as immanent in the world process itself, has been a part of all advanced religious cultures. It has been, until recent times in the West, a universal belief of civilized humanity. The opposite conception, that of a blind universe which is perfectly indifferent to good and evil . . . is characteristic only of the western world during the last three centuries and is the product of seventeenth century scientific revolution. That values are subjective and relative, that the world is not a moral order, is the fashionable belief of the intellectuals of our time. And this view of the world has seeped down to the masses. But since the older religious view persists under the surface, this gives rise to perplexities and contradictions in men's minds in contrast to the monolithic clarity and simplicity of the medieval mind.[1]

A naturalistic accounting for the operation of the forces at work in life is an increasingly dominant fact. What room this accounting may be thought to leave for the affirmation of the existence of God, for the reality of spiritual values and insights, for the influence in conduct of suprahuman purposes—all this has become for many persons a matter of profound doubt and for others of us a concern necessary if a coherent and rational expression of our belief is to be achieved. But even where teachers or students have positive theistic conviction, there is too often in the conduct of such "believers" an ignoring of the implications in their lives of the deeper spiritual insights which seem to have lost sufficient vitality and appeal to evoke profound and beneficent differences of conduct.

A second questioning, ultimately deriving from the first, is whether, even if there is somehow a body of human loyalties and moral standards which had better be served on prudential grounds, there is any need to assume that men will be better persons if somehow they feel able to relate their moral struggles to any direct or indirect support from suprahuman sources. Will not a purely humanistic interpretation account for all the motive power which individuals need for ethical striving, to the extent that such striving is deemed desirable or obligatory?

[1] W. T. Stace: *Religion and the Modern Mind*. Philadelphia, J. B. Lippincott Co., 1952, p. 49. I am indebted to this book for aid in clarifying the orientation of this chapter.

It is questions of this kind which young people in college are asking in their own language and which some teachers are discussing from various points of view and with divergent or ambiguous conclusions. And it should be obvious that the developing of spiritual insights in this climate of skeptical sentiment is not easy. Other teachers are even saying that this kind of inquiry is an impossible, an irrelevant, or an unimportant task. They are saying, in short, that spiritual insights are either untrue or illusory.

I believe, however, that there are a number of propositions—on which there may be reasonably wide agreement—which may illuminate this dilemma. I shall make no attempt to elaborate or "prove" these affirmations, many of which fall admittedly into the realm of "faith" and are not provable by logical argument. Perhaps such a body of hypotheses or principles will suggest a further sensible basis for saying something constructive about educational policy and program possessed of a spiritual outlook and calculated to have a deep and valid appeal for the students themselves.

"The Everlasting Yea"

I affirm that it is possible for a rational and intelligent person to hold the following beliefs:

1. A spiritual interpretation of the universe is valid—that is, a view and faith that our world is most richly intelligible in terms of the Spirit and of the creative processes, divine and human, which can be sensed as divine Outcome and Reality.

2. It is possible to attain a direct, immediate awareness of this spiritual Reality in terms both of personal identification with it and of an ineffably sensed consciousness that this Reality is a Source, a Law, a Power, a Process, in all of which we may dimly but progressively share as participants, no less than worshippers.

3. The way of loving kindness and tender mercy to all our fellow men gains its strongest sanction and deepest meaning in and through our belief that all men are the common heirs of this unutterable Spiritual Reality, are co-workers in a process to create that which we come to realize is true, good, beautiful, loving and holy—something for which men's selfhood has an innate, intrinsic affinity. It was St. Augustine who phrased this truth thus: "Thou hast made us for Thyself and our hearts are restless till they find their rest in Thee." And the "rest" which he identified has, I shall interpolate, its dialectic in the active, creative effort of all of us.

4. The world thus accepted is a moral order requiring human responsibility for the discovery and application of a moral law or a body of "natural law" in and through the fulfillment of which is the measure of the realization of our human destiny. This natural law deeply interpreted is ultimately not relative. There is rather an absolute demand made upon all men to the extent that they are progressively able, by virtue of their deeply felt and continuous intellectual and emotional search, to discern the "law" and to grasp its implications for the responsible conduct of each person. And the mandate imposed to pursue this search, although it is relative in its actual practical effectiveness, is absolute in the *striving* toward truth and goodness which it entails upon each one of us. There is, I believe, truth in the statement that the problem here posed is one of being relatively absolute, not of being absolutely relative.

Although this moral insight is absolutely needful in order to assist all men toward the relative and partial applications they have the capacity to achieve, men remain in this divine ordering free to make choices. And they continue responsible as individuals to make wise judgments in the interpretation and fulfillment of the "law," as applied to personal conduct. Failure to order one's life up to the measure of one's discernment (as re-enforced by education) is what we mean by sin. Sin is failure to obey the dictates of the vision of righteousness and of the creative processes which can be at work if we will strive to understand and share in the required individual collaboration with the Creative Intention.

5. The approach through science is but one partial, albeit essential, avenue to the understanding and experiencing of Reality. Our obligatory moral efforts are progressively informed and enlightened by the use of scientific methods and our application of the findings from such inquiry. Scientific inquiry and knowledge thus have indispensable moral value. And the view of the processes of nature and of human nature which a naturalistic interpretation supplies is the necessary condition of a progressive growth of scientific and also of spiritual understanding. But our judgments of "how things have come to be this way," "what value they have," and "how we can make them better" are distinctive judgments not alone of fact but also of value. And this distinction is a constantly valid one which the moral struggle has to keep clear and which education has to help to clarify. In other words, we are required persistently to ask two kinds of questions: (1) What are the facts? (2) What is meaningful and

valuable in the perspective of our individual scientific and spiritual awareness?

Obviously these propositions fail to take account of numerous additional beliefs which many with organized religious ties would add as integral to their own body of faith. But these "overbeliefs" differently characterizing every religion and sect, however valuable and true they may appear to the believer, are in some measure unacceptable in their stated formulation to those of a different traditional doctrine or of no doctrinal background. And this is why they are not here considered.

If, as is my purpose, the basic intent is to center attention upon the underlying ways and means of developing a spiritual grasp which clearly have some validity for students with varied or no religious traditions, I believe the most profound insights of history and of our contemporaries have to be advanced in as universal an idiom as possible and in as comprehensive a frame as can be widely meaningful. For this kind of universalism should certainly encourage some deep rapport to be established between a heterogeneous body of faculty, personnel workers, and students on our campuses who are in fact exponents of every important religion in the world and of every sectarian branch of the Jewish and Christian faiths.*

Surely one of the profound spiritual truths which has to be grasped is that the insights which are common to every great religion—the aspirations and the resulting moral claims upon its members—need to be acknowledged, to be clarified, and to be strengthened by an effort at recognized common acceptance and identifying statement. In this view there is One World of faith and hope to which allegiance can be given. And it is far more important that this all-embracing Reality be sensed and cherished than that partial insights doctrinally stated be held up as final truth—whether these derive from science, from mysticism, from revelation, or from some other avenue of what appears to be convincing experience.

If we want the assumption of the highest quality of human responsibility and a vivid sense of absolute obligation to develop in students as in ourselves, if we want for us all that profound purposiveness and self-direction which can have a kind of support *sub specie aeternitatis*,

---

* Elaborative of this view from somewhat different outlooks are two recent volumes: W. T. Stace: *Op. cit.*, and Edmund W. Sinnott: *Two Roads to Truth: A Basis for Unity Under the Great Tradition.* New York, Viking Press, 1953.

there are outlooks and commitments beyond the realm of reason and there are decisions of commitment to accept, and there is a positive faith as an adventurous leap of insight. All of which require conscious nurture.

My present purpose, therefore, is to express the need for some statement, all too brief, of the ways and means which might be educationally organized toward realizing in the life of many more students than now the cultivation of these resources and powers which the phrase, spiritual insights, intends to connote.

I shall refer to five aspects of possible program approaches.† These are:

1. The knowledge of religion as an historic fact;
2. The philosophic and reflective aspects of religious inquiry and concern;
3. The place of organized religious bodies on the campus;
4. The spiritual life of teachers and counselors; and
5. The role of meditation and contemplation.

1. The Knowledge of Religion as a Fact

There is wide agreement among all who have reflected on the place of spiritual development in college teaching that the first requisite for each student is some factual, historic knowledge of the role religious life, ideas, institutions, different religions, and personalities have played in civilization's unfolding drama.* In the earlier American tradition something of this awareness—at least as far as the King James Bible is concerned—could be taken for granted among a great majority of students because of the ministrations of home and church. This assumption of prior familiarity can no longer validly be made even among those young people who come from avowedly Christian homes.

The point does not need to be labored that spiritual insight is not a new and original revelation made afresh to every generation.

---

† The supporting literature on these five points is, of course, extensive, and is increasing rapidly. I have myself in *Character Building and Higher Education* (New York, The Macmillan Co., 1953) elaborated more fully on several aspects of program and have there supplied further bibliographical suggestions.

* See, for example, *The Function of the Public Schools in Dealing with Religion*, Washington, D. C., American Council on Education, 1953; *Moral and Spiritual Values in the Public Schools*, National Education Association, 1951; William Clayton Bauer: *Moral and Spiritual Values in Education*, Lexington, Kentucky, University of Kentucky Press, 1952; and Ward Madden: *Religious Values in Education*, New York, Harper & Brothers, 1951.

Rather, in each generation we build and rebuild upon a rich body of humanity's spiritual sensitivity and progressively disclosed insights. And for the young person in search of spiritual clarification to have to start his own search without benefit of any background of historic tradition and experience is unfair to him. Indeed, even the need for such a search is unrecognized by many students amid today's secular preoccupations.

Suffice it to say that in courses in history, philosophy, sociology, anthropology, social psychology, esthetic appreciation, and the like, every student might at least become aware of the religious influences which have permeated our historic cultural growth. At the least, the phrase, "spiritual insights," should come alive for today's young people as having some realistic connotations which are not in the realm of the superstitious, the obscurantist, the purely "mythical."

2. THE PHILOSOPHIC AND REFLECTIVE ASPECTS OF RELIGIOUS INQUIRY AND CONCERN

It is impossible briefly to do justice to the truth that all the great religions have implications which are philosophic or metaphysical in nature. One has but to mention the inroads which "scientism," the various determinisms (evolutionary, psychical, economic, historical), logical positivism, scientific humanism, anthropological naturalism, and others have made toward creating scepticism about the reality, validity, and potency of spiritual insight, in order to realize that college students are peculiarly subjected in the nature of their intellectual environment to influences which can readily encourage blind spots about the life of their spirits and of the Spirit.

Indeed, within the departments of philosophy, to say nothing of the outlooks of teachers in other fields, the metaphysics taught or implied can too often today be of a sceptical and unspiritual character. Moreover, the value of any metaphysics may be stoutly denied by highly regarded teachers.

Problems of the validity of rational faith as distinguished from knowledge; of the absolute character of scientific knowledge; of decision, commitment and dedication, as compared with a "take it easy" attitude; of established criteria as to right and wrong; of the meaning of a Law of Love; of the reality of a basic and pervasive orderliness in the universe—all these aspects of human tension not only can be but are ignored in the instruction (and comprehension) of too many college teachers. Or, in a more generous interpretation, some of them believe (mistakenly, in my judgment), in a separation of their personal religious convictions and of their presentations of instructional content and emphasis. The former is thought to be private and personal; the other is intellectual and "scholarly." And even the inconsistency of such a dichotomy all too rarely receives critical scrutiny by teachers who should know better.

It nevertheless remains true that recently more and more of the most profound scientific scholars are voicing convictions which are basically infused with spiritual insights and theistic interpretations. The obsessively "objective," "neutral," and hyperesthetic preconceptions of some of the humanists and social scientists are being left behind by the convictions and pronouncements of these wise exemplars of the deepest disclosures or intimations from the natural sciences. There is still, however, a long way to go if the historic insights of the human spirit are to be given their day in the court of the college classroom of scientists, humanists and social scientists. And I see no way for this advance to be hastened unless and until more college teachers have clearer beliefs about the aims and goals of their own instruction and about the overtones of conviction and insight about basic life outlooks which they feel able sincerely to articulate.

3. The Place of Organized Religious Bodies on the Campus

The potency of the church groups on college campuses in developing spiritual sensitivity among students depends upon a variety of factors. The number of young people who come from homes with vigorous church affiliations is certainly not increasing—is, indeed, probably a minority of the whole. And without some prior church connection of students, the chaplains and religious directors are likely to meet with some indifference in efforts to reach such unchurched individuals because of their unfamiliarity with the vocabulary of the spiritual life. The personal quality of the religious leaders can also have varying degrees of appeal even for church-affiliated students. The degree of influence may have to do with personality factors, with the degree of their theological liberality, or with the extent of their acceptance and tolerance of leaders and students of other religions or denominations.

I must register reservation with respect to too great stress in the conduct of these religious activities upon sectarian separatisms, upon denominational doctrines, upon special ritualistic emphases and elaborations. The world, I believe, is at a point where it is more important to stress those deep and abiding affirmations of faith which are virtually common and universal than those which are special to a particular religion or denomination. I know and would in some measure stress the need for and value of religious tradition and roots where they are already an experienced reality for the student or teacher. But I believe, none the less, that these can on occasion be stressed and promulgated by professional protagonists at a too great cost in relation to the strengthening of the sense of commonality of conviction and program shared by all men of good will and good mind. *The companionship of good will which unites men in agreed good action is always more important to espouse than that which may divide them in terms of doctrinal formulation.* This is to me one necessary affirmation in my own religious creed. And whatever ministers to the perpetuation of complacent separations and to a sense of spiritual superiority, or—even worse—of spiritual monopoly of the right and true, seems to me a defeat for the most generous spiritual insights of our day.

4. THE SPIRITUAL LIFE OF TEACHERS AND COUNSELORS

I believe that the student's spiritual welfare is greatly helped (or harmed) by the degree of spiritual maturity of those who teach him, and by those who counsel him beyond the instructional efforts. I have elsewhere* written upon the problem of the college teacher and his philosophy and religion in a secular society such as ours. Unless and until more teachers are, in their respective realms of discourse, more the prophet and less the priest, we may not hope for too much progress in the impartation of spirituality to students. I do not confuse the role of the preacher and of the teacher. I am only saying that *the vision of the deep human meaning of every subject* is the priceless spiritual asset of the gifted and profound teacher to whom the lines may rightly be applied:

> We touch him in life's throng and press
> And we are whole again.

That both the teacher and counselor shall measure up to this kind of stature is always our hope and prayer, but by no means can it be a complete realization in such a society as our own.

*"Spiritual Problems of the Teacher," *Harvard Educational Review*, Oct., 1945; "College Education and Character," *The Educational Forum*, Jan., 1950; "The Faith That Makes Men Whole," *The Educational Forum*, Jan., 1951; and *Trustees, Teachers, Students: Their Role in Higher Education*, Salt Lake City, University of Utah Press, 1951.

Far short of this ideal, however, it should be possible that the friendly human relations of personnel workers with students would exemplify a quality of deep and loving concern which would indirectly generate spiritual influences. The counselor who sees the student as an end in himself and as a human being possessed of autonomy and dignity as a person is almost certain to transmit and induce some real conviction within those he touches that they are co-workers together, collaborators in the search for a deeper reality which the student consciously or not seeks as a foundation for his faith, courage, and effort. Human relations at a sensitive level of interpersonal solicitude have their own sheer impact of value and enhancement. And I would not be interpreted as saying that the discourse between older and younger persons thus associated has to have any theological or doctrinal overtones unless their mutual inquiry is concerned with such matters due to some direct questioning on the student's part.

It is, of course, true that the counselor may not have the same continuing impact upon the student as the teacher in matters of systematic inquiry as to religious interests. But he or she has the priceless advantage of usually being sought by the student at some critical moment and hopefully—spontaneously—becoming aware in ways which words will but dimly convey, that the right counselor can also be a guide and friend. And the counselor's personality will be influential if he can manifest in his person and his human relations a total conviction, sincerity, earnestness, and concern for the student's welfare which shine through all he says. "We are not heard for our much speaking." We are, as counselors, listened to and followed for the patent integrity, courage, and strength of our characters. And it is to enhance the permanent undergirding of such courage and strength of character that this entire chapter is written. Spiritual insights thus reenforce attributes which can make the counselor's work especially meaningful and rewarding.

5. The Role of Meditation and Contemplation

One meditates upon the meaning and significance of that which may be existentially familiar. One contemplates the beauty, nobility, glory, mystery—of that which is not necessarily an objectively sensed reality but is deeply felt and realized by those who are sensitive.

There manifestly are established "disciplines" or regimens that forward both processes, especially the second or contemplative. Also there are forces in the psychic life and sentiment of our times which are discouraging to the moods of meditation and contemplation—

indeed to prayer and worship. To be able to resist these forces no doubt requires exceptional personal fortitude. Yet the development of spiritual insight in the deep meaning of that phrase does require some self-disciplining and some regimen beyond the immediacies of our usual activist programs of living and learning.

We have in our colleges too many courses each semester for each student. The "required" reading and writing is too imperious and voluminous. The claims of extracurricular activities are numerous and insistent. The encouragement to independent spiritual orientation becomes unappealing and obscure, if it exists at all. The physical circumstances of places of quiet and withdrawal where there is the likelihood of some evocation of the Spirit rarely exist and certainly are not stressed and given sufficient attentive concern by teachers and counselors. The difficult resolve to look within to discover one's deeper self, to be open to the influence of the Other, to "be still and know that I am God"—all this takes place not usually by chance or accident but by high and deliberate intent. And who is now helping this intent into being?

The body of our shared experience in college—hopefully shared by student, teacher, counselor, and administrator—which would further the insights toward the Spirit beyond the deliberations of the Mind (and the two must ultimately come much closer into the deeper unity of the all-encompassing Spirit), all this, in short, is not achieved without conscious striving and plan.

The need is real and urgent to vitalize the student's will to be and to become, his sense of upreach and outreach as a person and as a "son" of the manifest forces of Creation and Love which seemingly have placed us here on earth for ends toward which we are required to seek and labor.

The ultimate touch, the deep justification of all student personnel work, has to do with the strengthening, the rehabilitation, the resonant affirmation, of the integrity of the individual spirit as related to an ultimate Master Spirit in and through and for which it appears that our striving means, and means well and good, means better, stronger and finer for the good of men, as this can become organically related to what is, in our ineffectual vocabulary, God.

"The Spirit beareth witness with our spirits, that we are sons of God." Ultimately it is this sense within the individual that something in him is responding productively to Something he apprehends to be at work in his world, that is the true justification of a faith that grows as it experiences its own validity of enduring satisfaction, through apprehending "that by which it is apprehended."

No one in the role of counselor should tamper with the lives, careers, and destinies of young people, who has not a deep realization of the sanctity of the enterprise on which he or she is embarked. The contact of mind with mind and spirit with spirit has always hopefully to lead in what are believed to be Godlike directions. Only in a mood of humility and of reverence for life are other personalities to be helped toward spiritual strength and depth.

I am aware that I have not focused on the specific functioning of personnel workers in higher education. I have deliberately gone at that functioning obliquely to try to convey a sense of depth and "field" out from which alone fruitful contact with students can emanate. The roots of our human dealings are of the spirit, and unless and until that is realized by members of the personnel staff nothing profound in influence will be generated. If something of the ways in which the ministrations of the Spirit to self and to others may occur can be realized by us all both in our conviction and in the content of knowledge and faith we may embody in character and action, a truer work of healing and of helpfulness should be possible of realization.

18. Utilizing Every Resource

GEORGE E. McCABE

THE importance of utilizing all resources in work with counseling clients has been emphasized more often and for a longer period of time by the social work profession than any of the other human relations disciplines. Psychiatrists, psychologists, and personnel workers are paying increasing attention to the importance of using community resources, however, and are becoming less content with working individualistically or in clinical isolation. In the past twenty-five years our thinking regarding the use of resources has undergone major modification. The social worker, for example, no longer regards intake and referral as simply a kind of social switchboard which dispatches clients from one agency to another. No longer are needs and services thought of as static forces which need to be matched. Now we read and hear of the importance of helping a client to mobilize his inner resources so that he can more effectively seek and make use of the services in a community. By the same token, the literature on community organization no longer deals with resources as "given" amounts of community services but as potentials which can be developed through a process of cooperative consideration of community needs. In fact, the term "utilization of resources" no longer is adequately descriptive of a process which is now expanded to include the *development* and *mobilization* of resources as well as their utilization.

Thus far we have mentioned the development, mobilization, and utilization of resources "in the community." We have "looked outward" rather than inward. Such a tendency is consistent with the history of student personnel administration in this country. The emphasis on "utilizing every resource" has been on using *other* people's resources. The secondary school teacher has looked to the guidance counselor or the child guidance clinic, and the college faculty adviser has looked to the institution's counseling bureau.

Guidance has become a specialized function outside of the educational process itself. Personnel workers have encouraged this development while at the same time protesting its results—a lack of interest in or understanding by the instructional faculty of students as whole persons.

In seeking to utilize every resource we should first "look inward"—we should first explore the possibility of developing the untapped resources of our own staff.

The Price of Specialization in Student Personnel Work

Across the country, over the past twenty-five years, there has developed a markedly increased awareness of the importance of providing our schools and colleges with personnel services. With this awareness has come a tremendous increase in the number of persons trained for personnel and guidance work. This new recognition of guidance has been apparent in the myriad of specialized services established for students. This is particularly true at the college level where, in many institutions, the personnel head and his relatively large staff are completely independent of the dean of instruction and his staff. In the high school a small staff of counselors attempts to meet all of the guidance needs of the student body, assisted, in large systems, by badly overcrowded child guidance clinics. In short, personnel work in the past twenty-five years has glorified the specialist. While specialized personnel services have been established within the administrative framework of our educational institutions there has been a tendency for them to be adjunctive to the educational process, rather than an integral part of it. The educator has been encouraged to "look outward" for help for his students. This acceptance of specialism in guidance has been at a price. Because the price has been in terms of undeveloped, unmobilized, and unutilized resources within the educational system itself, it is important that we take a longer look at the results of specialization and generalization in a discussion devoted to *utilizing every resource*. What has it cost us to "look outward" to the exclusion of "looking inward" in our search for resources to meet the needs of our students?

Student personnel workers have long bemoaned dualism in education—the dichotomy between intellectual and personal-emotional development. They have emphasized, rightfully, that what we know about learning makes quite clear that it does not take place in disembodied intellects—that the student cannot be compartmentalized into the intellectual and the emotional. Yet they have defeated their own holistic approach to education by the dualistic administrative structure they have advocated for bringing personnel services to students—by their efforts to establish autonomous little empires free from the meddling fingers of academic deans who do not have the "personnel point of view."

The results of specialization and centralization are rather clear, I think. By coming in as "experts," personnel workers have absolved the instructional faculty of any responsibility for the personnel needs of their students. They have facilitated the process by which instructional faculty project all responsibility for the nonacademic needs of their students onto an inevitably overworked personnel staff. As specialized services become overburdened the cry goes up for more budget; for more staff. Costs go up, the empire grows, and still only a small proportion of the student body receives individualized attention. By dint of necessity personnel and guidance programs concentrate on service to the deviant. The personnel program becomes a negative, rather than a positive force in the educational process.

"Generalism" in Student Personnel Work—An Emerging Trend

A few institutions training personnel workers have resisted this pull toward ever-increasing specialization and centralization. They, and the colleges and schools in which they have placed their workers, have emphasized the personnel worker as a "generalist" rather than as a specialist. They have resisted the "service station" approach to personnel work. They have argued that personnel work should be an integral part of the educative process itself. They contend that generalism develops otherwise untapped resources within the staff. There is evidence that this point of view is being given wider credence; that there is an emerging trend toward decentralization; that the reorganization which is currently taking place in a number of colleges is in the direction of making personnel work inseparable from education, rather than adjunctive to it. This trend has been given a boost by developments in the field of group dynamics which have many implications for the guidance process.

The advocate of "generalism" believes in the "whole school" approach to personnel work: in services for all rather than specialized services for the few. He is concerned with the development of a hygienic climate in all phases of an institution's functioning; he is concerned with faculty staff development because he knows that a student spends much more time with his teachers and his residence hall supervisors than he does in the clinic office; and he knows that the quality of a student's daily interpersonal relationships can complement or undermine what is being done clinically; that it can often create or erase a need for clinical service.

The generalist is concerned with developing all of the resources within the situation in which the student has daily interpersonal relationships. He knows that his goal of staff development, out of which will evolve a hygienic climate, is dependent upon involving the faculty and entire staff in the personnel program. He knows that a sure way to abort the development of the internal resources of his institution is to allow a staff of specialists to assume total responsibility for the personal and emotional needs of students. Furthermore, if he is secure himself, he will be able to accept the fact that any staff, regardless of how psychologically unsophisticated, has valuable insights and understandings which should not go untapped.

In developing and mobilizing the resources of his own institution the generalist conceives his role to be that of consultant and of coordinator. He realizes the importance of establishing channels of communication which flow two ways; of providing opportunities for members of functional groups to interact around common problems. He sees the importance of providing these groups with responsibilities, and the power to make decisions; he also realizes the importance of their being able to see the results of their decisions, and to learn from them. He further realizes that commitment to action is best obtained when all members of a group responsible for carrying out a decision are involved in the making of the decision. He thinks of himself as a catalytic agent who frees the group to develop to its fullest potential through interaction.

In the high school the generalist sees the guidance program built around the home room teacher. In the college it is built around the faculty adviser and the residence hall counselor. The generalist envisions holding periodic conferences with groups of home room teachers, faculty advisers, or residence hall counselors. He sees himself as the convener of case conferences concerned with the needs of individual students. In short, he sees himself as a coordinator of a teacher-centered, rather than a specialist-centered, guidance program. This he sees to be a personnel program dedicated to the developing and mobilizing of every resource within the school or college. Personnel work so conceived touches every aspect of a school's or college's operations. It is an inherent part of the administrative and instructional program of the institution. Such a program is one that would leave indelible traces on any institution, even if the entire personnel staff left the institution tomorrow.

We Still Must "Look Outward"

One of the responsibilities of the personnel "generalist" is to help the teacher-counselor recognize the limits of his skill, and the areas of his competence, through regularly scheduled conferences. He knows the importance of helping a teacher-counselor to realize when to refer a student to the personnel specialist—when to "look outward."

The generalist is not unmindful of the need for specialized services. He realizes the importance of not building the program around such services, however. Some students are in need of intensive casework or psychotherapy, and such treatment certainly cannot be given by teacher-counselors. On the other hand, it does not seem too important, as a matter of general principle, whether such clinical help is given to a student within the school or college community, or the broad community. It *is* important that good treatment facilities be available to students at little or no cost: it *is* important that the personnel coordinator be in a position to recognize a need for intensive treatment. It *is* important that there be well-established referral channels. It is likewise important that there be integration between the clinic and the personnel program of the school; that each group understand, accept, and work with the other. This may be easier to accomplish if the personnel coordinator is responsible for administering specialized services (such as the university counseling bureau) as well as coordinating the general program. This will depend on the individual community situation, and, even more, on the human relations skills of the coordinator.

The College as a Community Agency

Almost all communities of at least moderate size have a Council of Social Agencies whose function is to coordinate the services of the community agencies and to be the instrumentality for cooperative social welfare planning. In some communities this organization may have the title of Community Welfare Council or Health and Welfare Council, or something similar. Regardless of title, the function is essentially the same. Membership of the Council, which usually has a professional staff, is made up of representatives of the public and voluntary social welfare, health, protective, and educational agencies of the community. In most communities the Council is the professional arm of the Community Chest and advises the Chest on the distribution of funds to member agencies, in accordance with a master social welfare plan.

Without a question the college or university should be represented on this Council by one or more of its personnel workers. This befits the institution's role as a responsible resident of the community. Of equal significance is the fact that the personnel worker, engaged as a co-worker on community problems with staff members of other agencies, is establishing a relationship which will facilitate communication on future problems, will dispel mistrust and lack of understanding, and, in effect, develop professional resources for the college that might well otherwise be unavailable.

The question as to what specialized psychological services are to be provided to students by the college itself, or the extent to which such services may be made available to college students in community agencies, are matters which might well be decided within the Council of Social Agencies after a cooperative study of the total needs of the community, including those of the college, rather than by any unilateral decision by the college which would presume, in effect, that the college and its students exist in a vacuum, untouched by the community, and vice versa.

There can be no ideal pattern for integrating the services of the college and those of other agencies in the community. This will vary with each individual situation. It will be dependent upon such things as whether the college is public or private, financed by state funds or local funds, whether the students are permanent residents of the community, or, if nonresidents, whether they live in private boarding houses or in college dormitories, etc. The only general principle is that the college should plan its student welfare program cooperatively with the other agencies of the community through the Council of Social Agencies. By "looking together" the needs of the community, and the college as a part of the community, can best be met through the development, mobilization, and utilization of all resources in a "whole community" approach.

Knowing the Resources of Your Community

The most effective way in which to become familiar with the resources of your community is to become an active member of your

Council of Social Agencies; to work with representatives of these agencies on problems of concern to the community. It is through endeavors of this sort, and through informal social contacts, that one really begins to know his community. It has often been said that one can usually find more resources in a cup of coffee than in a directory of social agencies.

Most councils of social agencies publish directories which are useful for purposes of initial reference. These vary in size from several hundred pages for the directory of the Health and Welfare Council of New York City to ten- and fifteen-page volumes for smaller communities. Every personnel worker should have such a directory. It must be remembered, however, that listing in these directories usually does not mean that the agency has been evaluated and "approved."

Other directories which may be useful are:

Directory of Psychiatric Clinics in the U. S.

Published by the National Association for Mental Health, Inc., 1790 Broadway, New York, N. Y. This directory lists only clinics which have a psychiatrist in attendance at regular hours. Listing is not intended to connote approval by NAMH.

Directory of Vocational Guidance Agencies

Published by the Ethical Practices Committee of the National Vocational Guidance Association. All agencies listed have been examined and approved by NVGA. The training and experience background of professional staff members is given for each agency.

Directory of Member Agencies

Published by the Family Service Association of America, 192 Lexington Avenue, New York, N. Y. Agencies listed in this directory meet the standards of the national association.

Directory, American Psychological Association

This directory lists fellows and associates of the American Psychological Association. Membership in the Division of Clinical and Abnormal Psychology certifies that the member has met minimum requirements for the performance of psycho-diagnostic studies and psychotherapy. Membership in the Division of Counseling and Guidance certifies that the member has met minimum requirements for the performance of counseling and vocational guidance. Listing of a psychologist as a Fellow signifies recognition by his colleagues of his professional eminence. The directory likewise lists psychologists in the various specialties who have passed the examinations of the American Board of Examiners in Professional Psychology and who have, therefore, been designated as diplomates of that Board. A brief biographical sketch is provided for each member listed in the directory.

Directory, American Psychiatric Association

This directory lists "physicians specializing in the practice of psychiatry." A brief biographical sketch is provided for each Member or Fellow listed.

Directory of Medical Specialists

This volume is compiled by the Advisory Board of Medical Specialties of the American Medical Association. Of particular interest to personnel workers is the listing of diplomates of the American Board of Psychiatry and Neurology. This is the highest paper certification of competence obtainable in psychiatry. A brief biographical sketch is provided for each diplomate.

One is inclined to ask, immediately, whether the listing of a psychologist, psychiatrist, clinic, or agency in any of these directories is sufficient evidence of professional competence. The answer is a forthright "No." The fact that a psychologist or a psychiatrist is a diplomate of a professional board certainly raises the presumption of competence. Unfortunately, psychiatrists, psychologists, social workers, and personnel workers are no different in this respect from the members of any other professional group. In all professions there are incompetents possessing the highest of paper credentials.

How, then, can we evaluate the professionals in our community to whom we may want to refer students? The answer, of course, is that there is no magic formula. Probably the most effective means is to gain acceptance by the professionals active in the social welfare program of your community, in the manner already described, and to rely heavily on their judgment. The social worker in a good family service agency, for instance, probably is very uniquely qualified to evaluate the psychiatrists in your community because she has probably worked closely with them. The analytic consultant retained by a family service agency over a period of years is likely to be highly regarded as a psychotherapist. By the same token you can usually find, from the same source, whether the local mental hygiene clinic offers little more than categorical diagnoses—either because it is understaffed, or because the psychiatrists and psychologists on the staff simply do not know anything about psychotherapy. Unfortunately, a great many public and low-cost clinics fall into this category.

It is no secret that there are many psychiatrists who do little more than "hang a diagnosis" on patients, or administer electroshock treatments. Their training has largely been in state mental hospitals, where they have had little in the way of intensive, formal supervision in psychotherapy. It is likewise no secret that there are many psychologists who are little more than psychometrists, and who are inadequately trained to work with clients in a treatment relationship. In general, this is less likely to be true of recent graduates in clinical psychology. It should be remembered, nonetheless, that many colleges training clinical psychologists do not believe that the four-year graduate training program leading to the Ph.D. is sufficient to qualify a graduate to engage in private practice. They advocate additional formal training, or intensive clinical supervision.

For the very reason that adequate psychotherapeutic service is often almost unobtainable, except at fees ranging from ten to twenty dollars per hour, the family service agency is often the best resource available. The social work profession has done a much better job than its sister professions (with the possible exception of clinical psychology which has greatly strengthened its training program since the war) in providing a training program which has been standardized nationally. All graduates have had two years of graduate training, including three days a week of intensively supervised field experience. In addition, because of the fact that social workers do not characteristically engage in private practice, it has been possible to provide graduates with opportunities for continued professional growth through intensive supervision throughout their professional careers. The result is that a corps of highly competent professionals staff the better voluntary family service agencies. It is no exaggeration to say that for the person who is not severely disturbed the family agency may be a far better resource than the local psychiatric clinic.

In the opinion of the writer the background of the private psychotherapist should meet two criteria: one, it should include several years of formal, intensive supervision in psychotherapy; two, it should include personal psychotherapy. Unfortunately, psychology and psychiatry have not done as well as social work in standardizing the kinds of experiences their workers receive. Because of the variability of supervision standards one cannot be sure that a psychiatrist's residency was an adequate training experience except in those instances where one is personally familiar with the training program of the resident institution. The psychologists are in an even less enviable position, except for the fact that their pre-doctoral training program is much longer and more intensive than that for the psychiatrist who does not begin to train for his specialty in any meaningful way until after he has completed medical school.

The one notable general exception is the program of the psychoanalytic training centers which consumes three to four years, is very intensively supervised, and which requires a personal psychoanalysis. Unfortunately, only a few of these centers will accept psychologists for training. There are notable exceptions such as the Institute for Psychotherapy, the National Psychological Association for Psychoanalysis, and the William Alanson White School of Psychiatry in New York City. Reference to such training in the biographical entry of one of the directories raises a strong presumption of competence merely on the basis of the scope and intensity of such training programs.

While in the area of vocational guidance there is considerable variation in the quality of service offered by the various agencies, listing in the National Vocational Guidance Association Directory does attest to minimum competency, at least, and to ethical practice.

Helping the Student to Accept Help

We have discussed the importance of "looking inward"—of developing the personnel resources of our educational staff. We have mentioned, likewise, that there will always be a need for specialized services beyond the function or competence of the generalist. We have discussed the manner in which the college can develop the resources of the community and integrate them with those of the college. It seems appropriate, now, to discuss the manner in which we can bring together the student in need of help and the agency in a position to offer it. It has already been emphasized that this is not a mere matter of dispatching. Often the student needs to be helped to accept help. Often he needs help in mobilizing his own inner resources before he is ready to use the resources of an outside agency— whether it be the college or university counseling bureau, or the local family service agency.

The referral interview, or series of interviews, is a counseling interview with particular emphases and problems. General counseling principles are as applicable to the referral interview as to any other.

The general counseling principles listed below are taken from an unpublished article by Dr. Claire Grauel, formerly of the Guidance Laboratory of Teachers College, Columbia University:

1. Try to create an atmosphere which will help the counselee to be at ease, and free to discuss the problem. What to do (and not to do) depends upon your hunches regarding this particular counselee. (Dominating, submissive, etc.)

2. By being receptive and willing to listen (rather than asking questions or making irrelevant "remarks"), give the counselee an opportunity to present the problem as he sees it. If he is rather vague, inarticulate, or timid, take notice of that and try to draw him out rather than do the thinking for him.

3. Listen closely (and as silently as you can) while the student attempts to describe the problem, always remembering that he is much more likely to describe the symptom (the thing that hurts) rather than the problem.

4. No matter how clearly you may see through the individual's confusion, start where he is—help him to recognize where he is and indicate your understanding (rather than sympathy) for his attitude and feelings in the matter.

5. One needs to keep the focus on how the student feels about what has happened to him, and to what extent he is trying to protect these feelings through being inarticulate, overly voluble, or through distortion of facts. Such behaviour represents the student's needs, and is to be understood and respected.

6. If the problem seems unbearable (or of no moment) to the student, try to understand why in either case, rather than giving (false) reassurance, brushing the problem aside lightly, or forcing out points he is obviously keeping back. Respect the student's need for self-preservation.

7. After the student has done his best to present the problem, make pertinent comments, or ask questions to bring out further information, attitudes, values, etc., with regard to (a) the length and onset of the difficulty, (b) efforts made to cope with the problem, (c) what help, if any, has been sought previously, with what outcomes, and (d) his present attitude toward a possible solution (optimistic or pessimistic).

8. Draw out all his ideas as to what he might be able to do, by encouraging him to present alternative courses of action, weighing values involved, and possible solution (optimistic or pessimistic).

9. Once the counselee prepares a plan of action help him to appraise it on the grounds of (a) his feelings, and (b) external reality.

10. Even at the cost of time, let the counselee work out his own problem in his own way, regardless of what you think he should do. Be patient. His job is to grow . . . not merely to obtain information or be

told what to do. If he had been "on his own" more in the past, he wouldn't be so dependent now.

11. Work for a good interpersonal relationship which is objective, collaborative (vs. cooperative), friendly, but not familiar, with understanding rather than sympathy (which might defeat your desire to help).

12. Beware of getting interested in the content of the counselee's material, or the situation may degenerate into a dramatic episode without any basic understanding of the student's feelings.

13. Watch the immediate situation. The student brings his habitual and characteristic problems of behaviour into the counseling situation and here you have them under the microscope for first-hand study. His timidity, aggressiveness, negativism, etc., are all in evidence and should be understood, not "corrected," by the counselor. They are "handles" for constructive work, not for moralizing or "preaching." These are evidences of his inner, and therefore, basic needs.

14. Try to understand what role you are playing—parent, sibling, pal, etc., and try to respect the counselee's need to project upon you. Never succumb to that role, however, if you wish to be a counselor.

15. Keep the counselee rather than his problems as the center of the counseling process (without, however, discounting the reality of the problem).

In addition to the general counseling principles listed by Dr. Grauel, the writer believes those listed below to be of specific pertinence to the referral process:

1. Referral often cannot be effected in one interview. Do not hurry the tempo of a relationship. Guard against leaping ahead in your own mind to the ultimate goal faster than the student is able to follow.

2. Oftentimes your first problem is to make the counseling situation sufficiently understanding and "safe" to enable the student to admit to himself, and you, that he has a problem. This may take time.

3. People aren't always asking for what they seem to be asking for. Don't be too quick to respond to the content of a question. Help them to express the underlying feeling.

4. Referral is not a process of logical exposition. Emotionalized attitudes must be recognized and the counselee must be helped to express them fully. Skillful counseling will help a student to lower his defenses sufficiently to enable you to get at the business at hand (recognition of problem, willingness to work on the problem, willingness to accept the help of a referral agency).

5. The referral interview is a counseling interview with a situational focus (the referral, per se). Attitudes and feelings must be skillfully related to this focus.

6. The student should not be "given" a plan. He should be involved in the planning; be given a sense of participation.

7. Sometimes we formulate "a plan" without really listening to what the counselee is trying to tell us. (He may not be able to verbalize it, directly.)

8. We cannot just deal with reality. We must begin with the student's distorted perception of reality. At the same time you have a responsibility to give the student full information regarding the individual or agency to whom you are referring him. Referrals should not be made unless you have made a reasonably thorough investigation of the resource.

9. Agencies have symbolic significance for individuals. Each person will have his own perception which, for him, is reality. There are certain general perceptions which we can anticipate: a) feelings of fright and shame, often covered with hostility or indifference, about being referred for psychiatric help ("Do you think I'm crazy?"); b) feelings of shame about going to family agencies ("social worker"; "family welfare"—these connote charity); c) feelings of debasement and worthlessness associated with using public agency services. Individuals must be helped to express the full intensity of these feelings, before they can be helped to "handle" them. They cannot be "convinced" or "argued" out of them.

10. A student's permission should be obtained before his name or other identifying information is used in a telephone conversation with another agency. His written authorization should be obtained if you intend to send a summary. The first telephone contact with the agency should preferably be made in the student's absence, for obvious reasons.

11. If the student is to cooperate in the referral, it is necessary that he understand and cooperate in the transaction. A clear interpretation must be given to him of the reasons for the referral, what may be involved in treatment, the nature of the service, the procedure and cost involved, etc. In addition to giving correct information at this point, it is helpful to make clear that "treatment" is not something applied or injected from the outside as in somatic medicine, and that solutions to problems usually depend most upon the deevlopment of the applicant's own resources.

12. Agencies oftentimes will not definitely commit themselves to accepting a referral until they have read your summary, and have spoken with the counselee. If an agency does not accept the case the individual is likely to be lost in the shuffle. It is advisable, therefore, to schedule a follow-up interview with your counselee, at the time you make the referral. Such an interview might be scheduled for two weeks or a month hence. If the referral is "successful" the student can cancel the appointment.

13. Don't "dump" counselees. Try to develop an understanding with the agencies in your community as to the kind of people to whom they can be of help. Your most difficult problems may be beyond the function or ability of the agencies in your community. This suggests sys-

tematic conferences with agency personnel to develop criteria for the most effective use of resources. Promiscuous and undisciplined mass referring will "burn out" the agencies in your community as an available resource.

Summary

1. Our first, most important, and often overlooked step in utilizing every resource is to explore the possibility of developing the untapped resources of our own staff. Centralization of the personnel functions in the offices of personnel specialists tends to thwart the development of resources in our own staffs.

2. The personnel generalist is dedicated to the developing and mobilizing of every resource within the school or college. There appear to be emerging trends toward decentralization and "despecialization" in student personnel administration.

3. The generalist is not unmindful of the need for specialized services. Planning for these services should be undertaken by the college in cooperation with other agencies within the framework of the Council of Social Agencies, in terms of the needs and resources of the total community.

4. The most effective way to *really* know the resources of your community which might not otherwise be available to your students is to become an active member of the Council of Social Agencies.

5. Probably the most effective way in which to evaluate the resources of your community is to gain acceptance by the professional people active in the social welfare program of your community, and to rely heavily on their judgment until such time as you feel you can confidently rely on your own judgment drawn from experience with these resources.

6. Referral is not a process of logical exposition. The referral interview is a counseling interview with a situational focus—the referral, per se. Attitudes and feelings must be related skillfully to that focus.

BIBLIOGRAPHY

American Psychiatric Association: *Biographical Directory of Fellows and Members of the American Psychiatric Association.* New York, American Psychiatric Association.

American Psychological Association: *Directory.* Washington, D. C., American Psychological Association.

Coleman, Jules V.: "Distinguishing Between Psychotherapy and Casework." *Journal of Social Casework* 30: June, 1949, p. 244.

Corey, Stephen M.: *Action Research for Better School Practice.* New York, Bureau of Publications, Teachers College, Columbia University, 1953.

Davies, Daniel R.: "Organizational Patterns for Today's Schools." *Teachers College Record* 52: Nov., 1950, pp. 90-97.

deHuzar, George B.: *Practical Applications of Democracy.* New York and London, Harper & Bros., 1945.

Family Service Association of America: *Directory of Member Agencies.* New York, Family Service Association of America.

Family Welfare Association of America: *Training in Family Social Work Agencies: Report of the Committee on Training.* New York, Family Welfare Association of America, 1933.

Fink, Arthur E.: *The Field of Social Work.* New York, H. Holt and Co., 1942.

Follett, Mary P.: *Dynamic Administration.* New York, Harper & Brothers, 1942.

Harms, Ernest: "Varieties of Psychotherapeutic Competence." *Nervous Child* 8: Jan., 1949, pp. 3-8.

Kasius, Cora (ed.): *Principles and Techniques in Social Casework— Selected Articles, 1940-50.* New York, Family Service Association, 1950.

King, Clarence: *Organizing for Community Action.* New York, Harper & Brothers, 1948.

Lippett, Ronald: *Training in Community Relations.* New York, Harper & Brothers, 1949.

Lloyd-Jones, Esther M.: "Centrifugal and Centripetal Guidance Programs for Children." *Teachers College Record* 51: Oct., 1949, pp. 7-13.

Marcus, Grace: "Family Casework in 1948." *Journal of Social Casework* 29: July, 1948, p. 261.

McMillen, A. Wayne: *Community Organization for Social Welfare.* Chicago, University of Chicago Press, 1947.

National Association for Mental Health: *Directory of Psychiatric Clinics and Other Resources in the United States.* New York, National Association for Mental Health.

National Vocational Guidance Association: *Directory of Vocational Counseling Services.* St. Louis, Ethical Practices Committee, National Vocational Guidance Association.

Simcox, Beatrice: "The Social Service Exchange: Its Function and Operation." *Journal of Social Casework* 28: Nov. and Dec., 1947, pp. 331 and 388.

Taft, J. Julia: *Family Casework and Counseling: A Functional Approach.* Philadelphia, University of Pennsylvania Press, 1948.

Trecker, Harleigh B.: *Group Process in Administration.* New York, Woman's Press, 1950, 2nd ed.

19. Legal Implications for Student Personnel Workers

THOMAS B. SHREWSBURY

Case No. 1: You are an assistant dean of men. During an interview, a disturbed 18-year-old boy mentions his intention to commit a felony. You take no action beyond referring him to the college psychiatrist. Later the crime is committed and the boy apprehended and brought to trial. You receive a subpoena. When questioned about the interview, what will you say?

Case No. 2: You are head of a women's residence hall. A student trips over a loose stair runner and falls the length of the stairway, suffering a fractured leg and internal injuries. She sues the college for negligence. Has she a valid case?

Case No. 3: You are a dean of students on the disciplinary committee. You hear vague reports about a girl causing trouble in her dormitory. You talk with her, but she denies it. The reports continue and reach other committee members who, feeling she brings no credit on the college, recommend immediate expulsion without a hearing. With no clear evidence of guilt, do you feel the board's decision is valid, legally and otherwise?

Case No. 4: You are appointed for a two-year term by the state legislature as Director of Veterans' Counseling in a state university. After one year the legislature abolishes the position for lack of adequate funds and prohibits further allowance of pay. Can you sue the state for breach of contract?

Each of the above examples depicts one of the many problems whose legal implications personnel workers should understand. While definitive answers in each case are admittedly somewhat difficult to set down, due to variations in state laws and inconsistencies in past judicial interpretation, why not jot down your reactions anyway at this time? Later, as we cover the areas in question, you can compare them with prevailing legal opinion.

Educative Responsibility, Deeper Teaching, and a Philosophy of Ethics

Why such stress on legal considerations? Why burden busy personnel workers with a responsibility for which colleges and universities specifically retain professionally trained attorneys? These are good questions, for lawyers are patently employed for but one purpose: to provide expert guidance in legal matters. But how effective can that guidance be when the necessity for immediate decision precludes consultation until *after* a crisis has passed? If a counselor, for example, should suddenly find his counselee making amorous advances, might it not be somewhat difficult for him to stop time completely while he telephones the college attorney and asks, "What next?" There is no denying that lawyers play a valuable role in the administrative regime, or that their advice should be utilized whenever possible, but there will inevitably be critical situations wherein the personnel worker can act only according to his own understanding of the legalities involved.

Nor is it a lawyer's duty to assume for clients the responsibilities of adult citizenship. Personnel workers, like anyone else, are citizens and employees in an interdependent society and, as such, are obligated to live by and work within the legal structure designed for the protection and well-being of that society. While it is not incumbent upon them to be "legal eagles," such a point of view does logically demand on their part a general knowledge of existing legislation and its implications for their work.

Furthermore, as contrasted with less strategically placed citizens, personnel people exist primarily for an *educative* purpose, with a responsibility for helping maturing students develop the intelligent attitudes and moral habits required for leadership in a turbulent world. Students look on college officials as examples, as persons whose influence can mark them for life, but they will not look with confidence on those who abrogate through ignorance the very laws they expect others to understand. For personnel workers, whose effectiveness depends so heavily on students' confidence, and within whose program lie so many special opportunities for this deeper teaching, such a mandate makes imperative a knowledge of legal implications relative to their own positions.

Then, too, since personnel people do not attain maximum effectiveness within their own program by operating in an educational vacuum, but rather according to a "generalist" philosophy, by maintaining close integration with all branches of the administration they must also be acquainted with the legal concerns of other institutional members, and must be ever appreciative of the possible effect of their individual actions upon the total college structure. A sympathetic dormitory supervisor who unwittingly gives illegal advice may win the momentary appreciation of the advisee, but she will receive no administrative pat on the head if that advice ultimately brings against the college a parental suit for damages.

Lastly, if the student personnel profession is to continue its advance as a vital force on the educational scene, personnel workers must not only keep abreast of significant developments in the field, but must also work actively toward improving conditions where necessary. This may well necessitate their being prominent, as educational leaders have been in the past, in promulgating local, state, and federal legislation, and in continuing to influence the trend in jurisprudence from the "punitive" to the "preventive" and the "educative."* It will also necessitate their doing their part in facilitating harmonious college-community relations and in effectively interpreting their needs to the local citizenry, since the adoption of amelioraive measures will ultimately depend upon the voting public's understanding of what is desired. For the attainment of these future goals, a knowledge of present practices and trends is similarly essential.

But is "knowledge" enough? Is it sufficient to say that a familiarity with legislative implications automatically equips one to handle campus legal problems? Does a dean of men, for instance, in attempting to discourage an irate police chief from legally booking a scared prankster, or in persuading a congressman to introduce a new bill, need more than factual knowledge on his side?

Moreover, is it not obvious from the above paragraphs that such problems will frequently involve conflicting loyalties, where the personnel worker will find it impossible to divorce strictly *legal* considerations from *moral* and *ethical* values? "Is my responsibility in this case," he will have to ask himself, "to the student, the college, society in general, or to myself?" Wrenn[1] and Thorne[2] emphasize this

---

* This trend, which has been fostered to a great extent by the rapid growth of local and state mental hygiene societies, is evidenced by such recent bills as those advocating more understanding treatment of sex offenders, juvenile delinquents, and inmates of mental and penal institutions.

[1] C. Gilbert Wrenn: "The Ethics of Counseling."

[2] Frederick C. Thorne: *Principles of Personality Counseling.*

as to counseling in particular, but these critical conflicts can and do arise within much of the personnel scope. And when they do, is knowledge enough?

If personnel work is indeed deeper teaching, then, as in all effective teaching, the value of knowledge per se can only be measured in terms of the constructive quality of its application. What is needed are persons whose sound informational base is buttressed by two very necessary attributes. First, situations of a legal nature will generally demand not so much abstract dealing with cut-and-dried statutes as they will active collaboration with all types of people in preventing and resolving the inevitable escapades of rambunctious college youth, and in educatively interpreting the involved aspects for the best interests of all concerned. This calls for a singular adeptness at that most important single criterion for successful personnel administration: *facility in the art of human relations.*

Second, a personnel worker can resolve the dilemmas of conflicting loyalties only through an *intelligently formulated ethical value system.* The decisions in such cases will be his and his alone, and the quality of his assessments will depend solely on what system of values, what code of ethics, he has integrated into his personal philosophy of life. This could mean, for some, cleaving rigidly to a path of traditional conservatism, bowing constantly to self-preservation and administrative convenience without due regard for student interests; or, for others, adopting an equally rigid policy of rash, foolhardy impetuosity that forever favors the student over self, society, and institution. However, when handling touchy situations no two of which will ever be exactly similar, we agree with Wrenn that neither of these extremely narrow approaches will be consistently effective in engendering wise and equitable analyses.[3] Nor are fumbling, patchwork methods any more advisable.

But if a personnel worker has acquired, through training opportunities and life experiences, an ethical philosophy that combines courageous, independent ideals with a balanced perception of individual and group requirements, he will be much more likely to operate instead with a *flexible consistency*—i.e., his approach to problems, and his ultimate decisions, will be governed not by a constant favoring of one party to the blind exclusion of all others, but by a flexible, unbiased appraisal of all relevant components and, most important, by a consistent application of personal principles that can never be compromised.

[3] C. Gilbert Wrenn: *Op. cit.*, p. 176.

If, then, personnel people can work effectively with others in interpreting legal problems, however complicated, according to a knowledgeable understanding of their educative responsibilities and the legal implications involved, and according to fairly conceived ethical convictions, their actions will surely reflect a high degree of professional performance and will guarantee that the rights of no interested person or institution will be unjustly denied.

Legal Opinions, Practices, and Trends

We will now consider, respectively, various legal implications relative to (1) general areas of responsibility with which all personnel workers are concerned, and (2) specific positions within the personnel program. Our reason for such a division is twofold: first, according to our previously stated philosophy, personnel workers have responsibility for both individual and group requirements; second, according to a psychology of learning which views perception of the whole as essential to complete understanding of the parts, it seems logical that familiarity with the points contained in the first section can facilitate fuller comprehension of those involved in the second.

The following *broad areas of legal concern*, then, have direct implications for all personnel workers, regardless of their particular functions:

COUNSELING

Several legal restrictions are imposed upon those who operate anywhere along the counseling continuum of informal chats to clinical psychotherapy. In mental cases, they cannot legally diagnose. Nor can they escape liability for damage if they give medical or legal advice, advise a married person to leave his spouse, or assist a minor to act contrary to parental wishes.[4]

One of the most important and far-reaching limitations involves the point of "privileged communication." Unlike lawyers, doctors, or ministers, counselors in many states possess no legal immunity from revealing confidential information before a court.* Some counselors feel that this immunity will ultimately be won only by a test case in which a counselor, risking contempt charges by refusing to

[4] Ernest R. Groves, and Catherine Groves: *Dynamic Mental Hygiene.*

*In June, 1952, a Chicago Circuit Court Judge ruled that a psychiatrist could not even be subpoenaed to relate intimate facts a patient had revealed to him. The judge, calling this the first such case in legal history, further disallowed the introduction of pertinent records. (Case No. 52 C 2535, Circuit Court of Cook County, Chicago, Illinois—Samuel Binder vs. Nathaniel S. Ruvell, June 24, 1952.)

divulge information, is accorded by the court a privileged status consonant with his professional ethics. But there is also the principle of "hearsay" evidence, not admissible in court. Without more substantial proof of injury than the mere relating of an incident by one party to another, as would be the case in a counseling session, a court could well consider interview data purely "hearsay" and inadmissible. Either of these possible rulings would establish a legal precedent most favorable to the conscientious and ethical pursuit of the counseling process.

Similarly, counselors are not legally required to release their records to any state or federal officer except upon issuance of a warrant. If they do otherwise without the client's consent, they can be sued for malpractice. Contrarily, should they flout the legal authority of a warrant, they are once again caught in the whirlpool of possible contempt of court, "hearsay," etc. Furthermore, even if they do relinquish confidential records when legally required, they run the risk of possible libel action if the records have been so faultily prepared as to contain damaging or untrue statements.* Every counselor is thus urged to be careful and accurate in preparing records, and to keep extreme confidences in a separate personal file which will "not become part of the official records of the institution or of his office (and which will) not have to be released when the personnel records of an individual are taken into custody."[5]

While a counselor, therefore, is not legally liable to divulge confidences except under oath, and indeed is professionally obligated to his client not to do so, he may frequently be faced with the kind of ethical conflict described in the introductory section. If he comes to possess certain "hearsay" evidence of criminal actions or tendencies, he will have to decide whether to handle the situation himself and become a possible accessory, or to insure society's protection by breaking his client's confidence and informing the authorities. Past legal decisions in this connection have generally favored society's welfare over that of the individual. Thorne, who cites several cases illustrating these conflicts, advocates a decision according to the degree of the crime:

. . . Where such asocial actions constitute only a misdemeanor or minor offense, some latitude in protecting the rights of society may be justified.

---

* See the section on "Libel and Slander" in this chapter, pp. 305-306.
[5] C. Gilbert Wrenn: *Op. cit.*, p. 164.

But in the occurrence of the more serious felonies, then it may be of serious consequence to disregard the rights of society.[6]

In situations of the latter type, the counselor cannot, it seems to us, shirk a clear responsibility for immediate referral to other appropriate agencies. If, unrecognized as he is by legal immunity, he conceals information and is subsequently indicted as an accessory, he may not be of much help to his client; and he will certainly reflect little credit on his institution or greatly further the recognition of psychology as a profession if the client's confessed asocial tendencies result in severe injury to others. No counselor would deny that his primary responsibility is to the client, and that where he is not competent to handle a situation he is morally obligated, for the client's welfare (as well as for his own protection against a possible malpractice charge) to refer him to a specialist. But his *ultimate* responsibility is to safeguard society from potentially dangerous influences, even though this necessitates severing the confidential relationship. In assessing these legal-moral conflicts of multiple loyalties, the counselor can be intelligently guided by the code of ethics of such organs as the American Psychological Association,[7] but, as we have emphasized, final decisions will be based upon his personal system of values.

Case No. 1, on the opening page of this chapter, illustrated several of these legal points. In the light of this discussion, what revision, if any, would you now make in your initial reaction?

TORT LIABILITY

Injurious accidents which occur on college and university campuses can frequently be traced to the tort[8] of some employee. Judicial decisions on subsequent suits for liability will involve two principles: *negligence* and *charitable immunity*.

As to negligence—"the failure to exercise that degree of care which an ordinarily careful and prudent person exercises under the same

[6] Frederick C. Thorne: *Op. cit.*, p. 62.

[7] The provisions of the code are described in *The American Psychologist*, Vol. 5, 1950, pp. 620-626 (Nov.); and Vol. 6, 1951, pp. 57-64 (Feb.), 145-166 (May), 428-452 (Aug.), and 626-661 (Nov.). A symposium of pertinent observations is available in Vol. 7, No. 8 (August, 1952), pp. 425-455.

[8] "A tort is a private or civil wrong or injury." Every individual has certain rights and obligations recognized by law, any violation of which, if resulting in damage, constitutes a tort. "The law of torts is concerned with the redress of injuries (to individuals only) which are neither crimes (against the public or state) nor arise from the breach of contracts."—Samuel G. Kling: *Your Legal Rights*, p. 280.

or similar circumstances"[9]—personnel workers, teachers, and other employees can be held personally liable (1) if they render more than emergency first aid treatment, even though disability results which was not caused by the treatment; and (2) if injuries occur on off-campus excursions of which they are in charge, even though parental or administrative sanction was granted, or on college property where the supervisory responsibility is theirs. Court decisions in such instances will depend upon the foreseeability of the injury by the person in charge, and upon any contributory negligence of the injured party.

Liability charges are usually brought, however, against the college or, in the case of a state university, the state, rather than against the individual. This raises the issue of "charitable immunity," whereby in most states, the state or the college, being a charitable, nonprofit corporation, cannot be held liable for the torts of employees. In the past the courts have generally acceded to arguments in favor of this principle: that funds granted for education should not be diverted for other uses, that persons accepting charity should waive their right to claim damages, and that public policy requires the exemption. But a study of recent cases cited in the literature reveals that while immunity is still granted more often than not, there is a growing tendency for social-minded magistrates to inveigh against discriminatory denial of indemnity to innocent persons—especially since colleges and universities can minimize their personal hardship through workmen's compensation laws or liability insurance.[10]

Within their purview of responsibility, therefore, and especially since the majority of accident cases occur in out-of-class situations, personnel workers are morally obligated to take whatever precautions will guarantee safety for others and will protect themselves and the institution from legal action. Negligence in one's assigned duties, particularly if it results in a suit against the college, is not advocated as a very effective means of ensuring pleasant administrative relations, personal security, or the education of students in positive moral values.

With this in mind, do you now feel any differently about Case No. 2?

[9] *Ibid.*, p. 281.
[10] Merritt M. Chambers: *The Colleges and the Courts*, 1941-45, pp. 112-128.
American Psychological Association Committee on Malpractice Insurance: "The Case For and Against Malpractice Insurance for Psychologists."

"In Loco Parentis" and Discipline

The principle of "in loco parentis" undergirds not only the educational and protective relationship of administration to students, but also the legal. In essence it states that as to mental training, moral and physical discipline, and public welfare, college authorities may establish regulations as would any parent; and that, as with domestic discipline, the courts will not interfere unless such regulations are so clearly unreasonable, arbitrary, or malicious as to violate divine or human law.[11] It has been legally tested primarily in suspension and expulsion cases, though it is equally applicable to other unreasonable disciplinary decisions.*

The college-student relationship is unilaterally contractual, similar to that of an insurance company to a policyholder—i.e., a student who is accepted by the college agrees to obey college regulations then in force or thereafter made, uphold specified moral, physical and academic standards, and pay necessary fees, in return for which he is promised instruction, welfare, and a degree. Furthermore, he can terminate the contract at will, but the college cannot except for cause. Such matters, needless to say, should be explicitly spelled out in the catalogue.

Where expelled students have sued for recovery on the grounds of malice, judicial decisions have been widely varied, but have generally reflected three conditions: (1) mere mistakes of judgment by college officials do not render them liable in absence of malicious, willful action; (2) college authorities are presumed to have acted in good faith; and (3) while no formal trial is required before suspension or dismissal, an informal hearing is advisable. There has been much inconsistency as to the last point, with higher courts overruling lower courts, but the issue is essentially one of moral interpretation. If a college catalogue specifically states—and some do—that students can be dismissed at any time with no notification of cause, then its officers are not *legally* bound to grant even a semblance of a hearing. However, the prevailing sentiment seems to be that, even with private colleges, the "power to dismiss is not arbitrary but discretionary," and

---

[11] Merritt M. Chambers: "The Legal Status of Pupils."

* For example, the courts have considered unwarranted any rules requiring students to pay for school property they have accidentally damaged or destroyed.

expulsion without a hearing is morally contrary to public policy, tending toward injustice and oppression.[12]

All this is important for personnel workers who view discipline as therapeutically inseparable from the guidance process. They may prefer not to be involved in extreme cases, but it is unrealistic to assume they never will be—particularly if the administration rotates membership on standing committees, if they serve as advisers to student councils possessing the power to recommend expulsion, or if they are sincerely interested in student self-discipline.

What is your opinion now about Case No. 3?[13]

COMMUNITY COOPERATION

Educational officials are not legally compelled to maintain good press, police, or general "town-gown" relations, but obviously they cannot do full justice to their various responsibilities without them. And the smaller the community, the more necessary does this become.

In line with the "in loco parentis" doctrine, strictly campus offenses, such as "pantie raids," should be referred to college security police who will summon additional aid as needed. But if students' illegal actions occur outside the college's jurisdiction, then the only influence college authorities can wield depends upon their relations with the municipal police. If these are not good, it may be exceedingly difficult to persuade a desk sergeant, for example, that a student's youthful exuberance (if such is the case) does not warrant a police record that could affect him adversely in later life. The situation will naturally differ according to the gravity of the crime, but in minor offenses it will help no end to have the various civic forces—tradespeople, police, and others—sufficiently sympathetic to the educational point of view that they will notify the college before taking action or preferring formal charges.

This can only be accomplished by reciprocal cooperation when requested. College-age crooks, wanted by the police, will sometimes attempt to work their rackets on campuses. F.B.I. agents will often seek information on students and graduates applying for civil service positions, or involved in subversive groups. In such cases, cooperation by college officials within the limits of professional ethics is essential for society's maximum benefit.

Many personnel workers will be dealing directly with community

---

[12] E. C. Elliott and Merritt M. Chambers: *The Colleges and the Courts*, p. 34.
[13] For the instance upon which Case No. 3 was based, see *Ibid.*, pp. 33-34.

forces in admissions, placement, curricular and activity work projects, etc., and all will live their personal lives as community members. If their relations with the general public are of the condescending, "ivory tower" variety that patronizes its intelligence, their chances of obtaining favorable press coverage and reasoned, unemotional support of projected legislation, even on items of direct public concern, will be materially reduced. But if they discharge their functions educatively and considerately, with due recognition of the necessity for mutual cooperation, they can inspire a public confidence and respect which can bear valuable fruit when capricious students and educational objectives stand in need of community consideration.

STAFF COOPERATION

There is likewise no law requiring a personnel worker to be responsible for his staff's actions, but he does have a moral compunction to educate them in their legal rights. Faculty advisers and teachers within the personnel program deserve to understand what constitutes legal negligence in counseling and student activities. And how many secretaries know that they are legally out of order in prescribing Grandma's "sure-fire" cure for a tummy-ache?

Personnel people hiring student assistants and clerical workers should be acquainted with state and federal wage and hours legislation and, if in municipal and state universities, the vagaries of inadequate civil service regulations. They should also recognize the legal prerogatives of union custodial personnel, so they will not, for instance, authorize students to paint what is not rightfully theirs to paint. Strikes can start from such minor misunderstandings, coupled with poor labor relations—and how some students love strikes!

Furthermore, since the full value of education demands the coordination of curricular and co-curricular elements, personnel people must keep pace with the legal aspects of state graduation requirements, accrediting and certification policies, and trends in curricular revision on all educational levels, including such items as the current furor over Communistic influences on textbooks.

LIBEL AND SLANDER

A most important aspect of effective human relations is circumspectness and irreproachableness in personal and professional conduct. In preparing reports, conducting collateral interviews, using records for teaching purposes, and in their personal lives, personnel workers must heed carefully the implications of *libel*, a legal defamation in permanent form (writing, pictures, and paintings), and *slander*, a temporary defamation (spoken words or gestures).

Both are similar in that the defamation (1) involves exposure to hatred, ridicule, contempt, or pecuniary loss; (2) must affect a living person; and (3) must, for purposes of recovery, be revealed to a third party. They differ in that any libel is considered injurious and immediate grounds for suit, while only certain types of statements—imputations of crime, contagious disease, female unchastity, and professional incapacity—are slanderous per se, requiring no proof of damages.

Ever since publisher John Peter Zenger, in 1733, was acquitted of allegedly scurrilous charges against the New York government, truth has been a valid defense in defamation suits. Merely repeating, not originating, a false charge, moreover, constitutes no defense. The plaintiff must prove not only the direct application of the charge to him specifically (the "colloquium"), but also, when required, whatever factors made the charge defamatory (the "innuendo")—a condition which, much criticized today, has in the past immunized from suit those who defame Jews, lawyers, or other large groups. At present, much disagreement also exists concerning the distinction between libel and slander, particularly as regards oral defamation via radio and television.

LOYALTY OATHS

This controversial topic is another example of how legal aspects are inextricably meshed with ethical considerations. The basic question is: How effective are loyalty oaths in guaranteeing academic freedom? The year 1952 witnessed three significant judicial decisions which are bound to have wide implications for future educational conduct and security.

1. New York's Feinberg Law, which empowers the Board of Regents to promulgate a list of subversive organizations, membership in which will be automatic cause for dismissal, was passed in 1949, but was originally held inoperative on the premise that it violated the Due Process clause of the Fourteenth Amendment and embodied a "guilt by association" principle. It was recently sustained by the U. S. Supreme Court, who ruled that the statute is aimed at persons who *knowingly* joined Communist front groups, not at those who joined them ignorant of their purposes. The Board is currently implementing the law's provisions, and in the process the Communist party may for the first time be ruled legally subversive—for while individuals

have been jailed under the Smith Act, and while actual party membership, and/or refusal to answer questions about it, have been held grounds for dismissal of public employees, the party itself has not previously been a defendant. If this happens, the party might well be outlawed in New York and other states.

2. The California State Supreme Court ruled unconstitutional a University of California loyalty oath on the grounds that the state Levering Act, which requires a similar oath, is sufficient. This has resulted in the reinstatement of eighteen faculty members who, in 1949, refused to sign the university's oath. Their reinstatement, however, is on condition that they sign the state oath.

3. On December 14, 1952, the Oklahoma branch of the Electoral College, assembled to ratify the results of the recent presidential election, stood and solemnly swore allegiance to a state loyalty oath. At that very moment, the U. S. Supreme Court unanimously declared the oath unconstitutional. Its decision revolved primarily around a provision requiring state employees to swear that for five years previous they had not belonged to the Communist party or to any group listed by the Attorney General as subversive. The court, which had formerly upheld other states' differently worded oaths (viz. New York's Feinberg Law), ruled that this provision does not differentiate between knowing and innocent association and therefore constitutes "unwarranted inhibition upon the free spirit of teachers"—such as the seven faculty members at the Oklahoma Agricultural and Mechanical College who had been discharged for refusing to take the oath.

This last decision clarifies greatly the nub of the problem: that *motivation*, not mere membership, is the decisive factor. By their own philosophy, avowed Communists are incapable of full dedication to the ideals of free thought. Similarly, while the Fifth Amendment guarantees a person the legal right to refuse to answer self-incriminatory questions, it was not designed as a cloak for those whose moral unsuitability is incompatible with the ethical honesty justifiably owed to the educational profession. Both counts legitimately call for the exclusion of such people from the profession, which is the one advantage of loyalty regulations—that they can root out those who have committed legal perjury under oath.

But loyalty oaths per se are no automatic safeguard of academic freedom. The possibility of political martyrdom through perjury action will not prevent subversives from signing oaths they are philosophically bound to ignore, and by the time investigative machinery has detected the fraud, irreparable damage may have been done.* The answer lies in the educational profession establishing its own sound code of ethics, and in colleges and universities enlisting personnel whose high and responsible ideals and whose personal and professional integrity are intolerant of such repugnant procedures. In this connection personnel workers have an obvious and responsible role.

PERSONAL AND PROFESSIONAL SECURITY

The judicial and legislative powers and dignities once held by the university professor have long since passed to lay governing boards, leaving him legally classed as a "mere employee" who "gives no bond, does not account for misfeasance or non-feasance in a legal sense, [and] has . . . no duties of a determinate character fixed by law."[14] This is advantageous in that, unlike a public officer, his contract cannot be annulled, nor his salary discontinued, simply by legislative abolition of his position.[15] But it also means that he is largely at the discretion of a governing board for those conditions of personal security which carry greater purchasing power than the admittedly valued esthetic rewards of the profession, and which, as an employee with personal and familial responsibilities, he is logically owed: insurance protection, provision for promotion and retirement, and a salary commensurate with living costs (as against the present 40 per cent lag). This does not mean, of course, that he should sit by idly, waiting for the mountain to come to Mahomet. Rather he must be aware that his dependent status may necessitate his lobbying for improved legislation on his own and others' behalf†—preferably via professional organizations rather than the legally acceptable but less socially approved teachers' unions.

---

* The nadir of misguided reasoning seems to us to have been reached in a recent resolution of the Harrison, N. Y., Board of Education, requiring loyalty oaths of private citizens—guest speakers and officers of community groups (Boy Scouts, Lions Club, etc.)—meeting on school property.

[14] John E. Kirkpatrick: *Academic Organization and Control*, p. 200.

[15] E. C. Elliott and Merritt M. Chambers: *Op. cit.*, pp. 71-73. It was on this principle that Case No. 4 was based.

† For example, the Joint Council of New York State Psychologists on Legislation is presently following this procedure in attempting to obtain legal recognition for the state's psychologists who now pay unincorporated business taxes, cannot be excused from jury duty, and whose clients cannot deduct fees for tax purposes. A bill for licensing psychologists was previously vetoed, largely because of opposition from medical groups who enjoy all such privileges. Similar movements are operative in other states.

Tenure considerations are also an important factor in academic security. Professors and staff personnel cannot legally be dismissed except for immorality, neglect of duty, incompetency, unprofessional conduct, or failure to obey reasonable rules of the governing board. In recent years, serious abuses of these principles by either faculty members or administrative authorities have been relatively few. Perhaps the most repugnant are those wherein political motives are unfairly utilized; when this happens, the strongest legal sanctions should be imposed. In all tenure violations, moreover, appropriate and vigorous measures should be taken by the profession itself, for legal regulations guaranteeing permanent tenure can be injurious unless all concerned "are in accord with the spirit of professional integrity; if such spirit prevails, enactment of legislation is hardly necessary."[16]

A final point involves copyright statutes—a necessary concern for educators whose promotion is in any way based on literary production, or whose teaching duties require reproduction of copyrighted material. Because of the intricacies of these laws, legal counsel should be consulted when questions arise but, as a general rule, permission should be obtained for all but the briefest quotations. To facilitate international distribution of materials without fear of violating complicated legal regulations, thirty-five UNESCO countries recently signed an agreement (which each must still ratify) granting to writers, artists, and scientists the same copyright protection abroad as they receive at home.

In addition to the above general considerations, all of which have implications for every college personnel worker, there are a few further legal aspects more directly pertinent to the following specific functions:*

ADMISSIONS†

Since education is a privilege conferred by the states and is therefore under individual state control, even private institutions must conform to state statutes as well as to the provisions of their charters.

---

[16] U. S. President's Commission on Higher Education: *Higher Education for American Democracy*, Vol. IV, "Staffing Higher Education," p. 55.

* This does not, of course, mean that there is no overlapping of interest or responsibility—e.g., an admissions officer will of necessity be concerned with the legal aspects of scholarships and foreign students, and a residence supervisor with those of student activities.

† See "In Loco Parentis and Discipline," pp. 303-304 in this chapter, for the student-college, landlord-tenant, contractual relationship.

New York, New Jersey, and Massachusetts, for example, have legally enjoined colleges and universities from requesting on admissions blanks data concerning race, religion, and national origin (except, of course, where the nature and purposes of the institution—e.g., Catholic or other sectarian colleges—rightfully necessitate the transmittal of such information).

Within the above limitations, then, private colleges may accept or reject applicants as they wish. Moreover, acceptance of certificates in lieu of separate admissions examinations in no way forces a college to surrender its right to set minimum standards. Similarly, while tax-supported colleges and universities are expected to be open to all qualified students, they can legally be selective should enrollment exceed facilities. State institutions may also require out-of-state students to pay tuition, but there is presently some doubt as to the social advisability of this procedure.

Admissions officers will be much concerned with the issue of segregation, now mandatory in 17 states and legally permissible in four others.* Most cases have arisen where Negroes have sought graduate or professional training in state universities. In 1938, the U. S. Supreme Court ruled that these applicants must be accepted *unless the state can provide separate but equal facilities*, thus guaranteeing all individuals equal protection of laws.† However, because of the tremendous financial burdens this has placed on the states, and because of continued contention that segregation violates the Fourteenth Amendment and places upon Negroes a stigma of inferiority, the issue has come to such a head that, at this writing, the Supreme Court is hearing five pertinent cases and is expected to rule unequivocally, for the first time, on the constitutionality of segregation. Should it be outlawed, some southern legislators are prepared to defy the court's edict by measures whose legality will themselves very likely have to be tested.‡

---

* Mandatory in Alabama, Arkansas, Delaware, Florida, Georgia, Kentucky, Louisiana, Maryland, Mississippi, Missouri, North Carolina, Oklahoma, South Carolina, Tennessee, Texas, Virginia, West Virginia; legally permissible in Arizona, Kansas, New Mexico, and Wyoming. In the District of Columbia, segregation has always been practiced—a fact that Congress has officially recognized without actual legislation.

† This "separate but equal" doctrine was first established in the Plessy v. Ferguson case in 1896; since then, the court has consistently reaffirmed its validity.

‡ South Carolina voters, for example, on November 4, 1952, approved a constitutional amendment, recommended by the governor, which would make it possible for the entire public school system to be sold or leased to private interests.

Other admissions considerations are: (1) applicants can be denied admission for physical or mental defects; (2) fraternity membership is no bar to admissions except by contrary state statutes (which are usually legally upheld as being expressive of the Fourteenth Amendment); and (3) students who have been accepted cannot arbitrarily be denied readmission.

Here, too, "ethical" and "legal" responsibilities converge. If, for instance, a personnel worker is not in sympathy with a college's policies that quite legally favor the subsidization of athletes, he should think seriously before assuming an admissions position there.*[17] Then, too, while private institutions need legally give a rejected applicant no reason for refusal, is there not a moral responsibility not only to explain why, but also to help refer the rejectee to some college which will accept him?

HOUSING

Although dormitory residents have the right of neither tenant nor ordinary lodger, they may be suspended for refusing to obey that part of the admissions contract which compels them to live in approved places, on or off campus, and to pay prescribed rentals.[18] They may also be summarily evicted for any infraction of reasonable disciplinary rules enacted before or after their assuming residence. Housing personnel, "in loco parentis," should keep sign-out sheets, conduct frequent room inspections, and, to avoid penalty, report all communicable diseases. They must observe community health and safety ordinances—fire prevention, dietary conditions, room space per individual, etc. Where an emergency operation is medically dictated and family permission cannot be obtained, the law would usually uphold a decision of life-saving intent.

While dormitory management is usually the institution's prerogative, the statutory provisions for the University of Kentucky, for example, specify supervisory details and method of room assignment.

---

* A case in point: A bill passed by the Florida State legislature in 1949 allows the net revenue from an extra day's racing at approved dog and horse tracks to be paid to the State Treasury "for the granting of scholarships for the purpose of attending the institutions of higher learning of the State of Florida." Arguments for and against the ethics involved are many, but all agree that "while the . . . law does not mention football, its primary purpose is to provide money for athletic scholarships."

[17] Fred Russell: "Football's Wildest Rivalry," p. 136.
[18] E. C. Elliott and Merritt M. Chambers: Op. cit., p. 28.

Residence personnel should naturally be acquainted with any such provisions as well as with legislatively sanctioned methods of dormitory financing—outright loans, endowment investments, bond issues, student fees, and others.

Residence workers are generally in such close and continual contact with students, maintenance personnel, and, in the case of off-campus supervisors, the community, that they must pay special heed to the many educative responsibilities related to legal considerations. Since campus difficulties so often stem from an ignorance of one's own and others' legal rights, housing personnel might profitably fulfill a deeper teaching function by holding joint discussions with house councils and other involved parties where these rights could be fully aired and clearly understood.

Similar preventive and educative functions devolve upon advisers to fraternities and sororities, and upon organizations like the National Inter-fraternity Council which, for fraternities, supplies the advisers. There is, however, the significant difference that while dormitories are universally approved, several states have legislated against secret societies in public education. In some states this applies only to high schools, with institutions of higher education being specifically exempt; in others, it is all-inclusive. Court decisions on this point have varied markedly according to the nature of each case, but have generally tended to uphold such regulations on the ground that the institutions are not natural rights, but public benefactions, and aspiring beneficiaries must obey whatever prerequisites to participation the law imposes. In line with this thinking, the trend has been (1) to disallow requests for exemption of fraternity houses from taxation; (2) to refuse Greek letter organizations any share in public funds for financing student activities; and (3) to deny consideration of "charitable immunity" in liability cases. Consequently, while residence personnel and fraternity advisers possess similar educational responsibilities, the latter's operations are somewhat more restricted in the eyes of the law.

Group Activities

As with residence personnel, directors of student activities have singular opportunities for developing to its fullest a philosophy of personnel work as deeper teaching. Not only will they be intimately connected with students in facilitating character-shaping and learning activities, but when those activities involve faculty sponsorship and cooperation with curricular and community interests, they will be enabled to exert an even wider educative influence. This means that activities advisers, more than perhaps any other personnel workers, can be directly involved with all the broad legal issues previously described.

Beyond those issues, they will be particularly concerned with the legal aspects of financing activities. Since a student, being a minor, cannot make a legal contract,* all possible protection of monies and persons using them should be observed. Whatever the origin of the funds—state, public, private, or any combination thereof—they should be audited by a bonded person employed by the governing and legally controlling authority. Within this ultimate limitation, student courts, student councils, and other organizational groups are, of course, encouraged to experience the values of budget balancing and other phases of financial management.

RELIGIOUS CONSIDERATIONS

Everyone is doubtless familiar with the U. S. Supreme Court's ruling in the McCollum case, in 1947, that any use of tax-supported institutions for classroom secular indoctrination is contrary to the First Amendment. Justice Reed's dissenting opinion, that "any use of a pupil's school time, whether . . . on or off the school grounds . . . falls under the law," has evidently, since then, been permanently shelved by increasing judicial permission for "released time" programs, now operative in some 33 states. In the most recently validated case, New York's Zorach doctrine, the majority decision, which claims that the First Amendment does not in all respects advocate separation of Church and State, would seem to indicate that "non-indoctrinational study of religion . . . will not fall under the ban."[19] This has definite implications for college personnel people who are attempting to further this nation's return to moral integrity by (1) assisting teaching faculty in the objective study of religious issues in art, his-

---

* While the law differs from state to state in this regard, in New York, at least, a minor can enter a contract with an adult person or firm, which contract will be held by the courts as legally binding upon the adult. It will also be held legally binding upon the minor unless, prior to legal execution of the contract, the minor does not, as he is permitted to do, void it by pleading "defense of infancy." Also in New York, a recent ruling places a person of 18 to 21 years of age in the category of an adult. The law is so intricate on this point, however, that anyone concerned should seek legal counsel.

[19] National Council of the Churches of Christ in the U.S.A.: "Supreme Court Validates New York's Released Time Plan," *Information Service*, No. 20.

tory, and other nonreligious disciplines, and (2) exercising direct responsibility for campus religious organizations.

While these organizations share with fraternal and political groups the dubious distinction of being denied public funds for promotional purpose, the above ruling should help increase membership, since the courts will undoubtedly continue to be liberal in permitting them the use of school facilities. Present discrepancies between law and practice in this regard are so wide that, in effect, religious activities may be carried on unless the public objects. And when illegal practices are conducted through ignorance, "cease and desist" orders are generally the only penalty. Needless to reiterate, such ignorance is not in keeping with an educative outlook.

HEALTH*

Lacking legal sanction, college governing bodies may not institute their own health measures, but are instead subject to community regulations governing public health, communicable disease control, sanitation, housing, etc. Since the Constitution of the United States makes no provision for health, they must look to their states and local communities for enactment of facilitating legislation, which has generally tended toward greater explicitness.[20] Here personnel people have an excellent opportunity to help bridge the gap between guidance and health services by assisting college health officers in fostering public awareness of legislative needs.

FINANCIAL AID

The administration of student aid calls for a sometimes hard-to-achieve combination of cold attention to legal technicalities and warm recognition of the human element. A student who applies for an emergency loan must be realistically advised that he cannot freely withdraw, as he can from a unilateral admissions agreement, and that the administrator's multiple obligations to the college, other applicants, and a loan fund's donor make legal action for recovery possible. Yet that same student must be viewed as a human being with human feelings, often including a swallowed pride, and with human needs which cannot be fully served by a flintlike attitude. For this reason, financial administrators will enjoy greater educative possibilities if the terms of scholarship, fellowship, and particularly

* See also "Tort Liability," pp. 301-302, and "Housing," pp. 311-312, in this chapter.
[20] W. S. Monroe (ed.): *Encyclopedia of Educational Research*, p. 533.

loan contracts are made humanly flexible as well as legally airtight.

Loans are advances with contractual obligations for repayment by a specific date with or without interest. Smaller loans are often made with little regard for scholastic achievement, while larger ones involve such contingencies as future earning ability, present need, health, reliability, and integrity. Where a student is a good risk, his personal signature is often sufficient security; otherwise a co-signer may be required. As to repayment date, a college may logically require small loans to be repaid prior to receipt of a diploma;* with larger ones, payment is often deferred until the commencement of gainful civilian employment.

Scholarship recipients may be reasonably compelled to maintain a certain level of attainment in the area for which the scholarship was granted. This could conceivably cause legal snarls where injury to an athletic scholarship student terminates his practical usefulness to the institution. In general, scholarship donors should be persuaded to make their grants unrestricted; otherwise, since administrators cannot legally distribute scholarship aid contrary to the terms prescribed, the funds could very possibly go unused for lack of qualified applicants, thus denying worthy students educational opportunities.

Financial aid administrators will also be directly concerned with the many legal complexities involved in all aspects of financing higher education. While a discussion of this broad topic is not within the scope of this chapter, attention is called to a recent report[21] which states, among other things, that if educational facilities are to meet an estimated 1960 enrollment of 2,500,000, an additional $226 million will be needed for scholarships. The report advocates that this sum be raised not by further expansion of government scholarship aid to individual students, but by college officials joining state and regional groups in soliciting philanthropic contributions from labor unions, corporations, and the like. Ensuring that such funds have no entangling legal strings attached is a direct responsibility of student aid administrators.

Foreign Students

Because of the continued increase in enrollment of foreign students on American college campuses, full-time positions as foreign student

---

* In which case, the college catalogue should so state (see "In Loco Parentis and Discipline," pp. 303-304 in this chapter).

[21] John D. Millett: *Financing Higher Education in the United States.*

advisers are being inaugurated in many personnel programs. These advisers, who have singular opportunities for deeper teaching on an international level,* have as a task of paramount importance the educative orientation of foreign students to a full understanding of American mores, including legal customs, as an aid to preventing inadvertent and embarrassing situations.

They also will be concerned with legal technicalities involved in admissions procedures, including implications of the McCarran Act, and with regulatory provisions anent visas and their renewals. For example, if a foreign student willfully disobeys college requirements for loan repayment or immigration authorities' stipulations as to part-time employment, his visa can be cancelled. Moreover, his visa is granted on condition that he pursue an explicitly defined purpose (viz., an A. B. degree); once that has been accomplished, he cannot renew the visa except by proper approval of another equally explicit purpose (viz., an M. A. degree).

VETERANS AFFAIRS

Despite an admirable desire to expand his profession's scope of influence, no personnel worker can be blamed for harboring mixed feelings about the acquisition of this area: on the one hand, a warm appreciation that his program includes service to such deserving persons, yet, on the other, an understandable regret that the need for that service ever had to arise. Be that as it may, however, a realistic view of today's world picture clearly reveals that veterans will be a significant part of the college scene for some time to come. Since this means a continuance of active federal interest in education without, fortunately, concomitant control, veterans' advisers must be especially observant of relevant legal aspects.

Obviously they should keep up-to-date reference files on (1) pertinent state regulations concerning bonuses, scholarships, and exemptions from academic preparatory work; and (2) current federal legislation re loans, service insurance, Public Laws 16 and 346, and, as with foreign students, the requirement that veterans specifically delineate their educational aims.

They must also practice effective personal and public relations, since their task calls for continual cooperation with students, Veterans Administration representatives, and community personnel in handling excessive absences, preventing legal difficulties through

* See Chapter 12, "Learning with Students from Other Lands."

educative orientation, establishing "continuing eligibility" for schools, facilitating mutual enlightenment as to V.A. and campus policies, and pressing for amended legislation as needed. Regarding the last point, an interesting trend is seen in the matter of elections. While away at college, a student of legal age has usually been denied voting rights in the municipality wherein the college is located, since his legal residence is considered to be his home town. But, in a few cases, contrary permission has been granted to veterans who, particularly if married, have been presumed legally to reside where they "hang their hats."[22] This seems reasonable when considering that, after all, college students are under the "pro parentis" protection of the college, and, consequently, under the jurisdiction of the local community.

Finally, students of college age, who are earnestly striving to formulate a philosophy of life, naturally seek some measure of security. When the present turbulent world situation, fraught with insecurity, is visited full force upon them in the form of notice of draft eligibility, it is no wonder that some become confused and tend to lose sight of the larger moral issues in favor of personal well-being. These students are often susceptible to the misguided advice of other students as to how to avoid the draft, how to obtain deferments, etc.—advice which in many instances will involve activity not sanctioned by the law. In such situations, veterans' counselors not only have a responsibility for informing students of their legal rights and of correct procedures, but they also have a mandate for moral guidance and deeper teaching which, for the interests of all concerned, they cannot afford to neglect.

PLACEMENT

As colleges and universities become more and more integrated with their local communities, part- and full-time placement officers will play an increasingly important role in promoting beneficial two-way relations, and in protecting and furthering both community and college interests—legal and otherwise.

Particularly in the part-time employment of minors, difficulties can arise if a student is assigned to a position which in any way violates established statutes. No such eventuality is possible, however, if placement officials keep informed regarding current federal and state legislation affecting the employment of women and minors. In

[22] Merritt M. Chambers: *The Colleges and the Courts*, 1946-50, pp. 30-32.

interstate industries, for example, child labor is regulated by federal wage and hour policies; but in intrastate matters, many states prescribe their own conditions as to place of employment (saloons are barred); frequency of salary payments; type of script (cash or negotiable checks); deductions for pension, breakage, and taxes; and compensation for industrial disease. Since states will vary in their interpretations, placement officers should regularly consult such pertinent resources as the Bureau of Labor Statistics monthly reports, the *Monthly Labor Review*, and the *Survey of Current Business Laws.*

Throughout this section on practical legal aspects we have stressed the necessity for personnel workers having adequate knowledge of the law and of when to consult experts. The following sources may be helpful in establishing a library of school law plus a digest of relevant legal decisions:

> State and federal acts and statutes (write state
>   departments and U. S. Office of Education)
> U. S. Supreme Court opinions (write direct; free)
> American Council on Education, Washington, D. C.
> Association of American Colleges
> American Association of University Women
> National Education Association (Research Division),
>   Washington, D. C.
> Superintendent of Documents, Government Printing
>   Office, Washington, D. C.

Also the following periodicals:

> *American School Board Journal*
> *Educational Administration and Supervision*
> *Journal of the National Association of Deans of Women*
> *Journal of Personnel Research*
> *Nation's Schools*
> *School Executive*
> *The American Psychologist*
> *Yearbook of School Law* (1933-42; 1950 to date)

Future Needs

Why have personnel people placed so little emphasis, both in publications and committee activities, on a problem area they are constantly facing? Does the word "legal" connote something so alien to a personnel philosophy that they must deny its importance or existence in their personal and professional dealings? Or do they perhaps feel that present legal practices are so perfect as to need no further revision? This chapter, which is at best but a cursory beginning, has cited sufficient evidence of judicial imperfections and inconsistencies to prove that much must yet be accomplished in the way of continuing evaluation and further ameliorative effort if the personnel profession is to discharge fully its educative functions.

Doctoral candidates could use this chapter as a springboard to more comprehensive analyses of the problem, utilizing more case illustrations than space has allowed here, and developing further ideas as to needed improvements in legislative policies. They could attack the whole problem globally, as we have, or could take separate aspects: a critique of state laws relative to residence halls; the legal implications of counseling; a compilation of case materials for teaching purposes; or many others.

Joint legislative committees of local, state, and national organizations could work on key problems relative to both personnel work per se, and, since the latter is no isolate in the educational field, education in its broadest sense: loyalty oaths; segregation; financing higher education; uniformity in interstate educational laws; professional security measures; and others. The combined influence of these committees on state and federal legislative bodies might accomplish in many instances what one could not achieve alone.

In addition, personnel workers could profit from a regularly featured column on legal matters in a periodical like *The Personnel and Guidance Journal*. This could be written "straight" or in a disguised, case-study style similar to this chapter's opening cases and to *The Saturday Evening Post's* popular feature, "You Be The Judge." If one concedes that an important function of the personnel profession is to inform prospective workers of inevitable problems in an educative way, such a column, provocatively presented and intelligently used, could have justifiable merit.

A Summation

In analyzing legal problems, mature and competent jurists rely not so much on rigid obedience to the law per se as on judicious interpretation of its moral intent . . . not so much on cold application of established statutes as on humane regard for the protection and welfare of all concerned. This philosophy of jurisprudence, which recognizes that moral and legal considerations are inseparable, is directly compatible with a conception of personnel work as essentially an *educative* task. For this reason, while our discussion of general and specific legal concerns has been primarily practical in nature, we have consistently stressed the necessity for a sound philosophy of ethical and moral responsibility.

In handling campus situations of a legal nature, personnel workers are frequently faced with multiple personal and professional responsibilities—to students, themselves, their institutions, fellow faculty and staff, local communities, the educational profession, and society in general . . . responsibilities they cannot, as self-respecting citizens, expect others, lawyers or anyone else, to assume for them . . . responsibilities which entail definite educative as well as protective demands. In the preceding pages we have pointed up several such situations and have emphasized how they often involve the reconciling of conflicting loyalties—a process wherein "moral" and "legal" are inextricably fused. Similarly, since resolving legal problems generally necessitates cooperation between *people* in effecting decisions equitable to all, something more is required of personnel workers than merely referring to abstract statutes and emerging with pat, mechanical solutions.

If, therefore, personnel workers intend their actions and decisions in legal circumstances to exemplify their function as educative agents and to reflect reasoned understanding of the above complexities, they must first possess a *workable knowledge of existing legislation and its implications* both for their particular positions and for their broader status as professional people in an interdependent society. Such a knowledgeable foundation is also required if they are to go beyond the *status quo* and, through writings and committee activities, influence the development of future legislation relative to educational and societal needs. In addition, if they wish to operate in such a way that all concerned will profitably learn from the experience, they must supplement this information with a practiced *facility in human relations* and with a *flexibly consistent application of sound ethical convictions.*

In any situation, effective teaching and learning depend upon the constructive utilization of these three abilities. Consequently, it is only through assiduous attention to this principle that personnel workers can, in situations of a legal character, wholesomely fulfill their educative obligations to individuals and institutions and thereby implement a philosophy of personnel work as deeper teaching.

BIBLIOGRAPHY

Books:

Blackwell, T. E.: *Current Legal Problems of Colleges and Universities, 1951–52*. St. Louis, Mo., Washington University, 47 pp.

Brody, Alexander: *The American State and Higher Education*. Washington, D. C., American Council on Education, 1935, 251 pp.

Chambers, Merritt M.: *The Colleges and the Courts, 1936–40*. New York, The Carnegie Foundation for the Advancement of Teaching, 1941, 126 pp.

Chambers, Merritt M.: *The Colleges and the Courts, 1941–45*. New York, The Carnegie Foundation for the Advancement of Teaching, 1946, 156 pp.

Chambers, Merritt M.: *The Colleges and the Courts, 1946–50*. New York, Columbia University Press, 1952, 202 pp.

Chambers, Merritt M. (ed.): *Yearbook of School Law*. Washington, D. C., American Council on Education. Published annually 1933-43; 1950 to date.

Elliott, E. C., and Chambers, M. M.: *Charters and Basic Laws of Selected American Universities and Colleges*. New York, The Carnegie Foundation for the Advancement of Teaching, 1934, 640 pp.

Elliott, E. C., and Chambers, M. M.: *The Colleges and the Courts*. New York, The Carnegie Foundation for the Advancement of Teaching, 1936, 563 pp.

Elliott, E. C., Chambers, M. M., and Ashbrook, W. A.: *The Government of Higher Education*. New York, American Book Co., 1935, 289 pp.

Greenough, W. C.: *College Retirement and Insurance Plans*. New York, Columbia University Press, 1948, 274 pp.

Groves, Ernest R., and Groves, Catherine: *Dynamic Mental Hygiene*. Harrisburg, Pa., Stackpole Sons, 1946, pp. 264-292, 415-425.

Johnson, Alvin W.: *Legal Status of Church-State Relationships in the United States*. Minneapolis, Minn., University of Minnesota Press, 1934, 332 pp.

Kelly, F. J., and McNeely, J. H.: *The State and Higher Education*. New York, The Carnegie Foundation for the Advancement of Teaching, 1933, 282 pp.

Kirkpatrick, John E.: *Academic Organization and Control*. Yellow Springs, Ohio, The Antioch Press, 1931, 246 pp.

Kling, Samuel G.: *Your Legal Rights.* Philadelphia, Pa., The Blakiston Co., 1945, 336 pp.

McNeely, J. H.: *Supervision Exercised by States over Privately Controlled Institutions of Higher Education.* Washington, D. C., U. S. Office of Education, Bulletin No. 8, 1934, 64 pp.

Millett, John D.: *Financing Higher Education in the United States.* New York, Columbia University Press, 1952, 544 pp.

Monroe, W. S. (ed.): *Encyclopedia of Educational Research.* New York, The Macmillan Co., 1950 (revised ed.), pp. 11, 229-236, 290-300, 533, 780, 1089-1098, 1438, and 1480.

Remmlein, Madaline K.: *School Law.* New York, McGraw-Hill Book Co., 1950, 376 pp.

Rosenfield, Harry N.: *Liability for School Accidents.* New York, Harper & Brothers, 1940, 220 pp.

Thorne, Frederick C.: *Principles of Personality Counseling.* Brandon, Vt., *Journal of Clinical Psychology,* 1950, pp. 61-80.

Trusler, Harry R.: *Essentials of School Law.* Milwaukee, Wis., Bruce Publishing Co., 1927, 478 pp.

U. S. President's Commission on Higher Education: *Higher Education for American Democracy.* New York, Harper & Brothers, 1948, 430 pp.

Wilson, Logan: *The Academic Man.* London, Oxford University Press, 1942, 248 pp.

ARTICLES:

American Educational Research Association: "The Legal Basis of Education." *Review of Educational Research* 3: No. 5, Dec., 1933, pp. 373-468.

American Psychological Association Committee on Malpractice Insurance: "The Case For and Against Malpractice Insurance for Psychologists." *The American Psychologist* 7: No. 11, Nov., 1952, pp 677-683.

Chambers, Merritt M.: "Legal Aspects of Personnel Administration in State Colleges." *Personnel Journal* 11: Aug., 1932, pp. 97-102.

Chambers, Merritt M.: "The Legal Status of Pupils." *Review of Educational Research* 3: No. 5, Dec., 1933, pp. 432-3.

Chambers, Merritt M.: "The Colleges and the Courts in 1946." *Educational Record XXVIII:* No. 2, April, 1947, pp. 173-89.

Cooke, D. H., and Anderson, H. W.: "Public Taxes for Private Schools." *American School Board Journal* 104: Feb., 1942, pp. 26-27.

Dabney, Virginius: "Southern Crisis: The Segregation Decision." *The Saturday Evening Post* 225: No. 19, Nov. 8, 1952, pp. 40-41, 101-104.

Decker, George C.: "College Housing Loan Program." *Higher Education* 8: No. 6, Nov. 15, 1951, pp. 69-71.

Himstead, Ralph E.: "The Colleges, Ethics, and the Public." *The Annals of the American Academy of Political and Social Science* 280: March, 1952, pp. 133-141.

Hungate, Thad L.: "Finance in General Management of Higher Education." *Teachers College Record* 54: No. 2, Nov., 1952, pp. 68-76.

Lane, David A., Jr.: "Student and Collegiate Contracts." *The Journal of Higher Education*, IV: No. 2, Feb., 1933, pp. 77-84.

National Council of the Churches of Christ in the U.S.A.: "Supreme Court Pronounces on Teacher's Loyalty Issue." *Information Service* XXXI: No. 11, March 15, 1952.

National Council of the Churches of Christ in the U.S.A.: "Supreme Court Validates New York's Released Time Plan." *Information Service XXXI*: No. 20, May 17, 1952.

Prescott, D. A.: "Problems of Staff Personnel." In *The School for Executives*. Washington, D. C., American Council on Education, 1942, pp. 134-147.

Quattlebaum, Charles A.: "Federal Educational Policies, Programs, and Legislative Issues." *Educational Record XXXIV*: No. 4, Oct., 1952, pp. 514-527.

Rosenfield, Harry N.: "Fraternities Can Be Banned." *Nation's Schools* 37: Feb., 1946, p. 47.

Rosenfield, Harry N.: "Recent Trends in Liability Decisions." *Journal of Health and Physical Education* 13: No. 4, April, 1942, pp. 232-233, 260-262.

Russell, Fred: "Football's Wildest Rivalry." *The Saturday Evening Post* 225: No. 21, Nov. 22, 1952, pp. 31, 136, and 138.

Saveth, Edward N.: "Fair Educational Practices Legislation." *The Annals of the American Academy of Political and Social Science* 275: May, 1951, pp. 41-46.

Sears, Jesse B.: "Ethics an Element in Administrative Authority." *Educational Administration and Supervision* 37: No. 1, Jan., 1951, pp. 1-24.

Soper, Wayne W.: "Planning in Finance and Business Administration." *Review of Educational Research* 14: No. 2, April, 1944, pp. 132-138.

Thomson, Proctor: "Ends and Means in the Finance of Higher Education." *Journal of Higher Education XXIII*: No. 8, Nov., 1952, pp. 429-433, 457.

Wrenn, C. Gilbert: "The Ethics of Counseling." *Educational and Psychological Measurement* 12: No. 2, summer, 1952, pp. 161-177.

20. Evaluation of the Student Personnel Program

CHARLES EUGENE MORRIS

Why Evaluate?

In any worth-while undertaking, evaluation is a vital, essential part of the enterprise. When Mary selects a new pair of shoes, or Joe plans a fishing trip with his buddies, some sort of evaluation has been going on in each instance. When shortcomings develop in virtually any life situation, it is not unusual to discover that fuzzy thinking and faulty value judgments are lurking somewhere in the shadows. This seems to be especially true in the case of educational and guidance endeavors.

On the other hand, whenever one encounters a thriving, dynamic, and successful personnel program which contributes in significant ways to the development of student life in the institution involved, it is almost certain that adequate provisions have been made for thoroughgoing evaluation all along the way. In fact, it is fairly safe to predict that the quality of any personnel program is, in the final analysis, but a reflection of the quality of the accompanying evaluative processes.

Evaluation of the personnel program should be a shared cooperative affair, for the aims of evaluation are coincident with those of action research: scientific inquiry and social action leading to social change. "The research program must be guided closely by the needs and interests of the group in order to bring about this change."[1]

Evaluation, then, is concerned with the cooperative formulation of goals, and assessment of progress toward them. As a cooperative endeavor, it is important that all those involved should be consulted and

[1] Harold M. Proshansky: "Projective Techniques in Action Research." In Lawrence E. Abt and Leopold Bellak: *Projective Psychology*, pp. 462-463.

given an opportunity to contribute their ideas. An office secretary is likely to be happier when she is asked about the merits of various grades of carbon paper. Students will use, and take care of, a new student union building to a far greater extent when they have had some share in the undertaking from the very beginning. Emerging research findings represent but one aim of the evaluative process. Evaluative methods applied to personnel programs must also have as their objective the sustained involvement, participation, education, and reeducation of at least representative students, faculty, administrators, and others concerned with and related to the guidance efforts of the institution involved. And representative students must be just that—students who *represent* appropriate segments of the student body. Otherwise, their participation in faculty and administrative consultations tends to become relatively weak and ineffectual. Only in instances of representative contributions can the process of evaluation reflect the best thinking of all constituents.

Parenthetically, the term "evaluation" is used advisedly. Within practical limits, it is possible to measure fields of physical force and energy. But personnel work deals with the intangibles—with human relations, with human programs and activities, with development itself, and with personality. Here, measurement, in the strict sense of the term[2] is not possible. As Cronbach points out, "there is at present no method of firmly established validity capable of measuring or describing personality."[3] Thus *evaluation*, rather than quantitative measurement, must be the basis for the assessment of personnel work.

In summary, evaluation of the personnel program ideally includes:

1. The democratic involvement and participation of at least representative students, faculty, administrators, and others related to the guidance efforts of the institution involved;

2. The cooperative formulation of goals or central purposes for the personnel program;

3. The selection of those methods which seem most likely to contribute effectively to the realization of these central purposes, and related goals for specific program features;

4. The assessment of progress toward these goals; and

5. The revision and expansion of original goals in the light of cumulative experience, new insights, and changing conditions.

[2] Helen M. Walker: *Elementary Statistical Methods*, p. 22.
[3] Lee J. Cronbach: *Essentials of Psychological Testing*, p. 452.

Steps in Evaluation

1. THE INSTITUTIONAL SURVEY

Too often, evaluation (so-called!) is inspired by crisis, dictated by expediency, or directed by personal bias or whimsical fancy. A "kidnapping" by rival fraternity brothers, a midnight raid on a girls' dormitory, or some similar student escapade flares into bold black newspaper headlines. College administrators and faculty unite in an outcry that "something must be done!" So policies for the personnel program are oftentimes forged in the heat of battle, when objective perspective is difficult to achieve. Or the college hits a lean year, when budget-balancing becomes quite a feat to accomplish. Presto, the "frills" represented by one or more features of the personnel program are ruthlessly pared away, without sufficient thought as to the hazards or deficits involved in such a policy of retrenchment. Or a personnel worker attends a conference, and becomes intrigued with some program feature reported as "wonderful" out at Blank University. Upon his return home, the personnel worker may move heaven and earth in order to put Blank's program into effect at his institution —without really having more than hearsay evidence at his disposal or questioning the advisability of this particular feature in so far as his own institution is concerned.

What a different climate of evaluation prevails when a more statesmanlike approach is undertaken! The process may seem slow and unwieldy at first, but is infinitely more productive than patchwork or piecemeal attempts at evaluation. When those concerned get down to fundamentals, the most basic question related to evaluation of the personnel program is this: "*What, essentially, is the institution trying to accomplish in its educational efforts?*" This is not always an easy question to answer, for catalogue descriptions and chartering provisions are not always too specific. Nor is it any answer when someone who writes easily sits down and writes out an eloquent statement of objectives for publication in the college catalogue. On the other hand, in one collegiate institution, a committee has been considering the problem for twelve years and still has failed to come up with any very definite conclusions (because of divided opinions and poor communications which result in ineffective problem-solving procedures). Despite the presence of semantic and other difficulties in specific local situations, it is imperative that this fundamental question be answered as an essential prerequisite to all other evaluative procedures.

The second question to be answered in a preliminary institutional survey is this: "Who determines institutional purposes and policies?" Legally, ultimate responsibility resides with the board of trustees. It is the trustees who adopt written policies which reflect the chief purposes of the institution. These board policies, in turn, provide blueprints for subsequent institutional practices and procedures.

Although institutions are guided by the decisions of the trustees, in common practice the trustees are frequently influenced by the recommendations of the president, along with the views of representatives of faculty, student, alumni, and other community groups. Thus, if institutional aims are to be reviewed, it is important to know who has been contributing to institutional policy-making in the past—and who else may be included with profit in a more systematic and inclusive examination of educational goals.

In such a cooperative institutional survey, sharp differences of opinion may develop in respect to educational philosophy and learning theory. Committee members do not always readily see that a concern for academic standards is quite compatible with a person-centered guidance approach. Such issues invariably come to the fore whenever central educational objectives are discussed. Interpersonal relations between specific individuals, and rivalry between departmental interests or other subsidiary "kingdoms" of the collegiate institution, may also seem to obscure or obstruct progress toward mutual agreement concerning central educational aims. Other pressures such as heavy work loads of the participants may contribute to the building up of a "hidden agenda" which for some participants establishes a prior claim on their energies and interest. On occasion, the personnel worker himself may not feel entirely secure in the situation, and therefore may tend to become somewhat defensive, to the detriment of the democratic problem-solving task at hand. Legal, safety, and welfare factors may delimit the far-flung aspirations of some participants.

However, these are all examples of barriers which are usually by no means insurmountable. Through the experience of working together in democratic fashion on the whole question of central educational aims for the institution, there is a good chance that a sound foundation will have been laid for even more productive shared activities as specific plans are made for implementing the goals which have been jointly determined by the representatives concerned.

2. Tentative Goals for the Personnel Program

In the light of such a cooperative identification of institutional aims, over-all objectives have thereby been determined for the personnel program, as well as for the formal academic offerings. The next task is to determine which institutional purposes may be profitably pursued by the personnel phase of the collegiate program. It is not unusual to find that classroom offerings and co-curricular activities go hand in hand. For instance, in one college the student-managed canteen provides an excellent field work experience for majors in business administration, and there is a close working relationship between the student personnel staff and those related to teaching responsibilities in the classroom setting.

Thus, goals for the personnel program must be explored in terms of their relationship to (a) institutional aims, (b) objectives of other departments or divisions of the college or university, and (c) the programs of other cooperating or competing institutions in the local community or wider geographical area. In the last instance, to cite one example, a certain eastern college has for some years sponsored a winter week end of sports and other festivities which attracts many visitors from other campuses. Obviously, a nearby sister institution would need to clear dates if it planned a similar affair—or better still, some other event might be planned if a need was felt to develop a similar extracurricular event. In the same vein, where a neighboring institution has already invested a great deal of money in the establishment of a first-rate remedial reading clinic, it might be better to work out a cooperative arrangement rather than undertake the expense of setting up a duplicate resource.

In the delineation of specific aims for the personnel program, it is also imperative to explore areas of actual or potential conflict. Should a consulting psychiatrist, for instance, be related to the health services of the institution, or to the personnel offices, or to both? What about the relationship between faculty advisers to students and those responsible for the administration of the personnel program? Such questions as these should be carefully, tactfully, and patiently explored so as to insure a teamwork approach on the part of all those concerned with and responsible for the welfare of the students.

It is also well to be sure that the proposed goals for the personnel program are sufficiently definitive and specific. A euphemistic aim like "helping the students" is much too general and ambiguous. "Helping the students to grow as persons" seems to be a better way of putting it, but here again it will be important to know in what particulars it is hoped that the students will be helped in order that they may help themselves.

Another important question is this: "Do the proposed goals for the personnel program provide sufficient continuity with the past?" Institutional traditions are of tremendous importance. To some people, Founders' Day or Prize Day or Sadie Hawkins Day or some other traditional observance may not seem to accomplish too much. The apparent purposes of such occasions may seem peripheral to the central objectives for the personnel program. To the extent that any past purposes or practices seem to have met a definite need, and continue in demand by students and alumni, to that extent it may be wise to broaden contemplated objectives for the personnel program so that these features may be retained (although in modified form).

Of equal importance is the necessity that proposed goals for the personnel program make adequate provision for the future. What is reasonable to expect insofar as fluctuations in student enrollment are concerned? Are the admissions policies of such nature that the college may make its maximum contribution in the light of the revised central purposes for the institution? With more and more students of mature years attending college on at least a part-time basis, has adequate provision been made for these people? Similarly, with increasing numbers of married students with new families joining the college community, what special aims should be developed for them? A kindred problem is posed by the increasing mobility of the general population, so that many students come from different regional, cultural, ethnic, and national backgrounds. What objectives are therefore envisioned for the personnel program? Finally, in common sense fashion, where an institution has financial problems, what can the personnel program do to help the situation? What kind of escalator arrangements can be worked out so that when and if temporary retrenchment becomes necessary, such a development will proceed according to a master plan without undue injury to anyone? These various possibilities are only suggestive, but in each academic situation certain contingencies will doubtless need to be provided for in outlining tentative goals for the personnel program.

3. The Exploration of Resources

Purposes must necessarily be related to resources. A thoroughgoing inventory of resources currently available is therefore highly advisable. Resources, of course, may exist in the local institution, the community in which it is situated, or in the larger society. Many resources are physical in nature—plant, facilities, equipment, and the like. Past, present, and projected budgets should also be analyzed in detail. In the same vein, the staff's own professional resources should be taken into account, in order that their respective abilities may be more fully developed and utilized.

Certain other resources undoubtedly exist, but often may be overlooked. Such intangibles as good will, established working relationships with others, and relative readiness for change are outstanding examples. Most personnel programs will also be able to take advantage of special resources peculiar to their respective locations. Rural, urban, industrial, or residential communities in each instance offer unique resources which may be utilized in the creative, imaginative personnel program. Near-by recreational facilities, including state and national parks, can contribute greatly to the resources available for the personnel worker and his associates. In almost any community, certain cultural and educational resources can be made available on a nominal basis, or without cost.

In addition to available resources of whatever nature, the next question is what other resources may be uncovered. Several methods for expanding resources immediately suggest themselves: (a) personal contacts, (b) gifts or appropriations, (c) re-allocation of existing resources used for the personnel program or for other purposes, (d) more efficient use of present resources, (e) sharing resources with others, (f) creative adaptation, and (g) a more systematic survey of the total picture. Other possibilities will doubtless occur to the enterprising group conducting a survey of possible resources. As a result of this exploration, tentative purposes should then be revised accordingly.

4. The Choice of Methods of Implementation

Methods, techniques, and procedures to be employed in the personnel program have no excuse for being apart from the objectives which have been agreed upon for that program. Thus, the choice of particular methods should be governed by careful consideration

of possible courses of action which offer the most promise of fulfilling those objectives.

Those engaged in evaluation should ask themselves, "Which
methods, related to revised purposes, have been used to date in the
local situation?" In the light of present goals for the personnel program, what evidence exists concerning the relative effectiveness of
these methods? Where sufficient evidence is not currently available,
how may such data best be obtained?

What methods have been used by other personnel workers with
comparable objectives? How have such methods worked out? How
may methods of implementation employed by others best be adapted
for local use? What locally devised innovations seem likely to serve
the specific purposes at hand?

From such an inventory of available methods, it is then appropriate to decide cooperatively which of the proposed plans for
implementation appear to be "sure-fire," and which methods seem
to be exceedingly doubtful in terms of outcomes.

Estimated cost and allied factors will also need to be taken into
consideration. A new dormitory, for example, may appear to be a
"must." Sometimes the planners overlook the fact that additional
facilities require extra maintenance and service personnel. The effect
of another living unit on the campus must also be taken into account.

Thus, for any new method which is to be introduced into the
personnel program, the apparent effect of this innovation upon other
aspects of institutional life is worthy of reflection. The establishment
of continuing discussion groups concerned with mutual problems
common to freshmen may represent a brilliant addition to the guidance program. However, in such a case it may be essential to consider
whether such a development may make a student feel stigmatized
when he finds it necessary to seek individual counseling and guidance.
Those planning any new developments should therefore make provision for overcoming in anticipatory fashion any untoward factors
which might thereby be introduced.

It may also be necessary to consider the best sequence in which
more extensive innovations should be introduced. Where should a
joint committee start, for instance, in its desire to change "hell"
week to "help" week? Along with this specific objective, how may
the Panhellenic council become in the process a more integrative,
service-featured force on the campus? Where neither organization
has existed heretofore, which should be developed first, dormitory

councils or a student council? Individual conditions will vary, and astute attention will need to be given to the whole question of sequence and tentative timetables for any changes of a major nature in the personnel program.

5. The Evaluation of Relative Progress

The preceding sections of this chapter have suggested processes and areas of exploration by which tentative answers may be arrived at with respect to where the personnel program is going, why, and how. This section will deal with some of the issues involved in the assessment of how fast, and how far, the personnel program has progressed in the realization of the outcomes envisioned.

Adequate evaluation of a given method of implementation must be related to the over-all goals, as well as to the specific objectives aimed at in the choice of the particular method under examination. Thus, if informal square dancing has been introduced in an effort to make some of the more shy students feel more secure in social situations, it would be inappropriate to jduge the success of such sessions on the basis of a numerical index alone. On the other hand, in view of budgetary considerations, it may be well to review the costs of various phases of the personnel program in the light of the size of the population served, along with apparent benefits derived by constituents.

Specific techniques for evaluation will therefore vary according to the phase of the personnel program under investigation. Questionnaires, interviews, rating scales, and similar devices are frequently employed to advantage. The field of group dynamics has produced many ingenious tools for assessing group interaction. Perhaps one of the most valid evaluative instruments is the situational test, where the subjects remain unaware of the specific aims under assessment. Whatever evaluative methods are used to check on the relative progress of the personnel program, as a general rule multiple "yardsticks" should be employed in the interests of validation and greater scientific accuracy.

Certain subjective elements, such as the insidious effects of personal bias, represent occupational hazards which must be carefully guarded against throughout the evaluative process. Infatuation with the new, or stubborn adherence to old, ideas and methods of implementation and evaluation of relative progress are equally fallacious positions. The cooperative, teamwork approach to evaluation therefore seems to offer the best opportunities for the development of proper balance and perspective. The value judgments of students in particular should always be solicited, for in the final analysis an adequate sampling of student opinion is probably the best evaluative source of all.

Furthermore, the evaluative methods and processes suggested all underscore the importance of critical, productive, and shared thinking and planning. Opportunities to share in democratic problem-solving experiences related to evaluation undoubtedly represent in themselves one of the most significant and important phases of any personnel program.

Evaluation as a Continuous Process

Evaluation of the personnel program represents a task that can never be completely finished. And this is as it should be. Once an institutional survey has been made, tentative goals identified for the personnel program, the best possible methods selected for implementation, and assessment of progress toward personnel goals has been made, each personnel worker and his associates will immediately begin to revise their objectives in the light of this experience. Some goals may prove to have been too narrowly conceived. In occasional instances, the original aims may have been a bit too visionary. In addition, in any growing program the improvement resulting from the evaluative experience thus far will in turn inspire further democratic problem-solving activities. When better provisions have been made for the freshmen, those responsible for the personnel program become more aware of improvements which may be made in meeting the needs of sophomores and upperclassmen. More objective research methods, including the use of more adequate criteria for assessing actual progress made, naturally result in the review of goals, resources, methods, and evaluative techniques.

Through such an ongoing process, all the participants in the evaluative enterprise have an opportunity to grow as persons and to develop new insights concerning the personnel program and its relationship to other spheres of educational endeavor.

As a final observation, it would appear that the cross-fertilization provided by an interchange of ideas and experiences between various institutional groups concerned with evaluation should further enrich the personnel programs of the institution, and make a significant contribution to the whole area of education and guidance.

BIBLIOGRAPHY

Benjamin, Harold (ed.): *Democracy in the Administration of Higher Education.* New York, Harper & Brothers, 1951, 240 pp.

Benne, Kenneth D.: "Theory of Co-operative Planning in Education." *Teachers College Record* 53: No. 8, May, 1952, pp. 429-435.

Benne, Kenneth D., and Muntyan, Bozidar: *Human Relations in Curriculum Change.* New York, Columbia University Press, 1946, 363 pp.

Bixler, H. H., et al.: "Conditions Affecting Personnel Work." *Review of Educational Research* 15: April, 1945, pp. 112-130.

Blaesser, Willard W.: "The College Administrator Evaluates Personnel Work." *Educational and Psychological Measurement* 9: No. 3, 1949, pp. 412-428.

Corey, Stephen M.: *Action Research to Improve School Practices.* New York, Teachers College, Columbia University, Teachers College Bureau of Publications, 1953.

Cronbach, Lee J.: *Essentials of Psychological Testing.* New York, Harper & Brothers, 1949, 465 pp.

Froelich, Clifford P.: *Evaluating Guidance Procedures.* Washington, D. C., Federal Security Agency, Office of Education, 1949.

Lloyd-Jones, Esther: "Some Current Issues in Guidance." *Teachers College Record* 49: Nov., 1947, pp. 77-78.

Myers, W. M.: "Evaluation of Educational Outcomes." *School Review* 55: Feb., 1947, pp. 99-102.

Proshansky, Harold M.: "Projective Techniques in Action Research." In Abt, Lawrence E., and Bellak, Leopold: *Projective Psychology.* New York, Alfred A. Knopf, 1950, 485 pp.

Raths, Louis E.: "Toward Better Evaluations." *Educational Leadership* XIII: No. 2, Nov., 1950, pp. 70-72.

Rhulman, Jessie: "Securing Faculty Co-operation in the Personnel Program." *Educational and Psychological Measurement* 9: No. 3, 1949, pp. 482-487.

Sharp, George: *Curriculum Development as Re-Education of the Teacher.* New York, Bureau of Publications, Teachers College, Columbia University, 1951, 132 pp.

Strang, Ruth M.: *Counseling Technics in College and Secondary School.* New York, Harper & Brothers, 1949 (revised ed.), 302 pp.

Strang, Ruth M.: "Major Limitations in Current Evaluation Studies." *Educational and Psychological Measurement* 10: No. 3, 1950, pp. 531-536.

Troyer, Maurice E., and Pace, C. Robert: *Evaluation in Teacher Edu-*

cation. Washington, D. C., American Council on Education, 1944, 368 pp.

Walker, Helen M.: *Elementary Statistical Methods*. New York, Henry Holt & Company, 1950, 368 pp.

21. The How
and the Who and the Why

ESTHER LLOYD-JONES
MARGARET RUTH SMITH

THE problem still remains of how to organize effectively the possibilities for broader and deeper teaching that have been presented in these chapters. In Chapter 1 questions were raised especially at the points of a dualistic concept of education and of specialization with its concomitant problems of organization. It was pointed out that some of the inadequacies in the development of personnel work within education have arisen directly because of the problem of giantism, and the prestige that America assigns to "bigness." But what to do about these problems is not so easily seen.

Human Relations

Basic to the development of effective personnel work and deeper teaching is the whole important matter of human relations. To re-study personnel work from a standpoint of human relations rather than from a standpoint of efficient services to students would quickly do much, we believe, to increase the educational contributions of student personnel work. Perhaps the fact that personnel work has been more concerned in its recent developments with measuring the abilities of students, advising students, developing special services, and efficiently serving their needs is due to the fact that personnel work has until recently tended to draw more heavily for its insights and techniques on an earlier psychology and a somewhat mechanistic idea of organization than on the social sciences and more dynamic methods.

If it is true, as cultural anthropology seems to show, that personality is almost infinitely modifiable in terms of the roles society permits or assigns the person to play and thus to learn, then the sort of society that exists on a college campus itself must be seen as one of the influences most powerfully affecting each person's concept of who he is, what abilities he possesses, and for what ends he might most profitably try to use those abilities. As personnel workers weigh grades and scores and ratings, for instance, of those applying for admission to their institution, it would extend their influence as educators if they could understand more perceptively the effect these judgments have on those about whom they are made. Each person must learn, of course, how to take and use for his growth the disappointments, frustrations, and even failures that he experiences, but should the admissions officer feel exempt from all responsibility for the consequences that his action will have in the reactions and thus the learnings of the persons whom he accepts or rejects?

Furthermore, as Havighurst so well points out, the admissions committee, as it makes its decisions, should have in mind not only the quality of book-learning ability the student possesses, not only whether he seems or seems not to be a potential trouble-maker as judged by his previous conduct, but also the fact that the members of the admissions committee are in a very real sense the constitutors of a society within which important values are going to be demonstrated, practiced, and learned.

What kind of people will make up a society that can be most educational for those who are members of it? What kind of values should be learned from membership for four years in a campus society? Should these four years of living teach individualism, ruthless competition, irresponsibility in group relationships, or social understanding, group skills, and social responsibility? Should campus living instill or subtly perpetuate contempt for certain races and socio-economic backgrounds, or should it increase each student's respect for all individuals and his belief that the world can permit each one to have a role of dignity and social worth?

All of this, involving the most complicated problems of social philosophy and educational purpose, is involved in every decision made by admissions officers or committees.

Because admissions is so much more than a matter of techniques and efficient administration, the admissions committee should take a great deal of care, with the help of technical experts, to develop policies and even make decisions that in the aggregate will result on their campus in the formation of a significant new society of people. Perhaps, in large institutions, most admissions decisions should be made by admissions committees in each of the various schools and large departments, with admissions experts serving merely as advisers to, coordinators of, and as executive officers for these several committees.

The Edward W. Hazen Foundation has under way a four-year project of encouraging colleges to study their student-faculty relations in all their complex manifestations. The hope, of course, is that the colleges that participate will be able to discover whether and how the quality of these relationships might be improved in the interest of educational outcomes. Mercer University is carrying on an especially thorough study by student-faculty committees to discover in what areas both students and faculty most enjoy each other and gain positively from their relationships. Which of the traditional social affairs, which student-faculty gatherings, athletic events, clubs, student government, publications, classrooms, etc., afford the best opportunities for students and faculty to associate together meaningfully, to evaluate the quality of their relationships, and to experiment with improving their quality? The assumption is that no college can subject itself to this kind of self-study without improving the quality of its campus life and consequently the deeper learnings of the students—and, as a matter of fact, of the teachers and personnel staff too.

A personnel consultant, appointed to review and suggest improvements for the testing, selection, admissions, orientation, records, advising, and placement services in a department of 700 graduate students within a professional school, ended by stimulating the department to make a thorough study of its student-student, student-faculty, and faculty-faculty relations. It became apparent that not only could the quality of education in the classroom be improved in this way, but also that this might be one of the most effective possible means for students to learn by actual experience just what democratic relationships truly are, the problems involved in developing and maintaining them, and how, when achieved, they release and stimulate personal growth.[1]

He found, through student group discussions and questionnaires, that students assigned to different faculty counselors in the same department wanted very much the same kind of thing from their counselors but had quite different experiences, depending upon whether they were so fortunate as to have one of the very interested,

[1] T. C. Clark: "A Plan for Improving the Student Personnel Program of the Department of Educational Administration."

effective counselors, one of the just average ones, or one who was little concerned with the counseling aspect of his duties. As a result of the consultant's report, the faculty were challenged to meet with their counselees, to try to get to know them better, and to find out what they wanted. Incidentally, then, the faculty began to work with each other and with the consultant on improving the records system for their own use in knowing and counseling students, sending better preregistration information to students, improving their departmental social program, etc. As the faculty gained a picture of how students saw them, and of the ratings they assigned to the human relations skills of the various faculty members, they recognized more fully than before how they could effectively teach their students democratic ideals and human relations skills by actually practicing them with each other and with the students, and by encouraging the students to do the same.

The Significant Community

Somehow human relations wisdom and skills are not learned so readily en masse as they are in encompassable situations that do not involve too many people. Brownell points out that the huge institutions to which almost half of our college students now flock are in no sense true communities. They may be made up of communities, but in themselves they are not communities and do not have the potentiality for education in human relations that the small community possesses. He says:

Human significance and value are created in the small community. . . . In this pattern and only in this pattern does the human being behave as a whole being in relation to other human beings. He participates here in the values that are called moral, intellectual, spiritual. Only in the true community is human integration possible.[2]

What implications are there in this for the education of the whole man and for the personnel worker and for educators interested in deeper teaching?

It behooves each college administration to examine its own situation to discover whether and to what extent it can truly be said to be a community. There are some small institutions that seem naturally to have excellent opportunities for teaching human significance and values out of the very stuff of which socially they are constituted. There are other small institutions that, by study and a

[2] Baker Brownell: *The College and the Community*, p. 248.

deliberate, designed cultivation of their resources, can deepen the educational influences they exert and broaden the educational outcomes which students in those situations derive.

Large institutions would do well to try to discover the small, true communities within them that seem to possess validity and vitality for those who are their members. Are these communities most promisingly the schools or colleges of the university or are they, perhaps, departments? Do the residence halls or groups of students living in the various parts of large residence halls constitute communities in which students behave as whole beings in relation to other human beings? Do the more apparent natural communities within the larger structure provide membership for everyone, or are there some nonresident students or some part-time students or others who seem left out?

In each case the answer will be different, unique to the particular institution that is trying to find and cultivate the natural lines of relationship that can result in true communities.

When these communities are discovered, it would seem that it is here that personnel work could be centered and practiced; it is here that human beings can be known as whole persons, can behave as whole beings in relation to other human beings, and can find human significance and value.

In such natural communities there is no need and certainly no justification for perpetuating on the one hand a program of instruction, and on the other a program of personnel work. There is no longer any excuse for dualism. Personnel work here can become integrated as a part of the plan for educating the whole man. The problem becomes one of how students and staff can work together to improve their community, to evaluate and re-evaluate the qualities that make it up, and to examine together how their human relationships may be improved and strengthened so as to contribute to total growth for each member.

It is in such small, cohesive communities that students and staff can discover and demonstrate together that "the health of a culture depends not on the volume of explicit teaching, but in the ability of its citizens to select from and recast the daily influences of normal life in the light of some system of values worked out for themselves."[3]

---

[3] Guy Hunter: *Residential Colleges: Some New Developments in British Adult Education*, p. 62.

Organization

With so much importance justly attached for educational reasons to the small community, the central bureau, the central department of personnel work in the big institution, must be seen in a different role. There would continue to be ways—and important ones—in which a central office or department could serve personnel work in these small communities. It could act as an office of central information, communication, and referral. McCabe's chapter, "Utilizing Every Resource," suggests how, in relation to information and referral functions, the central office might operate. It is in facilitating communication among communities, perhaps, that it can be most helpful.

As communities and subgroups within the natural communities develop strength, become self-critical, discover new problems, and invent solutions, they need not work in isolation from each other. There might be a council made up of representatives of the communities. This council might set up a rotating chairmanship from among its own members. On the other hand, it might want, either as chairman or chairmen, personnel consultants from a central office who would be related to all of the several communities and would consciously serve as cross-fertilizing agents, utilizing all the skills of group development in working with groups in each of the communities.

Large and small institutions would still need accessory specialists. These specialists would exist both within and outside of the institution's corporate structure. Specialists located within large institutions might still need a manager, somewhat in the sense that physicians who set up a group practice often hire a manager to take care of the many problems that detract from their services and to help them work together more smoothly. This person might be an "Executive Secretary of Student Services" or an "Assistant to the President." This same person might also provide an information service for possible users of the special services and might help work out appropriate referrals. If this person or these persons were still thought of, however, as having the "services within his office," as services now often are said to be located "in the office of the dean of students"; if this office derived power from control over the special services, then we will probably continue to have the sort of situation that now exists with the educational weaknesses that have been described.

How, more specifically, might we convert from the various patterns that now exist for carrying out personnel work to the general plan that has been suggested?

In the Case of "Divided Deans"

The organizational arrangements for personnel work that are still most commonly found in coeducational situations center around a dean of men and a dean of women. There has been great dissatisfaction with this pattern in some situations, especially in big institutions where special services have increased apace. This criticism has been especially loud when the dean of women or dean of men wanted to maintain a special service just for men or just for women when this seemed to mean unjustifiable duplication and expense. There has been dissatisfaction with this pattern, too, when there was sibling rivalry between the two deans under a patriarchal president, or when there was personal dislike or professional jealousy between them. Recently, accreditation committees have sometimes openly advocated that the dean of women, whether she be the more able or not, be brought administratively under the dean of men, and that the titles be changed from Dean of Women and Dean of Men to Associate Dean of Students and Dean of Students.

The various personnel specialists are then also made responsible administratively to the Dean of Students in what is thought to be a departmental arrangement similar to that which exists in the academic departments of the institution. Presidents sometimes like this, for it seems to them to relieve them of some of their problems, especially when the situation is really that of "divided deans," but other presidents prefer not to resort to "the Dean of Students" pattern, feeling that certain educational values may thereby be sacrificed to administrative efficiency and peace through suppression.

In the Case of Deans of Students

The title, "Dean of Students," has come to signify in the minds of most people that one person on a college campus "heads up" in a central personnel office a group of specialists who are appointed by him to perform certain expert personnel services for students. The job is a natural result of the concepts described in the first chapter of this book. Often this job, as presidents will frequently state, has been created because they did not know what to do with the many personnel specialists who had taken possession of their campuses and they felt the need of someone to curb their ambitions, settle their jurisdictional fights, and relate them effectively to each other.

How to convert from an arrangement that appeals to the self-preservation of presidents to one that is designed to further the educational program of the college in a somewhat new and deeper sense may prove difficult. It is not so much that presidents are more interested in their own survival than they are in education (although it is readily conceded that they are entitled to be concerned not only about education but also about survival—and about comfort) as it is that difficulty usually arises when an individual who feels he has superior status is asked to share it with others.

Furthermore, one accustomed to administering services may not have the educational vision and skills or enough commitment to the importance of human relations to enable him to change over from directing services to educational leadership of the sort which we are attempting to describe. The Dean of Students may professionally have become a captive to holding specialists in their places. The very fact that conversion to "the Dean of Student pattern" has usually meant the creation of one big job with the biggest salary supported by lesser jobs with lesser salaries also gives the Dean of Students a stake in maintaining the *status quo*. A few institutions that adopted the Dean of Student pattern, however, have now converted to the pattern of coordinate—not divided—deans of men and of women.

In the Case of Coordinate Deans

If there is a dean of men and dean of women who are coordinate rather than "divided," if they understand principles of human relations and have some skills in this field, and are cooperative in feeling and behavior rather than dominating or submissive, then the situation may exemplify some of the possibilities that we have suggested as educationally advantageous. The dean of men probably works informally, and sometimes more formally, with groups of men and women faculty members, with counselors of the men's residence halls, with groups of men students and with groups of both men and women students, as well as with groups of faculty and students working together, to help them analyze problems of group living and plan for the recasting of "the daily influences of normal life in the light of some system of values worked out for themselves." Similarly, the dean of women works with groups of women faculty members and mixed groups, with students, and faculty and students in the same general way and for the same general ends as does the dean of men. The dean of men and the dean of women compare notes, plan together, evaluate, and constantly demonstrate in their relationships with each other and with their colleagues that they understand good human relations and are able to practice them themselves.

The pattern of coordinate deans has the advantage of demonstrating to men and women students a truly cooperative, egalitarian kind of work relationship between men and women that students may not have had an opportunity to see in relationships between their parents, but that they may wish to try to practice both in their own homes, when they are married, and in work situations of which they will be a part. On the face of it, according to the American Association of University Women, who officially strongly favor this organizational plan, the coordinate plan may seem to hold more additional values for women students and women faculty members than it does for men, since men faculty and students in higher educational institutions usually outnumber the women, but there may be hidden educational values for men, too, in having an opportunity to observe and experience responsibility so fully and equally shared.

In one large university where, after experimenting with the dean-of-student pattern, the plan for coordinate deans was reinstated, the dean of men and dean of women make program plans jointly, appoint staff by mutual agreement, have a council relationship with their staff, and even make up a joint budget, not at all in the spirit of *Life with Father* but in the spirit that is advocated in all modern courses on marriage and family living.

Coordinate deans and their staff associates, in either a small or large institution, would properly serve as consultants to departmental or other groups of students, and to student-faculty groups. They would attempt by the application of the "best" group methods to help these groups define the problems that are continually arising within their common experience and that have, when perceptively viewed, a direct relation to the group's evolution of a system of values.

These might be such problems as are dealt with in preceding chapters of this book: How can a group help each member to feel a sense of belonging? How, in specific and concrete cases that are amongst us, should we handle problems that arise from our socioeconomic system of caste and class? How can we as a group deal both preventively and therapeutically with problems that many would label as apathy, lack of involvement on the part of group members, exaggerated individualism, disloyalty, or social irresponsibility? How can we adequately protect the rights of an individual to be different, to stick to his principles—even encourage him to do so—and encourage more appreciation by all for nonconformity that is based on principle? How can we, as a group, help an individual with his behavior when it is such (noise-making, property destruction, standard-smashing, crass insensitivity to others' rights, etc.) that others who must try to get along with him are in some way hurt? How does a group develop common agreement as to what its aims might most fruitfully be? How can it revamp and improve its aims as it goes along? How can a group democratically help each of its members evolve roles that not only are good for the growth of the individuals but that also contribute to the group's accomplishment of its goals? Answers to these problems are best found and skills for handling them learned by students in actually handling, with guidance, these problems as they emerge again and again in group life all over any campus.

Deans who are truly coordinate and who themselves not only know the theory of cooperative planning, action, responsibility, and evaluation but also practice it in their own work relations, are qualified to teach these important lessons both by precept and by skillful verbal interpretations. Personnel workers who operate individualistically as experts in some technical function, or as a coordinator of those who operate this way, may make valuable contributions to human welfare, but they are not as well qualified to provide leadership for this kind of an educational program in human relations.

Attempting to give groups this kind of consultative help can challenge all of the most creative insights and group skills that a personnel worker can command. It also imbues the campus society that practices this kind of democratic living with rich educational experiences for students and staff alike. It makes of the personnel worker an educator in the best sense of the word.

In addition to this sort of work with multiple groups in the campus community, the deans, of course, will be professionally concerned to see that each student is known as a whole person within some group of friendly persons (the natural community of which he is a member within the university, a class, his residence hall), and that there is within that group at least one older and wiser person (a teacher, a residence counselor, or some other member of the professional staff of the college)—as well as fellow students—who will see him regularly in the social context of the group, seek to know him well and sympathetically, and serve as an avenue for him whereby he can more readily find relationships with many sources that will be helpful to his growth and learning. This implies, of course, something in the nature of a faculty advisory system, but one quite differently ordered from the advisory systems found in most colleges at the present time.

Most professional members of the college staff who are related as counselors to students in the ways suggested above will find it a rewarding experience in terms of learning about individuals and human relations. They may not only be willing but even eager to try to learn how to put into effect the infinite possibilities there seem to be through counseling and group experiences for students to learn and grow.

At this point the deans have an important responsibility in devising ways of helping counselors to learn. Regular individual conferences with a counselor, especially when they center around a particular student whom the staff member is seeking to serve in a counseling capacity, and case conferences where several minds are brought together to pool insights and ingenuity, are excellent ways whereby understanding and skills are improved. Role-playing by would-be counselors of their counseling sessions, with tape recordings, may seem at first to contribute mainly to self-consciousness, embarrassment, or narcissism, but it has been reported by those who have stuck at it in a systematic way to have contributed ultimately both to insights and to skills.

Deans and personnel specialists must, of course, stand by to help with critical cases that always arise where more experienced help is needed quickly and over a more protracted period of time. In these cases the dean of men's help is usually, but not always, more acceptable for men students, while the dean of women can usually work more helpfully and tactfully in cases involving women students.

Furthermore, the coordinate deans, as generalists in personnel work, will serve as referral agents, watching every opportunity not only to see that the needs of students are met, but also that resources are strengthened, both within and without, as McCabe has emphasized.*

In the Case of the Personnel Councils

A considerable number of institutions report the recent evolution of personnel councils which have become central in the planning,

* All of the contributing authors were invited to criticize Chapters I and XXI. Many valuable suggestions were offered.

John Bergstresser, Dean of Students at San Francisco State College, explicitly action, and evaluation aspects of their personnel work. These councils seem always to include the personnel deans, and may include the president or an assistant to the president, an administrative or academic dean, the registrar, the director of admissions, the director of placement, one or more representatives of the health service, interested representatives of the academic council, and other interested and concerned members of the staff. The council usually selects annually the member it wishes to have serve as chairman of the council.

In large, complex institutions made from a number of schools and colleges, each unit may have such a council, with interlocking membership on a central council providing for desirable communication and reciprocal stimulation amongst the primary councils. The same functions and purposes described under the section above on coordinate deans can well be carried out in multiple ways by the various members of the councils in the situations in which each works with other staff and students.

As we become more expert in group methods it is probable that the council plan will provide a most effective method for furthering integration of personnel work with the total educational program of the institution as well as coordination of services.

Leadership

Each form of organization has its own distinct characteristics and can be variously evaluated depending upon the value context in which it is considered. There is no doubt, however, that the personalities of the people involved, their own personal needs and their skill or lack of skill in working with others will considerably modify each form of organization and contribute to or detract from its effectiveness.

---

dissented from the idea of coordinate deans. He believes that "the dean of students plan for the coordination and administration of all student personnel services is sounder in theory" and that "it can be made to function more effectively, and on a truly democratic basis—especially in colleges where the functions of admission, registration and record keeping, placement, clinical counseling, student health service, etc. are considered to be vital and integral parts of the total student personnel program."

Among the contributing authors who expressed agreement with the ideas outlined in this chapter was Frank C. Baldwin, Dean of Men at Cornell University. He said, further, "If you are referring on page 344 to Cornell University, you're absolutely right. Seven years ago Cornell University replaced the dean of students plan with the coordinate deans plan." Dean Baldwin says that "with a new coordinate dean of women at Cornell University during the past two years the advantages of this plan are as clear as ever."

A definite condition to developing the educational possibilities of personnel work has to do with conceptions of leadership that find expression in the practices of personnel leaders. One of the authors has described elsewhere[4] several types of leadership and their social consequences.

The status leader, for instance, tends to be a product of a social pattern that may involve subtly much of domination and submission, prescribed social distance, and hierarchical structure. The personnel worker who is a status leader tends to be absorbed in defining the needs that others, in this case students, may have, analyzing the functions that are to be performed by experts in order that these needs may be served, securing budget to pay the salaries of experts, employing the experts to perform the tasks, supervising their work, evaluating it, watching the relationships of these experts to each other, restudying the needs of students that should be further met, etc. He tends to operate in terms of line and staff relationships rather than in more dynamic work relations. He is concerned primarily with directing staff who will provide services for students; he is not so much concerned with educating students to meet their own needs better. There are those within the personnel field who feel most comfortable, however, in the role of status leader.

A type of leadership that fits well with the concept of the personnel worker as educator would be that of the chain-reaction leader. This sort of leader is less concerned with status and fitting people into niches and into echelons. He is more concerned with fostering processes that will develop leadership in others, and that will create in these others the desire to develop leadership in still others with whom they may be associated. This is the sort of leadership that is needed in a democracy. This sort of leadership develops the kind of human relations in which each person can find his greatest stature and the highest development of all of his abilities—which is the primary concern of personnel workers.

Guideposts

How can officers of an institution know whether it is moving toward personnel work as deeper teaching, and away from personnel work as an adjunct of education? There are several ways:

[4] Esther Lloyd-Jones: "Leadership in Guidance," p. 359.

Is the program:

moving away from:	moving toward:
1. a dualistic conception of teachers vs. personnel workers?	personnel workers and teachers working together as educators to accomplish common objectives?
2. a program of services to students?	a cooperative program by faculty, personnel workers, and students to improve the campus communities in which they share membership?
3. hierachical leadership?	chain-reaction leadership?
4. centralization?	centering the personnel program in the small, natural communities of the campus?
5. emphasis on organization, administration of services, and control?	emphasis on "deeper learnings" by both students and staff?
6. service by specialists?	consultation to help members improve group life and conditions of growth for all?
7. authority of expertness?	participation and sharing?
8. concern for efficiency of operation?	concern for the quality of human relations that are being learned?
9. importance at the "top"?	a concern for people at the "bottom"?

This book has attempted to present a changing conception of personnel work. Personnel work is described not as a collection of services to students, provided by a group of specialists who are administered by a "head," but rather as the extension and deepening of an educational program for the development of whole men for life in a democratic society. It is the hope and faith that these whole men, so educated, may, by their more intelligent living, contribute to and improve the quality of human relations in that society.

BIBLIOGRAPHY

Barron, Margaret, and Krulee, Gilbert K.: "Case Study of a Basic Skill Training Group." *Journal of Social Issues*, 4, Spring, 1948.
Baruch, Dorothy: "Therapeutic Processes as a Part of the Educative

Process." *Journal of Consulting Psychology,* 4, September-October, 1940, pp. 170 ff.

Benjamin, Harold (ed.): *Democracy in the Administration of Higher Education.* John Dewey Yearbook, Vol. 10. New York, Harper and Brothers, 1950.

Bradford, Leland, and Lippitt, Ronald: "Role-playing in Supervisory Training." *Personnel,* 22, No. 6, May, 1946.

Brownell, Baker: *The College and the Community.* New York, Harper and Brothers, 1952.

Burts, Annamarie: "Student-Faculty Relations in an American College" (doctoral project). New York, Teachers College, Columbia University, 1953.

Cartwright, Dorwin, and Zander, A. F. (ed.): *Group Dynamics, Research and Theory.* Evanston, Illinois, Row, Peterson, 1953.

Fenner, Mildred S.: "Improving the Group Process." *Group Dynamics and Education,* reprint of a series of articles which appeared in the *Journal of the National Education Association,* 1948-1949.

Gordon, Ira: "Creation of an Effective Faculty Advisor Training Program Through Group Procedures" (doctoral project). New York, Columbia University, 1950. Partially reproduced in *Educational and Psychological Measurements,* 10, No. 3, 1950.

Hall, Harvey: *How Would You Have Handled It?—A Case Book for Personnel Students* (doctoral project). New York, Teachers College, Columbia University, 1950.

de Huszar, George B.: *Practical Applications of Democracy.* New York, Harper and Brothers, 1945.

Homans, George: "Group Factors in Worker Productivity," in Newcomb and Hartley (eds.), *Readings in Social Psychology.* New York, Henry Holt and Company, Inc., 1947.

Learned, Edmund P., Ulrich, David N., and Booz, Donald R.: *Executive Action.* Boston, Harvard University, 1951.

Lewin, Kurt: "Group Decision and Social Change," in Newcomb and Hartley (eds.), *Readings in Social Psychology.* New York, Henry Holt and Company, Inc., 1947.

Lewin, Kurt: "Psychology and the Process of Group Living." *Journal of Social Psychology,* 17, 1943.

Lewin, Kurt: *Resolving Social Conflicts.* New York, Harper and Brothers, 1948.

Lewin, Kurt, Lippitt, Ronald, and White, R. K.: "Patterns of Agressive Behavior in Experimentally Created Social Climates." *Journal of Social Psychology,* 10, 1939.

Lloyd-Jones, Esther, and Kelley, Janet: "Social Development and Group Morale." *Encyclopedia of Educational Research.* New York, The Macmillan Company, 1950, pp. 1339-1345.

McGill, Ida Belle: *Social Competence for Teachers* (doctoral project). New York, Teachers College, Columbia University, 1951.

Metcalf, Henry C., and Murick, L. (ed.): *Dynamic Administration, The Collected Papers of Mary Parker Follett.* New York, Harper and Brothers, 1942.

Pflieger, Elmer F., and Weston, Grace L.: *Emotional Adjustment: A Key to Good Citizenship.* Detroit, Wayne University Press, 1953.

Prescott, Daniel, and Weber, Julie: "Peer Culture." *Illinois Education,* 36, No. 4, December, 1947—January, 1948.

Rahn, Grant: "Participation: Key to Education for Effective Living." *Bulletin of the National Association of Secondary School Principals,* 34, January, 1950.

Redl, Fritz: "Discipline and Group Psychology." *Journal of the National Association of Deans of Women,* 11, October, 1947.

Rogers, Carl R.: *Client-Centered Therapy.* Boston, Houghton Mifflin Company, 1951.

Russell, John Dale: "American College." *American Universities and Colleges.* American Council on Education, 1948.

Saddlemire, Gerald: *A Current View of Men Personnel Administrators in Colleges and Universities* (doctoral project). New York: Teachers College, Columbia University, 1949.

Sherif, M., and Contril, H.: *The Psychology of Ego-Involvements.* New York, John Wiley and Sons, Inc., 1947.

Shrewsbury, Thomas B.: *Selected Cases of Human Relations in Student Personnel Work* (doctoral project). New York, Teachers College, Columbia University, 1951.

Spencer, Louise: *Eleven Years of Change in The Roles of Deans of Women in Colleges, Universities, and Teachers Colleges* (doctoral project). New York, Teachers College, Columbia University, 1952.

Stensland, Per: *Guide for Group Leaders.* Institute of Citizenship, Kansas State College, 1949.

Strang, Ruth: *The Role of the Teacher in Personnel Work.* New York, Teachers College, Bureau of Publications, Columbia University, 1953 edition.

Strang, Ruth (ed.):*Unity Within Guidance.* Syracuse, Syracuse University Press, 1953.

Sutherland, Robert L. and others: *Students and Staff in a Social Context.* American Council on Education Studies, Series VI. Washington, D. C., American Council on Education, 1953.

Tead, Ordway: "Integrating Personnel and Teaching Functions in College." *The Educational Forum,* Vol. XVII, May, 1953, pp. 401-411.

Watson, G. B., and others: *Civilian Morale.* Boston, Houghton Mifflin Company, 1942.

Woolf, Maurice D., and Woolf, Jeanne A.: *The Student Personnel Program.* New York, McGraw-Hill Book Company, 1953.

Index